THE ROYAL HORTICULTURAL SOCIETY

GARDEN
book

THE ROYAL
HORTICULTURAL
SOCIETY

GARDEN
book

David
Stevens

Ursula
Buchan

conran
OCTOPUS

First published in Great Britain in 1994 by
Conran Octopus Limited
A part of Octopus Publishing Group
2–4 Heron Quays
London E14 4JP

www.conran-octopus.co.uk

Reprinted in 1994, 1995
Revised paperback edition published in 1997, reprinted 1998
This edition published in 2001, reprinted in 2002 (twice)

British Library Cataloguing-in-Publication Data
A catalogue record for this book is available from the British Library.

ISBN 1 84091 203 0

Illustrations by Vanessa Luff, Liz Pepperell, Paul Bryant (see page 352)
Art Editor: Helen Lewis
Designers: Sally Powell, Mary Staples
Senior Editor: Sarah Pearce
Project Editor: Kate Bell
Text Editor: Caroline Taylor
Picture Editor: Nadine Bazar
Editorial Assistant: Charlotte Coleman-Smith
Production: Mano Mylvaganam, Sonia Sibbons, Alison McIver
Typeset by Hunters Armley Ltd
Printed in China

The publisher would like to thank Valerie Buckingham, David Joyce,
Susanne Mitchell, Meg Sanders for editorial help; Sara Kidd for
design help.

Index by Indexing Specialists, Hove, East Sussex

CONTENTS

GREAT GARDEN STYLES 16

DESIGNING YOUR GARDEN 50

GARDEN ELEMENTS 142

THE TOP 100 GARDEN PLANTS 262

GARDENING TECHNIQUES 290

GREAT GARDEN STYLES

DESIGNING YOUR GARDEN

GARDEN ELEMENTS

THE TOP 100 GARDEN PLANTS

GARDENING TECHNIQUES

HOW TO USE THIS BOOK

ATTRIBUTION OF TEXT

Throughout the greater part of this book, the two themes of garden design and garden planting are interwoven, with David Stevens and Ursula Buchan each contributing their own special expertise. In order that the authorial voice should be clear in every section, the author's initials appear at the beginning of the text, as shown here:

DS Focal points can be used to add a sense of structure to the design. They are the visual hinges of garden design, the objects or features in a garden that draw the eye and lead the visitor towards them.

UB Flower and leaf colour alone will not make a satisfactory garden picture; the structure and shape of plants, especially those which make up the permanent plantings, are equally, if not more important.

The Top 100 Garden Plants and *Gardening Techniques* were written by Ursula Buchan.

CAPTION ATTRIBUTION

Each author has, in many cases, contributed separately to the picture captions. Their authorship is expressed as follows:

Picture captions in grey type were written by David Stevens, so relate chiefly to the structure and overall design of the garden shown.

Picture captions in serif type were written by Ursula Buchan, so relate to the planting of the garden shown.

I have spent the past twenty-five years enjoying myself as a landscape and garden designer. I omit the word 'professional' because in my chosen subject there may often be very little difference between those that are formally trained, as myself, and a gifted amateur. Working in any field of design is a rewarding and satisfying business, but particularly so in garden design. For in many ways, gardens are places where most people can have the greatest control over anything else they possess. The garden is our own space, and it is here that we have the unusual and unique opportunity to create something for ourselves. All this sounds exciting, and it is, but there are also a myriad pitfalls.

A garden is not simply a collection of isolated features, however attractive those may be in their own right, nor should it be born out of random binges at garden centres. To serve you properly, and reflect the needs of you and your family, it needs to be planned sensibly, simply, and practically. Garden design is a straightforward business, quite within the grasp of any garden owner.

My own philosophy of a garden is of a place to live outside. It should encompass sitting, dining and playing, the possibility of growing crops and vegetables, and also serve as a more mundane place that accepts dustbins, sheds, work areas and the drying of clothes. In addition, it should require as much work as you want to devote to it, never more. One of my prime rules of garden design is that you should never be a slave to that room outside.

Although a garden has many components and needs, it can be put together in an entirely logical way, from the initial survey and analysis of what you want, to the choice of 'hard landscape' materials for the basic construction. Plants and planting will, of course, breathe life into the garden, adding colour and interest, and bringing the overall picture into the third dimension.

One of the great strengths of this book is that it is jointly written. I have dealt with the subjects of design and construction, while Ursula Buchan has covered the vast subject of plants and planting design. This has proved both immensely rewarding and genuinely innovative. I feel we have both learned a great deal, which is one of the best reasons for passing that knowledge on.

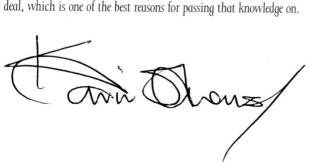

It has become almost customary for authors, when writing an introduction to a new gardening book, to take a rather defensive, even apologetic, tone. The temptation is understandable when there seem to be so many gardening and garden design books already on offer. This introduction adopts no such tone, however, for we believe that this book is genuinely different from those that have gone before.

The Garden Book will tell you both how to design and lay out your garden in the most efficient and satisfactory way, and also how to cultivate that garden once you have made it. This is unusual in itself, but the novelty really lies in the fact that equal emphasis has been given to the garden structure and to its planting. It is this synthesis of the two main areas of garden design that we believe will make this book so valuable for all garden owners, whether experienced or not.

This book does not assume knowledge or even, initially, enthusiasm. We see it as our task to try to give you both. Above all, this book offers you realizable ideas, created by two authors who have spent years involved in a practical way in the craft and art of gardening and garden-making.

Most garden owners discover through experience that much time and money can be wasted, especially at the beginning, in developing schemes that fail and effects that disappoint. This book has been written to show you a direct path to a well-designed, effective, and interestingly planted garden. We do not automatically assume that you have an infinity of time and money at your disposal; you will find it possible to draw out of this book that which you want and need, depending on your own particular circumstances. Care has been taken to give only information that is as up-to-date as possible, and to avoid repeating time-honoured formulae where these have lost their validity or relevance.

We are confident that this book will supply you with the information you most need to know in order to design and plant your garden successfully. Enjoy it, and your gardening.

GREAT GARDEN STYLES

There is a saying that 'there is nothing new in garden design', and there is certainly a degree of truth in the statement.

Any art form, including garden design, takes its inspiration from other examples that surround it. This will often create a strong regional or national style, and for that reason different countries have evolved quite different kinds of garden design. The influences driving that style are many and can broadly include climate, general land form, social factors and even religion. All of these can be further refined on a regional basis by such factors as microclimate, building styles and local materials.

Before travel between countries became widespread, these styles were both insular and protected, developing slowly over hundreds, if not thousands of years. As people became more mobile, art forms inevitably became intermingled. Sometimes this produced great results as with the development of the Japanese garden style from its earlier roots in China, or the creation of the West Coast American garden that originated from the Bauhaus and Modern Movement that started life in Germany.

The natural evolution of a style is a genuine and spontaneous affair, for which reasons it will almost invariably succeed. What is far more dangerous is the simple copying of an idea without fully understanding just what it is all about. This tends to result in the ludicrous mimicry of individual styles in the most inappropriate of situations.

The most important principle to grasp is just why these great gardens and styles were created, and then to draw inspiration from them. That inspiration is to do with appreciating the purpose of the garden and why it works so well in its particular location. Only then will you start to understand how to create a composition that will suit your requirements.

1 Flower is important in terms of planting design, but the shapes and relationship of foliage can be equally telling. Planting will provide many of the elements of your outside room, and here the floor is formed by a predominantly green composition, while planting and hedges at a higher level provide the walls. Overhead beams can provide a ceiling; here, the dark tree canopy plays the part. In a composition where light values are low, white blooms trap the sunlight and lift what might otherwise be a sombre glade.

What thrives in the climate will to a large extent dictate the garden style. Here much of the impact comes from bold, light-reflecting glossy foliage, but the stand of bright white arum lilies is crucial for the contrast it provides.

2 Light values change and shift dramatically in different parts of the world. In general terms, the hotter the climate the stronger the light, and the more vibrant the colours. The lower light values of temperate climates go with cooler temperatures and the greater frequency of mist and rain. While this may not be conducive to living outside, such conditions create ideal growing conditions as well as a soft and romantic atmosphere. Pastel colours, as here, often look at their best in such a setting.

Here the 'cottage garden' effect has been created using tender dahlias - which have been adopted successfully in temperate climates because gardeners are prepared to dig them up well before the frosts and then to replant them in spring.

2

Great Garden Styles

FORMAL GARDEN STYLE

DS A formal garden is, in strict terms, one that is entirely symmetrical, with one side mirrored by the other in a strongly conceived geometric pattern. There are many gardens of which this is true, but formality has also come to mean a composition that is laid out with a degree of regularity and geometry, and with stylized planting – not necessarily with mirror images.

Many historic gardens were formal in design, and geometry has been used in garden styles from the very earliest times. Egyptian and Persian gardens relied on a formal framework of hard landscape, often within a courtyard, in which pergolas, water and planting would be laid out in a symmetrical pattern. The great Moorish gardens were largely formal, and so too were the exuberant and lavish gardens of Renaissance Italy.

Such gardens reflected the architectural styles of the day, and were designed to provide a strong visual link between house and garden. Any garden should, of course, do just that, but a formal style relies heavily on the adjoining building for its inspiration. If the architecture of the house is classical, then formality in the garden should reflect this with clear axes related to the house, with stone paving, balustrading, stone or gravel paths, parterres, clipped hedging, formal pools and framed views. Urns on either side of a path, an obelisk at the end of a vista, an avenue of trees, a gazebo on either side of a lawn: all express formality.

Of course a building need not be classical or even old to possess an adjoining formal garden, but it does need to be a building with some character of its own. A formal garden could suit a Georgian house or a Victorian villa, and it could also suit a contemporary architect-designed building, reflecting the regularity of the house and providing a harmonious link between the inside and the outer world. It is less likely, however, to work in conjunction with a pre-war semi or a developer's house on a modern estate. Few modern houses have a balanced façade or strong layout, so an asymmetrical design would probably look, and certainly feel, more comfortable.

As well as creating a formal style, the materials used in the garden should link architecturally with the period of the house. While good-quality precast slabs could look well in the garden of a Queen Anne house, natural stone flags would look far better. Poor quality or coloured precast slabs would be a disaster, as would preformed ponds or plastic fencing. Yet any of these might look fine in another setting.

However, formality has more to it than just style. Historically, a formal garden was a place in which to stroll, parade or sit, and even today a formal layout is

1

2

1 Some of the most dramatic formal gardens depend for their success on direct contrast with the immediate surroundings. In itself this is a relatively straightforward composition, the surroundings, however, are anything but ordinary!

Shaped box and mown lawn: nothing could be simpler but the effect is striking. It requires regular maintenance, as it is important to match the shapes accurately and to keep them trimmed.

2 This is the classic formal path, simple but immensely strong in visual terms. It all has to do with balance; the great mass of the clipped trees to either side lead the eye straight down the path to the armillary sphere which has been elevated to bring it into scale with the avenue. Most focal points are placed to be viewed from the house; this composition works the other way round.

Formal shapes of yew are ideally trimmed twice a year, in the late spring and early autumn, to minimize the shaggy look. The use of juniper as horizontal contrast, but with similar colouring, is imaginative. Note the immaculate condition of the gravel: formal gardens need to be well maintained to perform their function properly.

22

Great Garden Styles

intended as a visual feast rather than as an active space. Formal gardens may be labour-intensive, but they preclude rapid movement. As the garden gets larger, the pattern can become less concentrated and can allow for the *allées* and vistas found in the largest formal gardens. But even so, a large garden, just as a small one, is to be walked, not jogged, through.

Formality need not extend throughout the garden. More formal or architectural areas close to the house can give way to less formality further away; and this offers the opportunity of creating separate garden rooms, each with a different character or style. But, as with any style, the prime rule is respect for the house, the setting and the adjoining surroundings.

A feeling of formality can be achieved by creating a symmetry and classicism in simple ways: by placing pots or urns on either side of a gateway; by planting two or a number of symmetrically placed trees; or perhaps by positioning clipped shrubs to flank a front door.

UB Such a severely architectural style requires that plants be used to adorn and emphasize rather than dominate. That is not to say that they are unimportant. Hedging, which can be close clipped, is the *sine qua non* of the formal garden. It can be evergreen or deciduous, though evergreen hedging has the edge because of its long season of colour and because the outline of the garden shape must be retained at all costs throughout the year. Of the deciduous trees, only beech and hornbeam retain their dead leaves in the winter. Evergreen hedging need not necessarily be tall: there are plenty of small sub-shrubs which can be clipped specifically to mark out, rather than hide, different parts of the garden.

Many hedges are, in reality, clipped and severely restricted trees, and these can be used in other ways too. Limes, for example, can be 'pleached' to make a kind of narrow hedge on clear trunks or 'stilts', while fruit trees, carefully pruned for the purpose, can be used

to form linear barriers and even *clairvoyées*. It is possible these days to buy fruit trees ready trained as 'espaliers'. In the case of 'stepover' trees, these need not constitute more than a nominal barrier.

Formal gardens rely heavily for impact on surfaces, and lawn is important for this reason. Grass is an effective and relatively inexpensive surface, and one that will take hard and regular clipping. What is more, as the formal garden is designed to be looked at rather than played on, it offers a splendid opportunity to make a good quality lawn, using a mixture of fine grasses to create an even and attractive sward. Colours are usually muted in the formal garden, with green predominating, and the lawn will act as a subtle foil to other shades of green such as the black-green of yew.

The purity of the formal garden ideal is often undermined by gardeners who wish to see informal planting within a formal (by which they mean geometric) setting. The result cannot, strictly speaking, be called a true

FORMAL GARDEN STYLE

2

1 A perfect example of a contemporary formal garden. The pattern is regular and geometric but very simply conceived. Water plays a major role, and the cruciform shape leads the eye from the rhythm of the outer circle to the stability of the central rectangle.

The inner and outer broken circles of hedging reinforce the circularity of the hard landscape. Note the extensive use of evergreen planting in the background, ensuring seasonal continuity.

2 Formality in the classical style demands symmetry, and here the composition is perfectly reflected from one side to the other. For such a positive treatment to work it needs to engender a feeling of movement, provided successfully here by the distant view between the far hedges and the centrally placed urn.

Even the clipped stems of trees add a vertical regularity to underline the formal theme, and the versatility of yew hedging is fully exploited. Because plants are subordinate to structure in this design, this garden probably looks almost as well in winter as it does in summer.

3 Clipped hedging provides a soft geometry that is impossible with hard landscape materials such as brick or stone. Traditionally, such patterns were simply filled with coloured gravels, but planting is a more modern alternative.

This is not a purist's formal garden, but one which reconciles a desire for geometry and a love of flowers. The laxness of the dahlias acts as counterweight to the stiffness of the hedges. Note also the extensive use of pots. The use of a small quantity of yellow-leaved privet gives the illusion of sunlight playing on the hedge.

formal garden; the introduction of any lax plant not amenable to clipping necessarily introduces a note of informality, however stylized the setting. Certainly, no plant should be allowed to flop over on to hedges and paths, or otherwise break up the strict architectural lines of the garden.

Realistically, however, anyone who loves plants will almost certainly want to bend the rules and plant informally within the formal framework. This often means planting in flowing drifts in the borders, and using a larger range of plant material than would be appropriate to the traditional formal garden. Such a course of action undoubtedly muffles the impact of the formal lines, but that loss is usually more than compensated by the beauty of the plants. This, certainly, is the view taken by generations of British garden writers and designers who happily choose to soften formality with the wealth of plant species which grow so well in a predominantly temperate climate.

3

Great Garden Styles

CONTEMPORARY GARDEN STYLE

DS Garden design in the twentieth century has become both a profession and an energetic contributor to the development of modern ideas about space and form. The term 'contemporary style' rather defies definition, but it is useful for drawing together the many different strands in garden design thinking, from the Bauhaus in the 1920s to the present day. Style has little to do with fashion, which is a transient thing, but the best contemporary gardens do capture the mood of society at a particular time, and reflect the particular lifestyles of their owners. They also show an understanding of the various components and materials used, both in hard and soft landscape

1

terms. This makes the best gardens timeless, although they were at their conception 'contemporary', that is, of their day.

Many, although not all, of the best contemporary gardens have been created by professionally trained landscape architects. Where such designers score over garden designers is in their educational background, which at its best allows for cross-fertilization with other professions. A talented landscape architect might be working alongside graphic artists, architects, fabric designers and a wealth of other disciplines, all at the forefront of current ideas. Just such a philosophy underlay the ideals of the Bauhaus, and certainly the Modern Movement has been a powerful influence on much contemporary garden design. Such brilliant designers as Thomas Church, Lawrence Halprin and Garrett Eckbo were all working within that discipline of austereness and functionalism.

Today a new generation is seeking to create landscapes that not only reflect their surroundings but also incorporate a far wider range of plant material. Form and texture of foliage are as important in a contemporary garden as flower colour, and the current trend

2

CONTEMPORARY GARDEN STYLE

1 This study uses one of the most important elements in contemporary planting design, employing a subtle combination of leaf shapes, colours and textures to gain effect. The simple decking, the adjoining water, and the broad leaves of the rheum all act as foils to each other. A positive focal point is provided by the terracotta pot, all the more effective for being left empty.

Rheum palmatum requires moist conditions, so is ideally suited to this position on the edge of water. Although the flower is secondary to the foliage, it does add a piquancy to the scheme, challenging the onlooker whose eye is inevitably drawn both to its leaf and to that of the purple Japanese maple. This is an arresting rather than restful garden picture.

2 Oehme and van Sweden are one of America's leading landscape design teams. Here they use a combination of very simple geometry and bold plant groupings to lead the eye and link the levels. The principles of the Modern Movement are here updated in a thoroughly contemporary way, where minimal detailing contributes to the strength of the design.

In this garden, plants are used not for individual beauty but for their form en masse. In that respect they approximate, though in a softer medium, to the timber decking and other hard materials. The trees in the background act as a link with the natural world beyond, providing security or invitation, depending on the onlooker's mood.

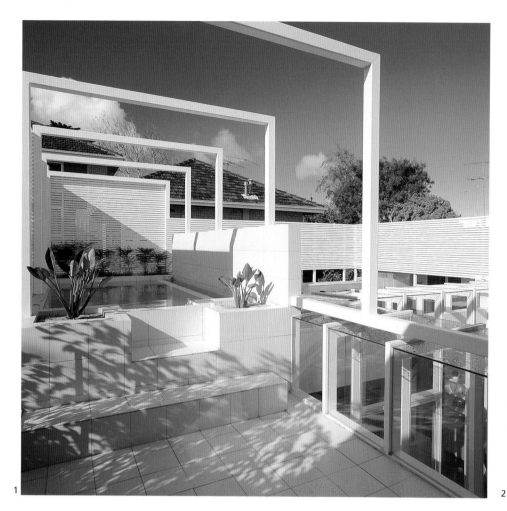

1

2

is to weave this into an increasingly simple hard landscape structure that bases itself on the geometry of the building, respects the materials used, and then flows into and integrates with the wider landscape setting.

There is also a welcome trend to introduce native wildflowers, to use indigenous plant material, and to encourage wildlife – at least in certain parts of the garden. This interest in the environment and in the naturalization of plants is sound and also refreshing. In many ways it is a culmination of garden thinking over many centuries: the desire to do away with the manipulation of plant material and the overcomplication of hard landscape design, in order to create something altogether simpler.

A number of designers, myself included, are also investigating the uses of materials that are common in other industries but not in the garden: plastic for flooring; polyester for fencing; lightweight alloys for buildings that can then be covered with non-rot translucent fabrics. Lighting, too, has enormous potential, and the use of lasers, holograms and fibre-optics is playing an increasing role.

Garden design should be an ever-changing art form; the most successful contemporary compositions embrace that philosophy to the full.

UB Paradoxically, plants are used in the contemporary garden in much the same way as they are in the formal garden: they play a subordinate role, and are merely components of an overall effect. In the formal garden identical plants are grouped, as in a hedge, to create simple geometric shapes; in the contemporary garden their task is to act as 'soft' architecture. In both cases their individual beauty is unimportant.

The obvious difference, however, is that in the contemporary garden the shapes formed by these plant groupings are usually fluid: irregular 'rivers' of colour.

The best known and most skilful exponent of this technique, which is used all over the world, is the South American landscape gardener, Roberto Burle Marx.

In the contemporary garden, ecological considerations are important. Stress is laid on the garden's place in the wider landscape. The wilderness has even been invited to invade the garden. This relatively new interest in native flowers, which can be traced to anxiety about the accelerating loss of natural habitats all over the world, is a departure from the desire garden owners have historically shown to shut out the world.

Contemporary garden style, and the minimalist approach in particular, does not appeal to those for whom the pleasure of growing a wide and associated range of plants ranks high. For others, the contemporary garden means the pursuit of a specialism: alpines, cacti, chrysanthemums, old roses. Here, the garden as a whole is less important than individual plants, although the results may be very pretty .

CONTEMPORARY GARDEN STYLE

2 Some houses sit very comfortably in the garden that surrounds them; this is just such an example. The long low roofline leads the eye into the natural landscape beyond, and stands out in sharp contrast to the trees. The groups of juniper provide a strong statement and help to offset the bulk of the building. The leaves, left on the lawn while their colour lasts, link with the warm tones of brickwork. Sculpture is a personal choice, and should be, the main thing is that it should elicit a reaction! Contemporary gardens use plants almost as artefacts. Trees have been chosen as much for their skeleton and bark as for their leaves: the silver birch with its two main, and probably scrubbed, stems is a good example.

3

CHOOSING PLANTS FOR SHAPE AND FORM

1 In this design, plants are entirely subservient to the architectural framework. Such a design is directly inspired by the Modern Movement and, though positive and refreshingly clean, is minimalist in its approach. Nevertheless, walls and overheads cast crisp shadows, and colour is provided by the blue pool which takes its cue from the sky. The few plants in this garden are very important; without them, the scene would be uninvitingly stark.

3 In this visual joke, multi-coloured balls are set in the gravel surrounding the building, helping to bring an otherwise austere picture alive. This kind of imaginative thinking should always be encouraged; it's the way that new ideas take root. The composition here is strongly dadaistic and provides an interesting link between painting and garden design.

Contemporary garden designers use bold, long shapes and plenty of contrasts of form. Here, spiky ferns are a counterpoint to the broad leaf shapes of hostas; and huge boulders make solid punctuation marks amidst the plants.

COTTAGE GARDEN STYLE

UB The seeds of the modern cottage garden movement were sown in late nineteenth-century English nostalgia. Influential garden writers such as William Robinson and Gertrude Jekyll extolled the virtues of the unpretentious gardens that they saw cultivated by rural cottagers, as a reaction to the exotic artificiality of large-scale country house gardens. They wished to return to what they considered to be indigenous small-scale gardening. In truth, the cottage garden had not existed since time immemorial but it appeared to be as traditional as the charming buildings it surrounded, and that is what mattered.

The cottage garden was profusely and closely planted with hardy flowers and bulbs, a good proportion of fruit bushes and generous, if monotonous, herbs and vegetables. Hedges, some trimmed into shapes, were important, but shrubs were not. The planting was luxuriant because the soil was kept in good heart by quantities of manure, but no attention was given to geometry or colour harmonization.

The true cottage garden would not do, of course, as a model without changes; it was simply too haphazard and the variety of decorative plants used too meagre, especially given the vast choice of plants available to us today. But thanks to a handful of sophisticated gardeners in this century it has developed into a style of its own, one that is much more visually pleasing and harmonious than its forerunner could ever have been.

DS The 'cottage garden' has become one of the most popular of all garden styles. Today's adaptations are particularly well suited to modest plots, and depend for their quaintly old-fashioned air, not only on the selection of plants, but also on the careful choice of vernacular materials that are both authentic and appropriate, and which create a strong link between house and garden. To achieve the most pleasing effect, it is important that brick paths match brick walls, stone paths echo stone floors, timber pergolas take their cue from a half-timbered house, and so on.

The design of cottage gardens can be surprisingly formal, with straight paths edged with hedges of box or lavender and symmetrically arranged beds for flowers and produce. However, it is the lax profusion of the planting, tumbling over the hedges and paths and softening all the hard edges, that gives cottage gardens their characteristic air of informality. It is precisely this element of controlled informality that is the true essence of the cottage garden style.

1

A COTTAGE GARDEN PLANTING SCHEME

This grouping uses just a few of the old cottage garden favourites. The rose at the back is the semi-double form of Rosa alba, *which has been grown in gardens for centuries. It illustrates the point that in cottage gardens the emphasis is on improved forms of those plants that have been popular, because reliable, for a long time – honeysuckles, lilies, violets and primroses, for example. Here the colour scheme is composed of pink, blue and white, but it is less important to harmonize colours than to present a cheerful flowering scene. Green, both of foliage and flower, is always an important component.*

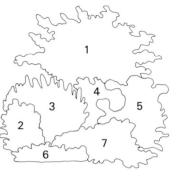

1 *Rosa* × *alba* 'Semiplena'
2 Annual mixed cornflowers (pink, white, blue)
3 *Nepeta* 'Six Hills Giant'
4 *Astrantia major rubra*
5 *Papaver orientale* 'Perry's White'
6 *Dianthus* 'Pike's Pink'
7 *Geranium grandiflorum*

1 Simplicity is important in a cottage garden. Here a straightforward earth path is flanked by a glorious jumble of plants. Pastel colours provide visual harmony. Flanking the path are mixed aquilegias (known by cottagers as 'Granny bonnets') and herbaceous geraniums.

2 Here, vegetables combine with decorative planting, flowers for cutting, and room for relaxation. The layout is simple, which makes for easy access and divides the space up into manageable sections. Thanks to boundaries blurred by planting, the garden itself appears of indeterminate size when you are in it. Although more sophisticated and on a bigger scale, this modern 'cottage' garden is still true to the tradition, with only simple, inexpensive hard features, and a profuse mix of flowers and vegetables.

UB The 'right' choice of plants is the key to success with a cottage garden. The large beds are planted with good forms of 'old-fashioned' flowers, particularly hardy perennials, and a few shrubs for structure. A wide variety of herbs, vegetables and fruits grow either amongst (what is known as 'integrated' gardening) or alongside the flowers. Scented plants are especially welcome, as are those which attract bees. Flowers may be left to seed and form informal drifts, but in a controlled way, for this is not a wild garden. One or two favourites may be used repeatedly as 'key' plants to give coherence.

Cottage gardening tends to be labour-intensive, relying as it does on good husbandry rather than modern chemical sprays; the garden itself can also look unappealingly dull and bare in the winter, for such a large proportion of the plants will be annual or herbaceous. But somehow the style is so satisfying to the psyche, so perfect an antidote to too man-made an environment, that it has adherents in country and city all over the world.

Great Garden Styles

1 The best cottage gardens display a subtle range of planting that is largely herbaceous in character. Here is a style very different from the more restrained planting of contemporary architectural gardens which rely more on foliage. Use is also made of biennials, such as the tall, untidy heads of yellow verbascums, and annuals, such as the sunflowers. One suspects that, in true cottage garden fashion, much has been allowed to self-seed. It is hard to know, in such a loosely controlled setting, whether the effective colour association, particularly of purple salvias next to orange marigolds, is intentional or accidental.

1

2

2 That this is a 'modern' cottage garden is obvious from the overall emphasis on plants that have attractive foliage as well as flowers, and from the restrained use of colour.
Because of their herbaceous nature, cottage gardens require relatively high maintenance. Much of this plant material dies down in the winter, and needs cutting back as well as regular division and thinning. In consequence, such gardens generally look at their best in summer, and the dormant period will leave large areas without a great deal of interest.

3 This proclaims itself as in the modern tradition because of the symmetrical, if lax, groups of planting and the subtle use of colour. The plants (*Alchemilla mollis, Geranium endressii, Rosa* 'Iceberg', for example) have been chosen carefully for their long and abundant season of flower. Foliage (hosta, rhododendron) is here given equal weight.
This delightful composition is all the better for having the clipped box as a pivot for the rest of the planting.

COTTAGE GARDEN STYLE

4 The planting is predominantly 'modern cottage': a large bed of mixed perennials with penstemons, phlox, and the grey-green furry leaves of *Ballota acetabulosa*. This Mediterranean plant would not have been available to true cottagers, but it and others, such as artemisias and santolinas, add greatly to the foliage interest of modern 'cottage gardens'.

The planting of this garden is fine but the drama depends on the arch that frames the view out to a meadow. In such a situation, a ha-ha would make the ideal boundary, leaving the view uninterrupted.

MEDITERRANEAN GARDEN STYLE

DS 'Mediterranean' gardening and garden design is not limited to that particular region but embraces all those places worldwide that share a similar climate: one that is hot in summer, with low rainfall; where winters are mild and frost unusual.

As far as design and living outside goes, conditions are wellnigh perfect. The main considerations will be ample room for sitting and dining, with provision for shade and enough irrigation to keep plants lush and healthy in such dry conditions.

Hot colours can be used successfully in both hard and soft landscapes, as the strong sunlight tones them down. Such drama in a temperate landscape would be garish. Strong sunshine brings with it positive shadows, which can be used as part of the design. Overhead beams cast traceries of light to filter through a canopy of foliage. Walls cast sharp dark shadows; the transition from full sun to black shade will produce a sense of high drama.

Trees, too, play their part, casting the shadow of their branches on the ground. With tall fastigiate conifers the shadows are correspondingly long, and can be used to provide visual divisions to an area.

Materials are often intricate and highly patterned. Glazed tiles descended from the Moors and Persians appear to sparkle in sunlight. Materials are generally local, and terracotta pots, white-washed walls and rough hewn pergolas all combine to produce a rich vernacular garden style.

Historically, the peoples living around the Mediterranean fully understood the benefits of gardens, and the pleasure of living in them. The Egyptians used water, walkways and pergolas, while the Romans created cool gardens within their houses, turning their backs on the harsh environment outside. The Moors too rejoiced in water of every kind, while the Persians built summerhouses called *glorietas* for eating, entertaining, leisure and lovemaking.

Today, the gardens of the west coast of America have taken over the mantle. Economy of line, harmony with the house and landscape, and the use of indigenous planting, all combine to form the perfect outdoor room.

There is also an increasing desire in the United States to use plants that will tolerate dry and arid conditions. 'Xeriscaping' is fashionable, whereby schemes are designed that require minimal water usage. Standard design ideas are still used, but sweeping areas of cobbles, boulders and bold planting of specifically chosen drought-tolerant plants are incorporated to make a contrast with the other surfaces.

1

UB If you garden on the Mediterranean, or in a Mediterranean-type climate, you can find plants from every semi-arid region of the world to suit such conditions. The typical Mediterranean plant has hairy aromatic leaves, and often short-lived but attractive flowers. Many bulbs, which flower early in the season and then die down, come into the same category. Mediterranean plants are drought-tolerant, liking hot sunny summers, dryish winters and a well drained, even poor, soil. They dislike humid mild winters, which encourage rot as well as soft growth, which tends to be vulnerable to late frosts.

However, if you garden in a temperate climate with mild wet winters, or where winter frosts are common, it is still possible to create a Mediterranean effect by choosing those Mediterranean and Australasian plants

1 Because of the quality of the light in hot countries it is possible to be flexible about colour combinations in the 'Mediterranean' garden. Here there is a cool background of grey-green foliage plants and olive trees.

2 All the elements of the Mediterranean garden are here: room for sitting and dining, overhead beams to cast dappled shade, and tough indigenous planting that will tolerate the dry conditions. The paving is made up from simple terracotta tiles, which would probably break up in a frosty climate, and the steps are sensibly broad and easy. But it's the view that is ultimately the dominant factor, and everything is turned towards it - the perfect 'borrowed' seascape!

The planting is simple and architectural, with colour provided by the mainstay of Mediterranean-type gardens, the ubiquitous and easy pelargonium. This colour would naturally draw the eye seaward, even if nothing else did.

4 The quality of light in the Mediterranean is strong and hard. In consequence, you can use very powerful colours as the bright light tends to tone them down. This exterior relies on pure geometry for its effect, and the delicate filigree windows and screens are perfectly set off by the blue walls and centrally positioned pot.

2

4

3 Courtyards are popular in the Mediterranean climate as they provide shade and turn their back on the harsher world outside. White painted walls help to reflect light and keep the house cool, while foliage adds more shade and provides movement in the rustle of leaves. Plants here are grown in pots and raised beds, so irrigation will be a factor, but the water will help to keep the courtyard cool. Among the palms, pelargoniums and jasmine are tubs of brightly coloured *Clivia miniata*, an easy-to-grow tender bulb which adds a welcome splash of orange to the sombre foliage.

3

Great Garden Styles

1 One of the most spectacular and vigorous of sub-tropical and tropical climbers: *Bougainvillea spectabilis*. The flowers are barely noticeable; the glory of this plant lies in the bright and long-lasting bracts which surround them. In colder climates, bougainvillea must be grown in a cool glasshouse or conservatory. Here, the bougainvillea has been trained to echo the strong line of the archway, and adds great strength to the design, where the concentric series of curves demand attention and lead both feet and eye in the right direction.

1

2

that will survive provided they are planted in poor free-draining soil in sun and, if necessary, given some protection in winter. Even many tender plants will survive if kept dry and protected *in situ* in winter. And species tulips and other dwarf bulbs will accommodate themselves to colder climates provided they get a baking from the sun in summer.

Mediterranean gardens work especially well where sunlight is strong and plentiful. They are particularly well suited to courtyards, terraces, dry hillsides, banks in sun, and sunny coastal areas.

Evergreens are an essential ingredient – important for casting shade on hot sunny days and for providing some colour in winter. The 'architectural' shapes of fastigiate junipers and cypresses will harmonize with plants from the Mediterranean area as well as with

'evergreen' cordylines, agaves, phormiums, yuccas, and semi-arid palms like *Phoenix canariensis* and *Chamaerops humilis*. Drought-resistant ground-covers and climbers, such as ivy, are invaluable.

Plant groupings in this kind of climate can be bold and colourful, even flamboyant, as the intense sunlight will temper any dramatic clashes of colour. Established shrubs can be supplemented with summer plantings of tender perennials like argyranthemum, *Lotus berthelotii*, trailing verbenas, cannas, and *Cosmos atrosanguineus*. Tender annuals are useful for ringing the changes.

In colder climates many other tender plants, such as cacti, citrus, and *Clivia miniata* hybrids, can be brought out for an airing in summer from the protection of conservatory or greenhouse.

Simple pergolas supporting vines, jasmine and other heat-loving climbers are everywhere in true Mediterranean gardens. In wetter climates this feature can be used, but with circumspection; it is not pleasant to sit under dripping foliage.

Nothing, of course, so clearly speaks of the Mediterranean garden as terracotta pots of all shapes and sizes. Some are available which will withstand winter weather in temperate regions, but it is usually wise to protect them against severe frosts nevertheless. Fill them with fleshy-leaved agapanthus, small sub-shrubs, dwarf bulbs and pelargoniums.

Scent, especially the fragrance of sub-shrubs such as cistus, lavender and artemisia, is another important element. It can be savoured best on cool evenings after hot days in a confined space.

2 Swimming pools lack attraction in cool and temperate lands, but not in the Mediterranean. This design is mercifully simple, and the blue door picks up the colour of the water. The stone bench is solid and practical. There is a domestic orderliness about the pots, and the way that the rose is neatly trained, which works well. The colour combination is unusually subtle for such a setting.

3 If the designer's prime role is to unite house and landscape, then the brief here has been perfectly executed. The walls have a controlled yet rhythmical pattern that echoes the hills in the distance. Paving is composed of a subtle combination of terracotta tiles and tiny glazed rectangles which effectively 'lift' the predominantly brown composition.

3

JAPANESE GARDEN STYLE

DS It is difficult for people from western countries to appreciate the garden art of Japan. It is an art born of religion and woven into the cultural history of the country over two thousand years.

The generic term 'Japanese garden' incorporates many different styles, but it is their underlying principles that are now copied throughout the world.

The essence of the Japanese garden lies in the recreation of nature within its boundaries. The classic example, with which most people are familiar, is the kind of rock and raked sand composition that can be seen in gardens such as that at Kyoto. In simple terms, the rocks form islands within the sea of raked gravel, with the gravel breaking as waves on the rocks. Even here plants play an integral part. Trees and shrubs are 'tamed' in the Japanese garden, but the aim is to retain the natural characteristics of each plant, not an artificial form. Western gardens attempt to imitate this but, unless undertaken by a Japanese master, they rarely come close to the real thing. Nevertheless, the idea of a 'dry' garden, with its contrasting surfaces of rock, stone, cobbles and gravel, lends itself to gardens all over the world.

However, water, too, almost always plays a part in the Japanese garden: from lakes and pools, that are again as natural as possible, to a clever manipulation of spouts and bamboo flumes.

The real lesson to be learned from Japanese garden makers is simplicity, whether revealed in the beautifully designed buildings and adjoining decks, the impeccable detailing of channels and gullies, or in an arrangement of stepping stones set among any number of different plantings.

The true Japanese garden is a place of quiet, of meditation, and of great calm. In the western garden we ignore these elements at our peril.

UB Because of the religious dimension to the real thing, any 'Japanese' garden made in the west must be something of a pastiche. Indeed, makers of the *jardin japonnais* tacitly admit the fact, preferring to develop their own laxer and more plant-oriented style, though keeping to predominantly Japanese plants. While using many of the ideas, they avoid the difficulties inherent in the symbolism of Japanese gardens.

Japanese gardens are tightly controlled by their makers; they depend heavily on pruned evergreens and azaleas, as well as on carefully manicured Japanese maples and cherries, with irises planted in blocks. Mosses are often encouraged as ground-cover.

1

2

1 Clipping shrubs and training trees is a specific element of Japanese garden art. Manipulation of this kind is all part of taming nature and bringing it within the confines of the garden.

Although obviously a western garden, the feeling achieved here is quite authentically Japanese. Flowering azaleas, clipped evergreens, water, stones and Japanese irises all contribute to the oriental atmosphere.

2 This is many people's idea of the classic Japanese garden. Such 'dry' compositions are highly symbolic. Planting acts as a simple backdrop, and the detailing of both boundary wall and paving is impeccable. The positioning of the hedges at two levels creates an interesting dialogue, and the trees in the adjoining garden are cleverly drawn into this intriguing composition.

3

3 Symbolism is a key element but, like any art form, can be interpreted by the beholder in many different ways. There is undoubtedly a visual dialogue between the smooth boulder, set carefully on the overlapping baulks of timber, and the more natural form of the rock.

This is the kind of static simplicity that many gardeners yearn for, even if they are a bit hazy about the symbolism involved. The horticultural input is slight, being restricted to mowing and clipping, although this must be done regularly to maintain the effect.

4

4 Stone lanterns are a familiar element in Japanese gardens, and were originally placed as votive lights in front of Buddhist halls. They were also used to light the paths to tea houses. In more modern gardens they are used as focal points; they come in many different styles.

The plants in this English garden are not specifically Japanese but the atmosphere is still sympathetic to the oriental theme; the orderly evergreens are clipped to make an overall shape rather than to define a space, as they would be if situated in a formal garden.

KITCHEN AND HERB GARDEN STYLE

1 This is a working vegetable garden of considerable size and productivity. The formal cruciform pattern of paths crosses below a group of fruit trees whose shade also helps to divide one area from another. Arches span the paths, and the frame of low clipped hedges provides a strong feeling of purpose and formality. Mellow brick walls enclose the whole area, providing both shelter and the opportunity to grow a range of fruit and climbers.

As the area is so large in this very attractive kitchen garden 'deep beds' are not necessary. This kind of gardening is labour-intensive, especially in the summer months, but rewarding because so productive. Care has been taken to keep the hedges neatly trimmed and the beds and gravel weed-free.

2 In design terms this little vegetable plot rather loses significance as the eye is drawn up to the pretty spire and beyond to the mountains.

Vegetables may not be very colourful but they have a quiet charm. Here they are sown in blocks, rather than lines, which has the advantage of cutting down on weeding.

3 Here, both horizontal and vertical space has been well used. The great mounds of clipped yew, form a monumental but at the same time rhythmical backdrop that helps to contain the space.

In the ornamental vegetable garden, productive plants also have a specifically aesthetic purpose: the vine on the pergola, for example, and the globe artichoke.

UB Throughout history, both rich and poor have used their gardens, at least in part, to grow culinary, medicinal and cosmetic plants. Such gardens were sometimes formal, and often decorative, but were essentially practical in intent. The Romans grew vines, fruit, vegetables, medicinal and culinary herbs all over their empire, and later, when the outside world was at its most unfriendly, these were fostered in the enclosed world of European monasteries. By Tudor times, the monk's productive gardening had become more ornamental: the Elizabethans took to confining these rather informal plants in trimmed geometric shapes called 'knots'. In the eighteenth century, kitchen gardens were unfashionable in Europe, amongst the rich at least, but, in the late nineteenth century, there was a revival in Scotland, where the necessity for walls to protect flowers as well as vegetables ensured the potager's enduring popularity.

The elevation of the kitchen garden to ornamental status, where fruit, herbs and vegetables are grown for visual effect, is a more modern phenomenon. The best-known example of a contemporary potager of this kind, at Villandry in France, dates from early in the twentieth century.

In Great Britain and elsewhere, ornamental kitchen gardening has slowly become popular; we have discovered that it can also provide a practical solution to the problem of space: even a small potager can be both decorative and productive, encompassing a variety of plant and garden features. Where space is very limited it can be composed entirely, or mainly, of herbs.

Moreover, ecological principles can be upheld by the use of organic manures, 'companion planting', 'deep beds', and flowers to encourage beneficial insects. The frequent and regular cultivation such gardens require lessens the need for chemicals.

Old techniques of fruit-training are back in fashion, and the restricted forms of fruit trees available today are ideal for smaller gardens. Antique vegetable and herb varieties have also been resurrected.

This more domestic type of gardening, neither ostentatious nor expensive to develop, is more in keeping with modern life than the agricultural landscapes in miniature of the past. The only possible drawback is that it is very labour-intensive. It is the ideal design for the keen gardener who wishes for ordered, peaceful, and fruitful surroundings in which to work.

As befits a garden style that owes much of its impetus to the growing of herbs, scent is important, and flowers of course are an integral part of the ornamental kitchen garden. These need not be restricted to flowering herbs, or edible flowers like marigolds and nasturtiums. Sweet peas are a must, but so too are artemisias, honeysuckles and tobacco plants.

Great Garden Styles

1 There are times when a softly planted scheme needs counterpoint and definition. Without the centrally placed pot, the fastigiate conifer and the surrounding standard clipped box trees, this composition would lack clarity. The central feature draws the eye and then allows it to range over the larger planted area.

Perennial flowers mingle informally and attractively here with herbs and vegetables. This is the ideal solution for those without space for separate kitchen and flower gardens, and who do not mind a rather muted colour scheme. Herbs are rarely colourful and can become tatty as the season wears on, but here, in midsummer, they look very well.

DS The need to produce food and grow crops has been a driving force in gardening since the very earliest times.

In the past, kitchen gardens were often laid out in formal patterns and enclosed within high walls to provide shelter and act as a support for climbing plants. Today, gardens can easily be planned to include the practical as well as the decorative, though this is often overlooked: herbs and vegetables are frequently relegated to an uninviting corner of the garden where, screened by a scruffy privet hedge, they are all but inaccessible and tend to be neglected as a result.

The fact is that if you grow vegetables you need to be able to tend and reach them easily. In many cases they can be sited in an area relatively close to the house, and if you want to screen them from view you can indeed use a hedge, but there are many to choose from; a better solution might be a wall upon which you could train fruit. Alternatively, you could form a very

attractive and at the same time productive boundary by growing fruit as espaliers or cordons, trained on posts and wires.

Good wide paths should be planned to service the area, to allow room for tools, barrows, and to tend crops. You may also need to plan space for a shed, greenhouse, cold frames, compost and incinerator, all of which will take up considerable space.

Vegetables, of course, do not have to be grown in isolation, and many are handsome plants that could be used to enhance a garden border or to create an ornamental potager. The French have practised the technique of growing flowers, fruit and vegetables together for years, and the idea of having things in the shrubbery that you can eat is hugely appealing. Globe artichokes, Florence fennel, savoy cabbage, marrows and pumpkins all contribute architectural shape to such a garden. The red-flowered runner-bean can be added for further interest, planted either in tent-shaped

groups or neat rows. Rhubarb, also, should not be maligned, as it provides a useful and good-looking source of ground-cover. Many herbs, fruits and vegetables thrive when planted in pots, and strawberries look particularly attractive grown in containers.

Herbs almost invariably look good – in early summer, at least – and have the bonus of flowers and, even more importantly, scent. A herb garden can form an important feature, and if positioned close to the house will offer easy access from the kitchen. Herb gardens can be designed formally in some kind of parterre or herb wheel, when the divisions will help to keep rampant root systems in check, or allowed to grow and spill over informally. Plants such as sage, rosemary and thyme are garden plants of the highest order and should be used as such throughout the garden. Many herbs also have fine architectural foliage and are invaluable when set within or close to major hard landscape features.

2 This formally arranged area is defined by low clipped hedges and gravel paths wide enough to allow plants to flop out on to the surface. A seat set among aromatic plants is ideal, and the colour scheme is built up from pastels that blend easily and allow the view to run out through the arch to the lawn beyond.

The planting of *Nepeta* 'Six Hills Giant' in quantity around the bench, will ensure permanent companionship from bees for anyone taking a rest in the summertime. The central bed is a tapestry of thyme varieties.

3 Practicality and productivity are the order of the day here. This vegetable garden positively glistens with health, and when kept as neat as this becomes a visual art form in its own right. The simple palisade fence is sturdy, easy to build and functional; it is also in perfect keeping with the overall purpose of the garden.

A bright splash of colour enlivens this utilitarian and simple space. The flowers planted against the far fence give a lift to a scene which, though admirably orderly, might otherwise be a little dull. The cabbages have been flanked by strong-smelling leeks, possibly to keep pests away from them.

COURTYARD GARDEN STYLE

DS Courtyards are found all over the world, and certainly formed the basis for gardens from very early times. The heart of a Roman house, the central open courtyard or *atrium*, had an enclosed *hortus* off it; both turned their backs on the often harsh environment outside. The great Islamic gardens of the Persians and the Moors, like the monastery gardens of Europe, were set within enclosed courtyards formed at least in part by the surrounding buildings: walled enclosures that provided protection from the elements and from attack. Today, the courtyard thrives in a thousand guises, from an enclosed Spanish patio to a backyard in New York.

The real prerequisite is that the space should be surrounded by walls, often those of the house or surrounding properties. Since these, mainly urban, courtyards are often not very large and, being protected by walls, have a climatic advantage over surrounding areas, they make ideal outdoor rooms. The potential for living outdoors is enormous, and the best courtyards take full advantage of this, with ample room for sitting and dining, barbecuing and relaxation.

Hard surfacing plays a major role, and this should be planned to provide a positive link with the interior of the house itself: paving to match the floor inside; an indoor colour scheme continued outside. Overhead beams running out from the house will provide dappled shade, essential in a hot climate, as well as support for fragrant climbing plants. They may also provide privacy – screening from neighbouring windows – and act as a ceiling for your outside room.

The smaller the space, the more important the attention to detail, as everything is close to hand and easily seen. In terms of walling or fencing, this will mean that not only is the choice of materials important, but also the way in which they are used. In a modern situation, brick laying and timber-work will need to be perfectly implemented, while surfaces such as exposed aggregate paving or carefully laid slate can look superb if used taking their cue from the adjoining buildings. There is a trend to try and create a feeling of space by the use of mirrors, false perspectives and murals. At their best, such devices can be great fun, at their worst, a pretentious mistake.

Courtyards need not be rectangular; many, particularly in towns, are formed in the awkward angles between adjoining buildings. Shapes like this offer all kinds of interesting design possibilities, including the opportunity to construct a wide range of features such as raised beds, built-in seating, lean-to buildings and conservatories, as well as water in all its guises. Creators

1

1 In a large courtyard such as this, there will be room enough for a diversity of paving, ornament and planting. Here a retaining wall is completely disguised with ivy, which has also been trained to fill in the bays on the surrounding walls.

The citrus tree close to the porch is a fine feature in a warm climate; it has been cut back to prevent it encroaching too far.

2 Such a superb floor, intricately laid in a traditional pattern of small cobbles, demands great craftsmanship. The cobbles are laid close together and the eye is led towards the central water feature where the circle of pots adds emphasis to the design.

Look what can be achieved with tightly packed planting in little or no soil. Even the hedge is grown in pots, and pots have been clamped to the house wall. The colour from pelargoniums and climbers is welcome amongst so much evergreen planting.

3 This tiny patio garden is completely enclosed by walls, while the ceiling is formed by rough poles slung across the space and softened by vines.

The planting is minimal and out of scale. However, it matters little in a setting whose impact depends on its singularity and clean lines.

4 Here is a delightful joke, for the boats are landlocked within their separate pools. The detailing is impeccable, with stout posts and ropes, solid overheads and crisp weather boarding. Such a feature could be simply visual or could double up as a swimming pool.

COURTYARD GARDEN STYLE

44

Great Garden Styles

of courtyards in hot climates have understood the advantages of water throughout garden history, and have used it in a thousand different ways. Even in a small space, it can be used formally or informally.

New courtyards are being built today, as architects increasingly realize their social potential, but many older ones started life with a very different role from that of an outside room for relaxation. Stable yards, storage yards, communal work spaces and farmyards were all working areas. Many, no longer needed for their original purpose, have now gained a new lease of life as a garden or leisure area.

Even relatively recent buildings of this kind can have an inherent charm, and the vernacular materials from which such places were built often reflect local traditions and are rich in pattern and style. So, approach such projects with care, and with restoration in mind; it is easy to rip up and discard history, and live to regret it.

Your design should be sympathetic to the original structure, and you should salvage materials wherever possible. Fine paving may, for example, have been covered up; if only part of it remains, try to match it with paving from a demolition yard. Walls can be restored and original doorways worked into the design.

UB A courtyard area that is used for other practical purposes can happily be made into a garden in one of a number of styles: you could have a 'Japanese', 'Mediterranean', 'formal', 'contemporary', or even a 'cottage' garden. You could also plant it up in no particular style but in response to the kind of architectural space, and to the aspect and climate that prevails.

The microclimate of a courtyard is often very mild, thanks to the protective walls. This may enable you to plant tender climbers but, since heat may also be more intense than outside the walls, you may have to choose drought- and heat-resistant plants.

1

In courtyards with solid walls on all, or especially the windward sides, damaging eddying winds can be a problem. If so, choose sturdy climbers and fasten them securely to the walls. Pots are a huge asset in the courtyard garden, but should be kept out of very windy spots or the contents will quickly dry out.

In general, however, plants flourish in courtyard gardens. There is much less likelihood of neglect as they are always on view and, since courtyards tend to be thoroughfares as well as sitting areas, there is a premium on keeping them tidy, and the plants deadheaded and in good condition. Containers can be placed on hard standing where they are secure, and can be positioned either singly (if large), in pairs at entrances, or in informal groupings.

For those who dislike bedding schemes, the courtyard can provide a longer-term and more 'natural' setting for tender annuals than is possible in the outer reaches of the garden. Foliage plantings can also be effective but, unless the area is shaded, I would favour a brighter effect in a courtyard.

Water is a feature in many courtyards and is usually used in a formal way. The planting will therefore be restricted to plants for a pool, and to waterside planting of those species which look like bog plants (such as many spear-leaved irises) but which do not require wet conditions and will tolerate heat.

Fragrant plants are essential in a courtyard, for the still air traps scent. This means climbing plants such as jasmine, of course, but also night-scented annuals like *Matthiola bicornis* and nicotiana. The range of scented plants for pots is vast, but herbs must be the first choice where a courtyard leads off from the kitchen.

On a warm evening and if lit effectively, the courtyard, even more than the terrace or patio, can provide the perfect outside room.

1 Granite setts provide hard-wearing no-nonsense paving, probably the original surface of this courtyard. Kerbs in the same material make fine steps, both for the change of level and leading up to the door. Generously planted raised beds are built from brick that provides a visual link with the wall behind.
Foliage plays a large and effective part in softening the hard lines of this courtyard setting. Note the pleasing contrast in shapes achieved here between bergenia, aristolochia, male fern athyrium, *Euonymus* 'Emerald 'n' Gold' and *Helleborus foetidus*.

2 In a tiny urban courtyard the centre of attention is the raised pool with its broad coping that can double as a seat. Foliage smothering the surrounding walls helps to frame an oasis set in the heart of the city.

Such a strong foliage planting in a small area might become rather overpowering if maintenance and pruning were neglected, and the loquat in the corner by the seat will certainly grow a lot larger. The contrasts are good, however, and there would be plenty to see in winter. It is obvious that this photograph was taken in the autumn, because the *Parthenocissus* on the wall is changing colour.

SECRET GARDEN STYLE

UB Ever since gardens were first made, emphasis has been laid on their seclusion; they were seen as retreats from the fierce world outside. The idea of the *hortus conclusus* has run through garden design since Roman times, and was influential in shaping both Moghul and medieval European gardens. The 'secret garden' has appeared in the literature of many lands. Hidden gardens within a garden were common in sixteenth-century England, and only went out of fashion with the 'landscape' movement in the eighteenth century.

A desire for intimacy and seclusion has reinstated the secret garden today. Although the need to keep wolves and bears at bay has gone, we still feel the need to retreat from the hectic, sometimes disturbing, world in which we live. Creating areas within your garden that are screened and essentially secluded, or indeed giving the whole garden an atmosphere of romance and secrecy, will make it a private retreat from modern life.

A secret garden could be reached by a winding, mysterious path under overhanging trees, or discovered by going through an opening in a wall or hedge. Plants within the garden can then be used to reinforce the sense of seclusion and romance: bowers and arbours can be protected from prying eyes by a curtain of foliage or flower from climbing plants; trees and shrubs can be used to divorce one part of the garden from another; hedges, in particular, can be used to make compartments so that all is not seen at a glance.

It is not just trees and shrubs, which we expect to form the structure of the garden, that can create or enhance an air of secrecy or separateness in a garden. Large-leafed plants can be used as living barriers, in the growing season at least. In boggy places, *Gunnera manicata* and *Rheum palmatum* may do the trick while in drier places much can be achieved with large clumps of vigorous grasses such as cortaderia and miscanthus.

In this inward-looking romantic garden there should be emphasis on scent, for scents are strongly evocative, and the sometimes fugitive fragrance is best appreciated in an enclosed space. It can be provided by climbing plants such as honeysuckles or roses, as well as by bulbs, perennials or herbs.

In the secret garden there is no room for brash modern plantings of annuals or complicated geometric layouts. Use lavender, rosemary, roses, honeysuckles, primroses and spring bulbs; use herbs and even wild flowers. Keep colours harmonious and muted: pinks, greys, blues, lemon-yellows. Foliage can play an important part, but use evergreens with forbearance; 'green shades' are fine in summer but turn to dank and dripping leafage in winter.

DS Space is often at a premium in the garden today, and with increasing pressure to use the area as an outside room, the need for privacy within it becomes ever more pressing.

Privacy brings with it those magical elements of mystery and surprise, elements which can themselves produce a feeling of space, and which add interest to the composition as a whole in a way that is impossible if everything is seen at a glance.

If the garden is relatively large and established, there may well be areas, already partially screened or tucked away, where a hedge or wall or arbour can quickly create a secret area. However, privacy is not enough on its own: the area needs sun and dappled shade; shelter from wind; and good planned access from the house or other parts of the garden. You may want to introduce a summerhouse or paved sitting area; and a

1

1 Hostas are the ideal ground-covering plants in this shady situation, though if it is an area to be visited in winter, it will need a planting of early shade-tolerant bulbs such as snowdrops or winter aconites which die down before the hostas get into their stride. Secrecy, mystery, tension and surprise are all here as the path winds its way between the trees from deep shade on to the brightly lit lawn beyond. Such an area should be crossed slowly to appreciate its character, and the uneven path cleverly ensures this happens.

2 The emphasis here is on attractive foliage plants: a golden elder, variegated hostas, prostrate junipers, and sempervivums in shallow troughs. The *Clematis* 'Nelly Moser' has been encouraged to scramble through the short shrubs.

SECRET GARDEN STYLE

3 This little building has an air of permanence and mystery, the latter brought about by the lush cloak of ivy. The box hedges frame intricate pathways that allow you to wander through the space while the stone column and ball acts as a central focal point to the area.

4 Woodlands are often secret and almost always mysterious. Here the shade is broken by dappled sunlight that filters through the overhanging foliage. The seat on the grass path offers a delightfully private place.
These plants are all excellent perennials for a place in moist soil and sun or partial shade. Tallest is the pink-flowered form of the meadowsweet, *Filipendula palmata* 'Rubra', with *Achillea ptarmica* 'The Pearl', and *Geranium psilostemon*. The flowers of this geranium are startling in their combination of deep carmine and black. It grows taller than other geraniums, up to 1.2 by 1.2m/4 x 4ft, and is also an excellent foliage plant, having leaves which change colour in autumn.

5 A common but very effective combination for a moist soil in semi-shade: *Hosta sieboldiana* with *Astilbe* 'Fanal'. These plants will efficiently smother weeds in the height of their growing season.

48 ▶

Great Garden Styles

hammock slung between two sturdy trees in a quiet and peaceful corner can be irresistible.

Children adore secret places, preferably those that are more or less inaccessible to grown-ups; if you can leave much of the planning of such areas to the young-sters, so much the better.

In a smaller garden, subdivision of space is ob-viously more difficult, but it is still possible to site screens and arrange planting in such a way as to create pockets of seclusion. If the garden is on a slope, you could cut into the lower part of the slope and then screen it with a combination of planting and trellising above. A path or steps for access could disappear gently from view around the screening, and become a feature in its own right.

As with planting, the kind of materials you use for the framework or screen to a secret area is important. While it would be possible to use crisp, modern materials in a contemporary setting, it is far more likely that you will want to use something altogether softer. Mellow brick or stone, with the patina of age, may be ideal, while an old thatched or peg-tiled summerhouse sets its own mood and invites seclusion.

Changing the levels in a garden, creating mounds and hollows, would allow you to introduce screened areas, reinforced by planting, behind the higher ground.

The essential point to remember is that any area, secret or not, needs careful planning at the design stage; unless your garden is old and large, it is wellnigh impossible to add such features later on.

1

SCHEME FOR A SHADY CORNER

1 *Jasminum officinale*
2 *Dicentra spectabilis*
3 *Hosta* 'Blue Moon'
4 *Alchemilla mollis*

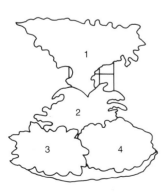

1 Pools of shadow always invite exploration, and this old and well-worn path beckons you towards a secret and shady arbour set about with foliage. Simply constructed from strong timber, such an arbour would provide welcome relief from the more open parts of the garden on a hot, sunny day.

Cornus controversa 'Variegata' is a very choice but slow-growing small tree which naturally takes on a horizontally branched and tiered appearance. It does best in a neutral or slightly acid soil. In the foreground is *Astrantia major rubra* and *Geranium pratense* 'Mrs Kendall Clarke'.

Shade-loving plants need not lack for colour or interest, as this planting scheme demonstrates. The trellis is covered with jasmine, which contributes the essential ingredient of fragrance.

SECRET GARDEN STYLE

2

2 This seat and arbour are cleverly wrought from strips of iron, painted black to merge into a background of foliage. White would have called attention to itself, spoiling a delightfully informal sitting area.

The ground-cover is the amenable and evergreen *Vinca minor*, scarcely without a flower the whole year through. The trees are hornbeam. which can be trimmed to complement the shape of the arbour.

3 A woodland clearing, even a gap among trees, brings a release of tension and a change of light values. Both of these engender surprise and a different mood, often encouraging a visitor to pause and relish the space. Trees set against the light of a clearing take on a more sculptural line, and the foliage stands out in sharp relief.

In a boggy setting such as this, good use has been made of bold-leafed plants like the American skunk cabbage on the left below the bamboo, and the gunnera on the extreme right. The trees casting light shade are *Cercidiphyllum japonicum*; these have leaves which turn a golden yellow in autumn. Astilbes have again been used as ground-cover.

3

DESIGNING YOUR GARDEN

1 Much of garden design is about making patterns, and the patterns must relate to both house and surrounding area. In a small space, a circular shape will help to temper boundaries that are visually 'static', particularly if it is softened by plants. Restraint has been exercised here when choosing plants to set off the paving. Green, glossy foliage and white flowers echo the white walls, underlining the principle that simple effects work best.

2 Certain plant shapes are more dramatic, and draw the eye more strongly, than others. Conifers, the punctuation marks of a garden, should be positioned with care as they form very definite focal points. Generous planting is a virtue in garden design, both for aesthetic and for practical reasons. In the foreground is an exuberant stand of *Rosa moyesii*. Its flowers are short-lived, but its foliage is attractive, and it has striking hips in autumn.

*V*irtually everything that surrounds us in our everyday lives has been designed. Your garden also needs designing if it is to look as you would wish it to look, satisfy your family needs, and work for you as a valuable 'outside room'. Whether it is a brand new plot, or an established garden, it will need careful planning to suit your taste and your own individual requirements. Unless this is done at the outset, you will find yourself squandering time, space and a great deal of hard earned cash on unsuitable plants and a garden that is difficult to maintain and unsatisfactory to use.

A well prepared design will help you to achieve the garden you want; it will allow you or your contractor to calculate accurately the materials needed for the job, and cost them accordingly; it will allow you to allocate a budget and it will mean that the project can be undertaken in phases, without losing track of the original concept.

Genius or perhaps good luck can of course make all the difference between a good garden design and a brilliant one, whether professional or amateur, but a garden designer will almost invariably be working to a tried and tested set of rules that are guaranteed to work in virtually any situation. Whether you call them design techniques or tricks of the trade, the rules are perfectly straightforward and can easily be learned.

The following section will first identify the factors that make a successful garden, and then suggest a logical sequence that will allow you to apply the design techniques to your own. There are a very few basic reminders before you start. The first is that a simple design almost invariably works best. There is nothing worse than 'design for design's sake', where a style is adopted or elements added with no regard to the garden as a whole. The second is that it is essential to keep the survey of what you have in your garden, and what you require of it, in mind. The third is that the principles that lie behind good design are timeless and remain valid, which explains why a well designed garden will survive neglect whereas a poor one will quickly begin to look tired.

These basic principles should be used not for their own sake, but with sensitivity and purpose in order to achieve a good design. They must be allowed to work together, to interlock as the scheme unfolds.

WHY YOU NEED A GARDEN DESIGN

DS In Part One we describe and illustrate a wide range of garden styles, and you will probably have your own idea of an ideal garden, gleaned from gardening books, magazines, or visits to show gardens, friends' gardens or gardens open to the public. However, dream gardens, like designer clothes, seldom suit without considerable adjustments, and it pays to take a close look at your plot and to work out carefully just what you require of it before dashing off on a random buying binge to the local garden centre on the first fine day of spring.

HOW DO YOU BEGIN?

The garden you acquire may be brand new, with very little in the way of features, or an already established plot, ranging from one that is wellnigh perfect for you and your family, to one that is tangled and overgrown. The first option is pretty straightforward – you have a clean slate and can start from scratch; the second may need a little in the way of modification; the third is more complicated. Resist the immediate temptation to 'slash and burn' everything in sight; trees can be felled in a matter of seconds but they take many years to grow, and some of that planting could form the mature basis of parts of the new design.

Old shrubs and trees that you have had the foresight to retain may later become a vital element of the restored garden. Old fruit trees are a typical example. It does not matter if they are beyond their best, although it is amazing what a good prune can do. Cleaned up, and propped up if necessary, they can become pure sculpture, a valuable screen, or a splendid support for a large climber. So by all means thin things out; but do it carefully. You can grub a tree or shrub out later on if it really is unwanted, but always leave it until your ideas have crystallized.

Remember, too, that some plants are invisible at certain times of year: hardy perennials die down during the winter, while most bulbs, appearing in the spring, are gone by midsummer. It can make sense, therefore, to wait before digging the plot over; those dormant plants could contribute to the ultimate garden design.

But whether your garden is overgrown or brand new, a breathing space is essential if your garden is new to you. You and your family need time to get the feel of it, to list your requirements, and to formulate ideas about the kind of garden you want. A little patience now will save a great deal of muddle – and expense – later on. This is the time for thinking and note-taking, before the action to follow.

WHAT DO YOU WANT FROM YOUR GARDEN?

Permanent factors such as shape, aspect and soil will all have a bearing on the final composition of the garden, but its character – unless you are ready to adopt an established garden with the minimum of alteration – will be determined by you and your needs. So start off by making an exhaustive list of the family's requirements. Leave nothing out; it is relatively easy to cut down, but much harder to add features to a finished layout. Details will be confirmed later, but listing your priorities for the way the garden is to be used is an essential first step. Use the list as a guide when you start work on your survey drawing. Bear in mind the amount of time you anticipate working in the garden, and the size of your budget. Some of the elements you may wish to incorporate are listed below.

Practical	Structural	Planting
Screen for bin/oil tank	Access to garage	Annuals
Compost area	Accommodation for bicycles/	Container planting
Night-time lighting	prams	Fruit trees
Noise minimizing	Built-in barbecue	Herb bed
Washing line	Built-in seating	Herbaceous/mixed borders
	Dog run/pet hutches	Raised bed
	Garden shed	Roses
	Greenhouse	Shrubs
	Lawn	Soft fruit
	Pergola	Trees
	Play area	Vegetable plot
	swings/slide/sandpit	
	Pond/pool	
	Preferred boundaries	
	fences/hedges/walls	
	Preferred paths	
	brick/concrete/stone	
	Rock garden	
	Steps	
	Summerhouse/gazebo/arbour	
	Swimming pool	
	Terrace/patio or sitting area	

DO YOU NEED A PROFESSIONAL?

The prime aim of garden design is that the plot should work in the way you want it, look good for 365 days of the year, and involve no more work than you are prepared to put into it.

The challenge of having to design in this way a space that is likely to be a good deal larger than the house itself may seem daunting if you have little or no design experience but, if you follow the guidelines in this section, there is absolutely no reason why you should not be able to do it yourself. There is no one better placed than yourself to know precisely your requirements, your likes and dislikes, and you will

1 This terrace, set against its glorious view, may seem to have little in common with typical garden plots; but it sums up many of the principles of good garden design. Its curving shapes, repeated in a low stone wall, sweeps of cobbles, circles of planting and shallow troughs, echo the curve of the bay beyond, showing on a grand scale the potential of linking features outside the garden with those within. The plants are appropriate for their stony home, and their low-growing mats help direct the attention to where it should be – beyond. The principles upon which the most successful garden designs are based, are fundamental, even if few gardens have a view as stunning as this one, and they underline the many reasons why every garden will benefit from a first-rate design.

1

achieve the result more cheaply. You will learn new skills, gain insight into the way your plot and its features and surroundings can work for you, and you will find the experience a fascinating and rewarding one.

You may, however, for a variety of reasons, prefer to use a professional garden designer, and a fresh – and practised – eye may indeed see solutions more quickly than you would yourself. A skilled garden designer will (like an architect) undoubtedly save you time; he or she will have all the tricks of the trade at their fingertips; will have contacts with the best contractors; and will also have the specialized plant knowledge to bring the whole composition to life. It is only important to remember that it is your garden, and that the designer is there to interpret your ideas, not to superimpose his or her own.

Garden contractors, incidentally, do not as a general rule undertake design commissions. They will carry out any work according to a properly drawn up plan – yours or the garden designer's – but beware of presenting them with a rough sketch on the back of the proverbial envelope and expecting them to read your thoughts; it will almost certainly lead to trouble.

There are many skilled garden designers at work today. The best way of finding one is by recommendation – from friends or a reputable garden centre; and in Britain the Society of Garden Designers can provide a list of designers whose work they have vetted.

Before employing a designer, arrange to meet him or her on site, and ask to see a portfolio of work, or to be put in touch with previous clients; it is important to feel that your designer's ideas are in sympathy with your own. Most designers will charge for this initial consultation, so ask about fees in advance. If you feel that his or her style or personality are unsympathetic to your own ideas, or that the cost will be too high, then say so politely. It is far better to part company at this point than to waste fees and emotion on an unsatisfactory result.

STAGES IN DESIGNING YOUR GARDEN

There are really four straightforward stages to designing a garden. You need first to consider how you intend to use it, and how much time you are prepared to spend gardening it. Next, you need to understand the technical practicalities of measuring, plotting and so on, in order to prepare a scale drawing. Then you need to consider the principles which operate in good design – not high-flown notions but simple rules which work. And finally, you need to apply the information and ideas you have gathered to create the plan.

MAKING A SITE SURVEY

DS Impatience is undoubtedly the enemy of the amateur designer. Instant gardens only exist at horticultural shows, and these often have a sterility about them that one would not wish to emulate. There are no short cuts; never be tempted to start designing your plot before your survey is completely finished. The information provided by an accurate survey is essential. It will form the basis of a scale drawing that will in turn form the outline of the finished scheme.

PREPARATION

You will need a clipboard with a pad of large paper, a 30m/100ft tape measure, a 60m/200ft reel of string and some skewers (tent pegs or metal skewers will do), some bamboo canes, and a compass.

On the pad, draw a very rough plan of the outline of the house and the boundaries of the garden; this enables you to mark on the actual measurements at the appropriate points. It does not need to be to scale, but it does need to show every detail, such as a chimney breast, an angled wall or a small outhouse. Back and front gardens should be plotted on separate sheets of paper.

Start with a large outline of the house at the bottom of the sheet. Include any projections, such as a conservatory, porch or bay window, the position of items such as an oil tank, fuel store or garage, and existing terracing or paths.

Next, draw in the boundaries of the plot to fill as much of the sheet as possible. Show the angle of the plot in relation to the house, and jot down what the boundaries are made from.

Mark in any existing trees or large shrubs, identifying the species if possible, and giving a rough indication of their height and spread.

MEASURING UP

Once you have completed the rough sketch you can begin superimposing measurements on the rough drawing. Using the house as a starting point, run the tape from one side of the garden (fixing it in place with a bamboo cane), across the back of the building to the opposite boundary. Pull it taut to remove any kinks and make sure it runs in a straight line. Now you can note down the running measurements.

In sequence, mark the distance from the boundary to the first feature you encounter – the edge of a terrace for example – and from there to the corner of the house. Measure and mark in windows, doors, projecting bays or porches, positions of drainpipes and gullies, and finally the distance to the second boundary. You can transfer the measurements to a scale drawing later on.

Next, provided that your garden has boundaries running at right angles to the house, run the tape at right angles from one corner of the house, lining this up with the side wall of the house by sighting back down the tape. Then take running measurements of anything you encounter along the length of the tape: the edge of a patio, a path, shrubs or trees, and so on to the end boundary.

By using these two sets of measurements, or 'base lines', you can check the shape and size of most small rectangular gardens, and plot in their key features.

If the plot is more complicated, you may need to employ a couple of other simple techniques. These are explained opposite. Triangulation enables you to locate accurately any feature that is some distance from one of the base lines, or a boundary that is set at an angle to the house. Offsets enable you to plot the shape of curved features in the existing garden. You may also need to measure the change in level of a sloping area.

WHAT TO MARK ON THE PLAN

Having taken the measurements of the garden, there remain a number of other pieces of information you will need for your survey. Manholes, drains, ventilation pipes and septic tank covers need to be recorded. Fix their position, using triangulation if necessary, and make a note of their exact size and angle.

The orientation of the garden – which way it faces in relation to the sun – is vital information. The direction of the sun will have a bearing on the choice of plants for particular situations and will also determine where you sit in the garden. So use a compass and mark magnetic north clearly on your plan. You should also remember that the sun swings higher in the sky during the summer, and that a wall or tree will cast correspondingly longer shadows in the winter. If you can mark the extent of the shadow patterns at different times of year, and indicate the arc of the sun across the garden throughout the day, this will provide invaluable information when it comes to planting as well as designing your garden.

Another detail that needs recording on your plan is the view beyond it, on all sides, for a good view from a garden can dramatically affect the finished composition. Good views – of a pleasing tree or perhaps a church spire – are a bonus but, unfortunately, bad views are rather more common. They can range from the obtrusive bulk of a neighbour's garage to the problem of overlooking windows, or the unsightly march of electricity pylons or motorways in the larger landscape. Inside the garden, an oil tank can be a real eyesore, and so can a poorly sited shed or dustbin store. Analyse just what views you have got, both inside and outside your garden, and record your observations on your plan.

Shelter, or a lack of it, is another point to record. Note down the places in the garden that are most affected by the prevailing wind or by draughts, for either could have a detrimental effect on both plants and people.

Another problem that arises in the proximity of any wall or building is lack of rainfall due to a rain shadow. The prevailing wind will drive rain along with it, and if a building stands in its path, ground in the lee will receive little or no moisture. A similar situation arises with overhanging eaves, trees or wall plants.

CONDITIONS AFFECTING PLANTS

There are further pieces of information that you need to note down before beginning to design your garden.

Climatic variations can be considerable within any country, and will depend on latitude, altitude and a number of other local factors. Some localities have their own microclimates, often with sharp departures from the norm. Subtle variations are such conditions as 'frost-pockets', in which frost, rolling down a hillside, gathers in a dip or 'pocket' at the bottom of the slope. Sometimes the problem is man-made: a dense hedge or building, for example, can prevent the colder air from draining away to a lower level. Sometimes a gap can be opened up to relieve the problem, or you may have to think about introducing tougher plants into these areas.

Next, soil. The soil that surrounds your home is the basis for all plant growth; a careful analysis may reveal that it requires some attention before you start to implement your planting plans. Topsoil is 'alive' with bacteria, insects and nutrients that plants need in order to thrive, while subsoil is, in effect, dead. Topsoil normally overlays subsoil but if building work has left it buried or absent, you are within your rights to demand that the top layers of subsoil are removed and replaced with good quality topsoil. Similarly, if the soil surface has been compacted by heavy machinery, forming a hard 'pan' that prevents drainage, you can demand that the ground is deeply dug over and levelled.

Finally, you need to check the water table – the level of water found naturally in the ground at different times of year – which can easily be checked by digging trial holes in different parts of the garden. Most roots grow in the top 450mm/18in of soil. If water stands higher than this then you may well have to think about solving the problem by draining the ground, or, alternatively, growing water-loving plants.

MAKING A SITE SURVEY

MEASURING YOUR GARDEN

Border edges can be softened

Bare walls can be softened with planting

Consider removing poorly sited trees

Neglected borders can be renovated or replanted

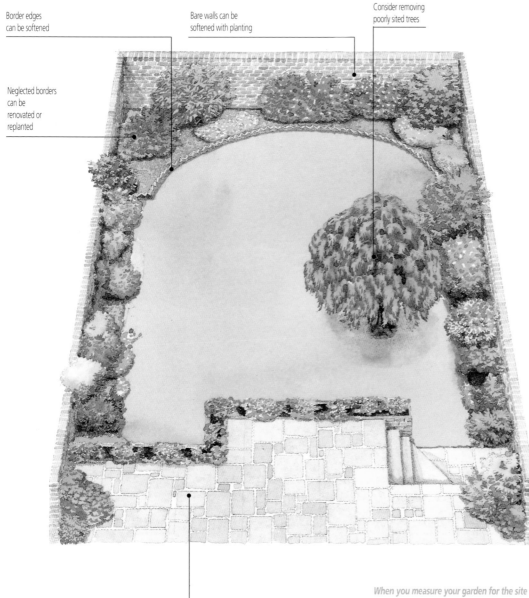

Areas of paving and steps can be reused in a new design

When you measure your garden for the site survey, note down the existing elements and decide whether you wish to retain, modify or remove each of them.

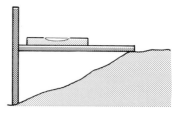

HOW TO MEASURE A SLOPE

An approximate gauge of the height of a steep bank can be made by standing at the bottom and relating it to your own height. For a more accurate measurement, you will need to use a pole, straight-edged plank and spirit level. Place one end of the plank on the ground at the top of the slope, position the pole vertically at its other end, then bring the plank to a level position by centring the bubble in the spirit level. Mark the level of the plank on the pole and record the measurement from the mark to the ground. Repeat the operation if necessary, placing the end of the plank each time in the position previously occupied by the foot of the pole. By adding the vertical measurements together you can easily work out the fall of the whole slope. If the garden slopes unevenly, you may need to repeat the process in different positions. Finally, plot the level lines on your survey as they will be useful if you wish to prepare contour drawings.

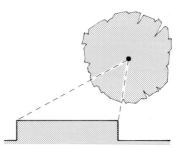

TRIANGULATION

Use this technique for free-standing features such as trees. It can also be used for awkward corners. Mark the tree roughly on your drawing. Measure to it from two known points, such as the corners of the house, and record them on your sketch. When you later come to make a scale plan, set a pair of compasses to the first measurement. Position the point on the house corner, and draw a short arc. Then repeat for the second measurement. The point where the two arcs intersect indicates the position of the tree.

HOW TO MEASURE A CURVE

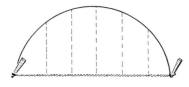

To plot the line of a curved boundary or wall, you use simple measurements known as 'offsets'. First plot the two ends of the boundary or wall concerned, using triangulation if necessary. Next, take your 60m/200ft line of garden twine attached to metal skewers and stretch this from one end to the other. Starting at one end, take a measurement at right angles from the line to the boundary at 1m/3ft intervals, clearly noting each measurement on the survey drawing. When these offset measurements are linked up, the curve of the boundary or wall will be reproduced.

Making a Plan

MAKING A SCALE DRAWING

DS You have measured the garden, have looked closely at its physical characteristics, and have noted things that will affect the final plan. You are now ready to transfer all this information on to a scale drawing.

Accuracy is vital. Only if you base your design on a plan drawn accurately to scale can you be sure that everything will fit in the way you intend. It will also allow you to make an estimate of the quantities of materials and numbers of plants you will require.

Use an A3 sheet of graph paper for your plan, choosing an appropriate scale for the size of your garden. Most gardens, up to a size of about 30 x 18m/100 x 60ft will fit. Larger gardens will fit better on a sheet of A2 or even

A1 paper. Each square or number of squares on your scale drawing will represent a measured square of garden, and the scale used will be determined by what fits best on your A3 sheet. The larger the scale, the easier it is to prepare and 'read'. The measured base lines on your survey will help you to work out which scale to use. Front and back gardens should be drawn up separately.

First tape the sheet of graph paper down on to a flat surface at the corners, then place a sheet of tracing paper squarely over the top of it and stick it down in the same way.

Working in pencil and starting approximately 2.5cm/1in in from the left-hand side and 2.5cm/1in from the bottom, number each 'metre'/'foot' square con-

secutively both across and up the sheet. In this way, if you are working to a scale of 1:100 (⅛ in = 1ft) the numbering will be approximately 1 to 25 across the sheet, and 1 to 35 up the side. If you are using the larger scale of 1:50 (¼ in = 1ft), with two squares per metre, the drawing will be twice as big.

When you carried out the survey of the garden you took running measurements along the base lines, across and up the garden. Now transfer these measurements to the tracing paper, link them up, and you will see the shape of the house and the position of the boundaries beginning to emerge. Mark in any outside buildings, manholes, drains, gates, paths and paved areas as well. If you have forgotten to take a vital

measurement, go out and check it; here you have an advantage over the professional designer who would have to travel miles to do the same thing.

Features on your survey, such as trees or awkward corners, that you measured by triangulation can be transferred to your scale drawing with the help of a pair of compasses as previously described.

Offset measurements can be transferred by drawing a straight line from the start to the finish of the curve concerned, and marking it off at 1m/3ft (or your equivalent) intervals as you did on the survey. Transfer the measurements you took out in the garden to the scale drawing. Join them up to plot your curve.

If your garden slopes you will have noted the levels on your survey. You

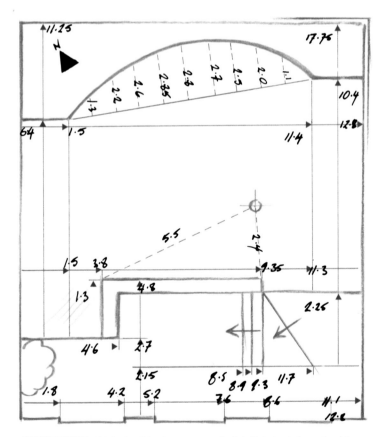

SURVEY DRAWING *This freehand drawing shows all of the relevant measurements taken during the survey. Triangulation and offsets are clearly indicated, as is the north point. These measurements will be invaluable when making the scale drawing.*

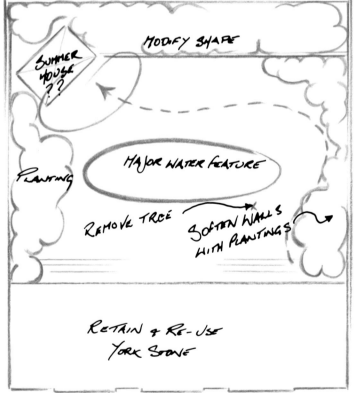

DESIGN SKETCH *Mark on the scale drawing the elements you want to include in the new design, as well as intended modifications to existing planting and paving. Use this as a basis from which to develop alternative design ideas (opposite).*

MAKING A SCALE DRAWING

DRAFT DESIGN: CIRCULAR *The circular theme turns in upon itself to detract from the rectangular boundaries. Steps drop down to the main level and a path sweeps past the pool that is a segment cut from the lawn. The seat acts as a focal point.*

DRAFT DESIGN: DIAGONAL *The design is turned at an angle to the house and boundaries, leading the eye away from the latter. The pattern is architectural close to the house, but fluid further away, providing a feeling of space and movement.*

DRAFT DESIGN: ASYMMETRIC *This whole design is based on a 1m/3ft grid with shapes and patterns overlapping one another. The pool forms a central pivot, while planting softens the various rectangles surrounding the summerhouse.*

now need to relate these changes in level to a known fixed point close to the house. Manholes are often used for what surveyors call a 'datum' point or 'zero', and from this point slopes up will be given as a plus measurement, and slopes down as a minus one. If you used the plank, tape and spirit level method in your survey, you can easily plot the measurements of the vertical drops, along with any contour lines.

Once the boundaries, levels and other measurements have been plotted on your scale drawing, you can mark the additional information that you noted.

When the scale drawing is finished, file the original tracing away. You can use this to make copies of your plan when devising possible designs. Never work directly on the original.

Your brief now, like that of the professional, is straightforward: to use all the information you have gathered to produce a strong design that will both suit you and suit your plot. You will have begun to formulate some pretty clear ideas of what you want, but you will also have understood the importance of doing the groundwork first.

Go back to your prepared list of items to include in your plan, and put them in order of preference. Number one might be a terrace, two a lawn, three a pergola, four a barbecue, five a water feature, and so on.

Then start to rough in the main features on one of the copy drawings. Mark in where the terrace might go – noticing where your plan indicates shade – the position of the lawn, a barbecue with built-in seating near the kitchen, a play area for the children, a vegetable garden. Group utility items together where possible: a garden shed, greenhouse, compost and incinerator or bonfire area, remembering to allow room for access and machinery.

Now you can go on to produce thumbnail sketches to map out various alternative designs for your garden, incorporating what you have and what you want in different ways. Make the shapes proportionate to each other by organizing them following multiples of your graph paper squares. The thumbnail sketches on this page will give you an idea of the possible variations that can be achieved using the same basic blueprint.

DRAFT DESIGN: FORMAL *This is the conceptual stage of the fully worked up scheme based on rectangles, but this time on a balanced and formal basis. The seat and pavilions act as focal points while planting softens and surrounds the composition.*

THE STRUCTURAL PLAN

DS You have now listed your needs for your garden, done a detailed survey, and transferred the information to a scale plan. You have drawn some sample designs, using different shapes and permutations, and come up with a solution that meets your needs for the garden, and pleases you aesthetically. You can now turn the rough design into a full structural plan, using the information on this page to plan the spaces. First, however, you will need to take into consideration some of the principles that underlie good garden design, which are discussed fully later in this section.

A structural plan is a detailed drawing, to scale, of exactly how the new design will look. It needs to be absolutely accurate, so that you can ensure the shapes you have created on paper will really function well in the garden. You will therefore find yourself refining and amending some of the ideas you had on your thumbnail sketches.

ASSESSING COSTS

This is also the time to decide exactly what material will be used to construct each area in the garden, and here you will have to think realistically about costs. It is virtually impossible to build a worthwhile composition on a shoestring. 'Hard' landscape features – paving, walling and so on – will take possibly 75 per cent of the total price, although if you do the building work yourself you will save much in construction charges. It is worth doing some serious market research at garden centres and builders' merchants to check the price of paving, walling and fencing materials. You will need to decide how to make the best possible use of the most expensive materials: brick, for example, is costly to lay, but can be used with paving slabs to reduce the expense. Paving slabs themselves vary enormously in cost, and you may be able to find a slab that achieves the visual effect you want, even if it is man-made, for a fraction of the price you would pay for natural stone.

Plants, seeds and turf are all relatively inexpensive, and do not require professional labour.

If the cost of the hard landscape materials turns out to be too high for your budget, you may have to adjust your design sights accordingly; but remember that if you are doing the construction yourself, you can spread the work and therefore the cost over a longer period. Areas that you would like to pave, for example, could be laid to turf, or planted with ground-covering plants, until funds become available.

Opposite is a list of all the paving materials you might choose, listed in order of expense (most expensive first).

THE STRUCTURAL PLAN

Draw the structural plan of your new design to scale, basing it on your original scale drawing of the garden. Accuracy at this stage is vital, as you will use this plan to assess the quantities required of your preferred materials, and thereby their overall cost. You may find yourself amending your original plan as a result of these calculations.

Square pavilions to continue rectangular theme

Sitting area moved to central position

Raised beds rebuilt to be wider for planting

Rectangular pool with water spout

Gravel paths to keep costs down

Trees sited to balance across garden

York stone paving to be relaid, to include gravel area

Balustrade to emphasize the change in level

As a general rule, all natural paving is more expensive than man-made; and the larger the size of each paving element, the cheaper it is to lay.

NATURAL MATERIALS IN DESCENDING ORDER OF EXPENSE
• Polished granite, marble and other specialist stone
• New natural stone
• Secondhand natural stone, in rectangular slabs
• Granite setts
• Cobbles
• Broken natural stone
• Railway sleepers
• Gravel or chippings
• Decking
• Log slices from fallen trees

MAN-MADE MATERIALS IN DESCENDING ORDER OF EXPENSE
• Bricks or clay pavers
• Terracotta tiles
• Stable pavers (new or secondhand)
• Concrete block pavers
• Precast concrete slabs, in many shapes and finishes
• Asphalt and bitumen
• Concrete in various finishes

CREATING FUNCTIONAL AREAS

No matter how beautiful your garden, it will be a constant source of irritation to you if the paths are too narrow for a wheelbarrow, or the terrace too small for easy movement around it. Working accurately to scale means you can assess how big all your spaces can eventually be, and adapt them as necessary.

Working ergonomically – that is, making sure that each space performs the function intended for it – relates to more than just the size of the spaces, however. Also important is access to each area: if you have planned in your compost heap in a certain place, can you get to it easily, without wearing bare patches in a lawn? If you intend to construct a pond, have you provided somewhere to

sit and watch the fish? Anticipating how the garden will be used and enjoyed is all part of garden design.

The following list gives some guidelines for how big or small areas need to be. Remember, however, that planting will form a part of your final garden, and may affect access around the garden. For example, a path edged with plants spilling over on to it needs to be at least

250mm/10in wider than a simple path edging lawn or a boundary. Planting areas need to be planned for easy maintenance, too. Narrow borders dry out quickly, and tend to force you to plant them in a single straight line – undesirable if you want to create interesting planting schemes. Conversely, very wide borders may need a path through them, to enable you to prune and maintain plants at the rear.

Even though you are working on a plan, boundaries need to be considered as an important part of the overall design. Ensure that any walls indicated are thick enough for their height, and allow extra space in front of any hedges to enable you to clip and maintain them.

If you follow all these guidelines, you should be able to achieve a garden that looks and works in the way you want.

SIZES AND DIMENSIONS

At this stage, you will need to work out precisely how big each area of your garden will be, and whether each will fulfil its required functions.

Paving

Minimum size for a terrace or patio is 3.6 x 3.6m/12 x 12ft. This gives sufficient space for a modest-sized table and four chairs.

All surfaces should be at least 2 courses of brick below the house damp proof course (150mm/6in).

Paving should 'fall' gently away from the house – not less than 1:100 to prevent water running towards the foundations of the house.

Paths should be no less than 600mm/ 2ft wide. For wheeled toys and ample barrow/power tool access, just under 1m/3ft is better.

Steps

Steps should have a riser of 150mm/6in and a tread of 450mm/18in.

Ramps – the maximum gradient should be no more than 1:10 or they will be difficult to negotiate with heavy barrowloads, or in icy weather.

Pools

The average garden pool need be no more than 600mm/2ft deep, with marginal shelves 225mm/9in below the surface. Shelves should be approximately 300mm/1ft wide. To calculate the area of a pool liner, add twice the maximum depth of the pool to the maximum width and length. Pools should be sited in full sun for water plants, but away from deciduous trees that will drop leaves into the water.

Seats

Built-in seats, seats around trees and raised beds used as seats, should be approximately 450mm/18in high.

Pergolas and Arches

These should always be high enough for head clearance, remembering that climbers will take up head room. 2.1m/7ft is a good average. The feature should be generously wide with posts a minimum of 450mm/ 18in from the edge of a path.

Barbecues/work tops

Height can vary slightly depending on personal choice but should be between 750-850mm/30-33in. Site carefully in relation to sun, wind and neighbours.

Lawns

Lawns need to be in sun or light shade, and the seed mixture should be chosen accordingly. It's a good idea to construct a mowing edge to your lawn from brick or other material.

Boundaries

Walls can cast rain shadows on beds beneath. Hedges planted at the backs of borders need to have 300mm/1ft access behind the planting for maintenance, clipping and so on.

Making a Plan

MAKING A PLANTING PLAN

262 The Top 100 Garden Plants

92 Soil and Excavation

UB It is easy to get stage-fright when you are about to begin making the planting plan. Plants can seem an unnecessary complication on what is otherwise a straightforward and clear-cut plan. Do not be put off: once you leap in you will find this as enjoyable an aspect of planning as any.

Before starting to work out a planting plan on paper, you need to decide what kind of 'look' you would like the planting in your garden to have; what kind of atmosphere you would like to create in particular borders or parts of the garden. For example, is that border furthest from the house going to be misty and indefinite in its summer planting, with the accent on cool pastel colours, or would you prefer it to make a more definite statement by using modern roses underplanted with spring bulbs?

You need also to decide how you wish the garden, or parts of the garden, to look in each season of the year. A neat and tidy spring planting, for example, could give way to a luxuriant summer border of herbaceous perennials overflowing on all sides. A pastel summer scheme could become hotter in colour as the autumn approaches.

Once you have established the 'feel' of the various parts of the garden (or perhaps the garden as a whole) try to stick to it. Integrity is as valuable an attribute in a garden as in a person.

It is useful to make a list of those practical factors which will inevitably affect your choice of plants in different areas, and keep it by you for reference: type of soil (wet, dry; heavy, light; acid, alkaline); aspect (not always straightforward: a sunny aspect may be shadowed by a building or a tree); climate (sheltered or exposed; direction of prevailing wind; average amount of rainfall; rain shadows; microclimates that exist or that could be created).

It is a worthwhile exercise, before you start designing, to cross-hatch those parts of the plan which you know (or can guess) will be in shade for some, or all,

PLANNING A COLOUR SCHEME

It may be helpful to visualize how an intended colour scheme works in practice. On a copy or tracing of your structural plan, try colouring in the areas for planting, to see how the garden looks overall; you may want to repeat the exercise for different seasons. In this way you can instantly see which flower or foliage colours are going to catch the attention. When choosing plants to fulfil a colour scheme, remember that while plants are often illustrated in flower in books and catalogues, many will not bear those flowers for more than a couple of weeks. If a particular colour scheme is important to the design of the garden, half-hardy annuals and later-flowering perennials and shrubs can be used to maintain it throughout the year.

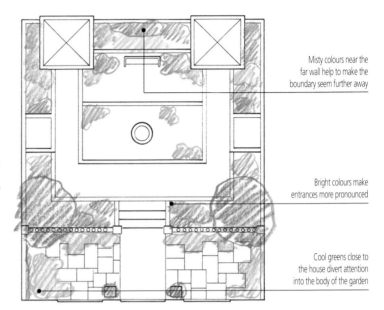

Misty colours near the far wall help to make the boundary seem further away

Bright colours make entrances more pronounced

Cool greens close to the house divert attention into the body of the garden

of the day. Although there are various plants which will grow and flower well in shade, this is the area of the garden most likely to cause difficulties and so should not be overlooked.

Next should come a list of all those plants which you particularly like, or have noted favourably, with their main characteristics: for example, their basic requirements and the time of year that they perform. Avoid going slavishly through a plant encyclopaedia, or you will end up with a garden composed entirely of plants beginning with A or B!

When putting plants on a plan, most people find it easiest to use a scale of 1:50, to avoid the risk of the plant groupings and accompanying names being too small to be legible. By now, having designed an outline plan, you should be quite used to using a scale ruler, and scaling up a drawing from 1:100 to 1:50 will cause you little difficulty. However, if you are short of time or it seems a waste of labour, by all means design to 1:100. You will need a piece of tracing paper to put over the outline plan, specifically for including the plants. Use a pencil for all this initial work; you can always ink it in, using drawing pens, later on. This is obviously

necessary if you wish to make copies. Put in not only the outline of the groupings but an 'x' where each plant is to go. That will enable you to use the plan, in conjunction with a measuring tape and bamboo canes, when you finally plant up your borders.

When deciding how much space each plant should take up on the plan (which is most important if money is not to be wasted by overplanting, or time wasted by underplanting), pay particular attention to its maximum height and spread on maturity. This information is usually available in plant encyclopaedias and sometimes also in nursery catalogues. These heights and spreads can only ever be approximate, of course, but they are a helpful guide. If in doubt, it is advisable to err on the generous side, especially in the case of trees. Most harm is done, in the long run, by planting everything too close together.

Start your plan with structural or framework planting; this usually means trees and shrubs, including hedges and dwarf conifers, but can also mean ground-covering plants, especially in the avowedly 'low-maintenance' garden. Next, begin to fill in with perennials, annuals and bulbs – the icing on the

cake. It is not obligatory, of course, to have every kind of plant represented in the garden (in a small garden a tree might well be a nuisance) but bear in mind that different kinds of plants perform different tasks, and sometimes more than one, at different times of year, so do not dismiss any one group of plants out-of-hand before you have considered very carefully.

The next stage is to crayon or paint in the flower or foliage colour, whichever is the more striking feature of the plant. Colours can be misleading, of course, tempting you to plan for maximum effect for only a short period of the year, and to assume that some plants flower together when they do not. No garden has (or should have) *everything* flowering at the same time, so you should expect some green areas on the plan. It will, however, give you a good idea of the overall balance in the finished design.

Do keep the design simple, especially if you feel you cannot spare much time on the garden. In this case, it is preferable to use repeating patterns of dependable plants. It is vaulting ambition, not lack of artistic sense, that usually makes for unsatisfactory or inharmonious schemes.

MAKING A PLANTING PLAN

THE PLANTING PLAN

A planting plan can be as simple or as complicated as you like. It may help you, for example, to use symbols and outline shapes that actually reflect, in bird's-eye view, the way a plant grows: spiky shapes for spiky plants, toothed outlines for shaggy plants. Such detail is helpful conceptually, but is often unnecessary if you will be planting up the garden yourself. The example shown here gives the minimum information you need: it shows a general outline for the area taken up by each species or variety, with actual planting positions, spaced as recommended, for each plant that will make up the total clump. For an informal effect, plant in long drifts. Generally, plant herbaceous perennials in odd numbers, both to avoid a boxy look and to ensure that the plants grow together into a group.

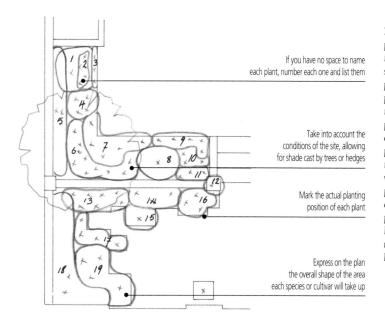

If you have no space to name each plant, number each one and list them

Take into account the conditions of the site, allowing for shade cast by trees or hedges

Mark the actual planting position of each plant

Express on the plan the overall shape of the area each species or cultivar will take up

Identifying the plants Choosing which precise species or cultivar should occupy which area in the garden depends on both the demands of the site, your intended colour scheme, your individual preferences, and the eventual height and form of the plant. You will probably find you make many revisions as you try to construct pleasing plant partnerships, or match favourite plants to particular conditions. For example, in the section shown, plants numbered 13 to 19 will be growing in relative shade, must be attractive enough to be viewed from the house, but should not outshine the plants beyond. Cultivars of hosta would be an appropriate choice, with ferns behind. The planting plan must be labelled accurately, and if you don't have room to write the full name on the plan itself, number the plants on the plan and list them in a key. Give the exact number of plants intended.

THE FINAL GARDEN

This illustration shows how the garden used as an example in this chapter might look, once it has had time to mature. In your own garden, the initial planting plan is never the final word, however carefully you have considered harmonies of colour and height. You will want to move plants around to achieve an effect that wasn't quite right the first time, fill gaps or dull areas with annuals and bulbs, introduce more seasonal variation, and make space for new plants that catch your attention at garden centres or nurseries. You may have to move plants that perform only poorly, too, or find substitutes for those that fall victim to pests, diseases or physiological disorders. Such constant re-thinking is all part of the pleasure of designing your own garden, and with plants, the changes are easy to make, and the choices almost endless. (For a full plant list for this garden, see page 103.)

PRINCIPLES OF DESIGN
TENSION, MYSTERY AND SURPRISE

DS There are three main ingredients that are essential to any successful garden design, and these are tension, mystery and surprise.

A garden that can be seen at a glance is far less attractive than one that is broken down into individual 'rooms', with 'tension points' that trap the attention on the way. A long narrow garden is in itself uncompromisingly dull; if you have to pass from one area to another through narrow gaps in high walls of hedging, stone or trellis smothered in plants, an air of mystery is added, tension is generated and released as you pass through, and surprise is achieved at the other side. Here we immediately have a composition that raises expectations of things to come, and the narrower the gap through which you pass, and the higher and more dominant the 'walls', the greater the amount of tension that will be generated.

Another way to achieve this would be to follow a path through a tunnel or pergola that had a focal point in the form of an ornament or seat at the end. Your eye would be attracted by the focal point, and not until you reached the end, and turned to take in the garden on either side, would you experience surprise and a release of the tension that had been generated by the uncertainty of what you might find at the end.

These elements can be combined. A path winding tantalizingly out of sight adds an air of mystery to any garden. If it also leads to a solid gate in a high 'wall' it adds to the tension and ultimate surprise. A partial view down a garden, with the vista interrupted by a circular 'moongate' or an opening in a wall or hedge, providing a glimpse of what is to come, will give a feeling of mystery and anticipation.

If your garden is large and has rising ground that hides the view beyond, the possibilities are obvious. A path that climbs the slope, either directly or by a tortuous route, will allow the view to burst out once the crest is reached. If you have the advantage of a woodland setting, you can often create openings to allow a glimpse of distant landscape, of an 'eyecatcher', or of the garden proper, as a taste of things to come. This will effectively whet the appetite, increase tension, and result in surprise.

Even the smallest garden can achieve the same effects. A narrow space can provide tension on a far smaller scale: a town yard with raised beds on either side or the placing of a protruding border in a modest garden will add to the sense of mystery and surprise.

Conversely, a bland garden lacks these elements. We have all seen the 'dead' square garden with its rectangular lawn and flanking borders; the dog-leg plot that fails to attract you into the hidden area; the large country garden with nothing to break the sight line and no secrets to hide.

It could be argued that the aim of all garden design is to fulfil these three criteria; that design principles are simply the means that allow us to form a composition that has inherent interest just because it places tension points effectively, creates a feeling of mystery, and provides in consequence an element of surprise.

1 A covered walk should always have somewhere positive to go. If the path can be constructed so that it disappears with a slight air of mystery, so much the better. A pool of darkness is always attractive, and here it acts as a real lure, drawing you irresistibly towards the end of the walk.

2 The most effective way for a view to build up tension is in a number of stages. This is why a wide open vista can sometimes prove an anticlimax. Here, there is ample foreground interest in the circular pool and centrally placed figure, and the eye can dwell here for a while before next moving on to the middle lawn, and finally to the simply planted tub in the distance. The drama is further increased by the cleverly contrived gap in the planting, and sensibly this has been left informal. If a rigid frame had been used here, it would have looked far too artificial.

3 A secret corner is always attractive in any garden. A well-positioned seat like this one can easily be tucked away behind a wing of planting or beneath an arbour. The metal seat in this picture makes an attractive pattern, and is thrown into sharp relief by the dark green conifers to either side and the evergreen hedge behind.

4 Gateways are the ins and outs of any outdoor room, and can separate quite different garden areas and styles. The solidity of this wall is pierced by a delicious opening offering a tantalizing view of the less formal landscape beyond. The various horizontal planes receding into the distance set up an interesting rhythm and create a real feeling of space.

1

2

2 There are fleeting moments in a garden that deserve to be remembered. A soft early morning mist that wraps itself around a finely planted border creates just such a moment, and the path, disappearing from view around the corner, adds a feeling of mystery.

3

3 Hedges can provide a strong framework in a garden, and an excellent background to planting. These solid blocks of yew act as buttresses and are carefully positioned to reinforce the underlying ground pattern. They also make links between the hard and soft elements – the granite setts in the foreground and the lawn. Just what is beyond those solid divisions is another question and something that begs to be investigated.

4 There is something slightly sinister about this grouping of tightly clipped trees, each one taking on a different character as they crowd the lawn. The drama is increased by the dusting of snow that throws everything into sharp relief. Such a hedge provides a virtually impassable barrier.

4

1 Garden vistas don't come much more dramatic than this. Here is a measured, well thought-out composition that relies on the gently rising ground and the strong framework of dark trees on either side. The impressive urn is set against the skyline for maximum impact to provide the ultimate punctuation mark in the landscape. Mixed sunlight and shadow cast across the broad grassy walk sets up its own pattern, mimicking a formal flight of stairs.

GROUND PATTERNS

DS The core of garden design is concerned with patterns, and the spaces within the patterns, based on an understanding of simple geometry. We can achieve this in different ways. Inspiration can come from many different disciplines – collage, abstract painting, architecture, furniture, Persian carpets, textiles or packaging, for example. Contemporary landscape architects look to the work of painters such as Mondrian, or Modernist architects such as Le Corbusier for ideas. They in turn were influenced by the Ancient Greek and Renaissance artists, whose work was inspired by abstract ideas of beauty expressed in geometry and the principle of the golden section. The latter, in simple terms, is the most 'comfortable' point at which one naturally divides a straight line or rectangle, almost two-thirds of the way down its length and not, as might be expected, in the middle.

By keeping your patterns relatively crisp and 'architectural' close to the house, and more fluid further away, you will achieve a logical progression of shapes as you move down the garden, which will in turn create a feeling of space. Rectangular shapes used near the house as a series of overlapping patterns based on the golden section, with raised beds, a pool, built-in seating, and planting to spill over and soften the outline, can make a fascinating pattern that links naturally with the shape of the building.

1 Nature has its own way of softening the hand of man, and here the underlying ground pattern has been tempered by planting of all kinds. The seat, with its flanking pots, is the natural focus of the plan, and the entire scheme is refreshingly muted by the absence of any harsh colours.

2 The small modules of brick paving set up their own geometric pattern, one that associates well with planting. This pattern is echoed by the low hedges, and the table and bench fit neatly into the composition.

3 There are situations that invite drama, and a setting such as this one is the perfect place for a swimming pool. Rectangular areas in the ground plan have been filled with the soft hummocks of *Festuca glauca* as ground-cover, providing a rich textural contrast to the water's smooth, reflective plane. Only the pine is allowed to give vertical emphasis, and it, too, is reflected in the water below.

1

1 The smaller the paving module, the easier it is to lay to an intricate pattern. Brick is an excellent hard landscape material, but make sure that you use bricks that will withstand winter frosts. Here, the floor pattern has been built up from a series of circular shapes that produces a great feeling of movement. The entire view is directed towards the pool, where the central figure acts as a focal point. Hedges and planting are used to reinforce the underlying shapes and soften the architectural framework. Mosses and other low-growing plants have started to colonize the brickwork, and this allows the garden to mellow and mature.

In the middle and more distant parts of the garden these patterns can become more fluid. Curves are one of the designer's most important tools, allowing features, paths and the underlying pattern to link and merge with one another. But curves in the garden should be crisply based on geometric radii, not on formless shapes provided by a hosepipe thrown on the ground. The one will result in a positive, strong design; the other in the weakest of lines that will disappear when softened by plants.

A design based on curves can be drawn with a pair of compasses so that one shape flows smoothly into the next. On the ground it can be reproduced by using a line attached to a metal pin or a cane, and marking the arc with a trail of sand.

Remember that any scheme will look stark on a drawing and when first pegged out on the ground, but a strong design will be enhanced by planting, whereas a weak pattern will simply look a mess. Remember, too, the visual difference between shapes drawn on a plan and actually laid on the ground. You will be hovering like a bird over your plan. When the same shapes – and curves in particular – are seen at eye level they appear sharper and flatter. A useful trick to try is to hold your plan at eye level and sight across it.

Formal gardens, fashionable again today (but not always suitable), are based on symmetrical patterns, with one part mirroring the other. Often laid out along a central axis with groups of plants echoing the underlying geometry of the composition, formal gardens can be used to reinforce the architectural style of a period building, and to provide a link between the house and the landscape beyond.

In a larger garden the component parts of a formal garden can be amply developed, but they are also effective in smaller, contained gardens; traditionally they were often intended to be viewed from an upstairs room. But they tend to be set pieces which sit uncomfortably next to contemporary architecture, and do not always accommodate a busy modern lifestyle or the needs of children.

Informal gardens depend on asymmetric designs. Here, instead of mirror images, you have to imagine two unequal weights positioned round a fulcrum. To achieve a balance, the heavier of the two weights must be placed nearer to the fulcrum and the lighter one further away. In garden design terms this means that the visual weight of one feature must always be offset by another smaller or larger one in order to balance the overall composition.

A rock garden, for example, might need to be offset by a group of trees in another part of the garden, and the associated planting surrounding them; a water feature may effectively be placed near to a screen heavily planted with climbers. The scale of these features will balance one another in visual terms, depending on their distance apart and size.

There is a growing trend towards creating total informality in the garden, which often favours the development and planning of wildlife and 'ecological' compositions. Although such areas should look as natural as possible, they require at least as much attention to planning as formal or asymmetric designs. Areas of wildflowers or dense shrubs will provide the ideal habitat for wildlife, but they can look messy. Try to maintain an area of formality immediately around the house, increasing the informality as you move away. Ensure that you balance each area of dense planting, and mow access paths through tougher grass so that the whole composition works as a cohesive unit.

Patterns of this kind, around which the whole basis of garden design revolves, are used to form the working spaces within the garden. For, ultimately, it is the spaces created by the patterns that are important, rather than the patterns themselves.

2

3

2 You have to be careful that a complicated floor pattern does not become too 'busy', confusing the eye with too many different shapes. There is some complex geometry at work here, but the materials have been kept to a sensible minimum of brick, timber and gravel. The pool and bowl act as the focus, with water trickling into the pool from a bamboo flume, giving slightly oriental overtones. The path is constructed from solid lengths of railway sleepers, separated by gravel, into which low-growing plants have been introduced. The steps are similarly constructed, and planting wraps the whole area, softening the overall picture and providing continuity among the hard elements.

3 Certain shapes lead you inevitably in a certain direction. Tension is always created when two circles are placed in close proximity, and the closer the radii, the stronger the effect becomes. Here, the lawn is progressively narrowed, leading feet and eye towards the stone seat and small sitting area. Granite setts, used for the edging and paved area, are set just below the level of the turf for ease of mowing. You need to be careful, however, with this kind of design, especially where grass is concerned: if the access route is too narrow, the surface will be worn out by concentrated traffic.

Principles of Design

SIZE AND SHAPE

DS The immovable parameters of the garden itself – its size and shape – will determine to some extent how patterns and spaces can be used. A long thin garden, a square, rectangular, triangular, or dog-legged one, will each need handling in a different way. The appearance and feel of the final composition, and the positioning of the various components, will depend to a large extent on how a ground pattern is created within the limitations of a garden shape.

Whatever the configuration of your plot, it will probably need modifying or strengthening in some way. A long thin garden, for example, if it is not to look as exaggerated as a tall thin man wearing a pinstripe suit, will need to be divided up into different areas or 'rooms', each with its own character and purpose. If

OBLONG GARDENS *Here the design opportunities are almost limitless, and the space can be sectioned into different areas or 'rooms', each having a separate theme or purpose. Changes of level can be used to good advantage, and in this relatively static composition, the eye is led up the garden by the trees planted at the far end.*

1

1 In this rectangular garden, the ground plan has been devised in such a way that it echoes the shape of the plot, rather than detracting from it. The simple York stone sitting area in the foreground leads on to a square lawn that is in turn flanked by a neat brick mowing edge. This fits in with the rectangular theme and prevents the planting from flopping directly on to the lawn. Space division in this design is created by the flower bed positioned halfway down the garden, and the paving gradually widens out into a broad brick path that leads into a less formal area. The well-positioned seat makes a final statement, drawing the eye towards the end of the vista.

2 Here, the opposite technique has been used, and a circular pattern has been introduced to positively detract from the surrounding boundaries. The rectangular boundary is, in turn, completely hidden by planting, which is the key to this kind of composition: such a juxtaposition of shapes will inevitably look uncomfortable if both can be seen at the same time.

2

the different sections are separated by hedges, low walls or screening of some kind, this will give it the sense of tension, mystery and surprise that we discussed previously, and will increase the overall feeling of space as well as providing practical areas for various different activities: sitting and eating, playing and utilitarian functions, for example.

Long narrow gardens have a strong directional emphasis. Square plots on the other hand are completely static. The solution here is to appear to change the shape of the garden. Designs based on a pattern of circles or on one of rectangles work equally well. A circular design distracts the eye from the straight lines of the boundary; a complex rectangular design uses the perimeter as part of the design and in breaking it up detracts from it.

Another way of dealing with square or rectangular gardens is to turn the design at an angle of 45 degrees to the boundary. A long diagonal line will immediately create a feeling of space, and paving near the house could lead further away into a series of strongly flowing curves. This creation of movement is the key to any shape of garden. In a dog-legged plot the aim will be to draw feet and eye into the hidden space. You can do this by leading a path into the dog leg or sweeping a lawn around the corner. Once you are there the rectangles themselves can be treated in one of the ways mentioned above. A triangular garden, on the other hand, should be considered simply as part of a rectangle, and so should be handled accordingly. Don't be fooled, just stand back, analyse the space at your disposal, and design accordingly!

SQUARE GARDENS *A feeling of movement' can be used to lead the eye away from box-like boundaries, provided the flow is continuous and unbroken by other features.*

MOVEMENT AROUND THE GARDEN

1 The way in which a space is planned has a great influence on the way you move through it. Paths, pergolas, arches and gateways all play their part, directing feet and eye in a particular direction. Here, the pattern moves from side to side, and is built up from a series of overlapping paved areas that are interspersed and softened by planting. Gravel acts as a link between the paving, and planting has been introduced to grow up through this surface. The path is low-key and not very obvious, but it still serves its purpose well, and you are drawn along it to see what lies at the other end. The view is terminated by the old wall, and the whole pattern of the garden is aligned with this ultimately dominant feature. The planting scheme is gentle and delicate, and this does much to soften the underlying geometry of the garden, making a perfect combination of hard and soft landscape.

2 Paths produce obvious directional emphasis, and the speed at which the eye is taken down a route is often dependent on the path surface and how it is laid. Brick paving, as here, is a delightful material, providing a mellow texture and a wide range of possible laying patterns. Because of their small size, bricks can be easily laid to a curve, and this will lead the eye in the direction of the bond. This path has been laid in a neat stretcher bond, sweeping around the garden and being set just below the level of the lawn, to act as a practical mowing edge. The seat provides a focal point to one side, balancing the two neatly clipped bushes, while the path continues beneath the pergola that helps to frame the view beyond.

MOVEMENT AROUND THE GARDEN

3

3 In the more distant parts of a garden, particularly in the country, paths can be quite informal, and grass is a perfect choice, provided traffic is not too heavy. They should of course be wide enough for a mower, and in this situation a hover type would be ideal, to avoid cutting off any planting that is flopping over the edge on either side. The route that a path takes is also vital in reinforcing the underlying design, and a straight vista, seen at a glance, can be spanned by a pergola and arch, perhaps with a well-chosen statue or urn at the end. Such an approach is formal, and this garden is the exact opposite. Here, the path gently disappears, with a slight air of mystery, towards the more informal garden in the distance.

DS Creating space has much to do with movement around the garden. The way in which different areas are linked together, by paths, pergolas, bridges, steps, or terraces, can enormously increase their apparent size and interest – a trick that 'Capability' Brown or Humphry Repton in the eighteenth century knew well. However, it is equally true that a linking element positioned carelessly and without proper regard to its surroundings, or the random placing of too many elements together, can confuse the eye and appear to diminish, rather than expand the available space.

Many elements in the garden encourage movement: entrances and exits, a disappearing path, a covered walk, a focal point, a pierced screen; or something as mundane as the washing line, dustbin or greenhouse.

In any garden there will be logical and favourite routes for getting from A to B. These are called 'desire lines', and should be respected, for they will not be deviated from, and will therefore affect your final layout. So if you want to introduce circuitous, meandering or zig-zag routes in order to increase the sense of space, the sense of mystery, or to lead the visitor from one viewpoint to the next, you must make certain that there are very clear reasons inherent in the design for following the line of the path.

Repton planted stands of trees so that his serpentine drives had a reason for winding round them; your garden path must also incorporate elements that appear to dictate its route.

However, the actual route around the garden is only one part of the equation. The way in which it is laid out, and the speed at which you traverse it, are also important. Within reason, the faster you move through a space, the smaller it feels, and you may wish to take this into account at the planning stage.

A gentle curve can be negotiated at speed, or at least at a brisk walk, but the tighter the radius becomes, the slower you tend to walk through it. This could be taken to absurd extremes, resulting in a garden full of convoluted loops and twists; there must, of course, be a balance between achieving a logical pattern and establishing a comfortable pace.

The width of a path also has a bearing on speed: just as the water in a stream accelerates as it passes through the narrows, so narrow paths encourage action. Doubly so, if your passage is restricted, either by planting closing in on either side, or by the flanking contours of a valley. In contrast, a wider path, meandering through the open space like a river meandering through a flat plain, will encourage much slower movement. By

manipulating these various elements, you can control the pace as you wish, allowing for variations of movement in different areas of the garden, all of which will create a feeling of space.

Levels also, of course, affect progress through the garden: steps, slopes, terraces all need to be negotiated, and can be used deliberately to slow the pace and direct movement.

Surfaces are important in determining the speed at which you travel along your paths. As we have seen elsewhere, both the type of material and the way in which it is laid should be carefully considered. Smooth, continuous, 'fluid' surfaces, such as concrete or asphalt, encourage speed; rougher, more uneven surfaces, such as brushed aggregate concrete, granite setts, small cobbles, brick, grass, or gravel, slow you down; and loose cobbles or even large, smooth boulders can, quite literally, stop you dead in your tracks.

The laying pattern also affects movement. If a brick path uses stretcher bond running away from you, down the path, this tends to engender speed. If the same bond is laid across the path, it has the opposite effect and slows you down. If a path is laid in panels of different materials, for example, brick and cobble, this too will slow you down.

76

Principles of Design

FOCAL POINTS

1 A great deal of thought and preparation has gone into this composition based on a Japanese theme. The carefully detailed timber fence acts as both frame and shelf, drawing the eye naturally towards the bonsai at the centre.

2 A succession of focal points can heighten the drama in a garden and lend added strength to a vista. This old copper boiler is an eye-catcher in itself, but raising it on a brick plinth helps to lead the eye upwards to the timber arbour and then through to the bust, positioned directly beyond the fountain. Rigorous planning is the key to achieving this sort of effect.

DS Focal points can be used to add structure to the design. They are the visual hinges of garden design, the objects or features in a garden that draw the eye and lead the visitor towards them. They play a dramatic role both in movement round the garden and in the composition as a whole, and the choice and siting of focal points is crucial to the success or failure of the plan.

A focal point can be achieved by the perfect siting of a simple garden pot at the end of a wall, or a dramatic fountain at the end of an avenue. It could be a bench under a rose-covered trellis; an urn or obelisk in a formal setting; a hammock swinging under an apple tree; a piece of sculpture half hidden in a border;

a gate leading out of the garden to the landscape beyond. At its subtlest it may be a pool set to catch a reflection or incorporating a small water jet to create the sound of gently running water.

It can equally well be achieved by careful planting: a well chosen tree or group of plants can be positioned so as to stand out in sharp relief against their surroundings, and it may also be possible to design the garden to take advantage of an existing, established feature such as the sudden explosion of a tree peony in flower, a little trough of species tulips beside the house, a stand of trees in a country garden, or a specimen shrub in a lawn.

A garden can only sustain a certain number of focal points; a small garden perhaps one, and a larger garden more, but in different areas. Objects in well positioned isolation are always more telling than a surfeit, which is both unrestful and counter-productive – the excitement goes and with it the manipulation of movement and emotion.

The essential factor is that the focal point should attract you to it for some purpose – whether to lead you on to some other view or some other part of the garden, to divert you momentarily from the area you are passing through, to impart an aura of mystery to a section of the garden, or to astonish you with surprise

3

4

5

6

as you turn a corner. A poorly sited object simply draws the eye at the expense of other things around it, foreshortens the garden and ruins the design.

The proportions of a focal point are also something to consider, as they are in the garden as a whole. In a small new plot the house may appear to dominate everything. Commercial developers often plant semi-mature trees to provide immediate bulk to redress the balance. That is an expensive option and you may have to be patient while your trees grow. An alternative would be to introduce a garden structure in the form of a summerhouse or pergola, which would both serve a practical purpose and help to balance the house.

3 An opportunity to exploit a feature outside the site as a focal point should not be missed, whether it be a fine tree, a striking building or a superb view. This is a splendidly clever approach, using the path of white chippings not only to lead the eye towards the lighthouse but also to echo its colour. Trellis to either side of the path helps to reinforce the line, and an arch frames the view.

4 Statues can be positioned to provide striking punctuation marks in any garden. This one is framed by a rounded open bower, over which grow climbers chosen to give colour or flowers most of the year. The clipped topiary pyramids add to the formality of the atmosphere.

5 The great architect Edwin Lutyens had an innate understanding of form and space. Here he created radiating tile courses on stone arches to set up a false perspective, which is then continued by a second arch to increase the tension and draw the eye onwards to the mysterious pool of deep shadow that lies beyond.

6 A powerful composition of spirals of contrasting plants, culminating in a natural focal point which could be a plant, pot or statue, demonstrates the potential for humour in the creation of focal points for a garden. The clipped box balls, trundling around bromeliads over loose cobbles, contribute a sense of both movement and fun.

1 The setting up of sight lines and focal points is one of the garden designer's most important tasks. Vistas should not be too obvious, and should work in both directions: a view from a focal point is just as important as the view to it. Here, the pergola is hardly visible, covered as it should be by an abundance of climbers, and the doors of the house are the natural focus. The view from inside the house would be just as attractive, encouraging you to go out and explore.

3

2 The designer of this really believed in making a point! The drama is inescapable. The fastigiate conifers make natural exclamation points behind the seat, while the wings of hedging in the foreground concentrate the view and act as a tension point. You could argue that this is all a bit too obvious, but viewed from a distance it will be brought into scale by the larger area of surrounding garden.

3 Humour is an essential element in any garden, but so too is practicality. The bell gives a distinctly nautical feel, but could also be used to summon the weary gardener when the sun is over the yard-arm, or to scare pigeons from the vegetable garden. The contrast of smooth metal and the natural delicacy of the leaves makes an interesting juxtaposition, and a charming pattern.

2

LEVELS

1 The use of a single material gives continuity to any composition. Natural stone has great visual strength, and here, great slabs and blocks have been used to retain the various levels. Smaller cobbles have been tightly packed together to leave minimal gaps between each module, and make attractive level areas in this composition.

DS The landscaping of a sloping garden will be far more expensive that that of a flat site if it involves building and levelling. On the other hand, a sloping garden has far greater inherent interest than a flat one, and slopes can act as host to many exciting garden features: steps, ramps, rock outcrops, scree gardens, and dynamic water projects in the form of streams, pools, cascades, waterfalls, or even water staircases.

In most smaller gardens, the creation of gentle flowing changes in level are more sympathetic and easier to stabilize and maintain than steep banks. Where steep areas are planned, it will probably be best to build retaining walls and subsequently soften them with planting.

Remember that gentle fluid shapes create a feeling of space and movement when situated in the middle and more distant parts of a composition, while any architectural and formal features often fit more comfortably nearer the house.

Allow your slopes to flow gently into one another. Keep them simple, and if your garden is small and the level changes not great, mould them into a pattern that will allow you to link the various garden elements together. A slope up from the house will appear visually foreshortened and therefore smaller, whereas a garden sloping downhill will appear larger.

Slopes have all sorts of possibilities, inviting the use of terracing and complementary features, but all the design principles discussed earlier will apply here also. It may be useful to 'lift' a low corner by positioning a group of trees or other plants there. This will have the effect of drawing the eye upwards.

Remember, too, that lawns and planting do not have to be on the flat, and an awkward gradient can often be counterbalanced by a strong block of planting to provide vertical emphasis at the lowest point.

If you do decide to terrace a slope, and retaining walls are used, they can be straight or curved to fit in

with the overall design. Or the whole garden could be constructed of steps incorporating platforms and terraces, even waterfalls and pools. Such a design could be based on rectangles, hexagons or circles, and each level could be surfaced in a different way.

In a flat garden it is possible to introduce artificial changes in level, either by importing soil, or by the 'cut and fill' technique – which involves digging soil out and mounding it up beside the excavation. The classic result is a mound or rock garden alongside a sunken garden.

In general, I believe in working with a situation rather than against it, and although you can create a hillside garden from a flat site, more modest changes of level will probably be more successful. Just remember that if you wish to create changes of level, or if other garden projects, such as excavating for a swimming pool, generate a great deal of surplus soil which has to be accommodated, it is vitally important to plan for this at the design stage.

3

2 Where the ground slopes up, away from a house, it has the effect of foreshortening the view. It makes sense, therefore, to provide a broad paved area adjacent to the building, to help balance the lower area visually. Planting softens the transitional bank before the slope is allowed to flow gently away up the hill.

3 Slopes can be treated formally or informally. Both methods are incorporated here. The lower area is formed into a broad geometric terrace of reflecting pools that has the effect of linking garden to house, despite the latter's elevated position. The bank, on the other hand, is informally planted to create a soft pattern of textured flower and foliage.

4 Even a slight change in level can provide interest. Here, broad shallow steps lead gently up to a secluded sitting area where the wooden structure, evergreen hedge and standard roses provide vertical emphasis. This is a tightly controlled composition, built up from rectangles but effectively softened by well chosen planting.

4

PRINCIPLES OF PLANTING
CHOOSING PLANTS

UB There are three main approaches to planting: the plantsman's; the garden designer's; and finally the gardener's, which is a mixture of the two.

The plantsman's approach usually results in a garden composed of singletons, planted where they are happiest, but independent of, and unconnected with, their bedfellows. This can provide the basis for a lovely garden, but there are likely to be problems. Not only are favoured places – like the sunny spot in a moist but well drained soil – usually crammed with plants while the shady dry areas are emptier, but, more seriously, there is no unity and the plants do nothing to enhance each other.

At the other end of the continuum are the garden designers, professional or amateur. For some, though mercifully not all, plants are an unpredictable, even unwelcome, quantity. In general, their preference is for a few well tried and widely available plants which will set off the hard landscaping without making undue visual or practical demands.

The third type of gardener has learned that his or her favourite plants can make far more impact if planted in a scheme, in association with each other, than they ever could on their own. In other words, that the whole is more than the sum of its parts. This is undoubtedly the most effective and satisfactory approach, but it is difficult to do really well because plants do not always obey the rules. Fortunately, charming and telling effects can often be created even when your carefully considered plan does not work quite as you intended.

Use the basic planting plan that you built up from the garden site survey as the blueprint for a more specific selection process. It is important to maintain an awareness of shape and form, considering how plants will interact when planted together, rather than simply how the colours of the flowers will look when positioned side by side. Consider too, the overall balance of contrasts and harmonizing elements; too much of either tends to result in a predictable scheme.

It is important to decide in what proportion you want bright or paler colours to predominate in your garden. In either case it usually works best if the predominant colours harmonize, leaving minor themes to contrast. Too much contrast tends to result in a harsh and busy scheme. If you wish to use 'complementary' or contrasting colours together, you will have most success if you choose those of different intensities.

Hot bright colours appear to reduce distance, while cooler, paler shades increase it. Hot colours will make a border seem shorter; cool colours at its further end will make it appear to recede into the distance. Planting

1

a small garden with predominantly pale colours, especially if they are situated slightly away from the house, will therefore make it seem larger.

Try to keep some sort of balance between deciduous and evergreen planting. Too many evergreens can seem gloomy and repetitive, while too much deciduous planting will mean there is little to provide interest during the surprisingly long dormant season.

Remember, too, the importance of foliage. It is often the height of foliage rather than flower which should influence the placing of plants. And when choosing plants specifically for the flowers, try to choose those that also have attractive foliage. Alternatively, place

them alongside plants with good foliage, so that they can be hidden or ignored when out of flower. However, do bear in mind that foliage can occasionally be a negative feature. Slug-chewed hosta leaves, for example, are inclined to stand out, and, if planting autumn-flowering colchium bulbs, bear in mind that they have large, fleshy strap leaves in the spring.

Scent, too, should feature prominently in your thinking: scent both of flower and foliage. Fragrance adds a further and indispensable dimension to a garden. Position scented plants where you are likely to sit in the garden, remembering that many flowers exhale their scents most strongly in the evening.

1 Good principles have been applied when choosing plants for this sumptuous border, pictured in high summer. There was obviously a clear idea of what was to be achieved: the planting is in groups, and in interlocking drifts which are not parallel to the border edge; one or two tall plants have been placed towards the front to avoid predictability; care has been taken to balance the various elements; there is an imaginative choice of plants (the vegetable, ruby chard, at the front, and *Rosa moyesii*, with its orange hips). The way in which bright colours have been handled is clever and assured, and so is the use of distinctive foliage.

2 This garden has been planted with due regard to the necessity of first making a structural framework: *Pyrus salicifolia* 'Pendula', climbing and shrub roses, hedges. There is a good balance here between plants which are principally grown for their foliage, and those which are grown for their flowers, such as *Allium christophii* and *Centranthus ruber*. Care has been taken to use the planting to set off, and soften, the 'hard' landscape. There is a good mix of deciduous and evergreen, so there is likely to be something to see at all times of the year. Scent is also well represented in, amongst others, the aromatic sub-shrubs, roses, and nepeta.

2

Other smaller considerations can promote the success of a scheme: plant early-flowering bulbs whose foliage dies down quickly where perennials will take over later on; remember that many plants which tolerate dappled shade will not tolerate the drip from evergreens in winter; be wary of plants that may swamp those growing nearby; put deciduous flowering shrubs where they will be hidden or can be disguised when out of flower; beware of introducing invasive plants – they may be difficult to eradicate later.

Even then you will find that the best-laid plans can be undermined by plants which refuse to flower when they should, or which fail to fill out the space allotted

to them. The flowering of many plants is influenced by temperature (roses are a good example): in a hot year two plants may flower together, and in a cooler year miss by days, even weeks. A plant that has been made the pivot of a planting scheme may die in an unusually hard winter, leaving a huge and unfillable gap.

On the other hand, marvellous effects can arrive quite accidentally – perhaps because you failed to remove self-seeded plants, or because a freak season caused a plant to flower longer and better than could be anticipated. There are disappointments of course, but the joy of the whole business lies partly in its very unpredictability. Unlike 'hard landscaping', you can

experiment with the planting each year if you wish, creating different effects without difficulty as circumstances change or new plants come to your notice.

One final comment: the most successful gardener is ruthless. His motto is – if thy scheme offend thee, cut it out. It does not pay to hang on to a plant which does not earn its keep or which no longer pleases you, even though it is a bore to remove and cost good money. You will be better off without it, and will then have space to experiment with something new. Moreover, however happy you are with your scheme, no garden or border remains static; over a period of years renovation and revision are not only desirable but necessary.

Principles of Planting

SHAPE AND PROPORTION

1 This is a cool scheme which depends for its appeal as much on form and shape as it does on foliage and flower colour. Unlike contrasts in colour, contrasts in shape must be striking and obvious to make a real impression. Here, on the left, the distinctive globe artichoke, *Cynara cardunculus*, with its jagged silver leaves and tall arching habit, has been planted to contrast with its neighbours – the shrubby elaeagnus behind, and the perennial *Stachys byzantina* ('lamb's ears') to its right. The leaves of the stachys itself contrast with the border pink, but are echoed by the purple-leaved sage beyond. Spikiness on a smaller scale can be found nearby in the eryngium on the right.

2 The original colour of the sedums in the foreground has almost disappeared by this stage in the year, yet their unusual flat-topped seedheads on fleshy stems still have something to add to the winter scene; especially when set in front of the Mexican orange blossom (*Choisya ternata*). This illustration clearly shows that successful plant design need not be simply a matter of putting together plants which flower at the same time and do not clash with each other.

1

2

UB Flower and leaf colour alone will not make a satisfactory garden picture; the structure and shape of plants, especially those which make up the permanent plantings, are almost more important for the maintenance of a year-round effect in the garden. Indeed, some marvellously successful gardens depend entirely on plants used in this way. We should remember that the garden will, in any event, be without its summer colours for more than half the year.

The shape and proportion of plants or groups of plants is important at all times of the year, but perhaps especially so in winter, when the bare bones of a garden can be most easily seen. Even in summer, however, it should be possible to discern the different shapes of plant groupings in borders. It is possible to be more adventurous with shapes than with colours.

3 Here is a simple, but pleasing, contrast in shape, which is easy enough for anyone to try. The common foxglove is seen here towering behind and over the popular peony, *Paeonia* 'Sarah Bernhardt'. There are not many plants that provide such a vigorous verticality in early summer as foxgloves do, which is what makes them so useful. They are also good companions for old roses. This kind of tempting and easily achieved contrast of tall and thin with short and round is effective, provided it is not done to death.

3

Plants can be used to alter or disguise the shape of a border: an evergreen shrub placed at the corner of a path; trailing plants at the edge of a planted area; prostrate plants spilling over on to paving, can all distract the eye from the rigid shape of the border and provide a degree of informality in a composition.

Try (especially with long straight beds) to break the tyranny of the instinct to position 'tall plants at the back, small at the front'. This kind of planting leads the eye down, and much will be missed on the way. Instead, introduce an occasional tall plant at the front, especially an airy one like *Verbena bonariensis,* which allows the eye to see partly, but only partly, through it. Use occasionally (but not invariably) narrow, vertical plants close to wider, horizontal clumps.

We are often invited to think of plants as individuals – even as distinct 'personalities' — and this encourages us also to consider their shape and structure in this way. But we should also be aware that there are plants (heathers spring immediately to mind) which create their maximum impact only when planted *en masse.* We should look to these plants to provide another kind of shape and structure in the garden: patterns, drifts which ebb and flow, and full stops.

Plants are usually more effective when planted in groups than as single specimens. This is sometimes true even of trees, but is especially the case with perennials, bulbs and annuals – which all look best if arranged in groups consisting of uneven numbers of plants. However, this rule is not immutable. A larger plant or a specimen of a tall imposing perennial like an acanthus can work effectively on its own at times, as can a smaller 'architectural' plant, such as the grass *Hakonechloa macra* 'Alboaurea', in a small area; moreover, it hardly matters whether you have even or odd numbers if you are dealing with large amounts of plants, for example, daffodils to be naturalized in an area of grass, or hedging plants. The repetition of key plants within a border or even throughout the garden – the tall, white, statuesque bulb, *Galtonia candicans,* say – can help unify the overall design.

Set plantings of perennials, annuals and bulbs at an angle to the edge of the border (except when you specifically want an edging of plants). Plant them in interlocking, overlapping drifts to allow one group to take over from another and ensure that when out of flower they leave the least gap possible. The exception to this rule is where you are planting in very formal situations, for example in an ornamental potager, a herb garden, or a rose garden, when blocks of plants are acceptable and appropriate.

For example, a spiky plant placed next to a prostrate or domed one, provided that their respective colours are reasonably harmonious, is likely to enhance the impact and drama of both.

The overall shape of trees and shrubs is important, but so too is their 'structure' – their branch framework or skeleton – especially in winter. Good structure will often allow the inclusion of a plant in spite of a short or insignificant flowering period: the common birch is a good example of a plant which is beautiful in both summer and winter, even though the catkins are not its main feature. If the plant also has fine bark, like the snakebark maples, or good autumn colour, so much the better.

Smaller plants, too, can be relied upon to provide winter effect in this way. In particular, grasses and ferns often add structural grace in winter to their summer charms. There is a substantial range of perennials and sub-shrubs which retain their leaves and also, therefore, their structure, in winter; and there are also many herbaceous and woody plants that can be relied on to make an impact, particularly when their sere stems and flowerheads are rimed with frost.

The importance of scale and proportion is crucial. Resist the temptation to plant only low-growing plants. The vertical plane is very important, even in a small garden; it is just that you have to achieve height with narrower plants. Think of your garden not as a flat landscape but as three dimensional. Planting in overlapping layers takes more planning and effort, but is far more effective. It may also help to obscure problem areas when plants do not do what is expected of them.

COLOUR

Principles of Planting

1

UB The handling of flower and foliage colour in the garden usually causes gardeners the most difficulty, but it also entails the most fun.

We all agree that some colours 'go' better together than others – though we may disagree which – and that in 'going together' these colours enhance each other. Good combinations are what we strive for, and that can involve both harmonies and contrasts.

When deciding how to plan a colour scheme, it can be helpful to refer to the chart called the 'colour wheel', which is based on the spectrum. On this circular diagram, the primary colours (red, blue and yellow) are separated from each other by related secondary colours (violet, green and orange). Whereas adjoining colours, say orange and butter yellow, are generally perceived to harmonize, those opposite each other, say yellow and violet, are 'complementary', that is to say, they provide the greatest contrast.

The colour wheel is simply a useful illustration of what many people instinctively perceive. If, for example, you were to plant the deep purple-blue *Salvia superba* 'May Night' next to the yellow *Argyranthemum* 'Jamaica Primrose', you would find that they made a lively and satisfying contrast, which drew your eye irresistibly. It would, therefore, come as no surprise, and is certainly no coincidence, that the two colours are to be found directly opposite each other on the colour wheel and are therefore complementary.

Flowers and foliage come in an almost infinite number of colour variations, and often the colours change as the season progresses and the plant matures. Flower colour, or our perception of it, is also affected by external circumstance: by the type and intensity of light (bright colours look paler in the twilight while pale ones acquire luminosity), by the background, and by the colour of neighbouring plants.

Brightness, or 'intensity' is another factor. The hardest colours to place in the garden are the bright ones, especially white, red, yellow and some blues. Bright colours tend to excite the eye and can dominate a scheme out of all proportion to their actual size, so should be used with forbearance. In sunny climates, with greater clarity of light, the use of bright colours is easily justified, while pale colours tend towards insignificance; under cloudy skies bright colours can look brash, even harsh, while the subtler paler colours (with more white blended in) not only show up to advantage but are easier to manage because of the wider range of colours with which they will harmonize.

We all know what we mean by a colour clash, though again we may not agree about what constitutes one. There are no immutable rules, but to avoid causing your guests to recoil in horror when you take them round the garden, take the simple expedient of

1 Most of the colours here are on the warm side of the spectrum; those that are not, principally the blue anchusa and violet-blue salvia, are directly opposite on the colour wheel, so they make a satisfying contrast. Note how your eye is drawn to the bright white flowers, which have a disproportionate, and not wholly comfortable, impact.

2 A soothing, gentle colour scheme for a moist bed in dappled shade. The relatively dark position gives these cool colours luminosity and depth, which they would lack in a sunny place.

3 This scheme works because of the conviction with which it has been done, the limited number of species used, the differences in colour intensity, and the green foliage which acts as a buffer between the warring colours.

4 A rich and successful scheme for a sunny place in early summer. On the right is the Siberian wallflower, *Erysimum hieracliifolium*, with its flowerheads in uncompromising orange, which has been toned down somewhat by the yellow of the iris flowers and blue-green of their leaves. These irises also act as a bridge between the wallflower and the lime-green golden feverfew, *Tanacetum parthenium* 'Aureum'.

Principles of Planting

1 The flowers in this border are mainly closely related tints on the cool side of the colour wheel. The result is harmonious, if not especially adventurous. The misty colours trick the eye into thinking the border is deeper than it is.

2 A deceptively simple scheme, achieved by using several different flowers of similar colour but varying widely in shape, texture and solidity.

3 Muted almost to the point of recessiveness, a planting like this is nevertheless welcome, if only as a relief from an area of hotter colours nearby. The grey-green of the lychnis leaves is echoed effectively in the fleshy ones of *Allium karataviense*.

4 Here, the complementary colours grey-green and strong pink, found in the same plant, *Papaver somniferum*, are toned down by the more pastel tints of salvia flowers.

5 Japanese 'candelabra' primulas and azaleas in a bog garden in late spring. The primulas have been grouped to present blocks of complementary colour of the same intensity. This clashing discord will not be to everybody's taste; however, there is a vitality in these colours, and conviction in the way they have been handled, which makes you want to see this garden 'in the flesh'.

5

keeping yellow-based reds (i.e. scarlet) away from blue-based ones (i.e. carmine) – or use a green, grey or white 'foil' of foliage or flower between them.

Pastel shades rarely clash but, used exclusively, can make for some pretty dull schemes: varying the intensity of colour within the scheme is therefore important. You can make a colour scheme more interesting by using flowers and foliage in one of the bright primary colours, toned down by neighbouring plants of the same colour mixed with white to give pastel colours, or black to give the browns, dark blues and purples.

Once you have decided in what proportions you want hot or cool colours in your garden, the choice of colour scheme depends first and foremost on personal preference, but it is also important to consider the surroundings. This can be as simple as enlivening a grey limestone wall by planting parthenocissus, with its bright scarlet autumn foliage, or as complex as softening all the 'hard landscape' of the garden with a variety of mixed plantings.

So-called 'one-colour gardens' have been popular ever since Gertrude Jekyll's day, and can work well, especially as components of a large garden. They are easier to handle than multi-coloured schemes but it is important to realize that the most successful are not truly 'one colour' at all. A white garden, for example, could also contain grey-blue, green, pale pink, and cream and gold variegated plants.

A single colour scheme can work well in a very small garden, but it is worth considering changing the predominant colours in mid-season. When the pinks and blues of early summer have faded, the emphasis could shift to the many bronzes, reds and yellows of high summer and autumn – perhaps with the blues and mauves of asters and tradescantias to act as contrasts to such a brightly coloured scheme.

Everyone has favourite colours, and the most successful gardens reveal the personality of their owners. That being the case, do not be side-tracked by any preoccupation with 'taste'. The widespread rejection of orange flowers, for example, seems to me inexplicable; deep orange contrasted with blue-purple can be dramatic and satisfying. Think how rich a picture you could paint with the purple *Clematis jackmanii* 'Superba' flowering alongside the orange-yellow of *Eccremocarpus scaber*. Even if a generous selection of colours does not please the purists, that does not mean that it cannot work for you. It is only important to pay due attention to context and proportion; problems arise chiefly if too many warring colours are introduced willy-nilly, without any concern for balance.

FOLIAGE

Principles of Planting

UB While some plants, such as potentillas, will flower all summer, most cannot be depended upon for more than three weeks – and in the case of peonies or irises for even less than that. How much more interesting is a garden where foliage – both of herbaceous and woody plants – is taken seriously and used intelligently. Few flowers can match 'foliage plants' for length of appeal, even if their impact is often more muted.

A 'foliage plant' is not necessarily a non-flowering plant such as a fern; it can just as well be one whose impact, and thus its place in the garden, depends as much, or more, on its leaves as on its flowers. *Fatsia japonica*, for example, has striking flowers but even more striking and longer-lasting leaves. 'Foliage plant' is simply a convenient shorthand term, and should not be taken too literally.

Plant foliage varies enormously in form and texture: from the huge and broad to the dainty and frond-like, from the fragile and matt to the sturdy and glossy. In colour, you will find leaves in every kind of green, as well as blue, grey, white, golden, bronze, purple and even black. Leaves can be speckled, edged, or splashed with cream, white or gold, or even a number of different colours, as in the leaves of *Ajuga reptans* 'Tricolor'.

The range of colour, texture and form is so great that it is possible to make charming and striking effects using leaves alone. They can provide sufficient contrast for the most adventurous schemer, be soothing or exciting just as flowers can be. Variegated leaves, for example, can be set against the denseness of single-colour foliage (say, of the background hedge) to lighten the appearance of a border.

Although truly restless schemes can occur when using only foliage plants, the eye usually tires less easily of foliage contrasts than of those created with flowers. The trouble usually comes when too much use is made of multi-coloured leaves.

Foliage plants seem especially well suited to urban gardens, perhaps because of the high proportion of 'hard' features such as paving and high walls which they usually possess. Large-leaved and imposing plants, such as fatsia, *Laurus nobilis* or *Yucca filamentosa*, are not lost in such surroundings in the way that delicate flowers are likely to be. If you couple this with the fact that many town gardens are shady, the value of foliage, being generally more tolerant of shade than flowers, becomes even more apparent.

Most gardeners, however, find that where foliage really comes into its own is in balancing out contrasting flower colours (in short, acting as foils and buffers) – just consider for a moment the importance in our gardens of the most widely planted of all foliage plants, grass. In a border, foliage can be used to reconcile the eye to a transition from cool to warm colours, or to rescue a brightly coloured flower grouping from garishness. Indeed, it is possible to argue that it is in the subtle combinations of a 'one-colour' scheme that the gradations of shading afforded by foliage plants really come into their own. Foliage can act as a recurring theme to unify a border scheme and can soften the harsh rawness of new 'hard landscaping' far more effectively than flowers. Moreover, plants with bold, long-lasting or ascending leaves can be used as cheap but effective focal points, accents and even boundaries.

Evergreens (and 'evergreys' such as the shrubby artemisias) give vitality to what would otherwise be a predominantly brown and twiggy winter garden, as well as providing an effective background for more ethereal perennials in summer. Roses, for example, never look better than when seen against the backdrop of a dark yew hedge.

What is more, most deciduous and many evergreen leaves change colour during the course of the year. The richness and variety of the autumn colour of deciduous leaves can, of course, hardly be overstated, even though the effect may not be entirely reliable, depending as it does on climatic variations and soil conditions. But many of the yellow-leaved conifers, which are insignificant, even a little drab in the summer, gain in brightness when the cold weather comes. And the colour of the new leaves of photinias, pieris, conifers, and many roses and rhododendrons often differs dramatically from that of the mature foliage.

1

1 This picture neatly illustrates the contention that foliage is indispensable if a garden is to be interesting all year round. Even in the depths of winter, the shape and colour of these leaves are striking, especially in comparison with the twiggy deciduous shrubs on the left. Moreover *Elaeagnus pungens* 'Maculata', in the foreground, boasts its brightest variegation in winter. Although gardeners would not be without the yellow winter flowers of the mahonia (right), especially as they are sweetly scented, this plant earns its keep as much for its statuesque shape and attractive, enduring evergreen pinnate leaves.

2 Two forms of hosta show how wide is the range of leaf colour amongst the members of this invaluable genus. They are dramatically contrasted here with spear-like leaves of *Iris sibirica*, and demonstrate clearly that foliage plants need not be merely the poor relations of flowers. The two forms shown here would make an excellent combination for planting in a moist or boggy place in a shady part of the garden. Contrasting foliage combinations such as this are especially valuable in shaded areas, because such conditions are not conducive to good flowering in many perennials and shrubs.

2

3 There is a wide selection here of foliage plants for all seasons of the year, showing clearly that foliage need not mean 'green'. In the foreground are *Pulmonaria saccharata* Argentea Group and iris, while behind is *Berberis thunbergii*, and at the back *Rhus hirta*, in its scarlet autumn glory. There is a balance struck here between deciduous and evergreen. Foliage plants are especially welcome in urban gardens, because their cool colours and abundant leafage are a positive antidote to excessive amounts of man-made hard surfaces.

3

SOIL AND EXCAVATION

SOIL AND DIGGING

UB Once you have completed your site survey, and worked out your garden plan based on the design principles discussed earlier, the next thing to do before you embark on major earthworks, is to consider the type of soil with which you are dealing.

Like the weather, soil is a constant source of interest and comment – not to say discontent – to many gardeners. This discontent is sometimes misplaced; although some soils are certainly difficult to cultivate, they may still be fertile, and most can be improved.

The ground in one's garden consists first of topsoil, ideally 450mm/18in deep but often much shallower, and usually dark brown in colour. In some gardens, and especially new ones, the topsoil barely exists at all; in this case it must be introduced. Topsoil is made up of a mixture of clay, sand and silt, stones of varying sizes, and dark brown decomposed organic matter, called 'humus'. Humus coats the soil particles, sticking them together in 'crumbs', and thus promoting air spaces in clay soils while retaining moisture in sandy ones. These, combined, form its 'texture'. The ideal soil, which few gardeners will ever admit to possessing, is a 'medium loam', which contains a balanced mixture of these ingredients, has a good 'crumb structure' (which depends on the humus content) and plenty of macro- and micro-organisms, from earthworms to bacteria. However, garden soils range from variants on 'heavy clay', 'loamy sand' and even 'peat'.

Topsoil overlays 'subsoil', which is yellower or greyer in colour, and, although containing some nutrition, has far fewer organisms and little or no 'crumb structure'. Plants will not thrive in subsoil alone, although the roots of large plants can penetrate it, enabling them to draw out the nutrients and moisture within.

Subsoil in turn overlays the 'bedrock' from which both subsoil and topsoil are derived, and the makeup of subsoil and underlying rock both affect the rate at which water will filter down through the soil. A topsoil overlaying highly permeable chalk, for example, will usually be very free-draining.

An ideal topsoil, a medium loam, is fertile, relatively easy to cultivate, and water-retentive without ever becoming waterlogged. By contrast, a very light sandy soil will have many air spaces which will allow water (and the nutrients dissolved in it) to drain away rapidly; it is therefore inclined to dry out, especially in summer. However, it is at least possible to cultivate it most of the year, even after rain. Clay soils are the hardest for the gardener to manage, yet also have advantages. The tiny particles of clay tend to stick together, so that there are far fewer, and smaller, air spaces than in sandy soil; this makes clay soils sticky and wet and difficult to work. This leads to them being described as soils of 'poor structure'. However, since water is retained well, preventing nutrients being 'leached' away in the soil water, clay soils are often very fertile, but they do waterlog easily, and when they eventually dry out, they tend to shrink and crack. They are also slower to warm up in springtime than other, lighter soils.

If the soil is clayey and readily 'puddles' after rain, you may find that there is a solid 'pan' in or below the topsoil, often caused by compaction from heavy machinery, or by always digging to the same depth. Breaking up the pan may be the only way to improve the situation. If it lies close to the surface you can either use a rotovator or double dig, incorporating plenty of organic matter to improve the soil structure. If it lies 60cm/2ft or more below the surface, or if drainage is poor for any other reason (perhaps because of a high water table) you will probably need to seek advice from experts. Laying drains to carry away water properly is a skilled task, and is discussed later on in this section.

Although it is not necessary to be *au fait* with the scientific ramifications of soil analysis, you should be aware that a soil can be 'acid', 'neutral' or 'alkaline'. The so-called 'pH' (measure of acidity or alkalinity) of a soil can vary from about 4.0 in a really peaty soil, to 8.5 in a very limy alkaline one; 7.0 is neutral.

You need to know what your soil measures because some plants will not thrive at a certain pH. This is because specific minerals are 'locked up,' that is, made unavailable to plants, at some pH values: the best known example is iron, which cannot be drawn up by plants in alkaline soils, and which iron-hungry plants like rhododendrons need in order to flourish or even survive. Such plants cannot really be described as 'acid lovers' but rather as 'lime haters' – 'calcifuges'. Other plants that require an acid soil, or at the very least a neutral one for this reason, include summer-flowering heathers, pieris, enkianthus, many maples, and camellias. 'Alkaline lovers' or 'calcicoles', such as dianthus, are usually less demanding, generally showing a preference for alkaline soils

IDENTIFYING YOUR SOIL

A standard technique for identifying the chief characteristics of your soil is to roll a lump between fingers and thumb, to see how it behaves. Soil types fall into three categories depending on the proportions of sand, clay and loam they contain.

Predominantly sandy soil	Predominantly clay soil	Predominantly loamy soil
• Immediately breaks up	• Can be rolled into a firm, pliable worm shape	• Can be rolled into a fragile worm shape
• Feels gritty	• Looks shiny	

SOIL PROFILE

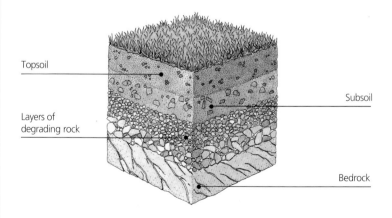

Topsoil

Layers of degrading rock

Subsoil

Bedrock

rather than a real intolerance of mildly acid ones. These things are a matter of degree, which is why, in the ideal world, most gardeners would choose a soil with a pH just below or about neutral.

Discovering the pH level of your soil is not difficult, for cheap and reliable testing kits are available from any garden centre. If you wish to grow mainly ornamental plants you need only establish in general terms whether your soil is acid or alkaline, and many people do this by observing what their neighbours grow; if there are no rhododendrons in the district you can safely assume your soil is not very acidic. However, if you wish to grow vegetables and fruit successfully, and especially if you have had to bring in topsoil, it is crucial to know your soil's pH. You should test the soil in different areas of the garden; you may be surprised to find how much variation there is.

Once you have established to your satisfaction what you have, you can alter the pH level of your soil by the addition of several different ingredients: peat, sulphur, lime and calcified seaweed. However, although organic products will have a long-term beneficial effect on the soil structure because they degrade to humus, these are all short-term ameliorants which will not alter the soil's pH permanently.

You will naturally want to know how to improve your soil, both before you start to plant, and in later years. The best way of improving both the texture and the structure of any soil is to add plenty of organic material, which will not only break down into humus but will also increase those all-important air spaces and make all topsoils easier to manage. Grit dug in does more or less the same job in clay soils, except that it does not have the advantage of adding nutrients and is likely to be more expensive.

'Green manures' can also be incorporated: these specific quick-maturing green crops help prevent nutrient leaching on otherwise fallow land, and, in the case of nitrogen-fixing clovers, tares, lupins and alfalfa, add nitrogen to the soil. They should be cut down and dug in when roughly 225mm/9in tall.

Organic matter does not necessarily have to be dug in. Indeed, many people believe that it is wastefully time-consuming and even damaging to dig at all – that you do more harm than good by walking on the soil because you can compact it, and that you are better off simply spreading large amounts of bulky organic matter about and leaving the earthworms to drag it down through the topsoil. There is a great deal to be said for this approach (favoured by organic gardeners), especially on light soils with good earthworm populations, although the organic matter is obviously incorporated more slowly than if it were dug in. On heavy clay soils, a thin planting layer can be created using organic matter, if digging the soil itself is not an option.

If you feel you must dig to incorporate organic matter, do so by hand rather than with a machine if possible, forking out perennial weeds as you go. A rotovator will chop up and scatter the roots of perennial weeds, which are capable of shooting once more. However, since in the ideal world even 'single digging' on light soil can be demanding work, mechanical digging is in some instances the only sensible option.

Cultivation by digging is obviously best done in the dormant season when there is little to obstruct you in the vegetable garden, and not much elsewhere to distract you. Heavy soils should be dug in autumn, light ones in early spring. The able-bodied have the choice of 'single' or 'double' digging. Double digging, the operation whereby the soil is cultivated to the depth of two spade blades (two 'spits'), is very hard work but is only necessary, or indeed advisable, if the soil has been long neglected, if it is compacted, if you wish to make permanent 'deep beds' in which to grow vegetables or if you wish to prepare completely new borders from grassland.

Whether you are embarking on either single or double digging, begin by taking out a trench to the depth of a spade's blade – one spit – across the width of the plot you wish to cultivate. Next, remove the soil in a barrow, wheeling it away over planks to minimize soil compaction, to the end of the plot in which you are working. In single digging this first trench should be 30cm/12in wide. Add roughly a bucketful of compost or other organic manure to each square metre/yard of trench, and if there is a lot of annual weed on the surface, skim it off and drop it into the first trench before making the next. Then, working back-

1 The secret of a healthy, vigorous and fruitful garden, such as this, is to choose plants which suit the soil in your garden. A suitable soil need not necessarily be a rich soil: the grey-leaved plants growing here, for example, would not thrive in such a soil, but rather prefer a gritty, free-draining one which approximates to the soil in which they grow in the wild.

Preparing the Site

wards and using the spade vertically to save your back and achieve as much depth as possible, dig the next trench, turning the earth over into the trench you have just made. Try to ensure that the soil from the top goes to the bottom. Only on heavy land will the soil come out in nice neat blocks which you can then stack in the trench for the frost to shatter; in lighter soils it will crumble as you turn it. Continue to work backwards like this until you reach the end of the plot, when you simply turn the original wheelbarrowed soil from the first trench into the last one.

In double digging your trench should be twice as wide, at least 60cm/2ft. Having taken out the first trench, fork over the bottom to the full depth of the fork's tines, incorporating manure or compost in this second spit. Then skim off any annual weeds from the soil that is to form the next trench, turn over the soil into the first trench (you will have to do this in several 'bites'), and work some more organic matter into it – many plants have roots which will not reach down into the second spit. Take care not to mix subsoil with topsoil if the topsoil is shallow.

This is the theory; in practice most people need time and experience to become really efficient, but perfection is not essential. You will, for example, find that the newly dug soil will stand proud of the surrounding area, possibly with bumps and depressions. Ignore these: some settlement will take place naturally, given time, and you can simply rake the soil level when it is workable in the spring. After all, part of the point of conventional digging is to make the topsoil sufficiently crumbly so that a 'tilth' can easily be formed with raking.

A 'deep bed' should ideally be 'double dug', but you will not need to repeat this for at least five years (some gardeners would say ever); thereafter you can simply topdress with compost or rotted manure each autumn, lightly fork over and leave the rest to the worms. 'Deep

beds' come into their own on heavy soils because the moisture can drain away more freely than it could on level ground, but even on light soils they have advantages: the amount of bulky compost added will act as a sponge to aid water-retention in summer.

Some tips: do not dig if the soil is very wet, especially if the land is heavy, because it easily becomes compacted if walked on. If the ground is liable to compaction, stand on boards to work. Do not dig in frosted soil because, once buried, it takes much longer to thaw out in spring. Do use a good sharp, preferably stainless steel, spade. Stop digging if you begin to tire or if your back starts to ache; several short stints of digging are far better than one long exhausting bout. Those with back problems should use an 'automatic' spade which can be operated without bending. It is highly advisable to wear gloves, to help prevent blisters, and to protect your skin from animal manures.

As for other additives: lime is helpful in increasing the alkalinity of acid soils, but do not raise the pH of a vegetable plot above 6.5 because other important nutrients will become locked up and some vegetables will suffer accordingly.

Lime should only be applied if, after a pH test, it is found to be absolutely necessary, and should be put on in the autumn in the form of ground limestone. Much larger quantities of lime are required to raise the pH of a clay soil than of a sandy one (read the instructions on quantity written on the bag of ground limestone you buy). Never combine lime with sulphate of ammonia or farmyard manure; they react adversely, and will give off ammonia. Applications of calcified seaweed also make a soil more alkaline, as do large quantities of spent mushroom compost.

Gypsum and seaweed meal help to draw clay particles together, leaving air spaces, so improving the structure of a clay soil and allowing water to drain more easily. Peat absorbs water and has, in the past, been recommended for making sandy soils more water-retentive; however, peat is a finite resource and other organic materials work just as well. Peat can also be used to acidify the soil for a time, but it is only really effective for growing lime-haters if they are strictly confined to containers.

Sulphur may be added to alkaline soils, but its acidifying effects are short-lived. It is really easier to treat specific

lime-haters that are suffering 'lime-induced chlorosis' (when their leaves turn yellow) with sequestered iron than to attempt to change the pH of the soil.

DRAINAGE

DS The water table is the level of water naturally found in the ground. It rises and falls between winter and summer, and can be easily checked by digging trial holes in different parts of the garden. A low water table can starve roots of waterborne nutrients, while a high one can be detrimental to plant growth. While the former can be eased by irrigation, the latter often requires drainage to rectify the situation. Bear in mind, however, that the process of improving the drainage, and thereby lowering the existing water table may, in turn, adversely affect mature trees. The water table can also be drastically altered by new buildings, roads or other major works, all of which can have a devastating effect on any existing, surrounding planting, especially trees.

The question of whether a garden needs drainage or not is a subjective one, depending on the use to which the garden is to be put. If your terrace collects standing water after rain it indicates that

SINGLE DIGGING

Keeping your spade as vertical as possible, dig out the soil to a depth of one spit, making a trench 30cm/12in wide. Barrow the soil to the end of the plot to be dug.

Dig a second trench in the same way, filling the first trench with the soil you dig out, and making sure that it is turned over. Add compost or organic matter as you go.

Repeat the process methodically, trench by trench, until the whole plot is dug over in this way, and fill your final trench with the soil you barrowed away from the first one.

SOIL AND EXCAVATION

its construction was poor and you should recall the contractor if you employed one; if your lawn becomes flooded, remedial action will be required, both to ensure that the area becomes usable as quickly as possible after rain, and to allow adequate aeration for grass to grow properly. Garden borders also require good drainage – unless, that is, you wish to grow moisture-loving plants.

In other words, first assess your garden and its needs: while poor drainage may well be a problem, it might in some instances prove a positive asset.

In many instances, particularly with new properties, poor drainage may be due to soil compaction as a result of heavy site traffic; on clay soil this can result in a solid 'pan' of clay which can usually be remedied by deep cultivation, either by mechanical rotovation or by double digging. Where the compaction is due to site traffic you are quite within your rights to ask the contractor to rectify the problem.

In a well established garden, poor drainage in a lawn may also be due to compaction – this time from mowing and rolling over a long period, or as a result of active games. Since the problem is often compounded by a 'thatch' of

dead grasses and grass clippings, remedial action should initially take the form of a well planned lawn care programme that includes scarification, spiking to improve aeration, and sensible weedkilling and feeding.

If, however, such relatively straightforward do-it-yourself remedies are insufficient, you will probably need to lay some kind of proper drainage system. The best, and the only one that is effective over a long period of time, is a herringbone system consisting of a central drain, either of clay pipes or of a perforated plastic pipe, into which spurs are run at an angle. The system should ideally extend over the whole of the area that needs draining, and pipes should run in a steady and accurate fall to a soakaway at the lowest point. Installing such a system is a skilled job involving considerable earth-moving, and is therefore best left to a good landscape contractor or drainage specialist.

IRRIGATION

DS Water is essential to plant growth and development, for the smallest alpine as for the largest forest tree.

Just how much moisture a particular specimen needs depends on such things

as rate of growth, size of leaf, and whether the plant is deciduous or evergreen. Some plants have evolved water-conserving characteristics, while others thrive in the moist conditions of marshy or marginal areas, and since most gardens offer a range of habitats, from open areas that receive any available rainfall, to those that lie in a 'rain shadow' beneath trees or under a wall, you should suit your planting to the plants' needs. Having said that, climatic conditions do vary considerably from year to year, and if there is a drought, plants may suffer however carefully they have been sited.

Irrigation is an obvious means of combating lack of moisture, and this can range from the use of a watering-can, to various kinds of hand-held hosepipes and spray guns, to manually positioned sprinklers and perforated seep hoses, right up to computerized systems that are purpose-designed to irrigate gardens of any size or complexity. Just which is suitable for you will depend on what you want to achieve and the amount of money you wish to spend.

Hand-held hosepipes can be fitted with a wide range of snap-together additions that make them very versatile.

Different heads provide a variety of spray patterns and can control the amount of water delivered; fertilizer can be incorporated; and moisture can be directed to a specific plant or location, preventing indiscriminate wastage.

Sprinkler systems are more often used for lawn areas, and the simplest can be connected to a hosepipe and placed in position to cover the widest area. If used sensibly, and moved at regular intervals, they provide an acceptable method of irrigation, but if left to run for hours on end, or even overnight, can become incredibly wasteful.

At the top end of the irrigation range all kinds of automatic systems are available, and these can be tailored to fit your garden. Some are installed by specialist firms and some are suitable for DIY.

Specialist companies will use a plan of your garden to work out a network of irrigation lines to service all areas. 'Pop-up' sprinklers can be neatly concealed beneath a lawn, and seep hoses positioned in borders and planted areas so that water is delivered exactly where needed. Systems can be simply programmed with a digital timer fitted to an outside tap, or fully computerized so that they can be set to come on at any time

DOUBLE DIGGING

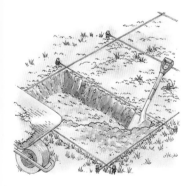
First measure out your plot into blocks 60cm/24in wide, using taut lines and pegs. Dig out a trench to this width and to a spit's depth, and barrow the soil away.

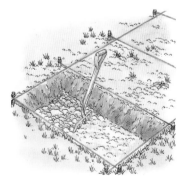
Fork over the second spit to loosen it. This stage is important as it will improve drainage and allow air to penetrate. Carefully remove any roots of perennial weeds as you go.

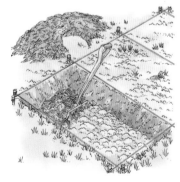
Add a bucket of manure or any other well rotted organic material to this second spit, at the ratio of one bucket per square metre/yard, and fork this lightly in.

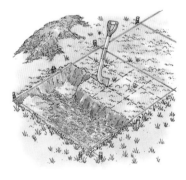
Dig out the soil from the second trench in 'bites', turning it and any annual weeds over into the first trench. Add more compost. Avoid mixing topsoil with subsoil. Fill in last trench with soil from the first.

of the day or night, or to look after the watering while you are away from home. A valve should always be attached to the tap. This is especially important if you are using plant food, to prevent it being driven into the mains.

With any kind of irrigation you should remember that even in temperate climates water restrictions may be in operation, and on occasions a complete ban. Water companies can charge extra for the use of sprinklers, and you may need a licence to operate them. In times of drought you may well bless your rain-water tubs.

Do not forget to drain and isolate, or lag, all outside supply pipes, to prevent freezing and subsequent bursting in sub-zero winter temperatures.

CREATING NEW LEVELS

DS Modest changes of level in a garden are quite within the scope of most people, provided the job is planned properly and plenty of time is allocated to carry the project out. If you do wish to include changes of level in your garden, or are encouraged into it because other garden projects have generated a great deal of surplus soil, you must decide first whether you want these levels to appear part of the natural landscape or as more architectural features.

If you look at the great parks of the eighteenth century you will see how landscape architects such as 'Capability' Brown dug lakes and created hills that were in complete harmony with the sur-rounding landscape. This landscaping was reinforced with large-scale tree planting, and although our domestic plots are on a far smaller scale, the prin-ciples of gently flowing contours rein-forced by planting can work just as well today. Base your design on nature, noting that you very rarely find a hill in isolation, a rigidly planted wood, or a dead-straight valley.

A vital point to remember is to strip off the fertile topsoil from the infertile subsoil before you start digging, and

stack it safely for future use. It is also worth remembering that, due to lack of aeration, topsoil in a heap does not stay in good condition for more than about six months. You may also need addi-tional new topsoil to supplement that which you have already used.

CREATING A CONTOUR DRAWING

DS Having decided where your new features are to go, and roughly how you want them to look, simple contours can be plotted on a copy of your site plan. You can of course build a mound by eye, but you need scale drawings if you are to visualize accurately how your mound will look, and to work out the quantities of soil that may need to be imported. The drawings should be carried out in two separate stages.

First, take a tracing paper copy of the previously prepared site plan and stick it down over the graph paper on which it was prepared, using the same scale of one square representing a metre or a foot that you used for the site plan itself. As you are going to show vertical distances as well as the shape of the mound, draw a series of lines, one within another, indicating the shape of the contours at different heights. You do this by joining up points of equal height. As an example, contours might be shown at 25cm/10in, 50cm/20in and a high point of 75cm/30in.

Slopes should be gentle, with a maximum gradient of no more than 35 degrees. The higher the mound is built, the larger the overall feature will be, and in most gardens the height should in any case be kept relatively low: 1m/3ft is usually enough. However, you can save quite a bit of space in a small garden if the back of the mound is held in place by a retaining wall.

Remember that a small mound close to the house or viewpoint will seem as big, or even bigger, than a larger hillock further away. And you may want to make the contours of a more distant mound rather more generous.

Once you have prepared the contour drawing that shows the *shape* of the mound, you will almost certainly want to see what the profile, or section through the middle, looks like.

To make a sectional drawing, take another sheet of tracing paper and copy on to it the contour lines you have just drawn. On the same piece of paper and exactly below the first drawing, draw horizontal lines across the page to ind-icate the vertical heights involved. Use the same scale as for the contour drawing, which will give you heights at 25cm/10in, 50cm/20in and 75cm/30in. Then match up the line of the retaining wall (or one side of the mound if you are not using one) on both drawings, and mark the height of the wall on the sectional draw-ing. Next draw a line AB on the contour plan across the section you wish to show. From each contour line that is crossed by this AB line, extend vertical lines down to meet the appropriate horizontal height line on the sectional drawing. Join these points up and you will have an accurate idea of the profile that the finished mound will present, and will also be able to estimate accurately the amount of soil that you may need to bring in.

To do this, you need to visualize each contour line as representing a column of soil. Work out the volume of each column by multiplying each dimension, length by width by height, as you would to find out the volume of a cube. Start with the highest contour. The 75cm/30in contour line, for example, measuring approximately 100 x 130cm/40 x 50in across, will have a column of soil 75cm/30in high. To calculate the volume of soil required for this column, multiply 100cm x 130cm/40in x 50in to find the area (= 13,000cm^2/2000in^2) and multiply this by 75cm/30in (= 0.975m^3/1.29yd^3).

Do similar calculations to find the vol-ume within the *overall* area of the next contour line, and so on down the slope, and subtract from your result the volume of the higher contour 'column' or 'columns' of soil as you go.

CAN YOU CARRY OUT THE WORK YOURSELF?

DS Whether you decide to create contoured mounds yourself or decide to call in a contractor really depends on the size of the job. You could hire a mini-digger but they are difficult for an amateur to operate successfully.

If you do employ a contractor to work from your contour drawing, make sure that you supervise the job. Not only may he deviate from the plan, with unsightly results, but you may want to make mod-ifications yourself as the work progresses. Remember that the shape needs to be as natural as possible, and that ulti-mately it is your eye that will determine what is right.

If you carry out the work yourself, carefully peg out the outer edges of the contoured area with canes, or mark its outline with sand. Either can be easily adjusted if you are not happy with the outline. Should you need a retaining wall, now is the time to set this out, to check its position, and then build it. If the mound is to be created over existing turf, lift the turf carefully with a turfing iron or sharp spade, and stack it with the topsoil for re-use once the job is complete.

Contours can be built up a layer at a time, and if the mound is a large one, subsoil can be used as a base, provided it is ultimately covered with topsoil to a good depth. Soil should be barrowed from the stockpile along a runway of boards across a lawn area. Each layer of soil should be well consolidated, and as the contours take shape, check the profile against the plan and sectional drawing that you prepared, making any minor adjustments as you go along. Inevitably the levels will settle slightly, so always build the mound slightly higher to allow for this.

The final stage is to place topsoil over the entire area and carefully grade the contours to their finished levels, making sure that the mound runs smoothly (is 'feathered') into the adjoining garden. This is a job that must be done by eye.

Last of all, either seed the mound with grass seed, replace the turf that you removed, or lay new turf.

If you wish to terrace a bank using retaining walls, this will be considerably more expensive than creating slopes. The pattern and line of such terracing will depend on the existing contours and on how these tie into the garden design.

ALTERING LEVELS AROUND TREES AND OTHER PLANTING

DS If you alter the levels in a garden you will inevitably affect the height of the existing water table, which may in turn cause trouble for any nearby planting and especially trees.

Raising the level of the soil will reduce the amount of available oxygen trees can take up through their roots, so at least a metre/yard of existing ground level should be left around the trunk of a mature tree. This can be done by building a circular retaining wall, which must subsequently be kept clear of rubbish, or by sweeping the retaining wall partially around the tree. In order to aerate the root system under the new higher ground, vertical tile drains should be put in to correspond with the limit of the root system, and these should link up with horizontal drains exiting through the face of the wall. Hardwood trees such as oak and beech are particularly susceptible to such changes in level.

If the levels are to be lowered around a tree you also need to think about safeguarding roots. The spread of a root system will not be more than the overall spread of the canopy above, so in this instance leave a platform of soil around the tree to match the circumference of the canopy. This can be supported by banking or by a retaining wall.

Smaller shrubs and hardy perennials can usually safely be moved during the dormant period, making sure that they are replanted, and staked if necessary, as soon as possible in suitably prepared ground. In dry weather, even in winter, it may be necessary to water.

MAKING A CHANGE OF LEVEL NEAR A TREE

Where a change of level is to be made close to a tree, it is important to maintain the water level as nearly as possible at its original level. You will probably need to build a retaining wall to hold the new level in place. This should be no less than a metre/yard away from the tree, and should be backed with crushed stone or hardcore, and neatly finished with a coping just below the level of the turf. Be very careful not to sever major roots while excavating for foundations; this could affect water take-up, and could also destabilize the tree in high winds.

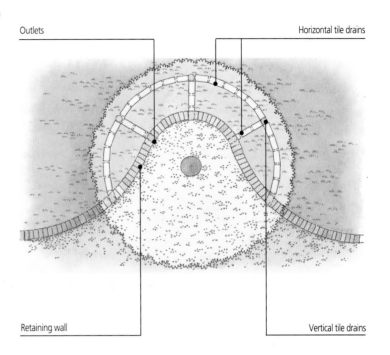

Outlets

Horizontal tile drains

Retaining wall

Vertical tile drains

ENSURING THAT TREE ROOTS HAVE SUFFICIENT OXYGEN

The root system of the tree will correspond approximately to the circumference of its canopy. Any roots covered by the new higher level of soil will need aerating. This can be done by inserting vertical tile drains at the outer limit of the root system, to link up with horizontal ones that also act as water drains, exiting through the retaining wall just above the existing ground level around the tree. Some trees are particularly susceptible to changes of level around their root systems. Oak is one, and if you own a fine specimen, it may be better to leave it alone and reconsider your plans for the garden.

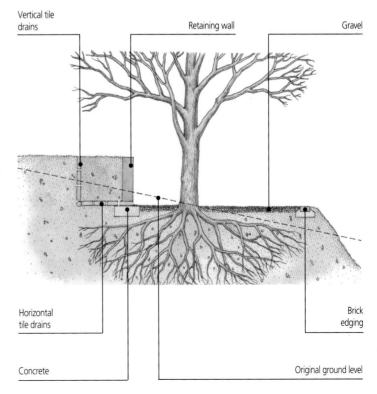

Vertical tile drains

Retaining wall

Gravel

Horizontal tile drains

Concrete

Brick edging

Original ground level

1 One of the strengths of a well planned garden lies in a positive use of plants. This in turn has much to do with the careful choice of colour, and the provision of visual continuity. As a general rule, hot colours draw the eye, while cool colours create a feeling of space, and are often best used informally further away from the house. Here the blue foreground planting helps to draw the more flamboyant tulips together, but also leads the eye further afield towards the trees.

In this semi-wild spring grouping under the trees, advantage has been taken of nature's generosity. Forget-me-nots, allowed to seed from year to year, create a carpet which tones well with the pink and white tulips. The large-flowered tulips, on the other hand, are best replaced annually, for they seldom flower satisfactorily the second time round.

3

2 Formality requires a measure of balance and control, clearly reflected here in the positioning of the pots and planting. There is humour, too, with the clipped hedge echoing the seat in front of it.
Here all the planting effects are achieved by the use of foliage. This demonstrates graphically how diverse are leaf shapes, and how useful leaves are in effective plant design.

3 Town gardens are often more formal than their country cousins. The hard landscaping of this scheme reflects the character of the surrounding buildings, and planting is simple but effective. A low level of maintenance would be required here.
This garden presents a challenge for the lover of plants: it is shady, and probably has a dry and free-draining soil. It shows what can be achieved with a few carefully chosen plants, and generous use of mulching material.

Designing a garden is fun, just in the same way as working out the interior design for a house or producing a particularly successful flower arrangement. For all of these disciplines to succeed you need to follow a planning sequence. Random planning rarely works and the creation of any situation on impulse inevitably leads to chaos.

Before making a start, you need to work out just what you already have in terms of the existing site, what you and the whole family wants, and to temper this with the amount of money you want to spend and the degree of maintenance you are prepared to undertake. Much of the latter is to do with the amount and kind of planting you incorporate: if you are a keen gardener then the pattern and species may be as demanding as you wish, but if you view your garden as an outdoor living space,

where plant material is subservient to the other activities that you enjoy, the scheme should be geared accordingly.

To illustrate this we have created twelve quite different garden designs, each of which has been evolved around a specific brief. In each we have travelled through the planning sequence, first analysing the site and situation before creating a structure of hard landscape that is subsequently softened and clothed by the soft landscape elements of plants and ground-cover.

We have not simply designed gardens of different sizes, but rather different situations where the contrasting needs of families, plantspeople and individuals can be catered for. We have considered soils, land forms, seasonal changes and the degree of maintenance involved.

Following on from each design are photographs that evoke each style of

garden in a different way, showing the numerous ways in which you can tackle any given site or type of garden.

One of the most important things to remember is that you should never copy a design directly from a book, magazine, television programme or anywhere else. Gain inspiration by all means, and by doing that understand the importance of all the factors that form the bones of any composition. For this reason we have created gardens that are themselves subdivided into different areas. Within each area the planting has been laid out in such a way that various sections and groupings can be taken out and used in situations elsewhere.

This is the perfect way to learn about garden design, and by following the guidelines and examples that we offer, you will start to evolve the style and expertise that is uniquely right for you.

THE DECORATIVE GARDEN

DS The concept of the decorative garden has relevance for anyone who wants their space outdoors to fulfil primarily an ornamental function. Of course, all gardens are decorative by their nature, but in these pages we have tried to present various options and ideas for the gardener who simply loves to create beautiful effects, whether using flowers, the layout, different materials, or added extras such as statues and ornaments.

Our first example is a potager. The design is for a garden of moderate overall proportions, approximately 21m/70ft wide and 27m/90ft long. It is set within a framework of 2.5m/8ft high walls along the sides, and yew hedges top and bottom. (Wattle hurdles 2m/6ft high could be used instead of the walls.) The far hedges can be tall enough to screen a bad view beyond.

A potager can be any kitchen or vegetable garden, although the term itself suggests that it will also be designed to look good. The underlying idea is simply that where bare soil will be visible for some of the year, as crops finish, there should be sufficient interest in the basic ground plan, and sufficient structure in the form of hedging and permanent feature plants or plant supports, that the garden is still pleasing. The results should be both decorative and productive.

This design is ornamental in every respect. The layout forms a symmetrical parterre, with four outer roundels centring on simple, metal, four-way arches. There are wide borders filled with both scented shrubs and climbers and plants that produce a crop, and these borders are interrupted by low buttressing hedges for structure. There is a central planting of thymes, intended to be walked on for their scents. The main focal point is a Lutyens seat, with two curved stone seats on either side of the garden. The surfacing is grass throughout – anything else would overcomplicate the garden, and detract from the decorativeness of the trees, flowers and edible plants themselves.

UB The idea behind this plan is a garden that includes a wide range of fruit, vegetables, herbs, cutting flowers and scented plants. Most find a place for their looks as well as their use in the kitchen.

A design as complex as this can be daunting, but it helps to consider it as a series of 'pockets' of planting, each one with a mirror image. Often, I have mixed productive plants with ornamental ones within the same pocket: for example, the two shapes opposite the bench feature tomato plants mixed with tagetes; down the left side of the garden,

lettuces grow alongside sages; and up the arches sited bottom left and top right, climbing nasturtiums romp with marrows and vegetable spaghettis.

There are several approaches to using productive plants ornamentally. Sometimes one can select a decorative form of an edible plant, such as the ornamental cabbages flanking the two *Pyrus salicifolia*. Or one can grow a traditional plant in a decorative way, such as training a gooseberry as a standard;

NORTH ▶

Shown in midsummer
Soil: fertile, free-draining loam; neutral pH

or one can choose statuesque edible plants, such as angelica and globe artichokes, and site them for effect.

All these approaches are reflected in this garden, and since symmetry is a vital principle of this design, so featured plants need to be balanced across the garden. The standard gooseberries oppose each other diagonally, likewise the raspberries trained up poles; and dwarf fruit trees have dominant positions at the four corners of the central area.

Herbs feature strongly for their scents and decorative value. The central motif contains three different thymes. Catmint forms low hedging to the surrounding beds, and there are two herb pockets within the central area.

The potager does not require enormous skill to achieve satisfactory results but it does need continuous attention, in particular the swift replacement of overmature crops, and dedicated weeding. Some form of crop rotation should be practised to prevent the build-up of pests and diseases in the soil.

PLANT KEY

1 *Malus floribunda*
2 *Foeniculum vulgare* 'Purpureum'
3 *Cynara cardunculus* Scolymus Group (globe artichoke)
4 Loganberry 'Thornfree' (trained on tripod)
5 *Salvia × sylvestris* 'Mainacht' ('May Night')
6 *Santolina pinnata* ssp. *neapolitana* 'Sulphurea'
7 *Buddleja crispa*
8 Tomatoes 'Alfresco' and 'Sungold' with *Tagetes* 'Golden Gem'
9 Arch covered with trailing marrow 'Long Green Striped' and climbing nasturtium; *Mentha suaveolens* 'Variegata' in pot underneath
10 Apple 'Sunset' (rootstock MM26)
11 Purple-leaved basil, chives and parsley
12 *Rosa* 'Mme Isaac Pereire'
13 Raspberry 'Glen Moy' (grown up single post)
14 *Borago officinalis*
15 *Rosa* 'Old Blush China'
16 *Nepeta × faassenii*

17 *Salvia × superba*
18 *Dianthus* 'Haytor'
19 *Hemerocallis citrina*
20 Central area planted with *Thymus serpyllum albus* and *T. serpyllum coccineus*; *T. serpyllum* 'Pink Chintz' on paths
21 Leek 'Blue Solaise' with radicchio
22 Arch covered with climbing French Bean 'Purple Podded' and Runner Bean 'Sunset'; Strawberry 'Pantagruella' in pot underneath
23 *Monarda* 'Cambridge Scarlet'
24 *Nicotiana* 'Sensation'
25 Gooseberry 'Whinham's Industry' (grown as a standard)
26 *Nicotiana* 'Lime Green'
27 *Levisticum officinale* (lovage)
28 Ornamental Cabbage 'Cherry Sundae' F1
29 *Ajuga* 'Rainbow'
30 Pear 'Onward' (rootstock Quince 'A')
31 Capsicum 'Golden Bell', *Allium cepa* Aggregatum Group (Egyptian or tree onion) and Capsicum 'Redskin'
32 *Artemisia absinthium* with *Helichrysum* 'Tall Mixed'
33 *Pyrus salicifolia* 'Pendula'
34 Pear 'Concorde' (rootstock Quince 'A')
35 *Lavatera trimestris* 'Silver Cup' with *L. trimestris* 'Pink Beauty'
36 *Angelica archangelica*
37 *Vitis vinifera* 'Purpurea'
38 Raspberry 'Glen Prosen' (grown on single post)
39 *Monarda* 'Croftway Pink'
40 Arch covered with vegetable spaghetti and climbing nasturtium; *Mentha × gracilis* 'Variegata' in pot underneath
41 *Salvia officinalis* 'Purpurascens', *S. officinalis* 'Tricolor', chervil and winter savory
42 Climbers on wall: *Akebia quinata*, *Lonicera periclymenum* and *Trachelospermum asiaticum*
43 *Argyranthemum* 'Jamaica Primrose' with *Anthemis tinctoria* 'E C Buxton'
44 Leaf Beet 'Rhubarb Chard' with lettuce 'Salad Bowl' ('cut-and-come-again')
45 Arch covered with climbing French Bean 'Climbing Blue Lake' and Runner Bean 'Painted Lady'
46 Apple 'Grenadier' (rootstock MM26)
47 Gooseberry 'Jubilee' (grown as a standard)
48 *Vitis* 'Brant'

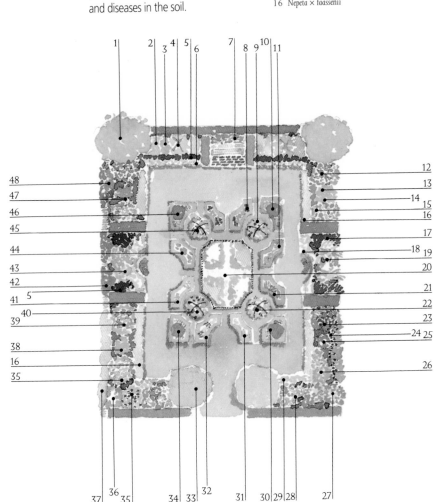

Garden Designs

DS This design for a town garden shows how a decorative overall effect can be achieved using the related disciplines of formality and symmetry. A formal design is essentially one that balances on both sides of a central axis. The garden can be small or large, rural or urban, and this style of design often looks at its best when it reflects a similarly balanced façade of a house.

The example here is surrounded by high walls, and the area immediately outside the house is elevated from the rest of the garden by approximately 60cm/2ft. Traditional materials have been used where possible: the upper terrace is paved in York stone, and a broad area of gravel leads out from the French windows. Gravel has been used as a major paving material and this is both easy to maintain and provides an excellent backdrop for planting, which can be allowed to grow through the surface.

Balustrade contains the terrace and broad brick steps drop down to the main garden level. The major feature here is the central pool, which is flanked by gravel paths leading down to the two matching pavilions that look back towards the house. Within these are set stone urns filled with colourful planting, while outside, raised beds help to interrupt the architectural outline and the surrounding walls.

The garden is strongly formal. The central axis, looking away from the house, runs straight down the middle of the steps, emphasized by the balustrade, and continues with the centrally placed bowl in the pool and the seat at the bottom of the garden. A cross axis is created by the two smaller raised pools and spouts, which are aligned on the central water bowl. As well as these dominant axes, repetition is continued throughout. The pavilions are balanced by the two trees nearer the house, and Versailles tubs topped with box balls flank the French doors. Such formality could be severe, but the overall effect is softened by the plants that spill over the gravel.

This theme is echoed on the terrace, where the paving is not set in a straight line, but has a 'crenellated' edge to allow for plants to intrude on to the stone area.

UB Such a symmetrical design seems to call for planting that both echoes that theme, and introduces some tumbling, sprawling elements to soften the hard lines. This is achieved by repeating groups of plants, maintaining the cross axes, but choosing plants for their habits and colours and taking aspect into account.

The garden is shady near the house, and sunnier further away. The soil is ordinary, but is moist near the house and drier at the far end. This, along with the sheltered conditions, gives the opportunity for growing plants such as teucrium, cistus, helianthemums and rosemary against the far wall. Sprawling into the gravel are groupings of plants that combine spiky leaves with spreading shapes: *Iris pallida* and hebes, for example. Also in the gravel are heat-loving bulbs such as tulip species, early crocuses and *Iris histroides* 'Major'. Although the garden is intended to be at its best in midsummer, these will help to create impact at other times of year.

In the moister soil nearer the house, the shade-lovers dicentra, ajuga and bergenia find a place under the trees, where climbers cover the walls. Facing the house are groupings of different

THE DECORATIVE GARDEN

NORTH

Shown in midsummer

Soil: ordinary garden soil; neutral pH

PLANT KEY

1 Tubs filled with *Milium effusum* 'Aureum', *Lobelia* 'Blue Cascade' and *Campanula* 'Birch Hybrid'
2 *Helianthemum* 'Jubilee'
3 *Indigofera heterantha* (pruned each spring)
4 *Cistus × hybridus*
5 *Trachelospermum jasminoïdes* (trimmed at top of wall)
6 *Pleioblastus auricomus*
7 *Rosmarinus officinalis* Prostratus Group (to trail over wall)
8 *Convolvulus sabatius*
9 *Phlomis chrysophylla*
10 *Teucrium fruticans*
11 *Helianthemum* 'The Bride'
12 In gravel, left-hand side: *Iris pallida* 'Variegata', *Salvia officinalis*, *Helichrysum splendidum*, *Sisyrinchium angustifolium*, *Thymus × citriodorus* 'Silver Queen', *Hebe* 'Youngii' and *Thymus pseudolanuginosus*
13 In gravel, right-hand side: *Iris pallida* 'Variegata', *Salvia officinalis*, *Acaena buchananii*, *Ruta graveolens* 'Jackman's Blue',

Alchemilla conjuncta, *Hebe* 'Youngii', *H. buchananii* and *Sisyrinchium californicum* Brachypus Group
14 *Acorus gramineus* 'Variegatus' with *Calla palustris*
15 *Pontederia cordata* with *Caltha palustris* 'Flore Pleno'
16 *Nymphaea* 'James Brydon'
17 *Nymphaea candida*, *Aponogeton distachyos*, *Iris laevigata* and *I. laevigata* 'Alba'
18 *Dianthus deltoïdes* 'Flashing Light'
19 *Fuchsia* 'Riccartonii'
20 *Parthenocissus henryana*
21 *Malus × robusta* 'Red Sentinel'
22 Underplanting of *Dicentra* 'Adrian Bloom', *Bergenia* 'Ballawley' and *Ajuga reptans* 'Burgundy Glow'; *Clematis* 'Kermesina' planted to climb up into the tree
23 *Itea ilicifolia*
24 *Acanthus spinosus*
25 Paving grouping, right-hand side: *Hosta* 'Shade Fanfare', *H. fortunei* var.

aureomarginata and *Pulmonaria angustifolia* 'Munstead Blue'
26 *Scrophularia auriculata* 'Variegata'
27 In tubs on wall: *Juniperus chinensis* 'Stricta'
28 Paving grouping, left-hand side: *Pulmonaria rubra* 'Bowles' Red', *Polystichum setiferum* and *Hosta* 'Shade Fanfare'
29 *Hosta fortunei* var. *aureomarginata*
30 *Heuchera americana*
31 *Rosa* 'Madame Grégoire Staechelin'
32 *Camellia* 'Anticipation'
33 *Hemerocallis* 'Pink Damask'
34 *Astrantia major* var. *rubra*
35 *Sedum* 'Ruby Glow'
36 *Vitis vinifera* 'Purpurea'
37 *Diascia rigescens*
38 *Dianthus* 'Devon Blush'
39 *Nepeta* 'Six Hills Giant'
40 *Convolvulus sabatius*
41 *Rosa* 'Silver Jubilee' (lightly pruned)
42 *Campanula lactiflora* 'Prichard's Variety'
43 *Digitalis purpurea* 'Sutton's Apricot'

hosta cultivars, with ferns and pulmonarias. Flanking the path are tubs of box and juniper, and the planting on one side of the steps echoes the other.

The design anticipates a certain amount of labour (sowing foxglove seed, pruning roses, clearing out water marginal plants and so on) for it is a garden where visual effects are generally more important than saving work.

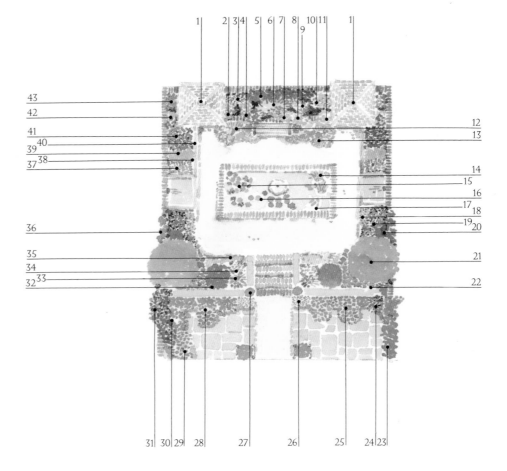

1

2

3

THE DECORATIVE GARDEN

2 The decorative garden in high summer can be a riot of colourful flowers and effects. A wide variety of plant material has been used in this garden, but the range of colours is much smaller. Limited amounts of yellow and white in a predominantly pink and blue setting lifts the whole scheme. The comparative lack of shelter has prompted the use of sturdy, self-reliant perennials, but often a decorative garden will mean a high level of maintenance, with plants needing to be staked, and lawns kept carefully mown. The results, however, justify all the hard work.

An informal scheme often engenders a feeling of space and movement. These borders, set at angles to one another, encourage a gentle stroll that takes a relatively long route within a comparatively small overall area of garden.

3 Pots filled with plants for the summer – here pelargoniums and glechoma – are always useful for bringing a decorative note to quiet corners. Nearby, permanent climbers including *Solanum crispum* 'Glasnevin' create a more sumptuous atmosphere.

1 Geometry is the basis of much design work. The layout here is strictly formal, with concentric rings of hedging and water acting as a central point from which the rest of the composition fans out. The hard surfacing is muted but has a fine texture; wedges of superbly laid cobbles are turned at angles to one another, and separated by bands of granite setts. Planting is architectural, and an outer framework of hedges helps to contain the space. But there is still ample room for sitting and dining, making this the ideal outside room.

There is a controlling hand in all this, which is necessary for an effective decorative garden where hard and soft elements are designed to complement each other. Maintenance of this type of garden is likely to be high.

4

4 I have always found busts amusing: both the expression on the faces and the poses. This series of four are looking in different directions. Change them around occasionally, so that neither they nor you become bored; you will find it makes a real difference to the look of the garden. Reflections are only one of the things that water has to offer, and here the juxtaposition of the vibrant tulips and the pure white statues sets up a fascinating dialogue. The busts also serve to frame the pool and keep the focus on this, rather than the wider lawn area.

Garden Designs

THE ENTHUSIAST'S GARDEN

DS This versatile garden incorporates several distinct areas to accommodate a gardening enthusiast's varied interests. There is a water garden, a large area for fruit and vegetable cultivation (including fruit trees grown as espaliers and also trained over arches), and two raised beds for growing different types of rock plants. All this is contained within an average-sized rectangular plot. This is the most common shape of garden encountered and one that many people find far from promising, as the overall shape and rigid boundaries seem dull; yet the shape has enormous potential.

Design solutions to this very common problem tend to follow one of two basic approaches. The first option is to create a layout based on a series of strong flowing curves, sweeping the eye round the composition and distracting it from the corners. The second option, illustrated here, follows quite the opposite course, positively revelling in the right angles in order to build up a montage of overlapping surfaces.

Brick paving, to link with the house, and York stone are used to construct the repeating series of interlocking rectangles which leads the way round the garden. A slightly sunken gravelled area marks the boundary between the architectural use of materials close to the house and the gentler planted areas further away.

On the other side of the lawn, a fruit tunnel leads to the vegetable plot, which is screened by a line of espalier fruit trees. On the house side of these is a seat in a small sitting area that links the upper and lower levels of the garden.

NORTH

Shown in late spring
Soil: moisture-retentive; acidic

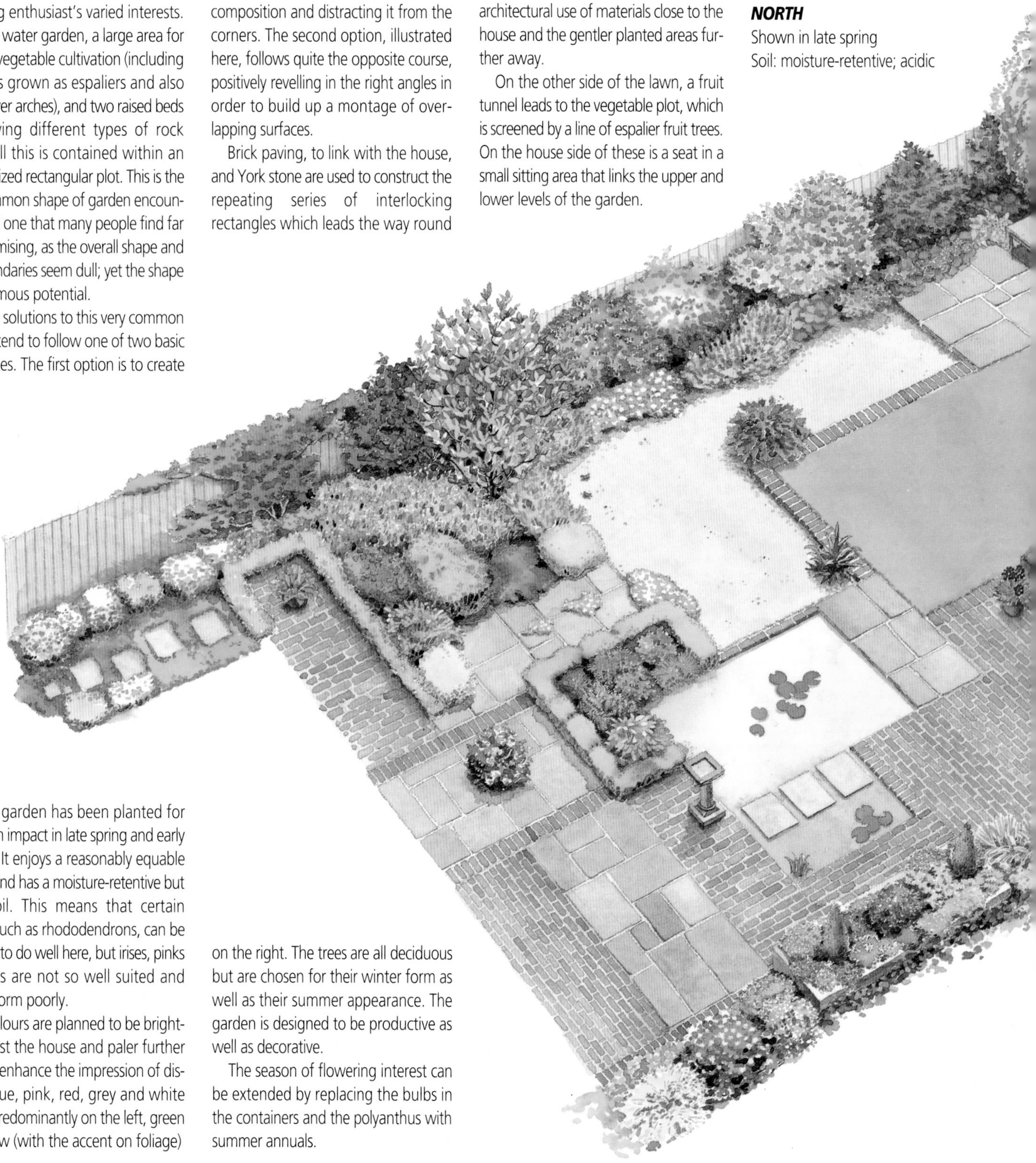

UB The garden has been planted for maximum impact in late spring and early summer. It enjoys a reasonably equable climate, and has a moisture-retentive but acidic soil. This means that certain species, such as rhododendrons, can be expected to do well here, but irises, pinks and roses are not so well suited and may perform poorly.

The colours are planned to be brightest nearest the house and paler further away, to enhance the impression of distance. Blue, pink, red, grey and white feature predominantly on the left, green and yellow (with the accent on foliage) on the right. The trees are all deciduous but are chosen for their winter form as well as their summer appearance. The garden is designed to be productive as well as decorative.

The season of flowering interest can be extended by replacing the bulbs in the containers and the polyanthus with summer annuals.

THE ENTHUSIAST'S GARDEN

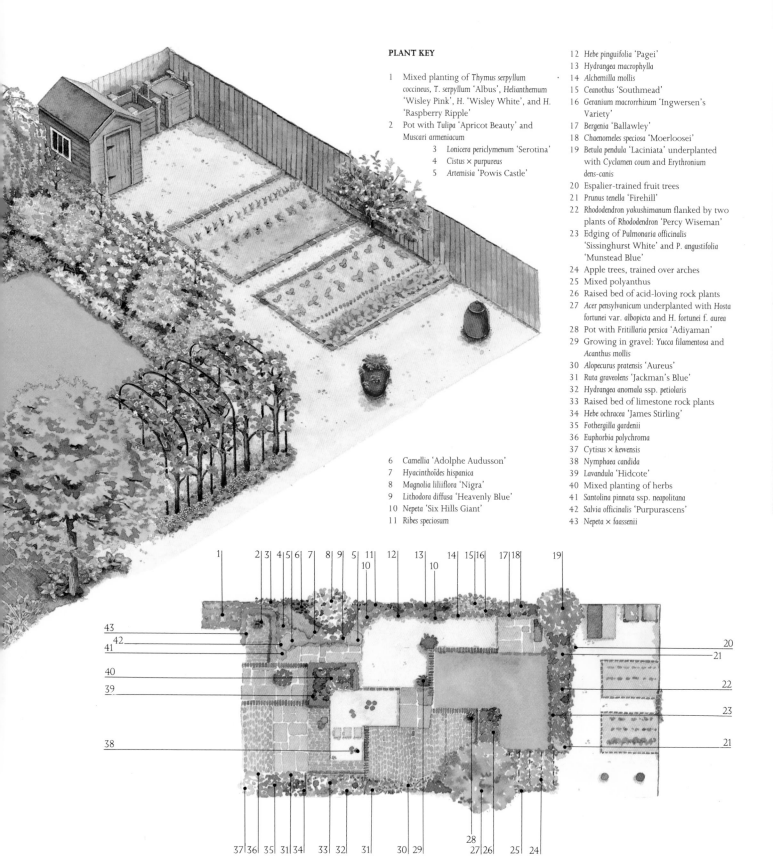

PLANT KEY

1　Mixed planting of Thymus serpyllum coccineus, T. serpyllum 'Albus', Helianthemum 'Wisley Pink', H. 'Wisley White', and H. 'Raspberry Ripple'
2　Pot with Tulipa 'Apricot Beauty' and Muscari armeniacum
3　Lonicera periclymenum 'Serotina'
4　Cistus × purpureus
5　Artemisia 'Powis Castle'

6　Camellia 'Adolphe Audusson'
7　Hyacinthoïdes hispanica
8　Magnolia liliiflora 'Nigra'
9　Lithodora diffusa 'Heavenly Blue'
10　Nepeta 'Six Hills Giant'
11　Ribes speciosum

12　Hebe pinguifolia 'Pagei'
13　Hydrangea macrophylla
14　Alchemilla mollis
15　Ceanothus 'Southmead'
16　Geranium macrorrhizum 'Ingwersen's Variety'
17　Bergenia 'Ballawley'
18　Chaenomeles speciosa 'Moerloosei'
19　Betula pendula 'Laciniata' underplanted with Cyclamen coum and Erythronium dens-canis
20　Espalier-trained fruit trees
21　Prunus tenella 'Firehill'
22　Rhododendron yakushimanum flanked by two plants of Rhododendron 'Percy Wiseman'
23　Edging of Pulmonaria officinalis 'Sissinghurst White' and P. angustifolia 'Munstead Blue'
24　Apple trees, trained over arches
25　Mixed polyanthus
26　Raised bed of acid-loving rock plants
27　Acer pensylvanicum underplanted with Hosta fortunei var. albopicta and H. fortunei f. aurea
28　Pot with Fritillaria persica 'Adiyaman'
29　Growing in gravel: Yucca filamentosa and Acanthus mollis
30　Alopecurus pratensis 'Aureus'
31　Ruta graveolens 'Jackman's Blue'
32　Hydrangea anomala ssp. petiolaris
33　Raised bed of limestone rock plants
34　Hebe ochracea 'James Stirling'
35　Fothergilla gardenii
36　Euphorbia polychroma
37　Cytisus × kewensis
38　Nymphaea candida
39　Lavandula 'Hidcote'
40　Mixed planting of herbs
41　Santolina pinnata ssp. neapolitana
42　Salvia officinalis 'Purpurascens'
43　Nepeta × faassenii

Garden Designs

1

1 This garden would verge on the over-complicated if the ground plan were less positive. As it is, the strong pattern of paving holds the planting of herbs and aromatic plants together, while the outer perimeter of low walls and higher planting act as a frame to this productive outdoor room. Vertical emphasis is provided by the standard trees set in the corners, and the trees outside, while the spirally clipped bush acts as a punctuation mark.

Herbs are definitely a speciality of this garden. The picture demonstrates that, if well looked after, they are quite in keeping in a formal garden. The standard trees add much vertical interest to what would otherwise be a predominantly low-growing scene.

2 The perfect combination of hard and soft landscape, with soft flower and foliage flopping over the gravel path and softening the formal stone piers and urns. The urns are well planted, and extend the use of colour to a higher plane. The path leads directly towards shallow steps, but the seat, set to one side, invites one to pause and sit. Behind it, the high wall provides shelter and also acts as a host to fragrant climbers.

This garden has a backbone of permanent plants (sedums, roses, climbers, free-standing shrubs). Half-hardy annuals have been added to these for the summer, in the foreground and in the large wall urns.

3 A simple scheme usually works best, and the path here provcides the perfect understatement to the subtly planted border. The two stone balls provide counterpoints, their solidity acting as a foil to the more delicate line of the picket fence.

Crammed with good herbaceous plants, and a few short shrubs, this front garden has been well designed to give plenty of colour and interest throughout the summer. Care has been taken to stake unobtrusively, and the planting is generous enough to discourage weeds.

THE ENTHUSIAST'S GARDEN

4 This is a glorious study in the subtlety of texture, form, and counterpoint, all set at different levels. The colours are wonderful, and the overall floor of gravel provides the perfect low-key backdrop.

The concentration of so many scrubbed pots of different kinds of houseleek, *Sempervivum*, together with a real stone sink filled with tufa rock and choice alpines, proclaims this as the garden of a real enthusiast.

THE LOW MAINTENANCE GARDEN

Garden Designs

DS For many gardeners, the overriding priority in a new garden is that it should require little maintenance. This design shows that such a brief need not compromise the overall look of the garden, nor restrict the choice of elements.

The design is for a long narrow plot, which is the perfect shape for sub-division into a number of separate 'rooms', each with its own identity. As you walk around the garden you will find it natural to pause in each area, increasing the feeling of total space. Separate areas also have an advantage in terms of maintenance: it is often easier to look after several smaller areas rather than one large space, as you can tackle a section at a time and see the fruits of your labours more quickly. If you leave one area to its own devices for a year or so, you can still have a 'finished' area in which to sit. A great psychological advantage!

Aside from creating 'rooms' within the garden, there are many ways in which you can keep work to a sensible minimum. Hard surfacing of an appropriate type is of course almost maintenance free, so close to the house I have provided a terrace of ample size. This is laid in a combination of blue-grey engineering bricks and precast concrete slabs in pale yellow. The terrace has raised beds around it, which are often easier to tend than planting at ground level.

A wall 1m/3ft high divides this first room from the next. Although you would easily see over this while standing, when you are sitting down it is just high enough to break the sight line down the garden. This increases interest from the house end, and gives a feeling of seclusion to the lower parts of the garden.

From the terrace, the path leads down the side of the next area and across it at the far end, so one's progress is slowed and a feeling of greater space is created. The path also provides a labour-saving mowing edge to the central lawn, as does the row of pavers on the opposite side. A trellis provides a screen between this and the third garden area.

The furthest part of the garden is given over to a more natural theme. Rougher grass, naturalized with bulbs and wildflowers, provides the main floor. Stepping-stones sweep across the area, terminating at the seat that acts as a focal point. Groups of birch and hazel provide an attractive, self-sustaining habitat, and the rose hedge can be left to thicken up, with little annual trimming or attention. This area, once established, will require very little regular maintenance but will be a pleasure to sit in.

Finally, at the bottom of the garden, there is room to accommodate a shed and compost heap.

UB In the low maintenance garden, it is most important that the plants should be as far as possible self-sustaining. They should require little or no pruning, not outgrow their allotted space, but cover the ground so that weeds are suppressed. Herbaceous perennials should be slow to need dividing; best of all will be those that prefer to be left completely undisturbed, such as the peonies.

Good preparation of the soil before planting is essential. Perennial weeds must be thoroughly eradicated, and plenty of organic matter dug in.

This planting scheme assumes a fertile soil, of neutral pH and deep enough not to dry out completely in summer. Half the garden is reasonably sunny, the rest in part or even dense shade.

The main eyecatchers in this garden are the trees: a gleditsia dominates the central area, with silver birches near the trellis. A fastigiate beech and a cryptomeria at the far end form important focal points near the seat.

However little maintenance a plant needs, it must still have decorative value. Examples are the hardy geraniums near the back door, the row of blue helictotrichon, which picks up the colours in the engineering brick, the senecio and 'bottlebrush' euphorbia that front them, and the alchemilla planted on either side of the low wall.

PLANT KEY

1. *Geranium* × *riversleaianum* 'Russell Prichard'
2. *Euonymus fortunei* 'Silver Queen'
3. *Ceratostigma willmottianum* underplanted with *Hebe pinguifolia* 'Pagei'
4. *Senecio* 'Sunshine'
5. *Helictotrichon sempervirens*
6. *Euphorbia characias* ssp. *wulfenii*
7. *Veronica gentianoïdes* with *Aster* × *frikartii* 'Mönch'
8. *Potentilla* 'Primrose Beauty'
9. *Geranium* 'Johnson's Blue'
10. On trellis: *Lonicera japonica* 'Halliana' and *Clematis flammula*
11. *Fatsia japonica*
12. *Betula pendula* 'Tristis' underplanted with bluebells (*Hyacinthoïdes non-scripta*) and hellebores
13. *Berberis thunbergii* 'Red Pillar'
14. *Euphorbia amygdaloides* 'Rubra'
15. *Polygonatum* × *hybridum* with *Bergenia* 'Eric Smith'
16. *Fagus sylvatica* 'Fastigiata'
17. Hedge of mixed rugosa roses
18. *Lonicera* × *purpusii*
19. *Viburnum* × *juddii*
20. *Cryptomeria japonica* 'Elegans Compacta'
21. *Prunus laurocerasus* 'Otto Luyken'
22. *Geranium macrorrhizum* 'Album'
23. *Ajuga reptans*
24. *Omphalodes cappadocica* 'Cherry Ingram'
25. *Euonymus fortunei* 'Emerald 'n' Gold'; *E. fortunei* 'Emerald Gaiety'; *E. fortunei* 'Coloratus'
26. Mixed planting of hazels: *Corylus maxima* 'Purpurea' and *C. maxima* 'Kentish Cob'; underplanted with primroses
27. *Digitalis purpurea alba* amongst *Hosta sieboldiana* var. *elegans*
28. *Carex hachijoensis* 'Evergold'
29. *Paeonia lactiflora* 'Duchesse de Nemours' underplanted with *Ipheion uniflorum*, *Scilla siberica*, and *Narcissus* 'February Gold'
30. *Gleditsia triacanthos* 'Sunburst' underplanted with *Omphalodes verna*
31. *Euphorbia polychroma* with *Alchemilla mollis*
32. *Alchemilla mollis*
33. *Juniperus sabina* 'Tamariscifolia'
34. *Acanthus mollis*
35. Raised bed with *Juniperus squamata* 'Blue Star' and *Ajuga reptans* 'Purpurea' and *A. reptans* 'Multicolor'
36. *Pachysandra terminalis* 'Variegata'
37. *Asplenium scolopendrium*
38. *Cotoneaster horizontalis*
39. *Geranium macrorrhizum* 'Ingwersen's Variety'

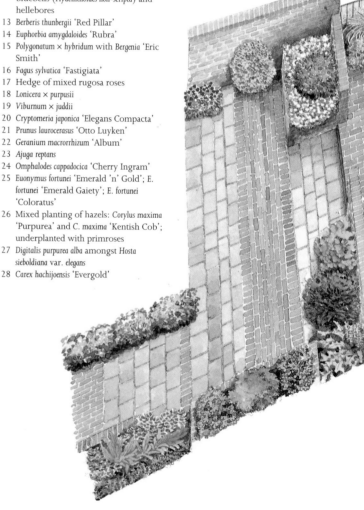

NORTH

Shown in early summer
Soil: fertile; neutral pH

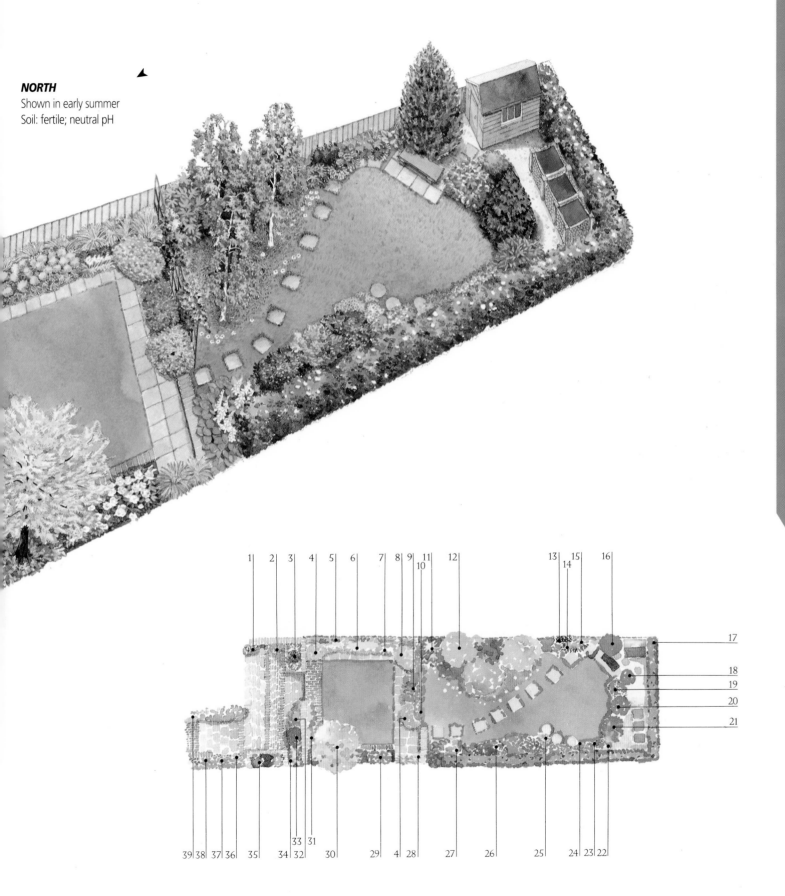

Garden Designs

1 You can do all kinds of things with colour, and garden design should relate to the house that it adjoins. But the question here is whether the startling red is too strong for the planting against the house? The answer is no, because the contrasting textures of foliage set up a different and more restful visual dialogue. You should never be a slave to your garden, and this composition will certainly keep work to a minimum.

The essence of a low maintenance garden is that the plants used in it should be, on the whole, permanent and long-lived. They should also require little or no pruning, feeding, support, or protection in winter; should be at least reasonably pest- and disease-resistant; and should cover the ground effectively to suppress weeds. This front garden has many, though not all, of the characteristics required. The tall ornamental grasses, the yucca, and the evergreen shrubs in the beds in front of the house, need little or no attention throughout the year, while providing continuous foliage interest.

2 The informality of the woodland setting here, and the use of vigorous weed-suppressing plants such as rhododendrons, both help to minimize the need for much close maintenance. This path disappears around the corner with a real hint of expectancy. The grouping of plants into drifts gives movement to the overall composition, guiding both feet and eye through the space.

3 The main tasks in this garden will be trimming off seedheads late in the season, to prevent too prolific self-seeding, and clipping the box hedges annually. It all goes to prove that you don't need a riot of flower to provide colour and interest; for much of this material is also evergreen. The pattern of paving helps to separate the different plants, and allow easy yet informal access through the space.

2

3

THE MODIFIED GARDEN

Garden Designs

DS For many people, a completely new design for their garden would be inappropriate. The existing garden may have evolved without any guiding plan, but often it incorporates features and elements that it would be a pity to lose. These pages show how an existing garden can be modified, by pulling together the best elements into a coherent and satisfactory whole.

The modified garden in its original form (below) is typical of many; it also serves to illustrate the drawbacks of a dog-leg shape, where one area is set at right-angles to the main space. The terrace of broken York stone is attractive but lacks definition; although it is the only sitting space in the garden, it does not catch a great deal of sun. The straight path and flanking flowerbed emphasize the length and flatness of the garden. A large but well grown conifer sits in the middle of the lawn and two wings of scruffy beech hedge project

into the garden from either side. The second lawn area is stocked with young fruit trees. The area to the right is completely undeveloped.

In the new design (right), modifications to the existing garden have resulted in a different approach as to how the garden is used and enjoyed. The terrace near the house has been made smaller, with the addition of a curving raised bed to contain its edge. Stone from the terrace has been reused to construct both the brick-edged path and the new, much sunnier, sitting area, which centres on a generous tree seat. The path now sweeps away in a strong flowing curve, using the conifer as a pivot to the design.

The beech hedge has been reclaimed, clipped to a good shape and linked together with two new short sections. These will grow together across the path into a low-cost arch. Its diagonal angle creates a feeling of greater space.

From here the path continues, sweep-

ing away around the bottom part of the garden and better quality lawn, drawing both feet and eye into the dog-leg part of the garden. Here there is another arch, leading into an informal sitting area and an attractive summerhouse. Beside them, the fruit trees have been repositioned in an area of rougher grass naturalized with bulbs and wildflowers.

Throughout the garden, the main lawn and border shapes have been remodelled into a series of strong flowing curves, providing a far greater feeling of space and movement.

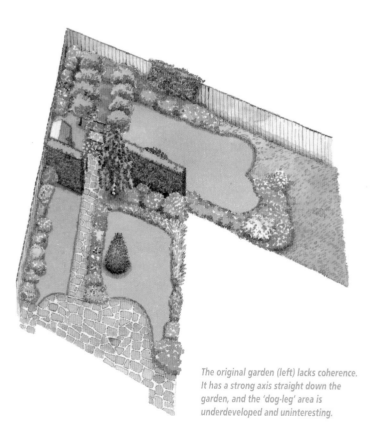

The original garden (left) lacks coherence. It has a strong axis straight down the garden, and the 'dog-leg' area is underdeveloped and uninteresting.

The new garden (above) has paths moving across and through it in generous, sweeping curves, bringing the entire garden together into one coherent whole.

THE MODIFIED GARDEN

NORTH

Shown in midsummer

Soil: ordinary garden soil; neutral pH

PLANT KEY

1 Crataegus persimilis 'Prunifolia'
2 Liquidambar styraciflua
3 Underplanting of Geranium phaeum, G. macrorrhizum 'Ingwersen's Variety', Dicentra 'Bountiful' and Geranium macrorrhizum 'Bevan's Variety'
4 Parthenocissus henryana (existing)
5 Hosta 'Halcyon'
6 Centranthus ruber albus
7 Aruncus dioicus
8 Rosa 'Nevada' (existing)
9 Fruit trees resited; rough grass with bulbs beneath
10 On pergola: Rosa 'Climbing Iceberg', (existing), R. 'White Cockade', Clematis 'Marie Boisselot' and C. 'Huldine'
11 Heucherella alba 'Bridget Bloom'
12 Grouping of Bergenia stracheyi with Astrantia major and Bergenia × schmidtii
13 Kolkwitzia amabilis 'Pink Cloud' (existing) with Pulmonaria rubra 'David Ward'
14 Astilbe 'Rhineland'
15 Abutilon vitifolium
16 Echinops bannaticus 'Taplow Blue'
17 Marrubium incanum flanking existing Alchemilla mollis
18 Hemerocallis 'Hyperion'
19 Geranium 'Johnson's Blue'
20 Helichrysum 'Schweffelicht' ('Sulphur Light')
21 Rosa 'Thisbe'
22 Ceanothus × delileanus 'Gloire de Versailles'
23 Clematis 'Perle d'Azur'
24 Achillea 'Taygetea'
25 Foeniculum vulgare 'Purpureum'
26 Potentilla fruticosa 'Vilmoriniana'
27 Santolina pinnata ssp. neapolitana 'Edward Bowles'
28 Viola labradorica purpurea
29 Saxifraga 'Carmen'
30 Veronica prostrata 'Trehane'
31 Geranium cinereum 'Ballerina'
32 Raised bed filled with Oenothera missouriensis, Euphorbia myrsinites, Alyssum saxatile 'Citrinum', Salvia officinalis 'Icterina', Hypericum olympicum and Helianthemum 'Wisley Primrose'
33 Rosa 'Golden Wings' (pruned to keep it within bounds)
34 Akebia quinata
35 Romneya coulteri
36 Hosta 'Frances Williams'
37 Salvia officinalis 'Icterina'
38 Berberis thunbergii 'Aurea' (existing)
39 Existing conifer
40 Origanum vulgare 'Aureum'
41 Lonicera japonica 'Aureoreticulata'
42 Sambucus racemosa 'Plumosa Aurea'
43 Beech hedge
44 Betula pendula (existing)
45 Grouping of Pulmonaria rubra 'David Ward', Filipendula rubra and Echinacea purpurea 'Robert Bloom'
46 Daphne × burkwoodii 'Somerset'
47 Grouping of Astilbe 'Fanal' and Gentiana asclepiadea around existing Berberis thunbergii f. atropurpurea
48 Rosa 'Madame Isaac Pereire' (existing, now trained against the fence) with Liriope muscari in front

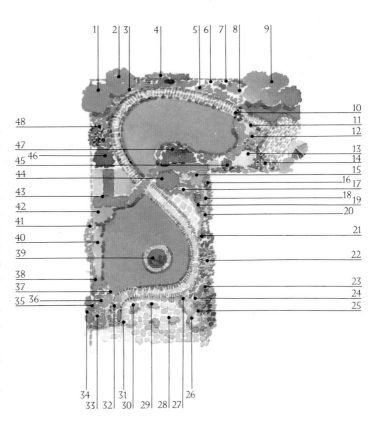

Most gardens include a few established trees and shrubs, if not climbers and herbaceous perennials, which it would be a pity to lose – the art lies in recognizing how they might play a role in a new, modified design.

The garden previously incorporated various examples of coloured foliage. These have been retained, with new planting around them to enhance their strong colours. The sambucus in front of the hedge, for example, now has a yellow honeysuckle alongside it, and a golden marjoram at its foot. Similarly, a pink kolkwitzia now has an underplanting of pulmonaria and pink flowering herbaceous perennials to surround it. The fruit trees have been resited into the area of rough grass, and even the conifer has been made into an important part of the overall design.

The new design shows how the separate parts of a garden can be 'colour-coded'. There is, for example, a white area near the summerhouse, with a pink one opposite it; an arch planted with roses and clematis straddles the two. This part of the garden lies on heavy soil, so moisture-loving plants can be grown. Nearer the house, the drainage is sharper, and gets sufficient sun in the course of the day to suit sun-loving plants well enough. Here yellow is the dominant colour, with romneya, roses, euphorbia, a yellow helianthemum and a variegated sage all included in the planting.

1

THE MODIFIED GARDEN

2 When modifying an existing garden, lawns are a flexible element and can be easily and quickly reshaped. Hedges are harder to redirect, though deciduous ones, as here, can usually be renovated successfully, even if overgrown. Small perennials, bulbs and bedding plants can be used to fill in gaps in borders, providing almost 'instant' colour while you wait to see what else will come up. You can also use them as an inexpensive and quick way to try out ideas for a more permanent colour scheme later on. Hedges form ideal boundaries, and although they need regular clipping, are far cheaper than walls or fences. They can also provide a sympathetic backdrop to planting, as is the case in the arrangement shown here, with its co-ordinated cool colour range.

2

3

1 Paving can be expensive to modify, but this simple solution is dramatic and humorous at the same time. The clipped box balls have been planted in strong counterpoint to the granite setts. Potted plants bring interest to the roof above.

A planting scheme like this one makes a strong impact in a terrace that is not needed as a sitting area. It is not a difficult effect to achieve, provided that the visible soil is well enriched to ensure that the shrubs grow well.

3 Moving a mature tree that is in an inconvenient place is unlikely to be a success. Instead, the specimen here has been integrated into a new design. The drama set up by bright light and cool shade can be telling. The deck is a shady retreat beneath branches that frame the view out to the wider garden. It is interesting to see how it has been cut to echo the bole of the tree, and how the crisp horizontal lines of timber form a contrast with the more delicate foliage above.

Garden Designs

THE SHORT STAY GARDEN

182 Surfaces

36 Japanese Garden Style

DS Many people need their garden to look established within a single season; they often don't have years to wait for it to develop and mature, and they perhaps don't plan to be living in the house for more than a couple of years. There are plenty of ways to tackle the garden design so that it will look good fast.

This design includes a good mix of surfacing materials that will quickly look established. Gravel looks good almost as soon as it is laid, and plants will quickly

DECKING

Wooden decking provides an instant and highly attractive surfacing, that is very easy to maintain. The seat around the tree makes an organic link between planting and hard landscaping.

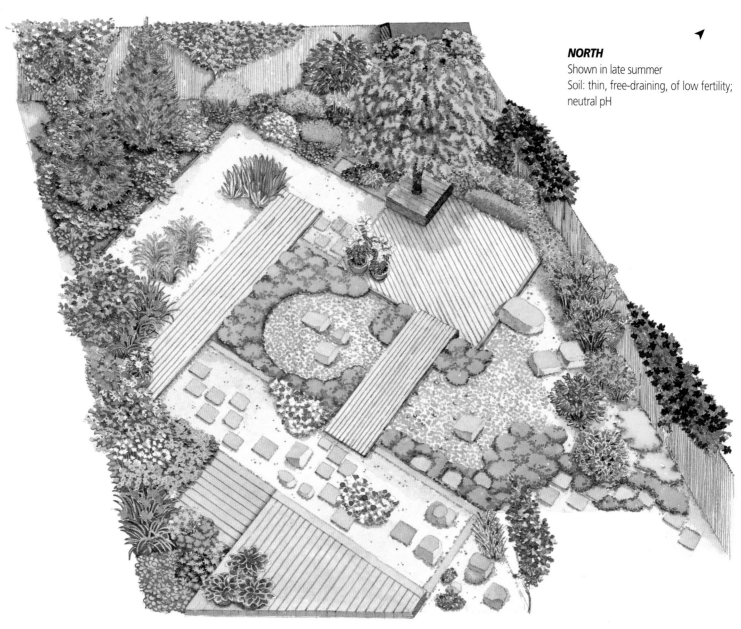

NORTH

Shown in late summer
Soil: thin, free-draining, of low fertility; neutral pH

THE SHORT STAY GARDEN

colonize it. Likewise the use of wood as the principle hard surfacing gives the garden an organic air that is very welcoming. The use of wooden decking, gravel, moss-like ground-cover, and in particular the bamboo fencing that forms the garden's boundary, all combine to reinforce the Japanese theme implicit in the overall design.

As the garden is virtually square, it is particularly effective to turn the design so that its main lines run at 45 degrees to the house: this utilizes the longest possible axis and detracts from the rectangular boundaries. The site is gently sloping, with a drop of approximately 45cm/18in between the house level and the lower right-hand corner.

The area nearest the house is shady, so only a relatively small paved area is appropriate. Here I have used railway sleepers, laid side by side. From here, stepping stones lead across a gravel and boulder area, giving access to the decked walkways that lead diagonally across the garden. The shorter of these crosses the 'dry stream', a typically Japanese feature, before dropping down to the main sun deck. Here a simple rectangular seat surrounds a tree.

The design creates triangular pockets of planting, which can be densely planted with fast-growing plants, summer bedding or spring bulbs to make a fast display. Fast ground-cover plants also have an important part to play. Throughout the garden, plants growing through the gravel, lilies in tubs, and carefully sited boulders all give movement and interest to the design.

UB The garden is planted to look established in its first year and mature within three years. Trees, shrubs and perennials all need to be relatively fast-growing, and also likely to flower young: this is particularly the case with the lavatera, buddleja, and the climbers. In such a garden, summer annuals and spring bulbs will play an important role in providing

colour and interest for part of the year, but this planting concentrates on those permanent plants that might quickly build into a pleasing framework.

The design assumes a new house, and a poor soil left by dilatory builders: there *is* topsoil, but it is thin, not very fertile and rather free-draining.

The difficulty with planting for the short-term is that, if you are not very careful, you can create problems for subsequent occupants. To avoid this, I have chosen plants which, though relatively fast-growing, never become too inconveniently tall (as would Leyland cypress,

for example). This is true both of the two picea at the end of the garden, and of the *Robinia pseudoacacia* 'Frisia'.

The emphasis is on Japanese plants (irises, hostas, and so on). *Saxifraga* 'Peter Pan' (a 'mossy' saxifrage) has been used extensively to give the impression of a Japanese moss garden, but one that is easier to manage and which has the added advantage of flowers in mid- to late spring. Herbs are grown close to the house and are chosen with attractive foliage in mind.

Annual and biennial climbers are invaluable in a fast-establishing garden:

Cobaea scandens features in this design, and *Eccremocarpus scaber* and *Tropaeolum speciosum* could be other good choices. *Clematis orientalis* is a particularly vigorous and useful form for this type of garden.

Maintenance requirements are generally low. The buddleja and caryopteris are best pruned right down every spring, but many of the other shrubs require little or no regular work. For a good supply of interesting annuals and annual climbers, a windowsill propagator would probably be a good investment to produce young plants each year.

PLANT KEY

1 Two trees of *Picea engelmannii* f. *glauca* underplanted with *Hedera colchica* 'Sulphur Heart'; *Lonicera periclymenum* 'Graham Thomas' on wall behind
2 *Perovskia* 'Blue Spire'
3 *Cistus* 'Silver Pink'

4 *Clematis orientalis* 'Bill Mackenzie'
5 *Hebe pinguifolia* 'Pagei'
6 *Aloysia triphylla*
7 *Argyranthemum* 'Mary Wootton'
8 *Buddleja davidii* 'Dartmoor'
9 *Humulus lupulus* 'Aureus'

10 *Ajuga reptans* 'Jungle Beauty' with *Milium effusum* 'Aureum'
11 *Robinia pseudoacacia* 'Frisia'
12 *Caryopteris* × *clandonensis* 'Worcester Gold'
13 *Clematis* 'Étoile Violette'
14 *Veronica prostrata* 'Trehane'
15 *Ceratostigma willmottianum*
16 *Foeniculum vulgare* 'Purpureum'
17 *Salvia officinalis* Purpurascens Group
18 *Artemisia dracunculus*
19 *Clematis* 'Étoile Violette'
20 *Salvia officinalis* 'Icterina'
21 *Thymus* × *citriodorus* 'Aureus'
22 *Cobaea scandens*
23 *Sisyrinchium striatum* 'Aunt May'
24 *Viola labradorica purpurea*
25 *Petunia* Resisto Series (blue and white forms) followed by *Myosotis* 'Marine' and *Tulipa* 'West Point' (for spring bedding)
26 *Saxifraga* 'Peter Pan'
27 *Hosta* 'Frances Williams'
28 *Saxifraga umbrosa*
29 *Alchemilla mollis*
30 *Asarum europaeum*
31 *Hemerocallis* 'Pink Prelude'
32 *Aster* × *frikartii* 'Mönch'
33 *Anemone* × *hybrida* 'Honorine Jobert'
34 *Lavatera* 'Barnsley'
35 *Lilium auratum* (in tub with ericaceous compost)
36 *Sedum* 'Autumn Joy'
37 *Lavatera* 'Burgundy Wine'
38 *Miscanthus* 'Silberfeder' ('Silver Feather')
39 *Iris japonica* 'Ledger's Variety' with *Iris japonica* 'Variegata'

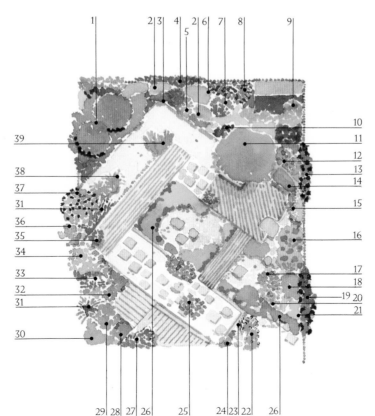

1

2 Here are quick-establishing perennials: two types of the ice-plant, sedum, together with *Stachys byzantina*, the easy ground-cover plant known colloquially as 'lamb's ears'. Perennials are an important ingredient, giving any garden which may be only temporarily occupied an air of permanence.

1 Pots and containers are essential constituents of the short stay garden; they quickly give the feel of an established garden. Here the half-hardy annual lobelia, together with daisies and pelargoniums, have been used to provide immediate colour. By themselves, they might give an impression of transience, but the reasonably fast-growing bulky shrubs behind them help to give a more substantial and permanent feel to the whole arrangement.

You can, of course, take pots with you when you move, but they have other far more important attributes. Here, a large selection has been used, and the real beauty lies in the wide variation of sizes, heights, and styles, all of which can be arranged and rearranged as the mood takes you.

3 You may not be intending to stay long in one place, but this does not mean that colour scheming should be abandoned in favour of quick effects. It would only take three years for a garden to reach this stage of maturity from scratch, and without the roses an even shorter time than that. This is a good example of a white planting scheme. The effect has been achieved with a subtle combination of silver, green and blue foliage, and white and pale pink blooms.

4 *Euphorbia polychroma*, the early spring-flowering spurge, and muscari make a very attractive and quick-growing combination for a spot in light shade. Plants will obligingly flower the first year, and both will increase in time.

Garden Designs

THE FRONT GARDEN

DS The role of front and back gardens is often very different. The latter usually provides space for relaxation, entertainment and play, while the former is primarily for access. More often than not, the lion's share of the budget and maintenance will be lavished on the space at the rear, leaving the front garden to be a low cost, low labour affair.

However, there are many occasions when the front garden is a sunnier and far more pleasant space than the back, and the design here illustrates just such a situation. It is for a large front garden facing almost due south; with the rear of the house in shade for much of the day, sitting at the front is an attractive proposition. The design therefore needs to allow for privacy and relaxation, while also providing efficient and easy access routes to front door and garage.

In this design, these two functions of the garden are consciously separated. The drive is wide, the gates being split between a small pedestrian entrance and a larger one for cars. Brick paving acts as an apron to the garage, then leads both feet and eye round to the front door, flanked by planting and tubs. The surfacing of the drive itself is exposed aggregate concrete, contained within large concrete slabs in a soft grey colour, offering the advantages of cheapness and practicality.

The brick leads out from the front door into the sitting area, which needs to be screened from the more public access areas. A wall 1.8m/6ft high and a hedge of the same height block the sight line for everything forward of the garage, while the hedge is decorative in itself. The wall is made interesting by a raised pool and spout, and a slightly lower raised bed interlocks with it.

The sitting area is now completely private, and enclosed within walls roughly 1.8m/6ft high. Brick and concrete slabs lead into a large lawn to create a feeling of space. A built-in seat fits into the angle of two walls, with a raised bed and box hedge on the other side of the terrace.

UB Like the overall design of this garden, the planting scheme works on two different levels. Bright, welcoming flowers make a bold impact as visitors approach the front door while, in the more private part of the garden, muted colours predominate.

NORTH ▶
Shown in summer
Soil: stony; mildly acid

THE FRONT GARDEN

The design is for a front garden close to the sea, with a mildly acid soil. It receives a great deal of sunshine, but also salt-laden winds all year round. The plants that will thrive here need to be reasonably wind and salt tolerant, but need not be hardy, for the coastal position ensures almost frost-free winters.

Full advantage has been taken of bright and cheerful tender annuals and perennials, even sub-tropical plants, such as the cannas, which will probably survive the average winter in this garden without having to be dug up in autumn.

In a front garden, the plants that mark the actual entrance are always important, and this particular example needs trees and shrubs that will do well in these coastal conditions. Flanking the drive are a species of tamarix, a hydrangea and a ceanothus. Facing each other are a male and a female plant of *Hippophae rhamnoides*: with both sexes present, the female should be thickly clustered with orange berries in autumn and winter.

The hedge of purple pittosporum makes up an important part of the living 'bones' of the garden. Its foliage contrasts prettily with the grey of the hippophae on one side, and the bright orange of crocosmia and yellow of anthemis on the other. Opposite is a tree tolerant of coastal conditions, *Acer pseudoplatanus* 'Leopoldii', a sycamore with mottled leaves turning yellow in autumn.

Initial care of the plants in this garden is substantial because the soil may well be poor and stony. However, the local availability of large quantities of seaweed will help. When rotted down, it makes an excellent fertilizer, rich in potash.

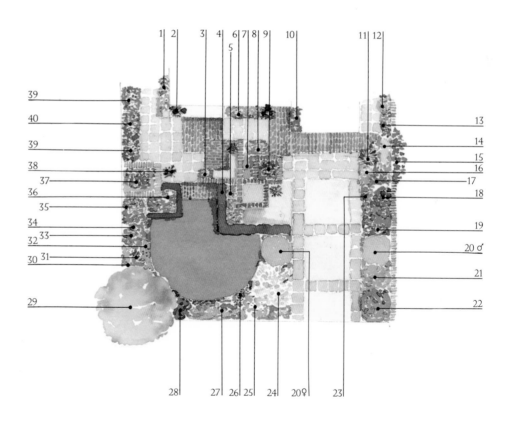

PLANT KEY

1 *Impatiens* 'Elfin Blush'
2 *Agapanthus* 'Headbourne hybrids'
3 *Osteospermum* 'Blue Streak'
4 Hedge of *Pittosporum tenuifolium* 'Purpureum'
5 *Crocosmia paniculata* with *Anthemis sancti-johannis*
6 *Gazania* 'Mini Star Mixed'
7 *Perovskia* 'Blue Spire'
8 *Potentilla fruticosa* 'Elizabeth'
9 *Pelargonium* 'Orange Beauty' and P. 'Flower of Spring' with *Lilium* 'Enchantment'
10 *Crocosmia × crocosmiiflora* 'Solfaterre'
11 *Phormium cookianum* 'Tricolor'

12 *Geranium wallichianum* 'Buxton's Variety'
13 *Sedum telephium* ssp. *maximum* 'Atropurpureum'
14 *Aster × frikartii* 'Mönch'
15 *Clematis* 'Jackmanii Superba'
16 *Convolvulus cneorum*
17 *Canna indica*
18 *Echinops ritro* 'Veitch's Blue'
19 *Canna iridiflora*
20 *Hippophaë rhamnoïdes*, male and female forms
21 *Ceanothus × delileanus* 'Gloire de Versailles'
22 *Hydrangea serrata* 'Preziosa'
23 *Achillea millefolium* 'Fire King'
24 *Tamarix ramosissima* underplanted with

Colchicum autumnale 'Pleniflorum'
25 *Lavatera* 'Barnsley'
26 *Penstemon* 'Garnet' (syn. P. 'Andenken an Friedrich Hahn')
27 *Ceanothus* 'Burkwoodii'
28 *Bergenia* 'Ballawley'
29 *Acer pseudoplatanus* 'Leopoldii' underplanted with *Brunnera macrophylla* 'Hadspen Cream' and *Heuchera villosa*
30 *Escallonia* 'Donard Radiance'
31 *Dierama pulcherrimum* and *Limonium platyphyllum*
32 *Dianthus* 'Cranmere Pool'
33 *Hibiscus* 'Blue Bird' (syn. H. 'Oiseau Bleu')

34 *Hebe salicifolia*
35 *Escallonia* 'Apple Blossom'
36 Assorted herbs enclosed by *Buxus sempervirens* 'Suffruticosa' hedge
37 *Petunia* 'Resisto Blue' and *Verbena* 'Silver Anne'
38 *Lilium* 'Pink Perfection'
39 *Hebe* 'Midsummer Beauty'
40 *Hebe × andersonii* 'Variegata'

124

DS In an urban setting a front garden is often little more than a transitional space between the street and the front door – a small dull area that has little money spent on it and next to no time. But neither lack of budget nor time need stand in the way of an inviting design that has plenty of interest in the plants and provides a pleasing view.

This is a typically tiny, sunless space requiring planting that is both shade-tolerant and good-looking all year round. Simplicity is the key, with low walls to the front that flank a 1.2m/4ft wide path, laid in neat precast slabs. This acts as the ideal foil to an attractive but low maintenance display to either side.

In a larger front garden, areas of nothing but planting may well become unmanageable. Large boulders or areas of cobbles could interrupt the gravel in place of plants, making access into the planted areas more possible.

UB Winter is a testing season in the front garden, for bare earth and denuded branches can offer a depressing vista for visitors to the house. The specific aim of this design is to show how even in a north-facing aspect, with relatively infertile soil and at a dead time of year, the planting can create plenty of interest and 'carry' the design.

The accent is therefore on neat and tidy evergreen foliage plants, but including many that flower at some time of the year. Apart from the two centrally placed plants of variegated box, which could be clipped into simple topiary shapes if required, the plants are mainly low and ground-covering, so ensuring that there is nothing to prevent light from reaching the house windows. Throughout the garden, pea gravel overlays the soil: this has the advantage of being both practical and decorative, making the garden look neat, allowing weeds to be easily removed, and showing off the foliage effectively. The gravel also makes it possible to walk amidst the plants to prune them where necessary; easy access to the climbers is particularly important.

THE FRONT GARDEN

NORTH

Shown in late winter
Soil: moist, infertile; neutral pH

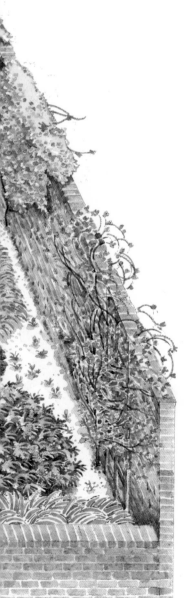

Many plants are repeated across the garden to link the two halves. Examples are the two plants of silver-variegated euonymus, each partnered by a clump of the yellow ornamental sedge carex; the variegated *Iris foetidissima* near the front wall – a plant noted for the way its seed pods curl open to reveal fat clusters of orange berries in autumn; and the use of two different hellebores. *Helleborus argutifolius* on the left has greyish foliage, while *H*. 'Wester Flisk' holds its slightly scented, greenish flowers on interesting red stems.

The repeated pairing of two very obliging and useful plants, waldsteinia with epimedium, offers a succession of attractive yellow flowers, the epimedium with heart-shaped leaves, the waldsteinia more profuse in its flowering (early summer), and bearing foliage similar to that of the strawberry plant.

Flanking the path at the entrance are two bushes of sarcococca, useful for its elegant foliage and scented winter flowers; after those come two different varieties of bergenia, used with heuchera and the purple form of tellima. The combination of bold foliage shapes and colours is intended to make a feature of the route to the front door. Repeated clumps of *Viola labradorica purpurea* and a swathe of ajuga continues the purple theme. The spiky-leaved *Liriope muscari* will provide blue, grape-hyacinth-like flowers in the late summer to autumn months.

Wall plants are useful for providing height in such a garden. Here ivy provides evergreen foliage; *Hedera helix* 'Glacier' has attractive silver and white variegations. Beside it is a honeysuckle that is semi-evergreen, and positioned on the opposite wall is the evergreen *Clematis armandii*.

Bulbs can be planted to push up in the small gaps deliberately left for them between plants. Crocuses, snowdrops, scillas and dwarf narcissi would be suitable, and, like the rest of the planting, require little in the way of maintenance.

PLANT KEY

1   *Carex hachijoensis* 'Evergold'
2   *Waldsteinia ternata*
3   *Viola labradorica purpurea*
4   *Euonymus fortunei* 'Silver Queen'
5   *Epimedium perralderianum*
6   *Heuchera micrantha* 'Palace Purple'
7   *Hedera helix* 'Glacier'
8   *Liriope muscari*
9   *Buxus sempervirens* 'Elegantissima'
10 *Bergenia* 'Bressingham Ruby'
11 *Ajuga reptans* 'Multicolor'
12 *Helleborus foetidus* Wester Flisk Group
13 *Lonicera japonica* 'Aureoreticulata' (on light trellis)
14 *Iris foetidissima* 'Variegata'
15 *Sarcococca hookeriana* var. *humilis*
16 *Clematis armandii*
17 *Helleborus argutifolius*
18 *Tellima grandiflora* Rubra Group
19 *Bergenia* 'Abendglut'

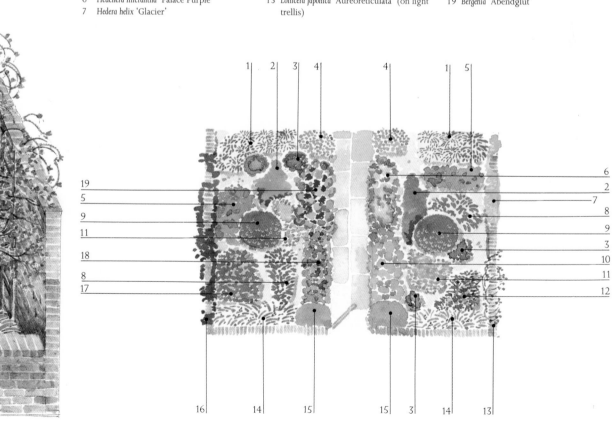

Garden Designs

1 Front gardens come in all shapes and sizes, and this one might be more at home at Versailles! However, this is a dramatic composition that is unashamedly formal. The paving has been thought out in great detail, and is well laid, reinforcing the geometric pattern of clipped hedging. The conifers provide strong verticality, and the whole composition focuses on the centrally placed and planted pedestal.

The hedges are of box, and the topiary cones are yew. A front garden is in a public position, and it would be important to trim the hedges carefully and frequently, at least twice a year. Feeding and watering in the growing season would also be necessary, to satisfy the demands of hedging plants. This may be labour-intensive, but the favourable comments from neighbours would make it worthwhile!

2 In a tiny urban space, climbing plants may offer the only chance to grow plants of a substantial size. Here a rose has been chosen to enhance rather than fight with the colour of the house wall. The result is alluring, although some trimming back will be necessary after flowering to prevent injuries to unsuspecting visitors.

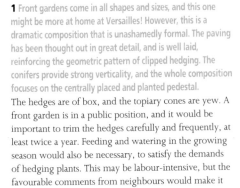

3 What a welcome home: straight from the street into a tropical paradise! The combination of planting and architecture is well handled in this situation, and forms the perfect link between house and garden.

The South African agapanthus, with its marvellous umbels of blue flowers above fleshy leaves, looks very much at home in this wonderful sub-tropical setting, but it will also grow in a sunny place, in containers or in the soil, in colder climates.

THE ROOF GARDEN

DS A roof space can make an exciting and interesting garden, as this design and photographs of real examples show. Usually the architectural surrounding is so thrilling that innovation in the design is both appropriate and necessary to cope with the practical limitations of the site.

Before any construction work is done, an engineer or architect must check the roof for its load-bearing capacity. Even if all is well, it is still prudent and practical to use lightweight materials in any construction. Strong winds can be a problem. Any design must take this into account, and if necessary provide for suitable boundaries. A roof garden is likely to be a dry environment for plants. Lawn is therefore rarely possible; but Astroturf can be rolled out and trimmed like carpet to achieve the illusion. Automatic irrigation systems are also an excellent idea for the beds and borders. Finally, rainwater must be directed into gullies or outlets, which could in turn be hidden beneath a timber deck.

The design for a roof garden measures just under 9m/30ft square, a space that is quite large for a domestic situation, as the available space at this height is usually smaller than the floor area of the house at ground level.

There are high walls around part of this roof space, but a boundary is also needed. The wall on the left is continued with a slatted fence, which will filter the wind and screen a bad view on that side. The remaining boundary is constructed from toughened plate glass screens, 1.2m/4ft high, bolted on to posts set approximately 1.5m/5ft apart. These break the wind, but allow the fine view beyond the garden to be enjoyed.

Access to the garden is provided by a door to the left. A timber deck is turned at an angle to the main garden plan to create a feeling of greater space. The boards are of unequal width to provide greater interest, and a built-in seat fits into the angle on the right-hand side. From here, the way leads under an arch, whose feet are set into the beds on

either side, over the Astroturf. Defining the far edge and creating an eye-catching feature with plenty of movement and interest, are sweeping curves of glass beads. They reflect the sky and the sun in a myriad sparkles, and are perfect for the lofty position of a roof garden.

Continuing the spirit of innovation, the central raised bed is made into a water feature, with a large fibreglass 'boulder' as its centrepiece. A good quality one will be very realistic. Set over a small tank where water is recirculated by a submersible pump, the 'boulder' is surrounded by cobbles and planting.

Raised beds are essential for planting and these are of a reasonable size and filled with a lightweight compost mix. The heights of the beds vary, which again provides interest. All the beds are constructed from timber slats, each about 5cm/2in wide and set vertically. The bed in the top left-hand corner is similarly constructed, but to conform to the curve the slats are bolted on to a metal frame, shaped to the correct radius.

UB A roof garden poses particular difficulties when it comes to planting. Most importantly, because of lack of shade or shelter, all plants (and especially those in pots) need to be tolerant of full sun and drought. There will be times when the planting medium will dry out, especially as the compost needs to be lightweight so will probably be loamless. (To avoid nutrient deficiencies, the compost could have a steady-release fertilizer added to it at the start of the season.)

The problems can, however, be turned to the planter's advantage. There are many beautiful and striking Mediterranean and sub-tropical plants that will thrive in these conditions, but fail in colder, wetter, ground-level gardens. Many, such as phormiums, kniphofias and grasses, are 'architectural' in nature, so fit in with the setting.

The other positive feature about a roof garden is that, if sheltered with a

wall and glass, warm summer conditions will continue for a long time. This garden is shown flowering in early autumn, when a garden at ground level would already be autumnal in atmosphere.

This garden lends itself to bold, striking plantings in strong colours – but with so much colour and drama in the design itself, too much plant colour could create a feeling of being hemmed in.

Climbers are important in a garden where high walls dominate. Here several climbers form the centrepiece for the planting around them. The pink-tipped *Actinidia kolomikta* becomes the focus amongst a grouping of pinks and purples, including artemisia, penstemon and sedum. Just beyond this, in a separate bed, abutilon has contrasting partners: kniphofia and pennisetum.

Much of the planting chosen would be too tender in a ground-level garden, but strong winds could still whip around, despite the elegant glass panelled boundary – so palms and other very tall plants are not suitable.

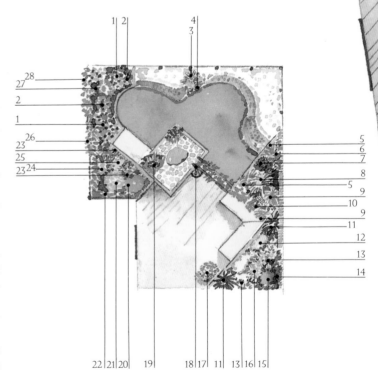

NORTH
Shown in early autumn
Soil: lightweight compost

1

1 Gardening in the sky can provide a green retreat in the heart of the city. The change of level is well handled, and overhead beams provide shelter and shade, and break the line of overlooking windows.

2 The interest here lies in the use of space, and in the handling of the backdrop. The geometry of the wall, and of the panel that echoes the shape, sets up a fascinating dialogue with the broad timber bench and generous deck. Planting is confined to pots, which can be moved and replanted.
Plants are indispensable in this otherwise rather stark roofscape. The use of containers allows some flexibility in an uncompromising situation.

2

PLANT KEY

1 Short bamboo tripods of climbing nasturtium
2 Ornamental vegetables, including Courgette 'Gold Rush' and Tomato 'Red Alert', and salad vegetables
3 Pot with *Phormium cookianum* 'Tricolor' and *Artemisia schmidtiana* 'Nana'
4 Pots with *Heliotropium* 'Marine', *Helichrysum petiolare* 'Limelight' and *Argyranthemum* 'Jamaica Primrose'
5 *Sisyrinchium striatum* 'Aunt May'
6 *Abutilon megapotamicum*
7 *Epilobium canum*

8 *Kniphofia* 'Little Maid'
9 *Pennisetum alopecuroïdes*
10 *Phygelius capensis*
11 *Yucca filamentosa*
12 *Sedum* 'Vera Jameson'
13 *Verbena bonariensis*
14 *Actinidia kolomikta*
15 *Artemisia ludoviciana* interplanted with *Nerine bowdenii* 'Mark Fenwick': the wide spacing should allow summer ripening of nerine bulbs
16 *Penstemon* 'Stapleford Gem'

17 Pot with *Convolvulus sabatius*, *Verbena* 'Silver Anne', *Helichrysum petiolare* and ivy-leaved *Pelargonium* (pink)
18 *Solanum jasminoïdes* 'Album' on pergola
19 Water feature planted with *Iris laevigata* 'Variegata' and *Lobelia cardinalis*
20 *Coronilla valentina* ssp. *glauca*
21 *Potentilla fruticosa* 'Primrose Beauty'
22 *Clematis armandii* 'Apple Blossom'
23 *Agapanthus* 'Headbourne hybrids' with *Lavandula angustifolia* 'Hidcote'
24 *Caryopteris* × *clandonensis* 'Kew Blue'

25 *Anthemis* 'E C Buxton'
26 *Rhodochiton atrosanguineus*
27 *Rosmarinus officinalis* 'Miss Jessopp's Upright'
28 *Passiflora caerulea*

THE GARDEN WITH NO VIEW

DS This design effectively copes with two commonly encountered types of site: it is intended for a garden in a town, where there is nothing beyond the boundary to which one would want to draw the attention; and it is wider than it is deep, so the boundary facing the house is relatively close.

In overcoming the latter condition, the prime task of the design must be to detract attention from the boundary, and one of the best ways will be to introduce a flowing pattern that will lead the eye around the space and create a feeling of movement. The treatment of the boundary itself is important: a fence with small, vertical slats is far less dominant than one with wide slats, for example. Hedging, fronted by a flowing planting scheme, would be a good choice, but avoid planting conifers, as these will inevitably draw the eye.

With such a broad, wide garden shape, it can be a help to divide off one section of it to create a more intimate and sheltered space to sit in. This has been achieved here with a trellis supporting fan-trained fruit bushes.

To compensate for the lack of view, there needs to be plenty of interest within the garden. Here the plants supply most of that interest, but set into an anchoring framework. For example, light-reflecting edging plants outline the curves of the lawn, and a raised planter for annuals and bedding is set beside a semi-circular bed.

If a focal point were to be introduced in the form of a statue or a seat, it would be best to site it to one side, so that it draws the eye diagonally, to increase the apparent size of the garden.

UB Plenty of shrubs, climbers and plants with coloured foliage ensure that this garden will look attractive all year round. It includes a shrub border, ground-cover for shady areas, and a striking collection of bedding plants for seasonal colour. Because this garden has no view, the planting must contain plenty of interest, and must hold the eye within the site. It assumes a soil that is light and not very fertile, and slightly acid. The garden is very much a gardener's garden, including many choice cultivars of plants and interesting pairings of fine shrubs.

A principle feature of the garden is a shrub border facing the house. Here the colours are kept pale and cool, to help give the impression of a bigger distance between it and the house than there really is. Blues and whites come from ceanothus, lavender and an edging of dianthus; pinks come from lilac and viburnum. Through the latter twines a late-flowering clematis, to extend the season of interest.

Stronger, brighter colours are used near the house. A bed of purple- and grey-leaved plants – *Heuchera* 'Palace Purple', a purple sedum, artemisia and rue – forms a permanent focal point. The raised planter offers the opportunity for a succession of colourful bedding: here, in late spring, wallflowers and polyan-thus mix with tulips, but later these could be replaced with summer bedding of fuchsias, pelargoniums and dahlias.

The tree's underplanting is green and white, including some variegated plants, to add brightness in an otherwise rather shady place. The epimedium and hellebore also have the advantage of glossy, light-reflecting leaves. Adjoining the brick paving is a bed which suits plants for moist, shady places; this is planted with ground-cover, including polygonum, ajuga and lamium.

On the other side of the garden, espalier-trained fruit trees disguise the fence, and a trellis dividing off the vegetable patch is made productive with fan-trained blackberries and loganberries, through which twine annual sweet peas.

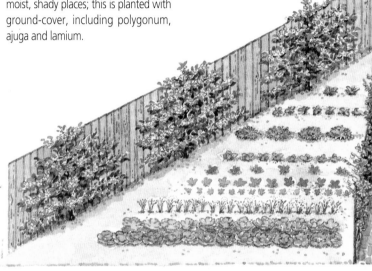

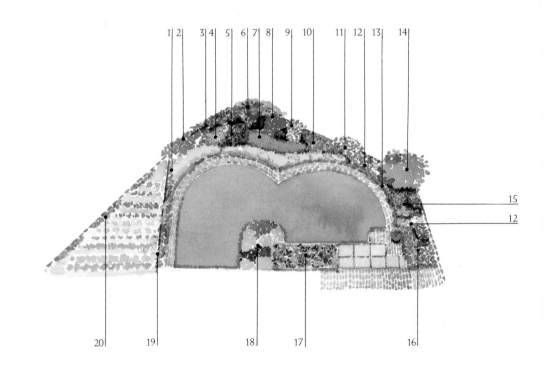

NORTH
Shown in late spring
Soil: light, not very fertile; acidic

PLANT KEY

1 Edging of *Dianthus* 'Doris' and *D.* 'Cranmere Pool'
2 *Jasminum × stephanense* (trained against fence)
3 *Clematis* 'H F Young'
4 *Viburnum carlesii* 'Aurora', with late-flowering *Clematis* 'Huldine' twining through
5 *Cistus × purpureus*
6 *Ceanothus* 'Delight' (trained)
7 *Lavandula angustifolia* 'Munstead'
8 *Osmanthus × burkwoodii*
9 *Syringa microphylla* 'Superba'
10 *Chaenomeles speciosa* 'Nivalis'
11 *Pyracantha* 'Orange Glow'
12 *Centranthus ruber albus*
13 *Epimedium perralderianum*
14 *Acer davidii* (three-stemmed)
15 Tree underplanted with *Helleborus argutifolius*, *Brunnera macrophylla* 'Dawson's White' and *Pulmonaria saccharata*

16 Bed planted with *Persicaria milletii*, *Ajuga reptans*, *Onoclea sensibilis* and *Lamium maculatum* 'White Nancy'
17 Raised bed planted with *Tulipa praestans* 'Fusilier', polyanthus (mixed) and *Cheiranthus* 'Fire King' (this planting to be followed by *Fuchsia* 'Thalia', *Pelargonium* 'Mrs Pollock' and *Dahlia* 'Bishop of Llandaff')
18 Bed planted with *Sedum telephium* ssp. maximum 'Atropurpureum', *Dianthus* 'Brympton Red', *Heuchera micrantha* 'Palace Purple', *Artemisia absinthium* 'Lambrook Silver', *Ruta graveolens* 'Jackman's Blue' and *Artemisia* 'Powis Castle'
19 Sweet pea varieties grown between Loganberry 'Thornless' and Blackberry 'Loch Ness' (as fans) on trellis
20 Apple trees (trained as espaliers)

1

THE GARDEN WITH NO VIEW

1 Walled gardens offer privacy and tranquillity. This essentially soft landscape composition uses a wide range of plant material to wrap the composition about in a soft mantle. The steps are hardly visible, being delicately smothered in a riot of sprawling plants that lead the eye up to the old timber bench. The box mounds and narrow lawn emphasize this view, while the borders to either side complete a picture that turns in upon itself to create its interest. The inward-looking nature of this garden is fostered by the use of pots round the bench, and by vigorous climbers that hide much of the boundary wall. There is so much interest within the garden that the lack of a view outwards is no hardship. Indeed, it becomes a virtue, protecting the garden visitor from the rough world outside.

2 The stunning tracery of this garden is a real eye-catcher, and helps to concentrate interest within the boundaries. The walls have been amply covered with climbers to reduce their impact, and this soft backdrop makes the central formality all the more telling. Such a strong composition is undoubtedly a very personal choice.

Intricate planting, which demands closer inspection, is a good way of dealing with an awkward-shaped or truncated garden. Here, trimmed box has been used to make a mini-parterre. The potential difficulty of a shady wall on the left has been tackled by planting ferns, hostas, and other shade-tolerant plants.

2

Garden Designs

THE HOUSE-SIDE PASSAGE

1 This potentially dull and shaded basement area has been brought thoroughly to life with gay tender and hardy annuals, planted mainly in pots and hanging baskets. Every bit of space has been used here, even to allowing climbers to scramble up the security bars on the windows!

2 The passage along the side of a house is often wasted, and becomes a dreary 'no go' area. Here, a neat brick-paved patio has been carefully designed, with steps to match. There is ample room for table and chair, while planting has been meticulously chosen and positioned. Note the generous raised bed.

DS All too often the area down the side of a house is a forgotten space, a dreary corridor that becomes a dumping ground for any unwanted objects. It is rarely seen as part of the overall garden, simply a way between back and front or to the side door. Yet the potential can be considerable, particularly if the gap between house and boundary is a reasonable one. Windows often look into the area, sometimes from the kitchen and sometimes from a living room, making the provision of a well thought-out scheme all the more important.

The design for a passage shown opposite suits a typical space: it is just

over 3m/10ft wide and 9m/30ft long, shady, and with a boundary formed by a high brick wall. A living room window looks straight at the wall, and the passage must accommodate dustbins. The design shows how the area can be exploited to become both more visually appealing and inviting.

As the area is dark, I chose a pale coloured precast concrete slab to reflect the maximum amount of light, and laid it in a staggered bond to help draw the area apart and create as much visual width as possible. Two sizes of concrete slab are used, 60cm/2ft x 60cm/2ft, and 60cm/2ft x 30cm/1ft. The slabs are inter-

spersed with courses of brick, to link the garden to the house.

As a focal point opposite the living room window I have suggested a simple bowl and spout that can be fed by a small submersible pump. To satisfy the practical requirements of the space, the bins are neatly housed in a purpose-built store, the top of which is a plant container.

Overhead beams span between the high wall and the house, playing host to climbing plants that help to soften the architecture to either side, and creating a sense of a vista. Planting softens and surrounds the pathway, while the pot and statuary add a personal touch.

UB A house-side passage can be a most ill-favoured spot; yet it offers many opportunities for planting, since, particularly in a town, such a space will be sheltered and reasonably frost-free.

The planting scheme for the passage opposite is designed to look its best during the late winter months, a time when the area might oppress most, and yet also a season offering plenty of scented plants. The fragrance from the pot-grown sarcococca, the *Mahonia japonica* on the left, and the winter jasmine growing on the far overhead beam are all chosen to make the job of filling the dustbins more agreeable.

Climbers are certain to be important plants in such a space. Various forms of clematis twine around the overhead beams, bringing cheerful flowers for later in the year; ivies, chosen for their ornamental potential, provide an evergreen background; there is a honeysuckle for summer scent, and a climbing hydrangea.

Winter-flowering pansies make a feature of the water bowl, to be followed in summer by the bluish-white bells of codonopsis; the pansies should be replaced by impatiens as they finish flowering. At the far left end violas, with a frost-tender bergenia, demonstrate how in such a sheltered spot plants can be grown that might not otherwise survive.

The planting trough over the dustbins needs adequate drainage, and plants that do not have deep, questing roots. It is planted here with lamium, polystichum, and a teaming of pulmonaria with anemones. In this unusual site, the plants will need regular attention.

Turning a gloomy space into an attractive one cannot be done without a little labour, so bulbs may need replacing; shade-tolerant bedding may need to be introduced; and the garrya near the entrance will need to be clipped over after flowering. The soil, assumed to be moist, acid and fertile, is nevertheless confined to narrow beds and will therefore need enriching every year, particularly around the climbers.

NORTH ◀

Shown in late winter

Soil: moist, deep and fertile; acidic

BIN STORE

The bin store is topped by a shallow trough planted with Polystichum setiferum; Lamium maculatum 'White Nancy'; and Pulmonaria saccharata 'Mrs Moon' underplanted with Anemone nemerosa 'Robinsoniana'.

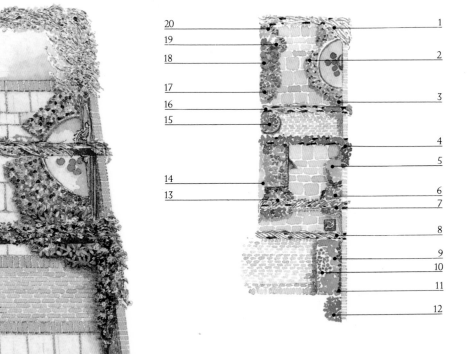

PLANT KEY

1   *Jasminum nudiflorum*
2   *Codonopsis clematidea* interplanted with *Viola* × *wittrockiana* Universal Series
3   *Convallaria majalis*
4   *Clematis cirrhosa* var. *balearica*
5   *Azara microphylla*
6   *Rhododendron* × *moupinense*
7   *Clematis* 'Nelly Moser'
8   *Clematis* × *triternata* 'Rubromarginata'
9   *Tolmiea menziesii* 'Taff's Gold'
10 *Hedera helix* ssp. *helix* 'Adam'
11 *Hydrangea anomala* ssp. *petiolaris*
12 *Garrya elliptica*
13 *Mahonia japonica*
14 *Hedera* ssp. *helix* 'Buttercup'
15 Pot of *Sarcococca hookeriana* var. *humilis*, with underplanting of *Erica carnea* 'King George' and *Scilla mischtschenkoana*
16 *Lonicera japonica* 'Halliana'
17 *Helleborus orientalis*
18 *Bergenia ciliata*
19 *Viola odorata*
20 *Helleborus argutifolius*

THE ROMANTIC'S GARDEN

DS This is a large garden that follows the contours of a valley. There is ample room to create a composition that is full of interest, with generous sweeping shapes, many secluded areas, and several changes of character as it extends away from the building.

The design incorporates some major existing trees, and a new orchard (on the left) and spinney (bottom). These create inviting 'secret' areas, ideal for picnics, children's play, or simply for getting away from it all. Sweeping around the garden and linking the areas of tree planting are paths, created by mowing a way between areas of rougher grass that has been naturalized with bulbs and wildflowers. These shapes have a natural fluidity that helps to create a feeling of space and movement.

The trees and mown paths represent the wilder parts of the garden; nearer the house, the design is more structured. The terrace is large enough for a wide range of activities from sitting, dining and entertaining to children's games and activities. The materials are a combination of random granite paving, which is local to the area, and brick, also used frequently in the locality.

The steps down from the terrace are turned at an angle to the house, and this helps to make a gentler descent down the slope into the lower parts of the garden. From the bottom of the steps a path sweeps down to the bridge over a newly formed lake. This has been created by damming a small stream and allowing the water to back up the valley.

Once over the bridge, solid steps constructed from railway sleepers pegged into the bank climb the slope, sheltered between new granite outcrops, created out of rock found on site during construction. On such a large site, a great deal of clearance and excavation is almost bound to be needed, and any materials uncovered during the operation, such as rocks, can often be 'recycled' and put to imaginative use by incorporating them into the final garden design.

The major focal point on this side of the garden is the arbour and barbecue area, which is surrounded by scented roses. This catches all the late afternoon and evening sun and is sited to take advantage of the wonderful view back over the lake to the house. It is cut into the natural slope to create a level area and this means that its back is retained by a sheltering wall.

THE ROMANTIC'S GARDEN

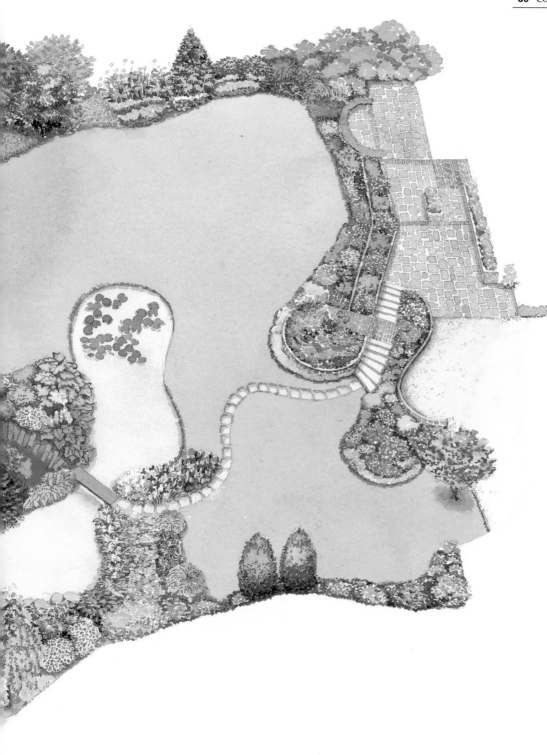

NORTH
Shown in early summer
Soil: heavy clay; neutral pH

UB Such a large garden offers an excellent opportunity to plant in sweeps for large effects, using a variety of trees and shrubs for a woodland effect, and a collection of wildflowers in the long grass. It is possible to accommodate larger, bolder plants than in a smaller garden, and one can happily tolerate plants that have only a brief season of display.

There is colour here for most of the year. It is shown in midsummer, with the collection of shrub roses around the arbour in flower. These are mainly English varieties, selected both for their powerful scents – making the arbour a delightful place to sit – and their repeat-flowering qualities, which ensure a succession of blooms during the months when the arbour is likely to be used. The colours of the roses and the purple clematis that scrambles up and over the structure help to draw the attention to this central feature.

Around the lake, bog plantings are possible, with many large-leaved plants such as rodgersia and gunnera. Flanking the path, on its right, is a collection of yellows, featuring lysichitons and primulas: mixed with the latter is blue *Iris sibirica,* chosen to contrast. *Clematis viticella* 'Abundance', not yet in flower, has been sited to encircle a prostrate form of juniper. This illustrates that clematis need not always be used to scramble up supports, but, where space allows, can be used horizontally to enliven an evergreen or dull shrub.

The top boundary has a colour scheme of pinks, blues, mauves and whites, with an amethyst-coloured campanula, foxgloves and astilbes. Shrubs, trees, herbaceous plants, and bulbs for underplanting all come together here in a free-flowing, unstructured border. Nearer to the house, the scheme is yellow and green.

Much emphasis has been put on reliable autumn colour from the shrubs and trees: there are four acers, for example, and the spinney includes a Turkish hazel (*Corylus colurna*) and a crataegus, both

Garden Designs

noted for their autumn colours. Winter form is provided by a few evergreens – a holly features along the top boundary, and the spinney has a *Picea* and an *Abies* – and several examples of ornamental bark. *Acer griseum* (top boundary) is the snake bark maple, for example. The bright winter stems of the three cultivars of cornus, sited on the far side of the lake will be visible from the house. Of all these trees, the only real giant is the metasequoia, sited on its own.

A feature of the garden in spring and summer is the long grass, interplanted with bulbs and wildflowers. The grass should be cut once in midsummer, then left to grow again in the following months. The garden has been planted assuming a heavy, moisture-retentive clay soil, with a neutral pH. The site is open, and exposed to the east, so everything that is planted needs to be frost-hardy; for this reason the orchard is restricted to apples and late-flowering pears. Maintenance requirements have been kept low: many plants can be left to themselves, and the more spreading shrubs, such as the *Prunus laurocerasus* near the spinney, and the *Viburnum rhytidophyllum* near the pond, will suppress weeds beneath them. The types of roses chosen need relatively little attention, and can be underplanted with forms of cranesbill to suppress weeds (such as *Geranium endressii* 'Wargrave Pink' and *G.* 'Johnson's Blue'). The bog plants, however, are likely to need regular attention, since they tend to spread.

PLANT KEY

1 *Prunus tenella* 'Fire Hill'
2 *Campanula latiloba* 'Hidcote Amethyst'
3 *Philadelphus × lemoinei*
4 *Aruncus dioicus*
5 *Geranium sylvaticum* 'Mayflower'
6 Mixed *Digitalis purpurea*
7 *Astilbe chinensis* var. *pumila*
8 Tree grouping (left to right): *Ilex aquifolium* 'J C van Tol', *Prunus padus* 'Watereri', *Acer griseum*, *Prunus × subhirtella* 'Autumnalis', *Acer davidii*, *Sorbus aria* 'Majestica', all underplanted with *Vinca major* 'Elegantissima', hellebores and *Pulmonaria rubra* 'Bowles' Red'
9 *Cephalaria gigantea*
10 *Euphorbia sikkimensis*
11 *Alchemilla mollis*
12 *Metasequoia glyptostroboïdes*
13 *Tellima grandiflora* 'Purpurea'
14 *Mahonia × media* 'Charity'
15 Mixed planting near house of roses and herbaceous plants, the beds edged with lavender
16 *Gunnera manicata*
17 *Salix hastata* 'Wehrhahnii'
18 *Cornus alba* 'Sibirica', *Cornus alba* 'Elegantissima' and *Cornus alba* 'Spaethii'
19 *Rheum palmatum* 'Atrosanguineum'
20 *Hypericum androsaemum*
21 *Lysichiton americanus*
22 Mix of *Iris sibirica* and *Primula florindae*
23 *Filipendula ulmaria* 'Aurea'
24 *Lobelia cardinalis*
25 *Carex elata* 'Aurea'
26 *Ligularia dentata* 'Desdemona'
27 *Potentilla* 'Moonlight' (syn. 'Maanelys')
28 *Rodgersia aesculifolia* underplanted with *Leucojum aestivum*
29 *Juniperus sabina* 'Tamariscifolia'
30 *Cotoneaster × suecicus* 'Skogholm'
31 *Cornus alba* 'Spaethii'
32 *Juniperus × media* 'Pfitzeriana', with *Clematis* 'Abundance' growing through it

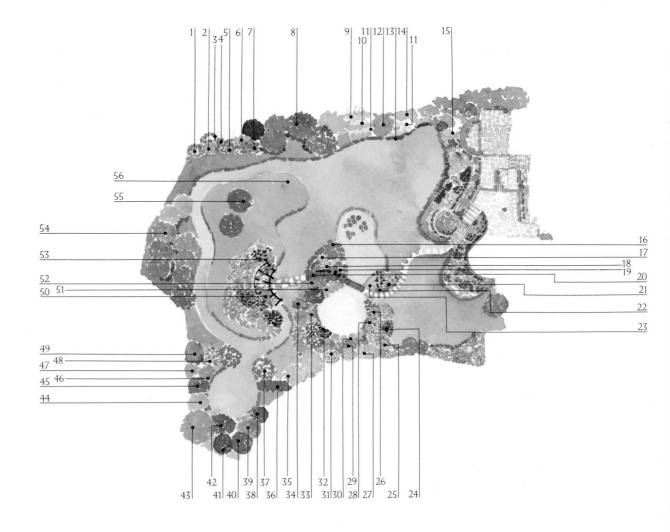

33 Mixed shrub planting (top to bottom): *Philadelphus coronarius* 'Aureus', *Rubus* 'Benenden', *Viburnum rhytidophyllum*, *Rhamnus frangula*

34 *Erica × darleyensis* 'Silberschmelze' ('Molten Silver') and *E. × darleyensis* 'Darley Dale'

35 *Betula pendula* 'Laciniata'

36 *Prunus laurocerasus* 'Zabeliana'

37 *Viburnum plicatum* 'Mariesii'

38 *Abies koreana*

39 *Acer palmatum*

40 *Pyrus calleryana* 'Chanticleer'

41 *Picea breweriana*

42 *Acer palmatum* f. *atropurpureum*

43 *Malus* 'John Downie'

44 *Crataegus persimilis* 'Prunifolia'

45 *Corylus colurna*

46 *Viburnum tinus* 'Eve Price'

47 *Berberis × stenophylla*

48 *Weigela florida* 'Aureovariegata'

49 *Salix gracilistyla* 'Melanostachys' with *S. hastata* 'Wehrhahnii'

50 On pergola: *Rosa* 'Leverkusen', *Clematis* 'Lasurstern', *Rosa* 'Alberic Barbier', *Clematis* 'Countess of Lovelace'

51 *Athyrium filix-femina* Victoriae Group

52 *Juniperus sabina* 'Tamariscifolia' surrounded by *Clematis* Viticella Group: 'Kermesina', 'Royal Velours' and 'Polish Spirit'

53 Mix of shrub roses in pink, white and red (top to bottom): *Rosa rugosa* 'Alba', *R.* 'William Shakespeare', *R.* 'Heritage', *R.* 'Mary Rose', *R.* 'Winchester Cathedral', *R.* 'Grouse', *R.* 'Felicia', *R.* 'Marguerite Hilling', *R.* 'Königin von Dänemark', *R.* 'Cornelia', *R.* 'Heritage', *R.* 'Partridge', *R.* 'William Shakespeare', *R. rugosa* 'Alba'

54 Orchard planted with: Apple 'Bramley's Seedling', Apple 'Discovery', Apple 'Sunset', Apple 'Spartan', Apple 'Greensleeves', Apple 'George Cave', Pear 'Conference', Pear 'Williams' Bon Chrétien', Pear 'Improved Fertility'

(apples grown on MM106 rootstocks, pears on Quince 'C' rootstocks)

55 *Carpinus betulus* 'Fastigiata'

56 Wildflowers in grass: *Ornithogalum umbellatum*, *Fritillaria meleagris*, *Saponaria officinalis*, *Cardamine pratensis*, *Centaurea*, *Primula vulgaris*, *Lychnis flos-cuculi*, *Ajuga reptans*, *Narcissus pseudonarcissus*. (This grass should be cut in midsummer.)

1 The essence of planting in the romantic garden is that it should be in drifts and unstructured groups. Cultivated forms of native plants, such as the Shirley poppies here, are ideal, because they add just that touch of showy sophistication that makes a garden more than just a natural landscape. Note the simple path leading away into the unknown; there are never straight lines in this kind of garden.

1 Here is the archetypal romantic garden, complete with a rustic pergola heavy with roses in full bloom. The roses, chosen to scent simple sheltered seats, also forbid a clear view of the end of the path, so that there is an additional air of mystery and potential surprise. The mixture of climbing and shrub roses is a happy one, for the shrub roses almost hide the bare lower stems of the climbers. The overall colour scheme is restrained and harmonious, thus giving a feeling of restfulness and peace.

Seclusion is one of the prime requisites of romance, and many different structures can provide this. Here, the arbour is admirably simple, with timber uprights, and overheads that frame the equally simple seats. The rustic construction just adds to the charm: architecture here would be all wrong!

2 Profusion and generosity are essential features of the romantic garden. Here, moisture-loving Japanese primulas, irises and ferns edge an informal pool, complete with water lilies. Roses and honeysuckle almost overwhelm the limestone buildings, giving a sense of permanence and continuity. This is a garden at its best at midsummer; the rose in the foreground, for example, will flower only once.

A cottage garden is always romantic, and the addition of water makes it more so. Materials here are undoubtedly those found locally, which provide a visually comfortable background against which the planting makes a softly modelled composition.

3 With its complement of roses, lavender bushes, and *Cleome spinosa*, controlled without being unduly restrained, this scented garden would make the perfect romantic setting.

Cool colour is often restful and romantic. This softly planted scheme tempers the harder lines of the brick paving which radiates out from the sundial.

4 In the romantic garden, the work of the gardener should remain carefully hidden. Although these roses have been pruned and restrained, it has been done with admirable subtlety.

Half-open gates are enormously inviting, and here the route encourages you to venture over an old timber bridge that is straddled by iron hoops festooned with climbers.

Garden Elements

A great deal of the garden design framework is built up from 'hard' landscape features. These include the boundaries that surround the site, the paving that forms the floor and pathways around the area as well as internal screens and dividers. It also encompasses such features as pergolas, arbours and arches, raised beds, buildings, barbecues and other decorative elements. All of these will have been selected from the checklist put together by you and your family. Just what these choices are and where they will be sited should have been broadly formulated at the design stage. The next job is to look at the options available within each category, which will have a considerable bearing on the visual finish of the garden, the overall cost and the ease or complexity of construction.

If you move into an established garden, some, or even all of these components may already be in place. You may have fences or walls, the paving may be laid and the paths already positioned. In an ideal situation, these will be just right but it is more likely that there will be a need for modification, extension or improvement.

If the latter is the case you will need to know how the new materials can be matched or blended with the old, but if the garden is a virgin plot you can start from scratch. In either case the way in which you choose and use garden elements is vital to the final character of the composition.

The order in which you build or lay these components often follows a set pattern: the boundaries first, followed by the paved areas and finally the various features that bring the scheme to life. Plants are woven into this sequence to soften and surround the garden, perhaps in the form of hedging for boundaries, screening material on pergolas or arches, or decorative features such as raised beds, rock gardens and bog gardens, all of which are contained within the overall plan.

We have already seen that the choice of materials is legion, and this means that many gardens suffer from overcomplication and a lack of respect for the surrounding environment. *As* a result they can not only look and feel uncomfortable but end up costing a good deal more than they need to. One of the keys to a well designed garden is simplicity, a tenet that may be easy to state but is not always so easy to implement!

1

2

1 Sloping gardens often call for terracing, and the steeper the gradient the greater the number of possible platforms. 'Shelves' such as these are perfect for placing pots and ornaments, and here they have been combined with dense planting set directly into the slope.

By using only terracotta pots, and planting them up mainly with a range of pelargoniums, an interesting and highly colourful effect has been achieved in what might otherwise have been rather inauspicious circumstances.

2 Where a garden drops away, you may wish to slow the eye down by setting focal points to stop the view. The simple column at the end of the path does just that, while the hedge in the background acts as a low level wall, stopping the view before it runs out into the landscape.

The length of border has been visually foreshortened by the use of bright colours at the end of the path, and paler ones nearer the eye. The small trees and the various shrubs planted in containers help to arrest the eye.

DS The fact that we still have and want boundaries around our gardens reflects our primitive instincts. Like our 'hunter gatherer' forebears many thousands of years ago, we build them to fulfil the basic function of keeping people and animals both out and in, and to give a feeling of security.

A boundary can set out to do a number of things. For example, it can:
• Delineate the limits of your property.
• Enclose a garden and provide security for or from people and animals.
• Provide a visual barrier by blocking unattractive views or preventing people from looking into the garden.
• Give shelter from wind, noise and pollution. A well-constructed fence or wall, backed by substantial planting, can help to combat both noise and pollution.
• Become an important part of the design framework by focusing a good view and screening a less attractive one, which may be part of the same aspect.
• Allow the view from the garden to continue out into the landscape by using a ha-ha or ditch to keep livestock at bay.

You should consider the particular type of fencing, screening, hedging or walling that would best surround your plot, while working out the overall design of the garden. If you install a wall or fence yourself, do try to respect both the surrounding materials and the levels of the site. A walk down any suburban or even village street will indicate just how insensitively materials can be chosen. And on a steeply sloping site with a high density of housing, the practical problems of the gradient often lead to a wide variety of fences and walls, many of which are erected with scant regard for a sensitive choice of materials or for the way in which the boundaries are constructed. In some cases fences or walls are 'stepped' at variance to the actual slope, so that fences go up where the levels go down, and vice versa. Planting can do a great deal to soften this kind of approach, but it is best avoided in the first place.

1

Boundaries

2

There is a vast range of boundary materials to choose from, and compatibility, both with the style of the house and with the surroundings, really is important. A cohesive street scene is far more telling than a hotch-potch of random styles; first impressions count, and the boundary of a property is often the first thing to be seen.

If your house is brick or stone, then carry these materials through to any walling if you can. It will provide a natural link, and allow the building to sit comfortably in its surroundings. Look for brick or stone to match that used in the house, and be careful to match the pointing. If your house is rendered, then rendered or fair-face (untreated) concrete blocks, or even concrete cast in situ,

can be used with superb effect. What is less sympathetic are the geometric blocks of white concrete whose harsh colour and busy patterns make them unacceptable in most situations.

Walling, however, is expensive, although it has an almost unlimited life, and a well-chosen fence will be a more economical alternative. Here, too, style is important, and what is appropriate in one setting may be quite out of keeping in another. Local fencing styles with a strong regional flavour often look particularly good in the country. Wattle or osier hurdles make a good foil for planting, and sturdy post-and-rail fencing fits well in an agricultural setting; wrought or cast iron railings are most effective in a more formal or urban setting.

Because the choice is so wide, and the outcome so important, take your time before deciding what to use. Keep your eyes open as you drive or walk about, and think about what particular kind of boundary would look most appropriate to your own property. Then, visit a good garden centre, builder's yard, or fencing specialist to see what they have to offer. Look at the patterns, compare the prices in relation to the durability of the fence, and consider which designs would best complement your house and garden, and the neighbourhood in which you live. Remember that you do not have to use an 'off the peg' solution; you may have seen something on your travels that you liked, and that you could, perhaps, make or modify yourself.

1 Boundaries need not always be high. Here they are below the sight line, and help to define the garden in a very controlled way, leading feet and eye out to the jetty and moored boat.

A fascinating vista has been made even more interesting by the cube of hedging which interrupts the path. Hedging is a useful, and inexpensive, delineator in many different situations.

2 The strong vertical line of the stems here is in direct contrast to the horizontal plane of water at ground level. A boundary such as this filters the view beyond, without blocking it out entirely.

Bamboo is almost always fast-growing; indeed, it can easily become too vigorous. Here, its height is an asset, and the thin stems allow light through.

FENCES

DS Putting up a fence is well within the scope of the home landscaper, and materials are readily available from local garden centres or fencing specialists. Uprights will be supplied cut to size and can be either concreted into the ground or set into adjustable metal sockets driven into the ground. Where possible, use 'hardwood' posts, as it is the post that takes all the strain. Posts should be the same height as the fence itself when sunk into the ground, so allow 450mm/ 18in extra for this purpose.

Close board and panel fences should be fitted with capping rails, post caps, and gravel boards which can be easily renewed if rot attacks the bottom of the fence. All fences will need an annual application of non-toxic preservative. Establish carefully where your boundary lies, in order to avoid disputes with neighbours. Make sure that the height of your fence is adequate; trellis fixed to the top is generally unsatisfactory.

Fences can be open, to embrace the view, or closed, to contain space and exclude the world outside. The essential requirement is that they should suit your particular garden and its setting.

Closed fencing is more expensive than other types but lasts a long time. Keep the posts and 'arris' rails on your side, leaving the flush side for your neighbour. (Arris rails are the cross timbers on to which the boards are nailed.) Stretch wires between the posts for climbing plants. These are detachable for maintenance, and keep growth away from the fence itself.

Interwoven panels are one of the most popular types of fencing. Panels usually come 1.8m/6ft wide, and in a variety of sizes up to 1.8m/6ft in height. Square panels can be fixed so that the laths run in alternate directions.

Close board makes a more durable fence than interwoven panels but is correspondingly more expensive. Posts 2m/6ft 6in high are usually set 1.8/6ft apart, with arris rails mortised into the posts, and feather-edged boards nailed on to the rails with a slight overlap. Close board fences may or may not have a capping, but gravel boards are essential.

Slatted fences use boards of variable width, fixed to arris rails in the same way as close board but without overlapping and without being feather-edged. They

1 A real rhythm is set up here by the sharp contrast of white picket fence tops as they swoop over the gate. The fact that the gate cannot open is unimportant.
Roses, with their arching habit, look attractive grown through a slatted fence.

2 Plants and wattle hurdles associate well together, and here there is a fascinating dialogue between the two clipped hollies and the laurel behind.
These hedges, well shaped and well cared for, emphasize the natural character of the wattle fence.

1

2

PUTTING UP A CLOSE BOARD FENCE

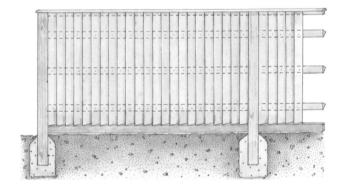

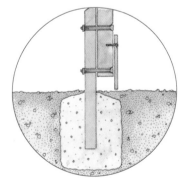

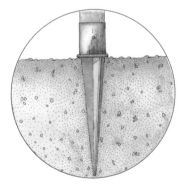

Close board fences are solid and durable. Hardwood posts 100 x 100mm/4 x 4in and 2m/6ft 6in high are usually set in concrete, and have arris rails mortised into them. Feather-edged boards are nailed on to the

rails, with a slight overlap. A removable gravel board at the bottom of the fence will take the brunt of any rot, and can be easily replaced, while a capping rail will provide protection at the top.

The wooden posts can be bolted on to concrete spurs, which are in turn set into concrete. This will allow easy replacement, should this become necessary, and gravel boards can still be fitted.

Another method is to drive metal sleeves with an attached spike into the ground, and fit the posts into these. This prolongs the life of the posts, as they are not in contact with the soil. Once again, they can easily be replaced as necessary.

3

4

3 Elegant timbers make an excellent foil for plants, and can form an ideal windbreak.

4 An open screen, painted white, makes an effective visual barrier. It throws the light back at you, disguising the view behind.

5 Repeating a theme can be very effective, especially when it is used in different design elements. Here, the trellis fence is cleverly matched by the pyramids in the background.

6 The Japanese are past masters at bold, precise, and simple detailing. This composition makes a visual link between the fence and the bamboo grove.

5

SLATTED FENCES

A variation of the close board fence is the slatted fence. Both use boards nailed to arris rails, but slats usually have gaps between them, and are not feather-edged. If the slats are set at an angle of, say 45 degrees, they set up an interesting pattern which could be reflected in paving laid at a similar angle to the house. The bottom of the fence should be kept just clear of the ground, and no gravel board is used, as it would break the visual line of the fence. It is important that the top is kept level.

6

1

2

3

4

1 A post and rail fence is ideal in a rural situation, as it allows a view of the surrounding countryside. Here, the slightly twisted timbers of the fence blend perfectly with the adjoining cottage.

Roses must be tied in when the stems are still young and flexible. The rails here would look stark without them.

2 This kind of bamboo fence is usually found in Japanese-style gardens. Here, it acts as a finely drawn screen in an altogether different kind of composition.

The planting, much of it evergreen, has the effect of encouraging the eye to run right through the fence.

3 These crisp, precisely sawn timbers frame the mop heads of the hydrangea, throwing them into sharp relief and keeping the woodland at bay.

This form of *Hydrangea macrophylla* makes an attractive informal 'hedge' for late summer and autumn.

4 The bamboo screen has a distinctly Japanese style, and the thin poles contrast with the visual strength of the smooth boulders positioned below.

This fence not only acts as a boundary; it also gives informal support to the accompanying planting.

can be set vertically or diagonally, with variable spacing. Wide boards tend to make a garden feel smaller, while narrow slats increase the feeling of space. Boards close to the house should be planed smooth, and painted or stained to pick up interior colour schemes. Rough-sawn timber might be used in the more distant parts of a garden. Slatted fences act as an excellent windbreak, allowing the wind to filter through the gaps, rather than hitting the face full on and causing turbulence on the lee side.

In ranch fencing, rails can be set, with quite wide gaps, either vertically or horizontally, and to any height. In 'hit and miss' fencing, boards are nailed on alternate sides of the posts, with no gaps, breaking the sight line completely.

Hurdles have a relatively short life of about eight to ten years, but look marvellous anywhere, and are ideal as a temporary screen to protect young plants. They are simple to erect, being wired to round posts.

Wattle hurdles, woven from hazel stems, and osiers (willow shoots) are usually woven horizontally, while reeds are set upright, wired on to rails. A vertical bamboo fence with its distinctive Japanese flavour looks wonderful for contemporary gardens.

Concrete fencing is available in panel or sectional form, slotted between concrete posts. It is unattractive but does have a long life, and can be transformed by a coat of brown paint.

Picket fences are halfway between closed and open fences, allowing a partial view through, and being low enough to look over. They traditionally come with pointed tops, or can be made with rounded tops and semi-circular cut-outs. They can be painted to tie in with planting schemes or to match the house.

Open fences provide a physical rather than a visual barrier.

Post and rail fences are stock-proof but clumsy, though if they are carefully sited along a fold in the ground, they can

FENCES

5 Virtually invisible chain link has been used here to make a post and rail fence pet- and child-proof, and yet allows the view to run on unhindered. The fence neatly picks up the half-timbering on the building, but uses it in a slightly less architectural way, which is very much in keeping with the increased distance from the house.

The planting here is informal to the point of wildness. These annual poppies will seed themselves year after year, without the need for any special attention. They succeed in providing a bright contrast to the simple structure of the fencing. Maintenance for this arrangement would be virtually non-existent.

virtually be lost to view. They can be either two- or three-rail, and sheep netting can be fitted from the bottom rail down to ground level to keep stock out and children and dogs in.

Single rail fences have a number of uses, from a well-detailed rail for a bridge or pathway, to a simple delineation around an open-plan front garden, when the height will usually be under 60cm/2ft. In a rural setting a half-round rail can be nailed into or on top of round posts; in a more urban situation a square rail can be mortised into the posts. If you use low single rails, back them up with planting to discourage children and dogs from using them as hurdles!

Elegant post and chain fences still work well outside smart town houses or along the drives of country ones. The posts should be 100mm/4in square, painted white, and the chains made from wrought iron, painted black. Beautifully detailed iron or stone posts are worth restoring. Avoid plastic.

Chestnut palings, often used to protect trees, or as temporary fencing on building sites, can form an excellent boundary, particularly between planted areas, or where the garden runs into woodland. The height is usually about 1m/3ft, and the palings are wired about 100mm/4in apart. They are cheap, easy to erect, and unobtrusive.

Chain link is greatly maligned, but the plastic-coated type has a long life, and if brown or black and sited within or against a planted area, becomes almost invisible. Posts can be metal or concrete.

Railings come in all forms, from grand to mundane. At their best, wrought or cast iron railings are superb; less satisfactory are the thin, lightweight affairs that grace a million suburban streets. Here, a well-detailed picket fence would probably look better. Iron railings need regular painting, and old ones can benefit from stripping, when a wealth of fine detail often comes to light. Black is almost invariably the best colour.

6 Picket fences come in many different patterns, and this design is particularly delicate. The entrance is emphasized by the bold posts and finials, and the gate has a slightly rounded top that draws attention to itself. The fact that the lawn extends to either side gives the whole composition continuity,

and the view through the fence reinforces this effect.

Elaborate and colourful planting would have detracted from the simple elegance of this wooden fence and gate. Sometimes restraint rather than exuberance gives the most successful results.

THE ADVANTAGES AND DISADVANTAGES OF FENCES

Advantages

Cheaper than walls

Quicker and easier to erect than walls

Can allow a view while still providing a physical barrier

Useful if only needed as a temporary barrier

Slatted fences can provide an excellent windbreak if built with a gap between each slat

Disadvantages

Less durable than walls

Less capable of reducing noise and pollution than walls

Ongoing maintenance may necessitate access strip or path at the rear of a border

1 This is the classic picket fence, with pointed tops and painted white. A fence like this can set up a changing pattern of shadows as the sun swings across the garden throughout the day, and is particularly effective in strong slanting sunlight. The russet leaves add perfectly to the artistic composition of the whole; enjoy this for what it is, and resist the urge to sweep them up!

2 It is important for a fence to echo the style of the building it adjoins. Here, the decorative pickets balance perfectly the delicate filigree of the verandah roof, and the colours are absolutely right, too.

The presence of beautiful roses effectively reinforces the silent invitation of the gate. Well-planted front gardens give a positive first impression.

3 Wrought iron is a fine, if expensive, fencing material. More architectural in feel than a picket fence, it is often ideal for a front garden on a street. It, too, allows the view to run in and out. The points have been picked out in a different colour for added emphasis. Roses with an 'old-fashioned' look and lax habit make a fine accompaniment to these elegant antique railings.

4 The lower internal screen echoes the complicated but well-worked out design of the boundary fence, providing visual continuity. The top is formed by an extension of every other slat, with a capping rail. The austerity of the fencing is richly enhanced by climbing plants. Both the clematis and the roses can be cut back hard when repainting is required.

5

6

7

8

5 The pretty timber balustrade surrounding the verandah is in perfect keeping with the architectural style of the timber-clad house. Fastigiate yews give a dramatic vertical element to the composition, screening the posts and standing out in sharp relief against the controlled and architectural background. They successfully lead the eye up to the delicately worked canopy supports.

6 Such beautiful and delicate wrought iron work is a testament to the skilled craftsmanship of the past. Sadly, it is rarely seen today; the cost is high and the talent hard to find. Railings like this have the additional attraction of allowing the view to run through almost uninterrupted. This has the effect of minimizing the boundary yet giving an impression of great visual strength.

7 This wrought iron has a far heavier and more Teutonic feel to it; the fence here undoubtedly says 'Keep Out!' The work is finely carried out but such a busy pattern needs to be tempered by planting. Flowering ground-cover goes a long way towards softening the stern and rather austere pattern of the railing. It can be trimmed after flowering.

8 This is pure magic, and embodies that prime rule of good design: simplicity. The rhythm is subtle, and has been reinforced by painting the hoops white. Planting is undeterred by the barrier.
The planting of annual poppies is so simple but extremely effective. They will self-seed, but need to be supplemented by other, later-flowering plants.

WALLS

1

DS Walling, although the most expensive kind of boundary, is immensely durable, and can form the perfect perimeter to any garden. There is a wealth of materials from which to choose, from natural stone, or reconstituted stone, to patterned concrete. Most walls are free-standing, but remember that retaining walls, supporting a bank or higher level, can also become an integral part of the garden framework.

Brick is the most widely available walling material, and the small modules of a brick wall give it an intimate and attractive character. Brick walls can make the perfect link between house and garden, but take care to match the bricks as closely as possible. Brick has a strong local character, and colours vary. For garden walls, a 'facing' brick will usually be the best choice, but where a

similar brick is used, perhaps on a nineteenth-century house, or in a modern architectural setting, crisp 'engineering' brick with a glazed or semi-glazed surface may be better. Go to a good builders' merchant or to a brick manufacturer; they will often be able to show you sample walls which give a far better idea than bricks in isolation. A free-standing wall, exposed to weathering on both sides, must be well built and protected by coping at the top, and a damp proof course (dpc) at the bottom.

Visually and structurally, a wall 225mm/9in, or two bricks thick, is best, and for heights up to 2m/6ft 6in buttresses will not normally be necessary. Coping, the capping along the top of a wall, often looks best with bricks laid on edge, but you can also use stone slabs, precast concrete, tiles, and certain

1 Brick is a mellow walling material that can provide an ideal visual link between a brick house and the garden itself. Bricks can be laid in a variety of ways, with different bonds, and walls of double thickness are stronger, and usually more satisfactory visually, than single ones. This honeycomb wall forms an ideal garden screen, and is a good host for climbers. It also makes a better windbreak than precast concrete 'screen blocks'.

Before planting anything close to a wall, it is important to prepare the soil deeply and well. Porous walls, such as brick ones, not only shield the soil from rain, but also draw moisture out of it. If the footings make it impossible to dig a deep hole, confine your choice of plants to drought-tolerant climbers such as ivies, or plant the climber well away from the wall and lean it towards it.

THE ADVANTAGES AND DISADVANTAGES OF WALLS

Advantages	Disadvantages
Visually attractive	Can be complicated to build
Provide privacy and shelter	Most expensive boundary
Reduce noise and pollution	Some materials difficult to obtain
Long lasting	
Link house and garden	

SINGLE THICKNESS BRICK WALLS

Single thickness walls more than about 1m/3ft 3in high will need piers or buttresses at roughly 3m/10ft intervals. Half round bricks, or precast concrete strips, make the best coping; buttresses or piers should be topped with slate or tile.

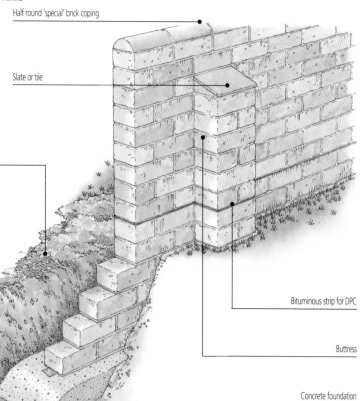

Half round 'special' brick coping

Slate or tile

Topsoil

Level pegs for foundation

Trench

Bituminous strip for DPC

Buttress

Concrete foundation

A coping of twice-weathered concrete, with integrated drip channels.

A wall-end pier for added strength.

specialist metal finishes. For runs of wall over 10m/33ft long, an expansion joint approximately 10-12mm/⅜-½in wide is necessary to prevent cracking. This can be left open or finished with mastic.

Single thickness brick walls are cheaper, but correspondingly weaker, and also lack visual strength. Walls higher than 1m/3ft 3in will need buttressing at regular intervals. Coping can also be a problem, and the best solution is to use a precast concrete strip. If you stand bricks on edge, they look visually uncomfortable on top of a single thickness wall.

A curved or 'serpentine' wall has greater strength than a straight run, although it requires quite considerable expertise to build.

Another variation on the single thickness brick wall is the 'honeycomb' wall, where bricks are laid leaving gaps in

DOUBLE THICKNESS WALLS

These are inherently stronger than single ones, and are 'bonded' together in various patterns. Flemish bond is the most commonly used, but you will also see English and English garden walling bond.

STAGGERED WALLS

Brick boundary walls, whether single or double, can also be built in a series of offset runs. This obviates the use of buttresses or piers for a single brick wall, and allows the wall to be built up to

1.8m/6ft in height, and wired for climbing plants. It also creates an interesting design and good protected areas for planting. Use bricks on edge for the coping of double thickness walls.

alternate rows of approximately 100mm/ 4in. Such a wall filters air currents, making an excellent wind screen, and provides a host for climbers, as well as partial vision. It is much better than the ubiquitous concrete screenblock wall.

As with any construction job, it is often the work that is hidden that is the most important. Foundations, or 'footings', should be soundly constructed from concrete. As a general rule they should be twice as wide as the wall, with a minimum depth of approximately 225mm/9in, and more if the wall is unusually high or the ground is soft.

If the ground slopes, the foundations must be stepped in level platforms so that the wall can be built vertically off them.

A damp proof course (dpc) is a physical barrier placed at the bottom of the brickwork to prevent rising damp and frost from attacking the main body of the wall. Modern bricklayers use a bitumenized strip that comes in rolls; it is virtually invisible once incorporated.

Brick bonds are the patterns in which bricks are laid, and which bind the whole wall together, to give it strength. All the recognized patterns – English bond, Flemish bond, English garden walling,

and so on – are more than strong enough for work in the garden, but today most bricklayers use Flemish bond, which is fine but lacks the interest of some of the other traditional patterns. If you are undertaking brickwork yourself, it will add interest if you choose your own bond. Alternatively, ask your bricklayer to try the bond you have chosen.

The joints between the laid bricks will need filling in, or 'pointing', with mortar, to provide added strength, and give weather protection. Good pointing will enhance the visual impact of a finished wall; poor pointing can ruin it.

Pointing can be flush, weathered, rubbed back, or raked out – each showing a progressively deeper joint between the bricks. The deeper the joint, the more shadow is created, and the more dramatic the effect. Bricks can be pointed with a matching or contrasting mortar mix, by using specialist additives.

In some areas, local materials such as flint or cobbles can be mixed with the brick or stone. Flint-faced walls with ends or 'quoins' of brick or stone can look superb; flint or cobbles can be set within brick panels along the face of a wall. If you are imitating or creating such a

1 Brickwork can also be painted in order to extend a colour scheme into the garden. Here, the crisp white throws everything else into sharp relief. Some paints also give protection from the weather.
The statuesque habit of Japanese maples (*Acer palmatum* and *A. japonicum*) makes them suitable subjects to grow against a wall. Here, shadows show up well against the white paintwork.

2 This flight of steps blends beautifully into the wall behind. The pots of santolina provide essential continuity and lead the eye from top to bottom.
A handsome old wall such as this one should never be entirely smothered in climbers. The task of the lonicera, hedera, and the santolina in pots is to draw attention to the beauty of the wall, rather than completely hiding it.

3

vernacular feature, look at the real thing first; you will learn a great deal about traditional skills and sound design.

You will need 100 bricks per square metre of double brick wall 225mm/9in wide, and half that number for a single brick wall. The mortar mix should be made up from four parts of soft sand and one part of cement, together with the addition of a plasticizer.

Because stone usually comes in uneven sizes, it makes a far less formal walling material than brick, and if it has been quarried in your area, will generally suit the surroundings.

Traditionally, stone was laid dry with no mortar between the joints; this was and still is a highly skilled job. A true dry stone wall is built so that the sides slope in slightly, known as 'battered', towards the top. Dry stone walling has the additional advantage of allowing plants to self-seed or be planted in the crevices.

Mortar can be used successfully in stone, preferably mixed on a clean board with stone dust from the same quarry, but the joints should be regular and not too wide. Avoid cement mortar squashing out like toothpaste, or, even worse, fancy pointing.

Stone walls can be either 'coursed', using similar sizes of stones, or random, in which stones of any size are used. If you intend to use stone, keep your eyes open, especially in your area, take photographs, and work from them.

Coping usually takes the form of stone set on edge, giving an uneven top. However, if the top of the wall is 450mm/18in wide, a double course of bull-nosed brick can be used, which sets a crisp top in contrast to the informality below. Dark engineering bricks will echo the colour of adjoining slate roofs, and pantiles or slates can be used to further blend in with them.

Concrete is a much maligned material, particularly in Britain, where it is seldom used to its full potential. In North America its worth is recognized as a durable, low cost, flexible and elegant landscaping material.

Concrete can be used either in block form, when it can be laid in a similar way to bricks, or cast *in situ*, when reinforced wet concrete is poured into a mould. Either could be faced with stone or brick to link with other parts of the garden.

Concrete blocks usually measure 225 x 225 x 450mm/9 x 9 x 18in, and are very easy to use. They come with rough faces for subsequent rendering, or 'fair', virtually smooth, faces.

Rendered blocks are ideal in conjunction with a house that has a rendered finish, look fine alongside a contemporary building, and the render can be painted to extend a colour scheme into the garden. An alternative, in areas where this is used, is to 'pebble-dash' the render. This involves covering the still-wet render with a layer of small stones or chippings. Fair-faced blocks are smooth enough to be used without rendering, and if they are carefully laid, with crisp joints slightly raked back, may not need painting at all.

Geometric, patterned screen blocks in white concrete, measuring approximately 300 x 300mm/12 x 12in, have been immensely popular for years. Yet

4

3 Cobbles are an immensely versatile material, equally at home on a floor as on a wall. Their texture allows shadows to become part of the picture.
In this hot position, drought-tolerant pelargonium, othonna and sword-leaved yucca are good choices for the top of this homespun retaining wall, where drainage is likely to be sharp.

4 Stone walls are perhaps the finest of all walls, and this one uses large pieces of stone that have been perfectly coursed. Raked-out joints throw each module into sharp relief, and pieces of stone set on edge have been used for the coping.
Parthenocissus tricuspidata does not need deep soil, and is self-clinging. It is fine for this situation where grass butts up to the wall.

1 Dry stone walling should always use material that is local to the area. The stone used here matches the adjoining paving, and the wall forms an attractive backdrop to the garden area. Such a wall is comparatively easy to construct, but it should never be built too high.

A gappy, rural-looking dry stone wall is suitable for native plants which naturally spread by seed, such as *Digitalis purpurea*, *Viola tricolor*, and ferns. Provided those plants with particularly strong roots, such as valerian, are discouraged, no harm should come to the wall.

DRY STONE WALLS

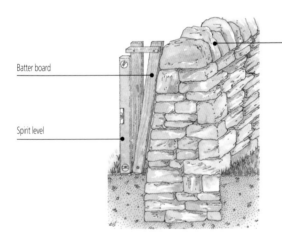

Cocks and hens coping

Batter board

Spirit level

Dry stone walls can provide a perfect boundary in a rural area where stone occurs naturally, but dry stone walling is a skilled job. The wall should be started from below ground level, and built with a slight taper, or 'batter', towards the top. The

finished wall should be no more than 1m/3ft 3in high, and the most suitable coping is formed by stones set on edge. Plants can be grown in the crevices of dry stone walls, to make such a boundary even more attractive.

2 This dry stone wall is randomly coursed, which sets up an attractively informal and natural pattern.

A retaining wall allows vigorous plants, such as this bougainvillea, both a good depth of soil, and somewhere to hang down pleasingly.

their harsh colour and busy pattern makes them visually uncomfortable in almost every situation, and the finished wall will need regular buttressing with special 'pilasters' that are also ugly.

Simpler block patterns are available, but do choose carefully, and smother with climbers to soften the whole composition.

Cast concrete walls can be superb, but you will probably need to employ professional help. Construction involves erecting wooden shuttering to contain the poured concrete, and reinforcing rods bedded into the foundations. The bottom of the wall should be wider than the top, and a 'toe' can be cast at the front, to act as a lever against pressure from behind.

Cast concrete walls can be immensely strong, and can be used as retaining walls as well as freestanding ones. The surface finish can be varied according to the way the shuttering is used. If, for example, rough-sawn boards are

3 Walls around a swimming pool provide necessary shelter and, as here, decoration. The stunning blue tiles are reflected in the construction of the pool.
A small-leaved, drought-tolerant, self-clinging climber is the obvious choice for this position. It can also be trimmed easily if it obscures the tiles.

4 A bland wall can be improved by trellis, which will disguise awkward angles and provide a host for climbers. The white walls provide the perfect background for the planting in different shades of green.
A low raised bed ensures a suitable planting environment for climbers and other plants grown against a wall.

3

4

positioned vertically, horizontally or even on a diagonal, the pattern will appear on the face of the wall. Carefully thought-out designs can result in something both crisp and contemporary.

The choice of facing materials for retaining walls should obviously match that used elsewhere in the composition, and will, in turn, need softening by planting to mould the levels together.

The general principles of building with brick still apply, but retaining walls also need to withstand considerable pressures of soil and water behind them. If you are planning to retain a change of level that exceeds 1m/3ft 3in, the job will almost certainly be best left to an experienced landscape contractor; and if you are in any doubt about the pressures behind a wall, or its integrity, *always* enlist the advice of a structural engineer; his fee will be money well spent.

The greatest pressure on the back of the wall will be towards the bottom, and consequently the wall should be wider at the base. The first six courses of a 1m/3ft 3in high retaining wall should be 450mm/18in thick; above this, the wall can be one course, 225mm/9in thick. If brick is used, vertical reinforcing rods can be set in the concrete foundations, and built into the brickwork as it progresses.

Weep holes should be included at the base of any retaining wall, to allow a build-up of water to escape. These can be formed from plastic or clay pipes, set at a slight downward angle, approximately 1.2m/4ft apart and 80mm/3in above the lower ground level, and finished flush with the face of the wall. To allow water to drain to the bottom and escape more easily, the wall should be backed with gravel, hardcore or similar porous material, laid over a sheet of polythene at the level of the weep holes; this will help prevent water seeping beneath the wall. The back of the wall should also be treated with a waterproof sealant.

RETAINING WALLS

Coping engineering brick on edge in mortar

Waterproofed cement/sand render

Hardcore backfilling

Weep pipe

Two courses of engineering brick DPC

Clayware drain

Concrete foundations

Retaining walls to hold back higher ground should have concrete foundations twice as wide as the wall itself, and be solidly constructed. The back of the wall should ideally be rendered and painted with a waterproof sealant. Back this with a filling of crushed stone or hardcore, and place a drainage pipe at the bottom. Run additional pipes through the wall, to emerge just above ground level.

HEDGES

DS Up to now we have been looking at the 'hard landscape' possibilities for boundaries. Now we should consider the use of hedges to surround the whole or part of a garden. Their main advantage over walls or fences is cheapness; their disadvantages include the length of time a newly planted hedge will take to reach maturity, and the regular maintenance in the form of clipping or pruning that they require. Different hedging grows at different rates, and it is also worth remembering that the style of your hedge can be changed over a period of time. Topiary is an obvious example, for the top can be scalloped or clipped to architectural angles and levels to pick up or reinforce a design theme within the garden. A fine hedge can form a superb and, if necessary, stock-proof boundary, and has an altogether softer line than any of the 'hard' materials. A thick hedge also acts as a barrier against the noise and pollution from roads, while providing a valuable wildlife habitat.

Alternating hedging with walls or fences can work well, as long as this is a planned rather than a haphazard arrangement. The hedge can be allowed to grow higher or lower than its hard landscape counterparts, or, alternatively, it can be clipped in curves or angles to meet the fence or wall.

Wattle or osier hurdles are ideal for protecting the young plants and creating a temporary boundary while the hedge is developing.

UB Good hedges can be either evergreen or deciduous, although in general, evergreen hedges provide the best defence against noise, animals and wind. Exceptions are beech and hornbeam, which are pruned in midsummer, and retain their dead leaves in winter. The neatest tend to be those which do not flower or fruit, such as coniferous hedges, but roses, forsythia and cotoneaster can all make good informal hedges.

In theory, any plant which will tolerate hard pruning can be used for hedging; in practice, some make more attractive hedges than others. It is best to buy 'hedging' plants in bulk as these establish quickly and will keep the cost down.

Although it is usual to grow a hedge of one species, you can also mix them to make an attractive 'tapestry hedge': use several types of beech or conifers with different coloured foliage, or a wider range of plants, including elaeagnus and green and variegated hollies.

Some hedges are invaluable for specialized use: *Griselinia littoralis*, escallonia, *Hebe speciosa*, and *Fuchsia magellanica* will only thrive in mild districts, but as they can also withstand salt air, are useful for planting near the coast.

Hedges composed of species such as hawthorn, blackthorn, field maple, holly, hornbeam and beech are useful for boundaries in country situations and will foster wildlife, some of which will be beneficial to the gardener.

Hedges not only have to last a long time, but are also subjected to severe annual pruning. It is necessary to prepare the ground well before planting, and to water plants until established. Mark out the line of the hedge using a garden line. Dig out a trench the length of the projected hedge using the line as a guide. For most purposes, plant in a single row (see chart below for planting distances). A staggered row of closely spaced plants is a good idea if you want a really impenetrable hedge, but remember that the hedge will also be rather wider.

Many types of hedge are in effect pruned trees or large shrubs, so their nutritional requirements can be substantial. A yearly mulch and application of general fertilizer in the spring is therefore advised. If not fed and mulched adequately, the hedge is inclined to draw what there is out of the soil, denying it to plants growing nearby. If you don't mulch, you may need to hoe weeds from the soil during the summer – although even weeds will languish in the dry shade of an evergreen hedge.

Most hedges need to be pruned after planting. The very vigorous and upright growers, such as privet and hawthorn, can be cut back to 150mm/6in. Other deciduous subjects, and the evergreens box and *Lonicera nitida*, should be cut back by one-third. The following year, trim all these species lightly, and in their second winter cut them back by one-third again.

During the following years, trim the hedge in late summer; for a formal hedge, or if the species is very vigorous, trim two or three times in the growing season. Once the hedge has reached the desired height, trim it back hard each time to within 6mm/¼in of the old wood.

With Leyland cypress and other vigorous conifers, including yew, trim only their side-shoots in the early years, leaving the leading shoots untouched; the most vigorous species may need this trimming two or three times in the growing season. Once the leading shoots

STRAIGHT LINE PLANTING

Deciduous hedges, such as beech, are planted bare-rooted in the dormant season, into a ready-dug trench to which organic material has been added. Hedge spacing depends on the species. Canes are useful for marking where the plants go, but are not necessary to support hedging plants once they are in.

STAGGERED LINE PLANTING

This technique is used where a very dense, impenetrable hedge is required, perhaps to prevent animals from pushing through. Make sure that the additional width of the hedge will not be a problem before planting in a staggered line, allowing 45cm/18in between rows and 90cm/36in between the plants in each row.

APPROXIMATE PLANTING DISTANCES

Berberis darwinii	45cm/18in
Berberis thunbergii	45cm/18in
Buxus sempervirens	30cm/12in
Carpinus betulus	60cm/24in
Corylus avellana	60cm/24in
Crataegus monogyna	45cm/18in
× Cupressocyparis leylandii	75cm/30in
Escallonia	45cm/18in
Fagus sylvatica	45cm/18in
Forsythia × intermedia	45cm/18in
Fuchsia magellanica	45cm/18in
Ilex aquifolium	45cm/18in
Lavandula	30cm/12in
Ligustrum	30cm/12in
Lonicera nitida	30cm/12in
Rosa rugosa	45cm/18in
Taxus baccata	60cm/24in
Thuja	60cm/24in

1 Although rather quick growing, and therefore in need of frequent trimming, the golden privet, *Ligustrum ovalifolium* 'Aureum' is a good choice here because the colour is enhanced by the variegated ivy below.

Hedges can provide both a physical boundary and great visual interest. Here, the fence has become virtually incidental, while the composition is dominated by the dramatic and effective foliage contrast between the ivy and privet.

2 To retain its sharp appearance, which echoes the sinuous lines of the balustrade, a hedge like this should be kept lightly trimmed throughout the growing season. Since the leaves are small, a hedgetrimmer can be used, although hand shears would be necessary for that part close to the railings.

This great organic shape has enormous power, and works in direct contrast to the delicate iron handrail. It helps to contain the flight of steps, and to balance the mass of the house and retaining wall.

FORMATIVE PRUNING OF A DECIDUOUS HEDGE

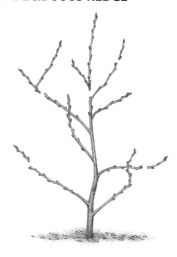

Cut back the sideshoots and main leader of average-growing deciduous hedging plants by a third after planting. The following year, trim back lightly several times to encourage the hedge plants to thicken up. In the second winter after planting, cut back the sideshoots and leader by one-third again.

FORMATIVE PRUNING OF A CONIFER HEDGE

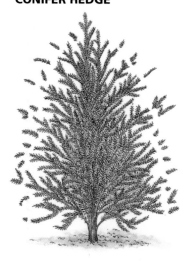

Conifers should be lightly trimmed in the early years, but the leading shoot should be left untouched until it reaches the required height. Only yew among the conifers commonly used for hedging readily regenerates from old wood. Yew is poisonous to animals, so should not be used in a stock-proof hedge.

CLIPPING AN ESTABLISHED CONIFER HEDGE

It is difficult to trim a hedge accurately by eye. Use string and bamboo canes as a guide to keep you straight. You will find the task of clearing up easier if you lay polythene sheeting on the ground before you start.

A 'BATTER' ON A CONIFER HEDGE

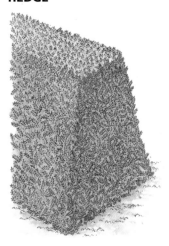

A conifer hedge with a 'batter', that is narrower at the top than the bottom, will allow both rain and light to reach the bottom more easily. If it is not trimmed in this way, the hedge may suffer from drought and die at the base.

1 Yew is the ideal hedging material where stock cannot get to it (both foliage and berries are poisonous). It can be close-trimmed into many shapes, and will ensure privacy, and shelter for the plants in front of it. Yew has a reputation for being slow-growing. This is not so, provided that it is fed and watered well. One of the advantages of a hedge over a wall is the fact that it can be clipped into any number of different shapes according to what is required. This upward sweep of green wall echoes the planted arch below, giving a delightful rhythm.

2 Roses make a charming informal hedge in a semi-wild situation. It is purely ornamental, making a symbolic break between the garden and the meadow beyond. Close pruning is not necessary; passing a hedgetrimmer over it in early spring would be sufficient. This is the ultimate romantic boundary, separating a country garden from the rural landscape beyond. The soft continuous drift of roses looks perfect, and will act as a surprisingly effective deterrent to intruders.

have reached the desired height, you can 'top' all the main shoots level to encourage a flat-topped, wider-growing hedge.

Flowering hedges can be trimmed after flowering if they flower on last year's wood, as most of them do. The exception is *Rosa rugosa*, which should be cut back hard in late winter or early spring. With fruiting hedges, such as cotoneaster and pyracantha, trim lightly either before or after flowering. You will lose some flower or some young berries, but the loss will not be serious.

Many flowering hedges, once established, need not require any work at all. Plant them in a double, staggered row, so that any bareness at the base is less obvious, then add dense planting in front, and plant climbers with a different season of interest to grow through the hedge (say species clematis or *Tropaeolum speciosum*). You should then be able to leave well alone.

Large-leaved plants, such as *Prunus laurocerasus*, are best trimmed back with secateurs; smaller-leaved subjects, such as yew and *Lonicera nitida*, can be done with hand shears (if you have only a short hedge) or electric hedgetrimmers. Strings attached to four bamboo canes, one at each corner of the hedge and set at the height required, will provide a cutting line and help to ensure a straight hedge. It is very difficult to judge accurately by eye while you are trimming a hedge; only when you have finished do the mistakes become obvious.

Close-leaved evergreen hedges, which do not allow rainwater and light to penetrate easily, are best clipped to a batter – that is, slightly narrower at the top than bottom – so that light can reach the lower parts of the hedge. If this is not done, the leaves on lower branches may turn brown and even drop. When trimming evergreens you will need to wear heavy-duty gloves, and goggles are also wise. Shears should be sharp. Many people favour mains-powered hedgetrimmers but these must be used with care; they can be dangerous if mishandled. Make sure that you have a 'residual current device' at the socket, to minimize the risk of electrocution should the cable be cut. Try to find a hedgetrimmer with a blade stopping-time of no more than half a second (two seconds is the British Standard requirement), and a two-handed switch, where the machine will only operate when both hands are on it. Blade extensions (which lessen the risk of a hand coming into contact with the blades) are also a helpful safety feature. If you have a broad and tall hedge you may need 600mm/24in blades; otherwise, 400mm/15in is adequate.

Cordless trimmers, which have batteries and a charger, provide some advantages, although they can be less powerful than mains-powered; you can also obtain petrol-driven trimmers.

Most hedgetrimmers have two-edged blades, so you can cut in sweeps to and fro. Always use two hands, and run the cable over your shoulder towards the power source. Never risk overbalancing by leaning too far over, and always make absolutely sure that your stepladder is stable before you start. Rest when your arms are tired. Lay polythene or similar sheeting down to catch the trimmings; raking them up is a long and tedious job.

Hedgetrimmers must be regularly cleaned to function efficiently; the two blades, which cut in a scissor action, easily become clogged, especially when cutting back resinous conifers.

It is possible to save time on hedge-trimming some of the faster-growing hedges by spraying on a chemical growth-retardant called dikegulac (avoiding other plants) in spring. Although not suitable for immature hedges, box, myrobalan plum, yew, viburnum and most roses, it may be helpful in restraining excessive exuberance in privet or Leyland cypress.

Neglected hedges can often be rescued, even if nothing has been done to them for some time. It is possible, for example, to cut yew back hard into old wood, and it will still sprout. So will laurel (*Prunus laurocerasus*), holly (*Ilex aquifolium*) and beech (*Fagus sylvatica*). Conifers are often more problematic, for example, Leyland cypress will take a long time to recover its looks after hard pruning, which is why you have to be so careful to trim it regularly. Generally, cutting back in spring one side of an old neglected hedge, and waiting until it has recovered before attempting the other, should prevent too violent a shock to the system. After any drastic cutting back, feed and mulch the hedge well.

1 These conifers have been allowed to retain something of their individual shape to make an effective barrier that possesses character. Nevertheless, great care has obviously been taken in their maintenance, for the top is ruler straight. A hedge like this will need several trims a year to keep the really sharp effect.

2 A striking alternative to a true tapestry hedge, in which species are clipped together. This beautifully manicured effect is ideal for a formal garden.
The alternating species provide a great contrast here, and the effect is dramatic. It would need careful maintenance.

3 The several different forms of escallonia planted together here make a lovely informal hedge. Although escallonias are a little tender in cold areas, they will tolerate salt spray, so a hedge like this would do well in those coastal areas where hard frosts are unknown.

4 Forsythia, as a spring-flowering deciduous shrub, should always be pruned after flowering. It will take hard clipping, which is why it is such a good subject for a hedge.
The dramatic colour of the forsythia makes a powerful statement, and the gate stands out from it in sharp relief.

HEDGES

5 Lime trees can be clipped into hedges on 'stilts', as shown here. To maintain this effect, the lower sideshoots should be scrupulously removed as soon as they appear. Formal hedges of this kind act as an orderly background to laxer flower plantings, creating a satisfying contrast in form and texture.

6 One of the advantages of yew is that it will tolerate clipping into its old wood. So these monumental shapes can be renovated, even if they grow too wide.
Yew, the king of hedges, can be clipped into startling and architectural shapes. Here, the cone contrasts with the tree behind.

6

7

7 This attractive, yet simply executed, tapestry hedge comprises two kinds of beech, *Fagus sylvatica* and its purple-leaved form, *F. sylvatica* f. *purpurea*. An advantage of using plants of the same genus is that they will grow in the same conditions, at the same rate, and can also be trimmed at the same time.

8 If trimmed in summer, beech (like hornbeam) will retain its leaves throughout the winter, thus providing interest for the greater part of the year.
Winter colour is one of the joys of the garden. This hoop of beech emphasizes the view and makes a lively division of space.

8

ENTRANCES

DS Entrances and exits can easily make or break an otherwise carefully measured composition. The choice of gates is vast, and you need to consider carefully the style and scale of your entrance, and the general impression that it will make. Where there is a fence, it works well to use the same material for the gate: a close board or picket fence could have a similarly constructed gate. Walls or hedges, on the other hand, obviously have to use a contrasting material such as wood or iron, and this will effectively help to emphasize the point of entry.

As with boundaries, gates can either provide an open or a closed view – in either direction – and to a large extent your decision will depend on the need for privacy or otherwise. My own home has solid stone walls but I have hung a

1 An open door is always inviting. The path is strongly defined by planting that leads one towards the opening with its undisturbed horizontal line along the top – simpler and more effective than a curved archway. The contrast of light and shadow is important.

2 This gate certainly draws the attention and focuses the view on the garden beyond, but it also attracts the eye *out* of the garden, so it is important that the view out is a good one. The hoop makes a natural host for climbers, and plants will draw the outline into the overall garden pattern.

well-detailed iron gate that allows the view from the road to run straight up a path to focus on a pool and fountain. Had this view impinged on my privacy, I might have chosen a solid timber gate. Simplicity and purpose apply to the design of boundaries and gates just as much as to other elements in the garden, and there are some practical rules that should be obeyed. You will find that if the top of the gate matches the general level of the top of the wall, fence or hedge, it makes a far stronger statement than if it is lower or higher, when it is almost invariably visually unsettling. Gates set within a wall work well if they fill the aperture adequately; those that have merely been given a feeble brick arch at a higher level than the walls gain nothing and smack of pretension.

Entrance gates often have to serve cars as well as people, and it is worth thinking about the problem. Five-barred gates are popular, but can be very inconvenient for pedestrians. It is often better to split a double gate into a small and large section so that pedestrians can use the small section and both can be opened for vehicles.

As a general rule, suit the gate to the entrance: grand entrances demand grand gates; modest entrances need something altogether less dramatic. But all the rules of good detailing, respect for materials, and scale, apply to gates as they do for walls. Rather than going to your local DIY or garden centre, look at illustrated books of garden detail; walk down streets in well conserved areas; observe what works and what does not; then you can decide.

3 This is a gateway on a grand scale. To reduce it to more domestic proportions, the arch has been infilled with timber, and a small gate introduced. Planting and climbers help to soften the outline, while flanking conifers act as punctuation marks and emphasize the pathway.
Wisteria hangs over the arch, and *Parthenocissus tricuspidata* on the right-hand wall will ensure scarlet tints in autumn.

4 Such imposing gate piers demand fine gates. The design has been kept simple; the swooping tops form a semi-circle when shut.

5 White walls demand black gates to increase the feeling of space. The strong horizontal lines of the path, laid with railway sleepers, complement the vertical pattern of the gate. Bold foliage plants are used to lead the eye towards the entrance. Ground-hugging plants solve the problem of using straight timber to make a curved path by filling in the gaps.

6 Many of the elements of a Japanese garden have been used here to good effect. The pale colour of the floor is thrown into sharper relief by the dark evergreen planting.

PERGOLAS, ARCHES AND ARBOURS

DS There are a number of garden components that offer vertical emphasis. Some are provided by the 'soft' landscape elements of trees and planting, while others, such as pergolas, arches and arbours, fall into the structural framework of the composition, although they can be vehicles for climbing plants.

Garden structures of this kind have a distinguished pedigree, pergolas being clearly recorded in the Egyptian gardens of the Nile. There, as in other parts of the Middle East, they were used as supports for vines, though it was originally the shade from the plants that was all-important. It was a logical development to use them as decorative elements.

While all these structures use overhead beams of some sort, pergolas and arches are primarily concerned with framing a walkway or point of entry into another part of the garden; they are associated with movement. Arbours, on the other hand, are static affairs, providing a place where you can sit in contemplation, a place where fragrance and shade come into their own. Arbours will almost invariably also be used as a focal point, and their scale and siting should be considered at the design stage.

A pergola will often be used to separate one part of the garden from another, but it must have somewhere positive to go. There are no rules to dictate its length, but it is worth remembering that the longer it is, the greater the visual tension. This can be used to advantage by siting it so that the walk ends with a release of energy, either opening out dramatically to embrace a wider view, or by entering a new garden area that is quite different in mood from the one you have just left. The run need not be a straight one; a pergola set on a curve gives a delicious feeling of mystery, and heightens the feeling of tension.

All too often you will see a pot or piece of statuary terminating the walk; a cliché of this kind will draw the eye and foreshorten the space, in direct contradiction to its original purpose.

As far as construction is concerned, simplicity is the key, and it should reflect materials used in other parts of the garden. Scale is also important. Massive brick piers and solid oak beams will look superb in a large country garden, but not in a smaller domestic plot. Conversely, the flimsy timber and wire designs offered at garden centres will look insubstantial in whatever setting.

Obviously, your choice will be determined by both the setting and your budget, but in most situations simple 100 x 100mm/4 x 4in uprights and 150 x 150mm/6 x 6in cross beams will look fine. Cast and wrought iron were traditionally used, but the price of these today is often prohibitive. Plastic hoops offer an alternative, but their dimensions are relatively light and lack visual solidity. Buy pressure-treated timber, or make sure it is soaked with a non-toxic preservative before erection.

The width and height of the structure should be generous; it is easy to forget how much room plants occupy when they are mature. Initially, the pergola will often look dominant and gaunt, but planting will very soon temper the outline. Simple wires up or around the posts are the least obtrusive way of supporting stems. If the pergola crosses a lawn, a continuous bed to either side of it will provide far greater continuity than spot planting at the base of each post.

The design and type of path beneath a pergola should be a continuation of that used elsewhere in the garden. Remember to keep any patterns as simple as possible, since too many materials lead to visual confusion. Set the level of the path just below the surface of an adjoining lawn to allow easy mowing.

An arch is, in effect, a mini pergola; it, too, demands movement through the space, but instead of providing an extended walk, acts as a point of tension between one garden area and the next. It forms a powerful focal point, with all the activity, visual and physical, compressed into a limited area.

The siting of an arch within the overall composition of the garden is crucial to the design as a whole. For example, if it is given a central position in a long, narrow garden, this obvious statement will merely exaggerate the shape of the plot; whereas if it is situated to one side, it will naturally lead you across the space, encouraging lateral movement, and resulting in a visual widening of the plot.

It is important not to site an arch in uncomfortable isolation. It will need a path to link it to the wider layout, and is best combined with wings or screens of some kind – fencing, walling or hedging – which should, in turn, be surrounded and set within planting. Any of

1 Dappled shade can be a welcome relief from hot sun, particularly in very hot climates. This simple construction of rounded beams and poles is echoed at a lower level by the screen. Vines are quickly becoming established on the screen, and will soon form a canopy over the whole structure.
The grapevine is the obvious choice for such a situation, but a deciduous scented climber such as jasmine would also be suitable, and provide a bonus on warm summer evenings.

2 This huge bonnet of flower has romance and a feeling of mystery. The deep pool of shadow lying underneath positively demands investigation.
Ceanothus, the Californian lilac, is one of the few shrubs with blue flowers. It is invaluable in those temperate or sheltered gardens where the slight tenderness of many of the species is not a problem. Ceanothus plants are not long-lived, but are worth growing for the generosity of their flowering.

3 Iron hoops often make the perfect pergola; their delicate yet strong construction allows planting to take centre stage rather than being dominated by the supporting structure. The receding arches give this composition a terrific feeling of perspective.
Simple planting is often the most effective. Here, climbing roses provide midsummer colour without hiding the arches or garden beyond. The rank grass may undermine the vigour of the roses, but it adds greatly to the semi-wild charm of this archway.

1 The construction of this arbour gives a feeling of stability to a perfect garden retreat. Flower, fragrance and foliage all have great appeal. For full effect, the roses must be regularly fed and sprayed.

2 Arches and pergolas can be made from many materials. Fruit is the perfect choice for a vegetable garden.

These 'restricted' apples are pruned in summer, to achieve a balance between leaf and fruit.

3 You have to be careful about the use of colour in the garden. The construction of this feature is fine, but planting will have to be meticulously chosen to team with such a dominant paint scheme.

PERGOLAS, ARCHES AND ARBOURS

6

7

8

6 The point of any overhead structure is that it should be a support for climbing plants and not just a feature in its own right. The great sprawl of clematis shown here will put considerable strain on the timbers, which are, fortunately, stout and well built.

The spring-flowering *Clematis montana* is one of the most vigorous of all clematis. It requires little pruning unless it gets out of hand, and this is unlikely here as there is plenty of space.

7 A leafy arbour is the perfect place in which to while away a summer's afternoon. The slightly haphazard arrangement of this simple but well-built structure merely adds to its considerable charm.

This is a fascinating use of different foliage plants, which have been clipped carefully back to make an enticing seat. The vigorous *Aristolochia* is making a bid to take over, and this may soon need to be restrained.

8 The pool and fountain provide a focal point in the cross-axis through the pergola, while the wings of hedging give a sense of perspective, effectively focusing the view on the lawn beyond.

Roses and clematis make a favourite combination for pergolas and arches, and look very ornamental when planted together. Both roses and late summer hybrid clematis can be pruned together early in the spring.

4 This classic pergola uses old stone columns, placed within the path for ease of maintenance, and sensibly stout overheads. It would look fine in a formal layout.

Unobtrusive vertical wires have been used to give support to these spirally trained roses. They have been pruned to ensure that they flower close to the base.

5 A terrific use of old timbers. Such a structure has enormous power, and the piers are large enough to prevent the roof from seeming visually top-heavy.

The structure is more than sturdy enough to support a wisteria, and is enhanced by the strong shapes of bergenia leaves and of the conifers on either side.

these materials could be used to form the arch itself, thus providing visual continuity with the wings on either side, but it would be just as acceptable to use, say, a timber arch in conjunction with wings of hedging, or hooped metal to link two areas of planting together. Whatever you use, the arch should make a positive statement, and its design and construction should be thought out with care.

Arches make an obvious vehicle for climbing plants; as with pergolas, allow plenty of room for the planting to develop. However, in a family garden, a well-built sturdy arch could start life as a swing, with the path diverted to one side. When the children have outgrown the swing, the prime purpose of the arch can be restored.

Arbours, with a more static role, and usually some way from the house, can act both as a retreat and as a focal point; though the view *from* the arbour will be equally important. Flower fragrance is often strongest in the evening, so a position that catches the late afternoon sun will be particularly attractive.

Once again, materials used in the construction should reflect the underlying theme of the garden. You will also want to incorporate a sitting area. This can be laid from a wide range of paving, and in a more distant part of the garden, mellow old brick, broken stone or random rectangular slabs, with low, aromatic planting between the joints, will all be in character. As with paths beneath pergolas, remember to set any hard landscaping just below the level of an adjoining lawn. Alternatively, you could raise the sitting area slightly, thus setting it apart from the rest of the garden and indicating a change of use.

Overhead beams, or 'overheads' as they are increasingly being called, are an architectural form of arbour, but usually connected to, or close by, the house. They can provide a useful link between architecture and landscape, and offer support for climbers, as well as the possibility of screening from neighbours' windows. Construction is usually crisp, using planed timber in a variety of sizes, and supports can be either timber or steel. If you paint the beams, pick up the colour used for woodwork elsewhere on the building, and remember to fix unobtrusive wires that will allow climbers to be tied in easily.

Avoid the temptation to roof the entire structure with an acrylic sheet, for not only does heavy rain sound like thunder on it, but leaves and debris are particularly difficult to remove. Overheads look excellent in conjunction with timber decking; or where a house is clad with boards, the link between architecture and garden will be a perfect one.

1 Pergolas need to be visually as well as physically strong, in order to make a positive contribution to the garden design and provide support for climbing plants. Often, supports are too flimsy, but these solid brick piers and heavy cross beams frame the generous walk and lead you, with a slight feeling of mystery, towards the far end of the tunnel.

Pergolas make marvellous supports for climbing plants. The Japanese vine, *Vitis coignetiae*, seen here, is suitable for a sturdy structure such as this, and is very hardy.

2 Unlike pergolas, which are freestanding, overhead beams, or 'overheads', are normally connected to the house. They are particularly useful on a roof garden, where they cast shade and help to provide screening from overlooking windows. This arrangement is painted white to match the colour scheme used elsewhere in the garden.

Wisteria complements the white structure beautifully, and makes an excellent choice, with its bright green leaves and sinuous habit. Its flower racemes are pendent and scented.

TIMBER PERGOLA

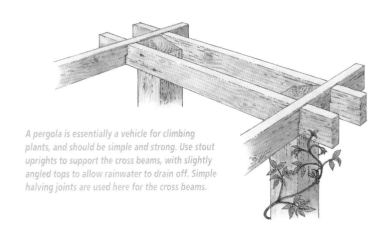

A pergola is essentially a vehicle for climbing plants, and should be simple and strong. Use stout uprights to support the cross beams, with slightly angled tops to allow rainwater to drain off. Simple halving joints are used here for the cross beams.

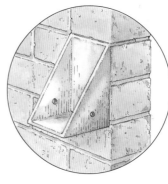

Joint hangers support overhead beams.

3 These overheads form a colonnade that extends the long line of the building out into the garden. The heavy, and unplanted, pillars provide a strong vertical emphasis.

4 Shade is an important element in any garden, and where the light is strong, drama is increased. Different shadow patterns cast by the overheads are thrown on to the ground and against the buildings.

5 The best pergolas act as supports for climbing plants, and the structure itself is therefore of lesser importance. They must, however, either lead somewhere, or include a focal point. This composition fulfils all the criteria perfectly.

PERGOLAS, ARCHES AND ARBOURS

2

3

4

5

SCREENS AND DIVIDERS

1

1 Moongates have enormous appeal, and here the brickwork has been beautifully laid. Notice how shadows reinforce the division between the sunlit garden rooms.
Young shoots of climbing roses can easily be trained to follow curves. Here the roses are used to adorn and accentuate the shape of the moongate.

2 What a delightful way to soften the architectural shape of a screen and arch! You would need to use hardwood for this structure, as rot could easily set in with such a tight clinging climber. The progress of the climber towards the top of the arch provides a great sense of movement.
Ivy is ideal for this kind of use, because the growths are so flexible, and it can be closely clipped.

3 Chinks of light add texture to the solid timber planks of this attractive screen. The sturdy gate continues the theme, and the wide brick path provides a practical and low-key foreground to this highly successful composition.
The yellow-flowered azalea emulates a patch of golden sunlight, in striking contrast to the shady and mainly dark green plantings nearby.

DS Provided a garden is of an appropriate shape and size, division of the space into a number of smaller areas can dramatically increase the apparent size of the overall composition. It may also provide a feeling of mystery and surprise, engender an element of movement, and create opportunities for a series of different themes. This kind of space division can be achieved either in a straightforward way, by using a solid barrier such as a wall, hedge or fence, or by using some kind of open screen that partially blocks a view but beckons you on with a glimpse of things to come.

Divisions of this kind do more than just block or deflect a view; by encouraging you to follow a planned route, interest is created in the different spaces along the way.

Planting can be planned to either side of a path; focal points can be carefully sited at the end of a vista; and overheads can compress the view so that tension is increased and then suddenly released. In this way, you are distracted from the garden as a whole, and led to concentrate on the spaces through which you happen to be passing.

The ultimate form of space division is a maze. Some gardens, over-planned and overcomplicated, verge on the maze mentality by breaking the design into too many set pieces. To achieve the right balance it is vitally important to look carefully at the size, shape, aspect and slope of your garden, and plan the break points and just what they are constructed from accordingly.

The decision about what to use for solid internal dividers is ultimately a personal one, depending on your own taste and practical requirements, but your choice of boundary material (which may

2

175

SCREENS AND DIVIDERS

4 The brick path here is superbly laid and naturally leads the eye towards the end. But the trellis arch helps to divide the long axis, and concentrates the eye on the bust and screen at the far end.

The clean lines of the trellis arch and the crisp planting have been effectively softened by the climber here.

3

4

A trellis screen will also be invaluable for disguising the mundane and utility areas of a garden. No pretension here; the simplest will allow climbers to do their job. However, never, in even the simplest trellis, sacrifice quality of materials or construction. Poorly made 'rustic' trellis screens look flimsy and quickly deteriorate, while larch poles covered with bark offer little support for a vigorous climbing plant, especially once rot sets in.

Basic trellis is made in a squared or diamond pattern from substantial slats that will give years of life if treated with a non-toxic preservative. Rather more complicated, but nevertheless acceptable, designs that provide greater visual interest can use wider slats of, say, 100mm/4in, set horizontally, vertically or at a diagonal. Whatever the size of the trellis, the same basic rules apply: always provide a sturdy framework, and use sound posts securely fixed into the ground to ensure it doesn't collapse.

Do not hesitate to seek ideas beyond the garden centre; you will almost certainly find better inspiration for the use of trellis in magazines, shops and public places.

As a final thought, remember to look at garden features in a lateral way, and do not rule out the use of 'unconventional' materials. I have even used scaffold poles to form an interesting and elegant divider. Set vertically, with about a 215mm/9in gap between each, painted black, and with the tops plugged to prevent water getting in, they are ideal for hosting a twining climber. A divider of this kind, made up from individual vertical components, has the added advantage that it can follow a curving pattern, both on the ground, and in the levels at the top.

Another contemporary divider could be made from long precast concrete building lintels, which are excellent for marking a crisp edge to a concrete terrace, or continuing the line of a modern building out into the garden.

itself have been determined by materials used in the house and surrounding locality) may well suggest what to use.

Stone or brick boundary walls might, for example, suggest similar walls within the garden, pierced by gates or gaps that focus on a particular view beyond. On the other hand, hedges could be used just as effectively. Yew, for example, will echo the solidity of stone but offer a softer backdrop to planting and a more gently themed approach.

Where a garden is surrounded by high boundaries, more open screens often work better than solid divisions, leading the eye down from the perimeter, either in a curving pattern that sweeps down, or a stepped design that offers a more angular approach.

Divisions of this kind need not divide an area in straight lines. Wings are particularly effective, and can, if they are staggered, allow a path to turn across the space, in front of one wing and behind the other. Dividers can also be set at a diagonal to a boundary.

Wherever a screen, hedge or wall projects into a space it will deflect a view and create a visual full stop. This is the natural place for a focal point of some kind, whether it be a well-chosen seat or a larger feature such as a pool, arbour or summer-house. These will be the punctuation marks of your garden, places to pause, places for something special to happen, before you continue with the rest of the composition.

Open screens can be made from a variety of materials, both soft and hard. A line of espaliered or pleached trees, for example, is essentially architectural in shape but has the benefit of flower and foliage both to temper the outline and provide an ever-changing aspect throughout the seasons of the year. The options for hard landscape dividers cover the whole spectrum, from honeycomb walls, open fencing of many kinds, and, of course, trellis.

Trellis, much in vogue, is often pompously referred to as '*treillage*' by garden designers and clients. Traditional *treillage* was incredibly complicated, solidly made, and always vastly expensive; what is meant by the word today is a kind of tarted-up trellis, swooping and swirling in an orgy of woodwork, overworked and frankly pretentious.

Simple things work best. Most trellis is used as a vehicle for plants, and although there are situations where a well thought-out and detailed piece of trelliswork will lie in perfect harmony with its surroundings, make sure it is designed as part of the overall plan, and not simply for design's sake!

CLIMBERS AND WALL PLANTS

UB Climbers and wall plants add greatly to a garden's aesthetic impact. They are a wide and disparate group, comprising all those plants (annual, perennial and shrubby) which naturally climb, together with woody shrubs which are too tender to put in the open garden, or which flower or fruit better when they have their backs to the wall.

Climbers and wall plants include many species which might not be hardy enough to survive winter in the open garden without protection. These contribute enormously to the colour, scent and interest in the garden, and since many are evergreen, they also provide a solid backcloth for deciduous climbers or other plants.

In design terms, climbers can provide vertical emphasis to a gardenscape which might otherwise depend solely on trees, tall perennials and spire conifers. They can even be used as thin buttresses to break up a long wall border.

Climbers can clothe internal screen constructions to help make distinct 'garden rooms' and cover ugly or unexceptional walls, fences, and buildings. They can be used on pergolas, arches and arbours, on tree stumps too big to remove, on fruit trees and conifers.

The more fragile climbers can be encouraged to grow through or over established shrubs and hedges to provide colour when the host is no longer in flower. This is particularly helpful in small gardens. Climbers can even be used as ground-cover.

Climbing plants achieve their purpose in different ways. Most noticeable are the barbs and thorns which give purchase to the stems of roses. Other plants do their climbing by twining, using tendrils (sweet peas), leaf stalks (clematis), or entire stems (lonicera). Then there are the scandent climbers, such as *Jasminium nudiflorum* and *Passiflora caerulea*, which climb by pushing long stems through other plants. This makes them useful for overlaying shrubs and for growing through open fencing, but they are not always satisfactory on a wall. Last, but by no means least, are the 'self-clingers', those plants which can attach themselves to a solid structure, either by sticky pads on the ends of tendrils (parthenocissus) or aerial roots (*Hedera helix, Hydrangea anomala petiolaris*).

The rewarding features of climbing plants have to be paid for. This kind of gardening is often time-consuming and labour-intensive, involving regular pruning, tying in and spraying.

You cannot simply plant and forget wall plants. They may grow and flower well, but will need more feeding and watering, and often more pruning and training, than comparable plants in the open garden. Walls alone will not always reliably provide the protection needed for tender plants, and it may be necessary to take additional protective measures in early winter.

Walls can cause their own problems: being solid barriers, they promote wind turbulence and eddying, which may damage the plants against them. Walls and fences both draw moisture out of the soil, and also create 'rain shadows', leaving the soil at their base very dry.

Pests and diseases thrive in the shelter of a warm wall, yet spraying tall climbing plants is not always easy.

On walls exposed to morning sun, early spring sunshine can thaw too quickly a slightly tender plant that has been frosted overnight, leading to death of the tissues. Many ostensibly hardy plants, like hydrangeas, can be harmed in this way. A wall in shade presents fewer risks, as the frozen water in the plant tissues can thaw more slowly.

Frost damage in spring can be minimized by planting only hardy plants against north or east walls. Nevertheless, it is difficult to prevent frost damage entirely, because growth often starts earlier in the warmer conditions of a wall than it would in the open garden. If shoots are frosted, cut them out.

1 A striking and unusual combination for a warm wall: *Actinidia kolomikta*, with its intriguing pink- and white-tipped leaves, together with *Clematis florida* 'Sieboldii', in summer. Both need a sheltered position to give of their best, and this brick wall will retain heat.

2 A simple but charming effect made with a good dark-coloured variety of *Chaenomeles speciosa*, the Japanese quince, which flowers in late winter and early spring. In some years the ornamental quince will set fruit.

ATTACHING CLIMBERS AND WALL PLANTS

a Trellis provides a neat and architectural support for climbers, often forming as much of a feature as the plant itself. Sound construction is essential, and panels should be screwed to battens, which will hold them away from the face of the wall and minimize rot.

b Wires fixed horizontally along the wall provide one of the neatest and least obtrusive ways of supporting climbers. Use vine eyes or hooks plugged and screwed into the joints. Plastic or galvanized wire will have the longest life. Climbing plants need regular tying in.

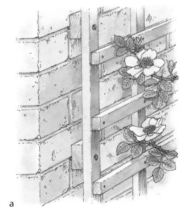

a

b

CLIMBERS AND WALL PLANTS

3 Roses fill a colour gap between the flowering and fruiting of fruit trees. They do need to be planted, as here, at a distance from the tree, in order not to interfere with the tree's roots, and to ensure that rain will be able to filter down to them. For ease of maintenance, they can be pruned at the same time as the trees, in late winter.

Climbers do not have to cover an architectural feature. In a natural environment they will scramble through any vertical structure, and trees are an obvious example. Swathing old apple trees in an orchard with climbing plants can produce charming results.

4 The long, sinuous, twining growths of the wisteria make it very suitable for growing along railings, although care must be taken if they are not to cause damage in the long term. Wisteria likes a warm situation, well sheltered from cold winds, and provided with ample soil for a vigorous root run. It must be concientiously pruned, and, if carefully nurtured, can be very long-lived.

Simple things nearly always work best, and here the visual strength of the wisteria works in direct contrast to the architecture. The combination of austere railings and tumbling climber makes a dramatic boundary.

5 No opportunity has been left unexplored here; the building is clothed with climbing plants. It is especially impressive because there does not seem to be much room for the rose roots. Feeding, watering and spraying in the growing season will obviously be more necessary than for plants growing in the open, but the results justify it.

When a climber, or a combination of climbers, completely hide their support, it is a wonderful sight. Occasionally, however, they can cause structural damage, and here it would be worth checking on a fairly regular basis to make sure that all is well.

1

2

Vigorous climbers are often used to clothe ugly buildings. Deciduous climbers can be more trouble than they are worth because their leaves clog gutters in winter; better, if shelter can be provided, to plant an evergreen like *Berberidopsis corallina*, the sweetly scented *Holboellia coriacea* or *Clematis armandii*. Do not even consider the pretty *Fallopia baldschuanica* (the 'mile-a-minute' plant): it can quickly engulf a building.

Many tender climbers need the protection of a conservatory in winter. Either plant them in the conservatory border, or in large pots which can be brought into the warm. Many of the less rampant climbing plants do well in containers, provided they are fed and watered regularly. Remember, though, that pests and diseases also thrive in conservatory conditions; and you will have to be scrupulous about removing, and sweeping up, faded flowers and dying leaves. There are ample compensations: the satisfaction, for example, of being able to train a pelargonium to climb up a wall.

Climbing plants do not necessarily require support. Several will do well as ground-cover. The large leaved ivies will grow thickly in shade under trees in this way, while clematis and roses can be pegged down to grow horizontally, and even honeysuckle and vines will happily scramble up or down a slope.

In our enthusiasm to grow a host of tender climbers, we are inclined to forget our best resolutions about plant associations where wall plants are concerned. However, the impact will be far greater if climbers and wall plants are thoughtfully combined. Consider just one example: the satisfying effect achieved by a combination of *Vitis vinifera* 'Purpurea', *Clematis* 'Étoile Violette' and *Buddleja crispa*.

While on the subject of colour, never ignore the colour of your house wall. Pink stucco will not be enhanced by the butter-yellow of *Fremontodendron* 'California Glory', whereas the blue of a ceanothus such as 'Gloire de Versailles' or *Buddleja crispa* would look fine. White

walls will detract from white flowers, but could look superb behind foliage such as that of *Actinidia kolomikta*, *Magnolia grandiflora*, or *Holboellia coriacea*. Likewise, the scarlet leaves of *Parthenocissus tricuspidata* will add to the attraction of a grey stone wall in autumn.

Scale and vigour are as important as colour. Strong growing and substantial wall plants are marvellous if there is space, but take care to avoid the really large growers, such as *Magnolia grandiflora* or *Ceanothus impressus*, if there is little wall space available between the windows; *Cobaea scandens*, *Passiflora caerulea*, or a regularly trimmed pyracantha would be more suitable here. If very vigorous or evergreen climbers are grown into fruit trees, they may affect the fruiting, so it is important to match the climber with the host.

Many climbing plants are richly or sweetly scented, and their fragrance can be all the more readily appreciated if they are grown to hang down from a pergola, arch, or porch. Amongst the best

climbers for fragrance are *Jasminum officinale*, most honeysuckles, many roses, and sweet peas.

Climbers that can be grown as annuals and sown in early spring to flower all summer, such as *Cobaea scandens*, are valuable for ringing the changes in a garden, and also for giving some semblance of maturity to a new one. We rarely think of climbing vegetables for use in the flower garden, but in a small space, one of the more ornamental varieties of runner bean, say 'Painted Lady', or a climbing French bean such as 'Purple Podded', can be used to give fruitful, short-term solidity to open fence- or trellis-work.

When planting wall plants, make sure that the soil against a house wall is well below the level of any damp proof course. Incorporate plenty of organic matter into the planting hole, and fork in 75-100g/3-4oz of bonemeal to aid root development.

Plants should be planted at least 30-45cm/12-18in away from a wall, to

3 *Fremontodendron* 'California Glory' is one of the most attractive summer-flowering wall shrubs. It needs a sunny aspect and well drained soil as it is rather tender, but little pruning beyond the removal of frosted shoots in spring.

1 Campsis is in its element in a Mediterranean setting, where the bright scarlet trumpet flowers look their best. In temperate gardens, this slightly tender climber will need a very sunny wall to flower in such profusion.

2 Ivy is the most versatile and amenable of climbers, especially for a shady position. Its aerial roots enable it to cling without help, but you must ensure that the wall pointing is in good condition before you start training the ivy.

4 The evergreen honeysuckle, *Lonicera sempervirens*, is a lovely sight in full flower, with its characteristic clusters of scarlet trumpets, orange-yellow within. However, it is a vigorous plant, and may well need curbing.

make sure rain can reach the soil around their roots. The plant should normally be put into the ground at the same level as it was in its container. The exception is clematis, which is best planted with the top of its pot compost about 10cm/4in below soil level; this should ensure regeneration from below ground if the plant suffers from clematis wilt and dies back. A bamboo cane tied to the plant and leaned against the wall will help direct the growth. In the case of clematis, it will also minimize wind rock.

Water well before and after planting, even if the soil is moist. Most wall plants will also benefit from mulching after planting, to conserve much-needed moisture; plants like cistus are an exception, as they thrive in poor droughty soil. Clematis and honeysuckle grow best where their roots are cool and shaded, so an organic mulch helps to provide these conditions. If you plant either in a sunny place, put large flat stones or tiles in a circle around the base of the plant to shade the roots.

Continue to water all wall plants at regular intervals for the first year, especially in dry weather, and especially those that require a lot of water, such as clematis, and those planted against large trees, since the latter will be competing strongly for moisture.

If you garden on heavy clay soil, a little extra care needs to be taken if you want to grow wall plants. Clay shrinks when it dries out, which can cause subsidence and cracking to permanent structures. A vigorous plant, such as a large shrub, planted close to a wall will take a great deal of moisture out of the soil and possibly leave the structure vulnerable to such damage. Choose less vigorous plants instead, and, since few wall plants thrive on really heavy clay, lighten the soil with sharp grit.

If you intend to replace one climbing rose with another, it is important to remove the old soil from an area 45cm/18in wide and the same in depth, and put in fresh soil from elsewhere in the garden. If possible, dig in organic matter with it. This precaution minimizes the risk of 'rose sickness', or 'replant disease'.

Some formative pruning is helpful after planting. All roses, with the exception of pillar roses, and climbing forms of bush roses, should have their main stems cut back to 30cm/12in or so. Vines should be cut back very hard, to within two buds of the base, and the resulting shoots trained to make a basic framework. Cut back all clematis to two good buds, 30cm/12in from the ground, in the late winter after planting.

Pruning established plants is unfortunately not a job that can be shirked, for wall plants and climbers can easily get out of hand. For this, and for spraying, you will need a lightweight but stable aluminium ladder with its feet placed on a board in the border.

Feeding wall plants is more important than it is for those in open ground, partly to make up for any lack in the soil, and partly because the situation encourages many plants to grow vigorously.

Nutrient deficiencies often show up more quickly on wall shrubs than on those in the open garden, especially if the soil is alkaline. A spring dose of fish, blood and bone, or a general balanced fertilizer, at a rate of 50g per sq metre/ 2oz per sq yard, is suitable. Liquid seaweed fertilizer is beneficial in late summer, for its potash content, which helps to harden wood in preparation for winter. Repeat-flowering roses benefit from feeding with rose fertilizer as the first flush of flower goes over.

However well you look after your wall plants, they will sometimes fall prey to pests and to damaging fungal diseases. You will have to treat them accordingly. Choosing plants with resistance to attack is plainly helpful. Roses such as 'Madame Grégoire Staechlin', 'Phyllis Bide' and 'Golden Showers' are mildew resistant; while 'Aloha', 'Compassion' and 'Dublin Bay' are little affected by blackspot. If you do have to spray, do it before the trouble is well established.

1

2

1 Here, the climber reaches up to link the simple façade of the house to the garden below. Support for the dense foliage is provided by unobtrusive horizontal wires, a lower-maintenance solution than trellis.

2 The autumn colour of the 'common' Virginia creeper, *Parthenocissus inserta*, looks particularly well trailing down in this attractive way against the pale yellow-grey of the stonework. Unlike the 'true' Virginia creeper, *P. quinquefolia*, it does not have adhesive discs, so needs wires to which it can become attached. Hand shears will keep it under control.
This climber forms a living wall through which the doors open. The delicate outline of the leaves contrasts strongly with the rugged grey stone of the building and the continuing line of broad steps.

3

4

3 Two contrasting colours of clay paver have been arranged in a satisfying, repeating geometric pattern, all set at a 45 degree diagonal to the outside edge. Using diagonals creates the illusion of a larger space and opens out this paved sitting area. The intricate patterning mixed with the structured, formal planting in pots, and the patterns cast by the overhead pergola, sets up interesting visual rhythms.

BRICK PATTERNS

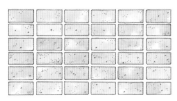

Herringbone – square

Soldier Courses

Basketweave

Stretcher Bond

Herringbone – diagonal

Stable pavers are another popular alternative to brick, and make a handsome non-slip surface, ideal for paths and terraces. Originally used as flooring for loose boxes and stable courtyards, they are approximately brick-sized, and made from extremely hard 'engineering' brick. Pavers are usually blue but sometimes red, and patterns vary. Some of the older ones are exquisite, but most have indented tops like a bar of chocolate, or in a diamond pattern. They make an excellent contrast material, but can look overpowering in a large area.

Because bricks and pavers are small modules, they take time to lay, and if you use a contractor the cost of laying will be relatively high.

4 Bricks can be laid in informal, almost fluid shapes. This path sweeps around the curved bed and takes you deeper into the more secluded areas of planting at the end of the garden. This type of brick path is deceptively complex and would require a good visual sense to lay well, as there is no set pattern to follow. Adding a restraining row of bricks at each side is important as half-bricks may have to be used in the main path. The planting here relies on evergreens such as box and ivies, so would look almost as good in winter as in the summer months.

OTHER SURFACES

1 Cobbles laid correctly are packed tightly together. Here they radiate out from the pot, the focal point of the area.
Rosemary and other scented shrubs partly obscure the cobbles. They enjoy the dry and sunny conditions.

LAYING A CONCRETE PATH

Concrete can provide a neat, no-nonsense and low-cost path that is very hardwearing. It will need some form of edge restraint, and timber boards, brick or granite setts can all be used. Lay the concrete on 100mm/4in of well compacted hardcore, level with the edge. Here, a straight-edged board is worked along the surface, with a gentle sawing motion, to produce a slightly raised finish on the completed path.

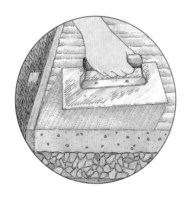

A steel float will give a smooth finish; a wooden float, a rougher one.

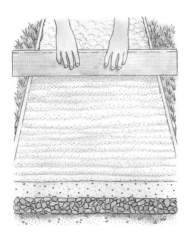

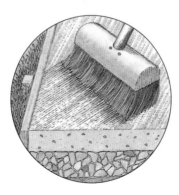

A broom will produce yet another texture. The concrete must not be too soft or hard.

DS Surfacing materials should be chosen to fulfil specific functions, as well as for their appearance. Cobbles can be uncomfortable to walk on, but very small cobbles can be used as inserts in contrast to other materials. Flatter cobbles can be set on edge, and used decoratively. Cobbles can be laid to form a solid surface, but use an edge restraint, such as a timber board. They are useful on drives or parking areas, where they effectively disguise oil stains. Use them loose as a ground-cover or architectural foil to planting, or piled up to stop people cutting corners!

Gravel looks equally at home in town or country. It can be used for drives, paths, awkward corners, or as ground-cover. It conforms easily to curves, and looks handsome with plants growing through it. It ranges in colour from golden to grey, and can be water-washed and smooth, or crushed from larger pieces of stone. Larger granite or marble chips are also available, often in striking colours. These can look terrific in a dark courtyard or basement area.

Concrete, being a 'fluid' material, can be laid to a variety of shapes, including curves, making it the ideal surface for areas such as drives or hardstandings. It is also a relatively economic choice.

Panels of concrete (to a maximum of about 3m sq/10ft sq) should be divided up and edged with courses of brick, paving or wood strips to act as 'expansion joints'. If laid to a curve, edging may be wood, metal strips, brick or other small modules.

Concrete can be given different finishes, and a technique widely used in North America produces one known as 'brushed aggregate'. Here, small stones in the mix are exposed, to give an interesting marbled effect.

Tarmac surfaces are useful for drives, paths and hardstandings. Whereas bitumen requires specialist equipment, and should be laid by a reputable contractor, asphalt can be bought by the bag from builders' merchants and is relatively easy to use for small areas. Tarmac must be contained within a framework of brick, boards or paving. Stick to black as a good, no-nonsense surface colour.

Finally, timber. The beauty of timber is self-evident. Decks look fine adjoining a timber building, and are excellent

OTHER SURFACES

2 Wooden decking is versatile and easy to lay. A good choice next to a timber-clad house, or for a roof garden.
A leafy, almost subtropical effect is achieved here, with hard and soft features complementing each other.

for building out over a slope where other materials would present a problem. Surfaces at different levels are easily handled, and existing trees can be allowed to grow through. Construction is comparatively easy. Prefabricated decking is available, but has none of the advantages of a purpose-built feature.

Hardwoods from the ever-dwindling tropical forests should be avoided, but good supplies are available from managed forest and woodland.

Softwoods can also be used, either 'tanalized' or pressure-treated, or treated with regular applications of non-toxic preservative – in a wide range of colours.

Timber railway sleepers are ideal for many garden projects, including hard surfaces, but are best used in more informal parts of the garden. Select ones that are clean and free from oil, which can present problems in hot weather.

Logs, which become available as a result of storm damage or tree surgery, are environmentally more acceptable than much sawn timber. They can be used as cross-slices to provide circular paving, or as lengthwise sections for sturdy and informal steps, paths, or

retainers. Hardwoods are the most suitable, and slices should be at least 80mm/3in thick. Wooden stepping stones can look perfect in a planted area.

Hardwood wood blocks are now being made again. They are usually cube-shaped, about 100 x 100 x 100mm/4 x 4 x 4in. They are not cheap, but this visually warm material can look very good close to a timber building.

3 A superb and dramatic use of railway sleepers is shown here. The strong directional emphasis links the edge of the pool and adjoining planting together, while the unusual diagonal line at which the sleepers have been laid provides a saw-tooth edge that is visually aggressive.
Strong foliage shapes help to mitigate the stark outline of this swimming pool. It makes a striking composition.

4 The gravel path leads the eye gently towards the powerful focal point of the old 'copper'. Gravel makes a fine ground-cover, and its neutral colour is an excellent foil for both flower and foliage.
If the vegetation were allowed to encroach any further, the path would disappear altogether. Daphnes, helianthemums, and other creeping rock plants are all happy growing directly in the free-draining gravel surface.

LAYING A GRAVEL PATH

Gravel should be laid on a sub-base of hardcore, followed by a layer of smaller stones, and then one of 'hoggin', a clay binder. The gravel itself is laid as a thin layer on top. Compaction and rolling are essential as each layer goes down. The final surface should always have a slight camber or cross fall to allow water to run off.

Any fluid material (gravel, tarmac, or concrete) will need an edge restraint. Here, bricks laid on edge are firmly 'haunched' or held in place with a wider base of concrete. Once again, the edging is laid just below the level of the lawn, for ease of mowing.

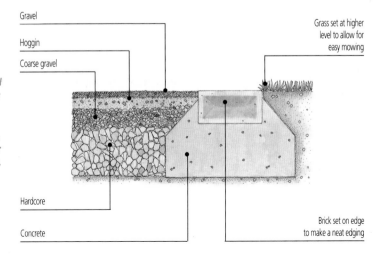

Gravel
Hoggin
Coarse gravel
Hardcore
Concrete
Grass set at higher level to allow for easy mowing
Brick set on edge to make a neat edging

Surfaces

GROUND-COVER

UB Ground-cover is self-explanatory, but the ways in which it is achieved are many and various. Plants which perform this function in the garden are those able to cover the ground (usually with foliage) sufficiently well, or for a sufficiently long period, to suppress or even eradicate weed growth. The word 'ground-cover' has for this reason become synonymous with 'labour-saving', and although that can be a misleading over-simplification, well used ground-cover can save the gardener from repetitive work, while achieving an agreeable, sometimes even beautiful, effect.

It would be foolish to deny that ground-cover has also acquired a poor reputation with many people. This is due partly to over-enthusiastic and misleading advice from nurserymen and other experts, and partly to the fact that some excellent ground-coverers cover the ground so well and so rapidly that they do not know when to stop. Space invaders such as *Lamium galeobdolon*, perfect for the far reaches of large gardens, become potential villains in more cramped and restrained surroundings. Among the most invasive (none of which appears on any list in this book) are: *Lamium galeobdolon*, *Rubus tricolor*, *Lamium maculatum* 'Chequers', *Hypericum calycinum*, *Rhododendron ponticum*, *Vinca major*, and the bamboos *Pseudosasa japonica* and *Pleioblastus variegatus*. A plant's habit can be a pointer: those plants which root very easily along creeping stems will probably cause problems, as will those, such as *Phlomis russeliana*, which seed excessively. If seeders are troublesome, you must either be prepared to dead-head punctiliously or else avoid them altogether.

But there are many positive benefits of ground-cover. The canopies of leaves of many plants conserve more moisture in the soil than they take from it, so it is possible to use ground-cover as a living mulch: for example, by planting pansies or geraniums under rose bushes.

Evergreen ground-cover can be used for areas of the garden where nothing else will grow satisfactorily: in a gap between wall and shed, for example, or under trees or large shrubs.

Ground-cover plants will hide, or disguise, ugly low garden objects such as manhole covers or tree stumps. Banks too steep to be mown safely can be planted with low, dense ground-covering plants such as *Cotoneaster dammeri*, which both flowers and fruits. (Do not overdo this, however, or your garden will soon resemble a council-planted roadside.)

Ground-cover need not involve the introduction of otherwise undesirable or uninteresting plants in order to solve a gardening problem. There are many beautiful plants whose dense prostrate or trailing habit makes them suitable for performing this function. Who would wish to garden without, for example, *Geranium macrorrhizum* 'Ingwersen's Variety' or *Heuchera micrantha* 'Palace

Purple'? Some will even grow in dry shade, that most challenging of garden situations: examples include hedera, pachysandra and *Euonymus fortunei*.

Attractive climbers, such as some ivies and clematis, can be encouraged to grow horizontally rather than vertically. Suitable cultivars of ivy could be *Hedera helix* 'Glacier' and *H. helix* 'Buttercup', and of clematis, any of the Viticella group. Even climbing roses can be pegged down to act as ground-cover. Moreover, many genuinely prostrate roses are now available, and more are being developed all the time, to join the long-established prostrate roses like *Rosa x jacksonii* 'Max Graf' and *R.* 'Paulii'.

It is not just prostrate or trailing plants which can perform a ground-covering function, however. Taller shrubs, provided that they are clothed to the ground, can do the same, as can bulbs with good leaf coverage, like *Cyclamen hederifolium*. Examples of shrubs which can be used for this purpose include fine

1

2

1 If the ground-cover here has been planted into weed-free soil, the only maintenance required would be a yearly trim with a pair of hand shears. Well-planned and maintained ground-cover gives continuity to a garden composition. The contrasts here are most effective.

2 Careful maintenance will be needed here. Mowing will be fiddly, but the gravel is easier to deal with. If hand-weeding is not possible, use path weedkiller in spring. The humour steals the show here, but the success of the chequered floor beside the four-poster depends on good maintenance.

3 The charming little *Viola tricolor* has been allowed to self-seed itself in profusion, with the result that the log path has almost disappeared. Both path and mixed planting would be excellent solutions for an informal or semi-woodland situation.

4 These are charming, if invasive, ground-cover plants for a semi-shaded place where weeding may be difficult or unwelcome. The periwinkle, *Vinca major* 'Variegata', is highly attractive with its blue flowers at most times of the year, but it will need to be controlled as it roots along its stems.

3

4

garden plants like hydrangeas, rhododendrons, elaeagnus, *Choisya ternata*, and *Berberis wilsoniae*.

Moreover, accent on ground-cover gives gardeners the impetus to use to the full those 'evergreen' perennials which retain their leaves at least in part through the winter season: stalwart garden plants like bergenias, most pulmonarias, *Stachys byzantina* and many of the euphorbias.

Ground-cover does not necessarily, however, demand an evergreen cover throughout the year. As weeds are mainly seasonal, the objective can still be achieved with deciduous plants, provided that the chosen herbaceous perennials, bulbs and shrubs come early into leaf. Weeds have the greatest difficulty competing with the large and numerous leaves of the herbaceous *Alchemilla mollis* and *Acanthus mollis*, for example; even those which germinate early soon languish under the weight of an acanthus leaf. Even annual plants can be used in this context: weeds cannot flourish successfully with a generous covering of busy lizzies (impatiens), and this plant will obligingly flower even in shade.

Since ground-cover plants will form a permanent planting, the soil where they are to go should be in good heart. When planting any ground-cover, but especially prostrate roses, be sure to see that all perennial weeds are first eliminated; it will be difficult to weed in inaccessible corners or amongst thorny rose shoots later on. Weeds poking through the canopy of an otherwise smooth planting of a single species of ground-cover plant will look particularly obvious and inappropriate.

Plant in autumn, if possible, to give plants time to become well established before the weed explosion in spring, and use mulches to prevent annual weed growth until ground-cover plants have had a chance to knit together.

5

5 Another energetic dwarf evergreen ground-covering plant, *Gaultheria procumbens*. It will grow happily in woodland, but does require an acid soil. It has pinky-white bell-shaped flowers in summer, followed by bright red berries. The leaves turn purple-red in winter.

Surfaces

UB Lawns, and their burdensome care, rank nearly as high in the gardener's list of nuisances as perennial weeds. The constant maintenance easily puts us off. However, lawns can be a major aesthetic asset, especially in larger gardens, for green is the perfect foil for hot colours; they are cheap in comparison with hard materials; they can be either smooth and neat, or wilder, acting as a bed for 'naturalized' bulbs.

A top-quality lawn will be composed of bents and fescues, both of which are fine-leaved and will need close and regular mowing to keep weeds out. An ordinary, serviceable family lawn, appropriate for most gardens, will contain fewer bents and fescues, but also meadow grasses and ryegrass, which are coarser, more hard-wearing, and more tolerant of occasional neglect. Precise seed mixtures should be chosen according to soil and site.

If you would like, with one bound, to be free of the tyranny of lawn care, then you will have to abandon all ideas of a striped billiard table and go instead for the latter type of lawn. It should be allowed to grow no more than 3.25cm/1⅛in long, and should be mown in the growing season once a week or less, using a rotary mower with the blades set fairly high, at 2.5cm/1in, and without the grass box. This will enable the lawn to return its nutrients gradually to the soil, but it does mean regular cutting. In wet weather, use the collection box to avoid tracking grass clippings into the house.

This minimalist's mowing regime should make for a reasonably healthy, dense-growing lawn, provided that you also apply lawn sand in the spring, to give a boost of nitrogen to the grass and to knock back moss and weed growth, at least temporarily. At least once every three years, in autumn, apply a mosskilling preparation. Once the moss is dead, use a motorized lawn rake to scratch it out, and with it any dead grass, known as 'thatch'. Then aerate the lawn by spiking it to a depth of about 8cm/3in: this allows the ingress of water and air to the roots. Use a garden fork or, far easier, a hired spiker on wheels.

Such an approach will not suit the perfectionist. If you have a flat lawn which you wish to keep smooth and weed-free, buy a good-quality cylinder mower with a back roller. A cylinder mower cuts lower and more cleanly than a rotary mower, and close cutting helps to eradicate coarse grasses and weeds. But do not mow lower than 1.25cm/½in, or you may 'scalp' the grass.

No one lightly takes on the task of making a new lawn, but there are occasions when it is necessary: either because you wish for a lawn where lawn there was not; or because it is in such bad condition; or because it is so uneven that there is no way of avoiding scalping the grass as you mow.

Sowing lawn seed is cheaper than laying turf, but it is less convenient and takes longer to mature. Sowing seed should be done in late spring or early autumn; otherwise you run the risk of dry weather causing the grass seedlings to shrivel. Prepare the ground for both sowing or turfing (and when re-seeding small worn patches) as if you were preparing a firm tilth for a vegetable seedbed, but do not incorporate organic matter. Once sown or turfed, water well if dry, until the lawn is well established.

However careful you are, over the years bumps and hollows will inevitably appear in a lawn. To deal with these, cut a cross in the turf with a halfmoon edger, peel it back, and either remove or add topsoil, before returning the turf.

LEVELLING THE GROUND

When seeding a lawn or laying turf, the ground should be made as level as possible. After cultivation and grading, divide the area up into 2m/6ft 6in squares and drive level pegs, marked with a band of paint 80mm/3in from the top, into the ground. Align the pegs using a straight edge and spirit level. Tie garden string around the pegs at the level of the paint bands, dividing the area into squares. The level of the ground should then be brought up to the height of the strings.

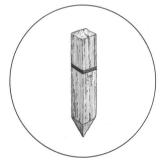

Level peg with painted line.

BROADCASTING SEED

When sowing grass seed, leave in place the taut strings used for levelling as area markers, or replace with bamboo canes laid on the ground. A few days before sowing, or turfing, apply a granular general fertilizer at 150-200g per square metre/4-6oz per square yard. When ready to sow, measure out the recommended amount of seed for a marked area, and working backwards, sow half 'broadcast', and the other half at right angles to it. Remove the strings, rake lightly, and water in dry weather. Lay down netting if birds or cats are a nuisance.

LAYING TURF

Lay turf in the autumn or in spring. Meadow turf is best for a hard-wearing lawn; otherwise buy specially sown turf. Lay turves in straight lines with alternate joints. Lay large turves at the edge of the lawn. Firm with the back of a rake, and keep well watered. To cut the edge of a curve, describe an arc with a peg or metal pin swung on a line from a central radius, peg down a hose along the scribed line, and cut along it with a half-moon edger. For straight edges, stretch a taut line along the full length, then cut along the edge of a plank.

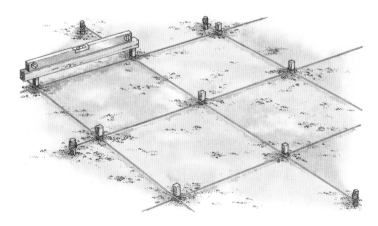

1 A well cared-for sward is not an everyday sight, but is the perfect accompaniment to cool and harmonious flower and foliage colours.
In most gardens, lawn is the major surface material, and grass grows well in a moist, temperate climate. You can suit the kind of turf to the situation: a tough ryegrass-based mixture will be ideal for play, while finer bents and fescues will be required to create the perfect 'bowling green' lawn.

2 Crocuses make good subjects for 'naturalizing' in grass, because their leaves die down within a few weeks of flowering, making an almost normal mowing regime possible. Although they multiply easily enough, they are small plants and should be planted in quantity. If you are going to do a job, do it well! So often bulbs are grown in isolated pockets; this is the real way to go about it.

LAWN CARE FOR PERFECTIONISTS

Spring

Sweep away wormcasts as they appear. Roll lawn if it has been lifted in winter. Mow when grass begins to grow, starting with blades high and lowering them progressively as the spring goes on. Collect mowings. Always cut the edges. Lightly scarify: scratch with a rake. Apply lawn sand to get rid of moss; rake up dead moss later, after it has turned black. If moss is not a problem, apply a combined lawn weedkiller and fertilizer suitable for use in spring. Repair broken lawn edges, and re-seed bare patches. Sow or turf new lawns.

Summer

Mow weekly or even twice-weekly, unless the soil is very dry. Trim the edges at the same time. Feed again with summer lawn fertilizer. Spot-treat weeds with lawn weedkiller, or dig out by hand. Water if there are prolonged dry periods and before the grass begins to go brown. If you go away on holiday, cut the lawn only lightly on your return, then cut progressively closer.

Autumn

Sow or turf new lawns. Repair existing ones. Mow less frequently. Rake up leaves. Scarify to rid lawn of 'thatch'. Spike the lawn, and brush in an autumn topdressing of sieved soil (or sharp sand) and compost (1kg per sq metre/2lb per sq yard). Apply high potash autumn lawn feed a few days later. Apply mosskiller and fungicide. Sweep off wormcasts.

Winter

Cease mowing. Continue to turf in open weather. Avoid walking on frosted grass. Service lawn tools.

Surfaces

EDGING

1

DS Any 'fluid' surface, whether concrete, tarmac or gravel, will need a firm edge to hold it in place while laying, and prevent it moving once it is down. This is particularly important with gravel. Small-module surfaces, such as bricks, setts or pavers, will also require some form of edging restraint to hold the bond together. This edging can become decorative in itself, provided it is kept simple and in keeping.

Various 'trims' can be used, ranging from lengths of pressure-treated timber

held in place with stakes, to brick, or granite setts, 'haunched', or set in concrete. The last are expensive but durable, and could link well with similar materials used elsewhere in the garden or near the house. The choice of even costlier trims includes thin strips of steel and, more traditionally, wrought-iron. This produces a beautifully crisp line, useful on curves or between lawn and hard surface. (Do not confuse this with the cheap 'roll-out' corrugated metal edging that looks frightful and should be avoided at all

costs.) It is important to remember that edging adjoining a lawn must be laid below the level of the lawn, both for safety, and ease of mowing.

Long edging units, such as precast concrete edgings approximately 900mm/36in long x 150mm/6in deep, or timber, generally look awkward if laid to conform to a continuous curve. A better solution is to use either a flexible edging, such as board or metal, paving slabs, or tightly laid small modules, such as brick or granite setts.

1 Edges to paths do not have to be hard. Indeed, an architectural treatment in this situation would have looked far too precise. The informality of the wider setting is wisely reflected in the delicious sprawl of white – the perfect choice of colour in this generally muted composition.

How charming is the effect of these massed *Viola cornuta* 'Alba' in a semi-shaded spot. They divert attention away from the indifferent concrete path, and their informal appearance accords well with the woodland setting. The only drawback is that they will not flower continuously all summer.

2 There are few neater edgings than a clipped box hedge, which can readily follow a flowing curve. The flattened cobbles in the earthy-coloured gravel suggests a pleasantly idiosyncratic approach to the garden.

The use of dwarf box hedging in such a neat setting is highly appropriate. A lax plant edging would be counter-productive here, especially if it had the effect of hiding the cobbles, and box can be clipped hard to retain its shape.

3 Architectural paths or other surfaces provide a perfect foil for sculptural planting. Here, the gravel is neatly laid to a slight camber, and contained by brick, laid in two different directions, to prevent the edges from becoming undermined with wear.

Here there is only a hint of informality in what is otherwise a restrained and ordered setting. The hosta leaves encroach on to the path, but in a controlled and tidy way.

2

3

UB Edging plays a useful role in a variety of important garden situations: where a hard surface like a path meets a lawn or flower bed, and where a border meets a lawn. These edgings can be invisible, but it is also possible to make a virtue of them, as, for example, when good quality stone paving is laid flat along the edge of a straight border. The purpose of edging is to facilitate mowing, to provide an important pathway, and to allow lax perennials to flop over without killing any grass beneath.

Edgings can be used either to define or blur the join between two surfaces, and plants offer as many opportunities to do this as hard landscape choices. For a formal edging to a border, a hedge of box, lavender or other clippable sub-shrub is an obvious choice. Santolina and *Hebe pinguifolia* 'Pagei' both make attractively sprawling mounds that still look neat and contained, while conversely plants with large leaves make good defining material: hostas and bergenias, for example.

Indifferent hard-surfaced paths and paving can be immeasurably improved by sensitive planting to soften the edges. Ground-hugging plants that creep and sprawl include violas, ajugas, or stachys. Where drainage is good, helianthemums or *Euphorbia myrsinites* work well. Moving away from ground level, it can be pleasant to brush against aromatic-leaved plants to release their scents into the air: rosemary, the sages, or catmint would be good choices. Ornamental grasses also make fine edging plants.

Some plants will tolerate being walked on occasionally, so could form an edging. Reasonably tough carpeters of this kind include the thymes, such as the forms of *Thymus serpyllum* and *T. doerfleri*, all of which release their delicious foliage scent when bruised. The non-flowering version of camomile, *Chamaemelum nobile* 'Treneague', can also be employed, but only where traffic is light. *Mentha requienii* is suitable for a moist soil in shade; it smells of peppermint when trodden on.

Surfaces

STEPS

DS Wherever you have a change of level in a garden, you will have to negotiate it in some way. In a formal situation, close to the house or between retaining walls, you will probably need steps. In an informal situation steps may also be an option, albeit handled in a different way, but smoothly graded banks and ramps will also play their part. The latter are a necessity when moving mowers or other heavy equipment up and down a slope. Keep them to a gentle gradient, and remember to make them wide enough to manipulate machinery and wheelbarrows with ease.

If you are considering building steps in the garden, make sure that you make them as wide and inviting as possible. Narrow steps are dangerous and visually uncomfortable.

Steps comprise a tread and a riser. An ideal step has treads that are 450mm/18in deep, and a riser of 150mm/6in. The overall width should preferably be greater than a minimum of 900mm/36in.

In steep gardens, the whole composition can be constructed from a series of steps filling the entire space. Such steps can turn into or be linked with level platforms or terraces, and designed as overlapping rectangles, hexagons, or circles.

The scope for steps in a sloping garden is enormous; they can be curved, to disappear with an air of mystery; doglegged to save space by turning through a right angle; straight and grand; or staggered and informal.

Just as there is an almost unlimited number of patterns, there is also a wealth of materials to choose from. Paving is, perhaps, the most obvious choice, but you could also choose timber, cast concrete, brick, railway sleepers, or log slices. What you choose will be dependent on where the steps are sited in relation to the overall garden design. Crisp rectangular slabs will form fine steps within an architectural terrace close to the house, while logs, pinned into a slope and softened by planting, will look perfect climbing a woodland bank, although they could become slippery in wet weather. Select materials of regular thickness to avoid ending up with uneven risers which could cause you to stumble or fall.

1

BRICK AND LOG STEPS

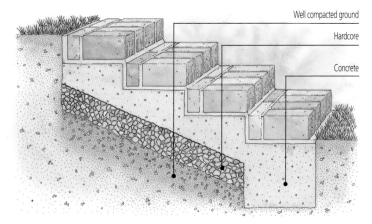

Well compacted ground

Hardcore

Concrete

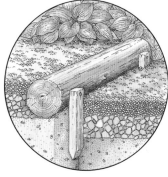

Brick steps provide a crisp, workmanlike flight. If a concrete foundation is first laid over a bed of compacted hardcore, the bricks can be neatly bedded in mortar on this base. This flight uses a combination of

headers and stretchers, with the joints rubbed back to emphasize each module. Choose brick that is frost-resistant, with a rough texture to minimize the risk of slipping in wet weather.

Hardwood logs from storm damage or tree surgery form easily constructed steps, pegged firmly into a slope. Treads can be surfaced with gravel or chipped bark, laid on compacted hardcore.

1 Some steps encourage a rapid climb; others a more leisurely ascent. These, with their shallow risers and ample treads, fall into the latter category. A flight like this allows you to take stock of your surroundings as you move along, involving you, at the same time, in the very fabric of the garden.

2 It can be fun to echo the line of a flight of steps with flanking hedges, clipped to a similar pattern.

Such a composition effectively reinforces the visual impact of the steps themselves. *Euphorbia characias* adds muted colour.

3 Concrete is a most versatile material. Here, precast slabs have been set in a staggered pattern to work their way gently up the slope which has, additionally, been softened by careful planting.

Plants are adept at colonizing small niches. Here they have been planted in pockets of soil in and around the risers of these informal steps.

4 Marble is vastly expensive, and when used properly gives a genuine feeling of theatricality. This is an imposing entrance to a garden, given emphasis by the flanking pots. The classical lines of these steps demand an appropriately formal approach as far as planting is concerned.

5 These really are fun! The drama is increased by the sharp contrast of colour, and the choice of material cleverly links with the old railings in the background. Such unusual steps need to be in sympathy with the rest of the garden, or they will look very odd.

6 Where steps are built to a curve you need to use materials that will conform. Here, logs form the risers, and treads are built with irregular stones.

Grass, one of the best colonizers of bare soil, has been allowed to stay, giving colour and softness to these steps.

7 This flight of steps has enormous rhythm, and although so architectural in design, associates well with the lush planting of ferns and ivies to either side. As a design element it also works well, disappearing from view, with an air of mystery.

3

4

5

6

7

PLANTING FEATURES

TREES

Planting Features

5 One of the finest of all small trees is *Acer griseum*, known as the paperbark maple for its characteristic peeling rusty bark. It has good orange-red autumn colour, and will grow in alkaline soil.

6 The attractive spiral stem of the large bay tree, *Laurus nobilis*, would have been achieved by the technique of twisting the stem around a round stake while the tree was still young and flexible.

1 These carefully pruned trees are the yellow-leaved form of the Indian bean tree, *Catalpa bignonioides* 'Aurea'. It is very late to come into leaf in spring.
The trees here are carefully positioned within geometric beds. The sundial marks the crossing of the brick path, and two little stone balls indicate where you should turn.

2 Here is a group of *Prunus* 'Ukon', one of the very best of all Japanese cherries for blossom. Greeny-white semi-double flowers are set off by bronze-coloured young leaves.
Blossom comes to perfection only for a short time each year, but what a bonus! Choose trees for their overall effect in the garden, and position them for maximum impact.

3 How we prize the sealing-wax red stems of the hardy *Cornus alba* in wintertime. The form usually grown is 'Sibirica', although 'Elegantissima', with white-edged leaves, is also good, as is 'Spaethii', with yellow-edged leaves. Cut the stems down almost to ground level at least every other spring, to get the best bark colour.

4 Forsythias are amenable and hardy, and give welcome, if somewhat obvious, colour to the garden in early spring. These standards will be trimmed to shape after flowering.
Forsythia is really a shrub, but is grown here like a miniature 'tree'. The plants have been trained on single stems to produce a head of flowers, and give balance to a formal garden.

5

6

UB With trees, you are planting for the future. Before you make a choice, check the eventual size of any tree you are considering – height and spread – after ten years. Choose, too, trees of varying growth rates to achieve variety. Reference books and catalogues will be of great value to you.

Remember that where you place a tree affects not only you, but also the future occupiers of your house, and even neighbours, for many years to come. This is no reason not to plant, but it is a powerful one for giving the matter careful thought.

If there is only room for one, consider growing a 'multipurpose' tree, which has more than one season of interest. *Acer griseum*, for example, is a small, slow-growing tree with a good shape, small green flowers, very good autumn colour, and a warm cinnamon-coloured peeling bark that glows attractively in late winter sunshine.

In small gardens, make use of fastigiate and columnar trees, and in very small gardens consider growing large shrubs as small trees, cutting all lower branches away. This is often done with *Buddleja alternifolia*, and would work with lilac. Some trees, such as salix and eucalyptus, can also be pruned to form shrubs with multiple stems. Trees that will withstand some drought and poor nutrition, such as birches, can even be grown in containers.

In country gardens it is often appropriate to plant native species – for example, in Britain, oak, birch, beech, holly, yew – to fit in with the landscape and encourage wildlife; however, much indigenous fauna adapts easily to exotic trees, so you will find that many of the vast range of beautiful foreign trees are just as suitable.

Avoid planting trees that look out of tune with their surroundings. For example, certain ornamental Prunus, such as 'Kanzan', whose stiff habit and strident flower colour make it difficult to combine harmoniously with other plants in the garden, have nevertheless become clichés, and are available everywhere. A better alternative would be the less commonly planted, but far lovelier, pink cherry, *Prunus sargentii*, which has the additional bonus of providing good autumn colour.

Trees can be used for different purposes. As a shelter belt to protect plants from strong winds, they should have 50 per cent porosity (that is to say, as much air space as leafage) in order effectively to break the wind without causing it to eddy, as a wall might. Suitable trees include airy conifers like *Pinus nigra, P. sylvestris* and *P. radiata*.

Denser trees would be appropriate if they were used to form a hedge: *Thuja plicata, Fagus sylvatica, Carpinus betulus, Crataegus persimilis* 'Prunifolia' and other thorn trees, or poplars and sycamores.

In coastal regions, plants with leathery leaves and a hardy disposition, such as *Ilex* x *altaclerensis* 'Hodginsii' and *Griselinia littoralis*, are suitable, as are tamarix, *Cupressus macrocarpa*, pines, willows, whitebeams, and crataegus.

The use of trees as focal points is obvious, although not all are suitable. Amongst the best for this purpose are *Carpinus betulus* 'Fastigiata', *Prunus* x *hillieri* 'Spire', and, for the larger garden, *Cedrus libani* and *C. atlantica* 'Glauca'.

Where height, speedy growth rate and density are required to screen or camouflage a building, or provide privacy, x *Cupressocyparis leylandii* is often chosen. More attractive are many of the poplars, although, if the screen is planted nearer to the viewer than to the object to be hidden, height becomes less important. A solid wall of foliage can often be dispensed with, if the eye is distracted by something striking elsewhere.

For gardens in frost pockets, especially where late spring frosts are commonplace, choose late-leafing trees such as *Catalpa bignonioides, Ailanthus altissima*, or native species which are attuned to your climate.

Trees in garden centres are usually sold as 'half-standards' or 'standards', although 'feathered maidens' and even 'whips' are also available, especially from specialist mail-order firms. 'Feathered maidens' have laterals growing all the

1

way up the stem, whereas 'half-standards' have up to 1.5m/5ft of clear stem, and 'standards', 1.8m/6ft. It is possible to get hold of 'extra-heavy standard' and 'semi-mature' trees from specialist suppliers, but these are very costly and can be slow to re-establish.

Many trees are 'grafted', that is, the wood of the species or form required is spliced on to a related species, which often controls its vigour and size. Pendulous trees are often grafted: the junction between 'stock' and 'scion' is usually clearly visible.

Not surprisingly, most trees need a greater depth of soil than any other type of plant. They will often survive in a shallow soil, but may not thrive and are less likely to be wind-firm. It is therefore important to work the soil deeply before planting, at least to 45cm/18in, and if you suspect a problem with compaction, then deeper still.

Do not plant a tree where one has been before if you can help it; if you must, replace the soil to a depth and width of 60-90cm/24-36in.

Plant trees in a place sheltered from fierce winds if you can, for they will establish themselves more quickly. Some, such as grafted trees (which have a tendency to snap at the graft union), trees with tall trunks and thick crowns, and eucalyptus and false acacias with brittle branches, are especially likely to be adversely affected by wind. Evergreen trees will benefit from windbreak material erected to the windward, at least for the first year, to stop the risk of desiccation and scorch.

It is always wise to plant trees at least as much as their eventual height away from walls or buildings. Some trees, such as poplars and willows, make substantial demands on available water, and the roots will grow a long way to find it, often damaging drains or foundations in the process. Plant these even further away from walls.

Where rabbits or deer are a problem, protect your 'whips' with spiral tree

1 Olive trees are not frost-hardy, but make very attractive trees with their crooked trunks. The spread is often as wide as the height.
These two trees provide a focal point in the garden, and frame the carefully positioned pot below.

2 Some remedial work may be needed here to pull the conifers back to an upright position for, to the purist, this kind of feature works best if the trees are vertical. Guy-ropes and pegs are the answer.
Clipped shapes like these form dominant features in the garden. Too many will make it restless.

3 Autumn colour comes in many shades and tints. Although it may disappoint in some years, it is an important consideration when deciding on trees and shrubs for the garden.

4 The thin trunks indicate that these are still young trees, yet they already achieve the intended effect. They will need frequent clipping to maintain it.
The formal geometric treatment of these trees helps to frame the garden at a high level, preventing the view from encroaching.

guards. Tree 'mats', or organic mulches, to keep down competing weeds are essential for quick establishment.

Check your trees regularly for damage or dieback, and remove or loosen tree ties if they start to bite into the bark. If you suspect any major problem, call in an accredited tree surgeon for advice. It is advisable to avoid carrying out any major tree surgery of your own, although small branches may be removed, preferably in sections, with a hand saw.

Ensure that heavy snow is not allowed to lie on the branches of evergreens, particularly conifers. The weight, especially if it has frozen, can break branches easily.

If you wish to remove an existing tree, be sure, especially if you live in a town, to check that there is no tree preservation order (TPO) relating to it and that it is not growing in a conservation area. If so, you must also inform and ask permission of the local authority before carrying out tree work. If a tree hangs

over from next door, you are legally entitled to remove those branches which overhang, but the wood belongs to the owner, so you must offer it to him.

Tree removal should be done by experts. Ensure that the tree stump is removed, either by winch or stump chipper if honey fungus is a problem in the garden, or killed with ammonium sulphamate poured into holes drilled in the wood. Alternatively, leave it as a support for climbing or trailing plants.

BORDERS

UB There are three classic types of border for any garden: shrub borders, herbaceous borders, and a mixture of the two. The reason for the popularity of shrub borders is easily explained. There is a huge range of tolerant, hardy, amenable shrubs of varying heights and habits available, and a border containing a mixture of evergreen and deciduous, flowering and leafing shrubs can be most attractive. It will also provide form and colour throughout the year – although it is often at its best in the spring and early summer.

Shrubs can act as a naturalistic under-storey to trees in so-called 'woodland' borders; and if they in turn are under-planted and edged with shade tolerant ground-cover plants, time-consuming weeding can be cut to a minimum. Most shrubs do not require much attention, except for pruning, and many do not need much even of that.

On the other hand, beds of shrubs can look remarkably dull, especially if the balance between glossy evergreen and deciduous is not properly struck. Everyone who knows the dreary repetitive planting found in car parks will know what I mean. However, even these would be improved if the soil was mulched so that the shrubs did not wilt in dry weather, and if bulbs and ground-cover were planted underneath.

When choosing shrubs, a balance needs to be made between those which offer a lot for a little of the year, and those which offer a little for a long time. Philadelphus and syringa (lilac) spring immediately to mind as examples of the first; they are wonderful in flower but have little to recommend them in habit or leaf form when flowering is over. An example of the second is *Elaeagnus pungens* 'Maculata', grown for its gold variegation throughout the year.

A solution to the problem of a dull deciduous shrub is to train a clematis through it, specifically chosen to flower at a different time from the shrub itself. Select a late-flowering hybrid which can

be cut hard back in late winter, when you will find that the long cut stems can just be easily pulled away without damaging the roots. Examples include any of the *Clematis* x *jackmanii* hybrids, the Viticellas such as *C.* 'Royal Velours' and *C.* 'Alba Luxurians', and *C. flammula*.

Some shrubs, however, earn their keep all year round, and examples of these should appear in every shrub border; I list these valuable plants in the Top 100 Garden Plants.

Shrub borders usually take up to five years to achieve a mature look. Attractive ground-cover plants are therefore especially useful before the shrubs have gained in stature. These ground-coverers may die out later under shrubs clothed to the ground, but that hardly matters. An alternative is to use a semi-permanent mulch, such as large bark chippings, which looks acceptable and, though expensive, lasts for several years in such undisturbed circumstances. It is in any case desirable to avoid annual digging round a shrub's roots, many of which are only just under the soil surface.

The great joy of the herbaceous border is its coherence and flexibility. Since the plant material itself is relatively homogeneous, it will enable you to plan sophisticated colour combinations; although some of the most successful schemes do in fact use a surprisingly restricted range of colours.

One glaring disadvantage to this kind of border is the fact that it looks bare for the dormant five months of the year. Even with so-called 'evergreen' perennials like bergenia, dianthus and stachys, it can look very brown and flat in the winter, and is thus only really suitable in a part of the garden which is not visible all year. What is more, although it is quicker to establish and to come to its peak than the shrub border, it also needs an overhaul at least every five years, for many herbaceous plants begin to falter if not frequently divided.

Although a true herbaceous border works very well visually, it is inclined to

1 This is a classic 'mixed' or 'shrubaceous' border, where shrubs, roses, perennials and even rock plants, grown together, will give an all-season effect. A double border such as this is especially valuable because, as demonstrated with the purple-leaved berberis, it gives an opportunity to provide visual echoes which help unify the scheme.

The contrast between hard and soft landscapes is often a telling one. Here, the path is of ample width, allowing both free passage and room for the plants to flop naturally over the edge.

1

2

2 Great care has been taken with the foliage planting here. The clipped shrub is *Cornus alba* 'Spaethii', and is surrounded by great foaming waves of *Alchemilla mollis*.

This careful orchestration of shape, size and foliage, to create an informal and contemporary shrub border, will hold interest for longer than flowers alone.

3

4

3 This is planting for bold effect, rather than for the individual beauty of the plants. The grasses work particularly well, allowing the sea to be glimpsed between the stems.
The strength of this composition lies in the great drifts of planting that echo the line of the ocean beyond. Trees help to stabilize the view from the house.

4 Here are the best-loved colours of early summer in a temperate garden. The effect is created mainly by using perennials (geraniums, *Stachys byzantina, Linum narbonense*)and alliums, with a few specimen evergreens added. The deciduous trees, such as the weeping willow, form an important background, giving a feeling of privacy.
A rural garden deserves a softly modelled planting scheme through which grass paths can be allowed to meander.

Planting Features

1 Short evergreen buttresses have been used in this border to compartmentalize the planting. This is an excellent idea if you wish to achieve different colour schemes in a restricted space. Buttresses are tools of the formal or semi-formal garden, for they are an architectural device, as can be deduced from their name. Here, they jut out into the lawn, which serves to emphasize their role.

2 The appeal of these borders lies less in the particular plants used, or the neatness of cultivation, than in the profusion. Weeds, except for the charming little self-seeded poppy and the useful foxglove, have little chance here. The border is essentially herbaceous, although there is a backbone of roses, and even of trees.

hit a 'gap' in flowering if the planting is designed to last for more than a few weeks. Then one can bend the purist rules in order to extend the season, and fill the spaces by planting annuals and bulbs in flowing drifts amongst the clumps of herbaceous plants.

Herbaceous borders do not have to be 'borders'; for many years 'island beds', cut out of lawns, have been popular. These are planted with the tallest peren-nials in the centre. However, unless done spaciously, and with conviction, these can look rather silly.

In most small gardens and many medium-sized ones, the mixed or 'shrubaceous' border may be a better option. This contains a variety of plant forms which complement each other: perhaps a tree or two, with shrubs, herbaceous and evergreen perennials, bulbs, and even annuals and biennials.

In theory, this is the most satisfactory kind of border of all: there is always something 'coming on', and large plants can provide a structural backcloth for more ephemeral ones. In practice, the more elements that you introduce, the harder it is to control. It can easily look a mess, and will always require firm plan-ning if it is to look its best.

Aesthetic difficulties with the mixed border can be minimized by planting perennials in substantial and convinc-ing drifts, and giving it a recurring shrub theme, so avoiding the impression of a mass of dotted and disparate plants. Large shrubs or even hedging can also be used to buttress or break up a long expanse of border and to segregate those sections whose colours clash.

Borders can be planted solely with bedding plants: half-hardy annuals in the early summer, replaced with biennials

are over. Taller annuals do exist, and should be searched out, together with 'everlastings', which can be cut and dried.

Popular, too, are seasonal borders, which contain several representatives of a particular genus (say, lupins, bearded irises, or peonies). These look best in concert, and only for a limited period, but provide enormous impact when in flower. Such a border can work well but should either be in part of the garden that is not seen throughout the year, or the plants must be strictly deadheaded in order not to attract the eye once they are over. Many people prefer to integrate individual specimens or small clumps in a general scheme, or simply to grow these plants in rows, for cutting, in the vegetable garden.

Borders composed entirely of herbs are sometimes suggested; in my opinion these 'go off' spectacularly after midsummer, so are only suitable for very small, discrete beds or, better still, as occupants of a more general border. Some herbs, such as angelica, bronze-leaved fennel and lovage, for example, make substantial contributions at the back of a herbaceous border.

All borders, except for annual ones, must be prepared for a long life, so incorporating organic material and removing all perennial weeds is essential, even if it means a delay of six months before planting. My advice is not given lightly; it is the fruit of bitter experience.

Do not plant in front of a wall or hedge without taking into account the consequences of substantial moisture (and in the case of a hedge, nutriment) loss. Never plant less than 45cm/18in from the hedge; planting too close undermines the perennials and can lead to defoliation or stunting of the hedge itself. Mulch in autumn or spring to keep down annual weeds and to minimize moisture loss by evaporation; this is important when so many plants are being grown in close proximity. Mulching also keeps tender plants insulated from cold spring and autumn weather.

Try, for your own sake, to choose plants which do not need extra support, although you must accept that some will need staking in late spring as their stalks start to elongate.

Do not plant too close to the edge of the border, if you do not want your grass killed by exuberant plant life. Follow the planting advice given in catalogues, so that there are no more gaps than is necessary between plants in the early years. Profusion is a virtue in itself.

Give a balanced liquid feed every month in the summer time. Feeding will encourage good growth, which can discourage fungal attack.

Herbaceous plants should be divided in early autumn or early to late spring. There are some plants, however, which do even better if left alone – peonies and Japanese anemones amongst them. Others – for example, old-fashioned pinks – are not by nature long-lived and have to be propagated every so often. In the case of herbaceous borders, the whole border will probably need overhauling every five years or so, in order to divide plants, eliminate perennial weeds and add organic material.

I cannot overestimate the value of deadheading, especially in the first year after planting. Often, as with perpetual roses, dianthus, and geraniums, this encourages a second flush of flowers; even if it does not, deadheading channels the plant's energy into leaf and root growth after flowering, which is especially valuable when you are bringing on young plants.

Tidy up borders, especially predominantly herbaceous ones, in the autumn. Many pests and diseases overwinter on old flower heads, in stalks and on leaves, so a good clear-out is helpful. At the same time you can protect tender plants, collect seed that you want to keep, and divide clumps. If you like to see the sere dead-heads of some perennials in winter, leave them when the rest is seen to. Leave all these tasks until spring, however, on heavy soils in cold areas.

and bulbs ('spring bedding') in mid-autumn. It can look stunning, but needs by far the most planning and work – both in the garden itself and in the greenhouse. Unless you sow biennial seed at the optimum moment the summer before, the spring bedding may start to flower just as it needs to be removed to make way for the summer bedding. Because many annuals are bred for uniformity of size and habit, bedding of this

kind can look fearfully regimented and unnatural. It is, however, many people's preferred option for narrow, sunny borders. On the positive side, annual and biennial borders offer a quick, easy, and interesting way of trying out new colour schemes, before deciding on more permanent plantings. Moreover, annuals often flower for many months in the summer, especially if deadheaded, at a time when many shrubs and perennials

Planting Features

RAISED BEDS

294 Plant Care

284 Alpines

UB Raised beds are especially suitable for Mediterranean and alpine plants, which thrive in extremely well-drained conditions. They provide a more attractive setting for these plants than the old-fashioned rock garden, and allow beautiful little carpeters and dwarf plants to be viewed at close hand. It is even possible to plan a miniature landscape.

In gardens on heavy soil, raised beds are recommended for anything which appreciates a reasonably light soil: many vegetables, herbs, climbers, and half-hardy evergreen perennials.

Best of all, in gardens with an alkaline soil, raised beds provide the opportunity to grow plants which will only tolerate acid conditions – and vice versa. Although this social engineering can look strange in informal country gardens, it does not look out of place in the typical town garden.

Raised beds offer more than one surface for growing. Many plants will grow happily in crevices in the side walls; indeed some, such as *Ramonda myconi* or *Lewisia cotyledon*, will only thrive where their crowns do not collect water.

If you wish to plant a raised bed predominantly with alpines, which are mainly spring and early summer flowers, you will need other plants to prolong the season: summer- and autumn-flowering bulbs, and dwarf perennials with attractive leaves such as ajuga, acaena, thymes, sedums and *Artemisia schmidtiana* 'Nana'. There are also a few winter- and early spring-flowering bulbs which die quite cleanly and are thus suitable: *Iris danfordiae*, *I. reticulata* and early dwarf narcissus, for example.

While in principle a raised bed, especially if it is to double up as somewhere to sit, should be about 450mm/18in high, what you plan to plant in it can determine its height. Alpines are, on the whole, shallow-rooters, so it is possible to get away with a bed 300mm/12in high. Larger plants need a greater depth, especially if the raised bed is laid on paving rather than soil.

1 Creeping yellow *Lysimachia nummularia* has been used to blur the distinction between raised bed and ground level. A vigorous waterside plant, it will nevertheless grow in dry soil.
Logs set vertically into the ground are ideal for making a curved or irregularly shaped bed. The tops can either be kept at the same height, or varied slightly to set up an interesting pattern.

2 Even the simplest raised bed can provide a suitable home for plants which like well drained soil, such as the stunning *Anemone* x *fulgens*.
If a raised bed adjoins a wall, the materials should be matched – as here.

3 This raised bed permits the use of some welcome soft green foliage.
Some compositions simply hit you between the eyes! The raised bed acts here as an extension of the building.

RAILWAY SLEEPERS

Railway sleepers can be laid either horizontally or, as here, vertically, to form raised beds or act as a low retaining wall. Choose sleepers that are clean and free from oil that can sweat in hot weather. Bed them in a 450mm/18in trench, either concreted in or surrounded by rammed soil. The tops can be left at different heights. If sleepers laid horizontally are more than three courses high, they will need to be drilled so that steel reinforcing rods can be inserted and driven well into the ground.

4 A wonderful position for plants, where easy access means that their needs can be almost individually catered for.
Railway sleepers are easy to use, and provide great physical and visual strength as a background for plants.

5 If lush growth is any guide, this raised bed suits its plants well. It also accentuates the trailing potential of these alpine campanulas.

6 In gardens on heavy soil, raised beds are invaluable for plants which like a reasonably light one. Good subjects for such a situation are herbs, many vegetables, half-hardy evergreen perennials, climbers and wall plants.
Beds of the same size and shape form a relatively static pattern here, flanking the lawn and helping to contain the space. On the far side, the long retaining wall also doubles as a raised bed.

3

4

5

6

Planting Features

Whatever the height, you will need 10cm/4in or so of small rubble, pebbles, or clay crocks to put in the bottom to prevent water lying and stagnating – unless the raised bed is built on poor rubbly soil, when this will not be necessary. Over that should be placed a sheet of permeable polyester or fibrous matting, or a layer of turves used grass-side down. Either will prevent the compost from clogging up the drainage layer.

Next you will need an appropriate growing medium: unless your raised bed is very small, you will need to buy in good topsoil as a basis for this. Try to find good quality loam, free of perennial weeds (even in winter, perennial weeds can be spotted in soil because of their persistent roots); ideally it should be sifted.

Alpines need more drainage than loam alone will allow. For them, mix one-third peat, one-third horticultural grit, and one-third loam, with a small dose of bonemeal. Alternatively, mix two-thirds proprietary soil-based compost (John Innes No 3, for preference) with one-third grit.

The same soil mixture will also suit Mediterranean plants, but omit the grit if you are going to grow a range of ordinary hardy plants in the raised bed.

If you are planning an acid-lover's bed, use half peat and half (preferably acid) loam. A more expensive but convenient option is to buy a proprietary ericaceous or even peat-based, multipurpose compost. Remember that acid-loving plants often like a shady and moist position.

Whatever the compost you use, it should be added gradually to the raised bed, and trodden down lightly before the next layer is added. Try to finish the preparation of any raised beds in advance of planting (spring to early summer, in the case of alpine plants), because there is bound to be some settlement of the soil. An alpine bed should have some flat rocks on the surface, partly buried, to provide a cool root run for the plants, and a topdressing of chippings to help to prevent neck rot.

How you plant depends on the type of plant, but it is best, when planting alpines, to remove the top chippings, spread out the roots of the plant before planting, firm the soil down, water the plant in, and replace the chippings.

All alpines will need watering until well established, and always in dry spells.

Alpine plants are quite happy under a carpet of snow, but extended periods of cold and wet may kill them, so vulnerable, hairy-leaved plants should be covered by a cloche in winter.

However careful you are, it is almost inevitable that weeds will appear. Try to keep on top of the weeding because

1 Raised beds offer the chance to grow acid-loving plants in alkaline gardens, and vice versa. It is important first to cover the bottom with small rubble, so that water can drain away easily. A generous mulch in spring is also a good idea. Railway sleepers used to form a raised bed or retaining wall should be laid with a staggered bond, like bricks in a wall, as shown here.

RAISED BEDS

weeds stand out in the tame neatness of a raised bed and, if allowed to get out of hand, can easily swamp the smaller plants. If weeds are taprooted, use a 'touch weeder' filled with systemic weedkiller to eliminate them, so that you do not disturb the *bona fide* plants by digging and delving.

A topdressing of grit is important for alpines, while a slow-release fertilizer works for everything else. Remember that many alpines live in nature on the stone dust of rock crevices and, if fed too richly, grow leafy, fleshy, prone to disease, and reluctant to flower.

Division of plants, deadheading, and removing dead leaves should be carried out as elsewhere in the garden. Plant labels, especially in alpine beds, can quickly turn a garden into a botanist's laboratory. If you have difficulty remembering names, either use a waterproof pen and bury the label by the plant so that you can find it if you really need to, or, better still, make a sketch plan of your bed after planting – though this requires self-discipline to keep it up-to-date.

DS To my mind, raised beds are an essential feature of every garden, and they can be situated in virtually any part of the composition.

Just what form and outline the bed takes will depend on its position within the overall design. Close to the house, in a terrace for example, it should be designed as part of the ground plan of the area, set perhaps within a modular pattern of brick courses and another material. A raised bed in a position such as this will have an inherently architectural feel, and if the terrace adjoins a wall or fence, a raised bed will allow plants to act as a bridge between the horizontal and vertical planes. Raised beds set in more distant parts of the garden can be far less formal, and this will be reflected in their shape and planting.

In design terms, there are all sorts of possibilities for combining raised beds with other features: barbecues, seating, water or play surfaces. A raised sandpit is particularly attractive to toddlers, and once children have got past the sandpit stage, it can easily be converted into a raised bed or pool.

Raised beds can be used to help frame a terrace or similar space, or to divide it visually from other parts of the garden. They will provide a feeling of intimacy and containment, and it may well be possible to link them with an arch leading through to the next 'room'.

If the beds are free-standing, they can also double as a useful occasional seat. In this case they should be built about 450mm/18in high, and be of double thickness 225mm/9in brick work, with a comfortable bull-nosed coping.

If the garden is on a slope, steps and raised beds can be designed as a series of interlocking platforms to link the changes in level, with planting tumbling over the retaining walls to soften the general outline.

The choice of material for beds will be partly dependent on the overall theme that you have already determined. If brick has been used in the house and part of the terrace, then brick raised beds may be a sensible choice. If stone is the overall background theme, walling for the beds may follow suit.

However, in any composition there is always room for contrast or change, and alternative materials can be attractive. Within a terrace built from brick and slabs, raised beds made from railway sleepers might well provide a welcome change of mood, bringing an altogether different character to the area. Ensure that you choose clean, oil-free units. Sleepers are an ideal self-build proposition and can be quickly stacked in a staggered bond to form a bed or low retaining wall, though if the walls are more than three courses high they will need reinforcement to tie them together. This can take the form of steel rods passed vertically through holes

drilled in the sleepers, and hammered at least 450mm/18in into the ground. Alternatively, the rods can be bedded into a concrete foundation. Shorter sections of sleeper can be set vertically into the ground, preferably concreted into position. The tops can be either cut flush in a horizontal line, or staggered slightly, which sets up an altogether different rhythm.

As far as construction is concerned, it is worth remembering that raised beds are in effect large plant pots. In other words, they need to be large enough to retain moisture comfortably, but also have adequate drainage to prevent waterlogging. An ideal size is about 1.8m/6ft square. If building the bed in stone or brickwork, you will need to construct suitable concrete foundations, twice the thickness of the walls. Drainage holes should be incorporated in the walls, just above the final ground level. Open joints left between every three bricks will normally be quite adequate for this.

BRICK RAISED BEDS

Raised beds are indispensable garden features. Build them of double brick, approximately 450mm/18in high, off sound concrete foundations, and leave some joints open at the bottom of the wall, just above ground level, for drainage. Lay hardcore or other free-draining material in the bottom of the bed, and top up with enough clean topsoil to allow for settling. The bull-nosed coping brick shown here will form a comfortable seat.

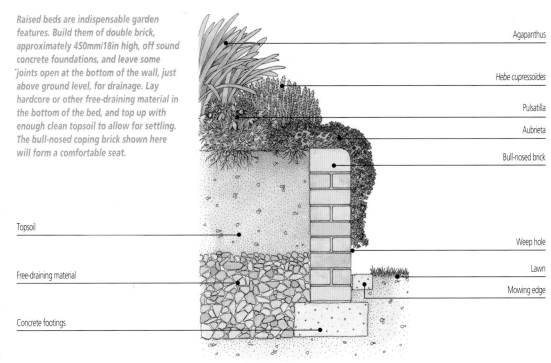

Agapanthus

Hebe cupressoides

Pulsatilla

Aubrieta

Bull-nosed brick

Topsoil

Weep hole

Lawn

Free-draining material

Mowing edge

Concrete footings

VEGETABLE AREAS

UB It is perfectly possible to make even the most utilitarian parts of the garden attractive in their own right, though a potager or ornamental kitchen garden will require rather more thought, and probably more labour, than a strictly practical one.

In an ordinary plot, vegetables are often left in the ground for some considerable time, even when they have become mildewed or pest-damaged. In the potager, some loss of productivity is therefore inevitable, since vegetables will be dug up when their decorative value has faded away.

Some vegetables are more stalwart than others. The winter-hardy leeks retain a handsome appearance throughout the winter; perpetual spinach takes a long time before it looks moth-eaten; and the coloured-leaved lettuces remain attractive for several weeks. However, brassicas, in particular, are prey to many pests, and vegetables such as summer spinach, summer lettuce, and Chinese vegetables run quickly to flower.

Care must be taken to remove needed vegetables neatly and inconspicuously, and frequent successional sowings are highly advisable.

1 No productive fruit garden need ever look strictly utilitarian, as fruit trees are so amenable to training over arches and into restricted shapes. Fruit trees in grass are reminiscent of the orchard, and are therefore a powerfully evocative image even for long established city dwellers. Here they provide the perfect combination of practical and ornamental planting.
There is no reason why fruit and vegetable production should not be decorative. Fruit tunnels are fun, and this one frames a highly attractive view along a well-laid old stone path to the white column and armillary sphere towards the end.

2 All cultivation of this triangular-shaped bed can be done from the path running along each side – an ideal situation. The apple tree has been beautifully and decoratively pruned.
Access paths are a practical necessity in a vegetable garden, and these old bricks echo the colour of the cabbages!

3 Old-fashioned 'forcing' pots are back in fashion, and modern replicas can be bought. The idea is to encourage precocious growth, and they are especially suitable for rhubarb. Note the lids, which are taken off as the plants grow.

4 The simple wigwams of bamboo canes, tied round with garden twine, make splendid supports for sweet peas, which climb by the use of tendrils. By high summer there will be little to see of the supports behind a mass of sweetly scented flowers. The flowering herbs in the middle and foreground are chives.
There are many ornamental ways of supporting sweet peas or runner beans. These wigwams have a sculptural quality in their own right.

VEGETABLE AREAS

To provide some kind of winter interest, use productive plants as short- or long-term structural elements: raspberries grown as 'exclamation marks' on single posts; Ballerina apple trees; restricted forms of fruit trees grown over arches or as see-through barriers; fruit trees and bushes used as standards, as boundaries, and to clothe walls.

Supplement these architectual elements with short-term summer plants: coloured cultivars of climbing French bean; ornamental squashes; and trailing marrows and vegetable spaghetti – all of which are equally suitable for climbing over arches or arbours.

Coloured-leaved herbs, such as the sages and thymes, are an invaluable addition to the potager garden. They are excellent as ground-cover, for edging beds, planted to spill over paving, or to grow in gravel.

Attractive cultivars of vegetables are legion: multicoloured cabbages; alpine strawberries with variegated leaves; striped tomatoes; coloured sweet peppers; even blue-leaved leeks. Many more can be found in seed catalogues.

A crab apple such as 'Golden Hornet' is primarily decorative but also has edible fruit; and even bronze-leaved fennel and the statuesque angelica and globe artichoke plants are valuable dual-purpose plants.

The way plants are arranged can also be attractive. Do not be afraid to mix flowers with your vegetables; not just marigolds and nasturtiums but scented flowers and foliage of all kinds. Just avoid poisonous plants; they are particularly unsuitable for this kind of planting.

The potager is in essence formal, but square or triangular blocks of plants look more attractive than long straight lines.

Traditional but ornamental objects can be used to enhance the appearance and atmosphere of this garden. Rhubarb and strawberry pots are widely available, but you may have to search further afield for bell and lantern cloches, and other *objets* from the heyday of kitchen gardening.

WILD FLOWER AREAS

UB In recent years, many people have become concerned about the wide-spread loss of natural habitats, resulting in the scarcity and even disappearance of wild flowers, and of the wildlife dependent on them. As a result, there has been an increased interest in growing wild flowers in gardens.

Never dig up or take seed from plants growing in the wild, but instead obtain seed from specialist mail-order seedsmen, or even garden centres – mixtures labelled 'hedgerow', 'meadow', 'cornfield', 'woodland' and 'pond-margin' are available. Many outlets also sell nursery-raised plants in pots, which are the easiest to establish.

You cannot, unfortunately, make a meadow by scattering the contents of a seed packet over an unmown lawn; wild flowers prefer poor soil, and the seedlings would soon be choked by strong-growing grass. You will have to clear the area first, preferably with a systemic weedkiller, before making a tilth and sowing a mixture of flowers and fine grasses in early autumn.

Better still, sow seed of 'meadow' perennials in trays, and plant out the sturdier plantlings into prepared ground, or even into cleared patches in the turf. Spring bulbs will thrive in the 'meadow', such as *Anemone nemorosa* and *Narcissus pseudonarcissus*, augmented, if you are not too much of a purist, by the striking presence of *Narcissus cyclamineus* and *Anemone blanda*. In the naturally artificial confines of the garden, closely related foreign or cultivated species can add to the impact of less eye-catching natives.

The meadow must not be cut until just after midsummer, when the main flowering is over and seed has been set. If the plants are well established, use a rotary mower with blades set very high; otherwise, use a scythe, shears, or a strimmer. Leave the mown grass to dry, like hay, so that the seed can drop down, then rake it off and add to the compost bin. Cut again in late autumn.

However you do it, be prepared to wait several seasons before wild flowers really take hold, and for the best results add to the planting each season.

'Cornfields' are made using only annuals such as corn cockle and field poppy. Sow on cleared poor soil in autumn; after the plants have flowered, let them drop their seed, cut off the debris, and fork over the soil to get another cornfield the next year.

A woodland can be an ideal place to plant wild flowers. Many common gardenworthy shrubs and trees will encourage wildlife: forms of hazel, crataegus and buddleja, coloured- and cut-leaved cultivars of the common elder, different forms of oak, birch, beech, holly and yew among them. Wildlife is undoubtedly encouraged by the presence of plants native to your area – sometimes all too well, for there are pests and diseases which require native hosts. Oaks and birches, for example, support enormous numbers of insect species which, while not all desirable, will certainly attract birds.

In wildlife gardening, take your cue from the way plants grow in the wild. Forget regimentation, straight lines, and the prissiness inherent in planting in clumps or drifts. In a wood, you are just as likely to find a single plant as a whole carpet of the same species. Use seed mixtures for carpets of flowers, or transplant self-seeded individual plants, such as primroses and bluebells, from other parts of the garden. And, as we are still, after all, dealing with a garden, do not hesitate to grow coloured primroses, white foxgloves and pink bluebells.

'Woodland' has to be managed, and the balance maintained for all its inhabitants. Native understorey plants will only do well in light dappled shade, so periodic thinning of trees and coppicing of hazels may be necessary.

Water gardening for wildlife with wild flowers can also be fun. Remember that informality is important, and take care that plants such as the yellow flag

1 This is halfway between a wild flower meadow and a wild perennial border. Note the lupins and the marvellous foxtail lilies, eremurus. Maintenance and grass-cutting need to be carefully timed to keep such an area at its best. It would not be wise to scythe the meadow off until

midsummer at the earliest. After that, the flowers should be left to drop their seed before raking off the hay.

The trend today is to create wild flower meadows to show off the beauty of these plants. Wild flowers make ideal underplanting in an orchard, but can be grown in smaller areas.

iris, *Iris pseudacorus*, do not become dominant. Fish, water insects, and even water fowl can be introduced, while frogs, toads and newts can be encouraged by providing shelter with marginal and bog plants, and easy access to and from the water.

However you grow native and other wild flowers, you will have to keep an eye out for weeds; not just the wolves in wolves' clothing, like thistles and nettles, but also charming plants that are simply too promiscuous, such as the lesser celandine and Welsh poppy. Systemic weedkiller, applied with care, and a watchful eye, are the best defences against a native uprising.

2 A mixture of grasses is allowed to flower and seed here, on either side of the mown path. It is likely that this area was deliberately ploughed and then sown with a grass mixture; if this were not the case there would probably be more field weeds. That is certainly the most successful method, rather than just letting the grass grow up.

The re-creation of a hayfield is a joy, especially when it is filled with grasses of different kinds. The beautiful example shown here makes a perfect rural foreground to the cottage. Random paths can quite simply be mown at will through such an area. They need no formal edging and their gently meandering routes create a delightfully relaxed feeling of space and movement.

2

3

3 *Fritillaria meleagris* was a once common sight in grazed water meadows, but, with the advent of chemical fertilizers which encourage grasses at the expense of these beautiful bulbs, there are only a handful of natural sites still in existence. Here, this lovely moisture-loving flower in its white and purple forms is associated with the equally beautiful hoop petticoat daffodil, *Narcissus bulbocodium*, which likes much the same conditions.

ROCK AND GRAVEL GARDENS

UB The badly sited artificial mounds of non-indigenous rock that once gloried in the name of 'rock garden' have mercifully in recent years given way to increasingly naturalistic treatments. Rocks, boulders, cobbles or stone chippings not only provide sheltered habitats for plants, but also add another dimension to the garden itself.

Rock gardens have traditionally catered for alpine plants, and for those loosely called 'rock plants' – either because they naturally grow in stony and hilly ground, or are dwarf and, coincidently, happy in those conditions. Dwarf plants which do not naturally thrive in free-draining conditions can be accommodated in pockets of a suitable soil mix. So a very wide range of plants can be grown in a rock garden.

If you have an existing rock garden, it is essential to remove all perennial weeds, such as couch grass, before planting it afresh. Here, systemic herbicides are almost compulsory; weed roots are often impossible to extract by hand.

Once the rock garden has been built, or an existing one cleaned of perennial weeds, you can decide where plants are to go, by putting the pots in different places to see how they look. Planting areas should be dug out and filled with 10cm/4in or so of small rubble, crocks or stones, and a compost consisting of one-third horticultural grit, one-third peat or peat alternative, and one-third good quality sifted loam, with a dash of bonemeal. Tamp the soil down as you add it, and topdress with a layer of chippings to help prevent collar rot.

Spring to early summer is the best time for planting alpine and 'rock' plants, as the plants are growing actively and will establish most quickly. Water the plants in their pots before knocking them out, to avoid tearing the roots, and if possible tease some of the roots apart. If plants are to be planted into a crevice, find the smallest viable plants in the nursery or, if growing them yourself, keep them in a very small pot before plant-

ing out. Then dig out a hole slightly larger than the root ball, and push the roots to the back of the crevice. Alternatively, gently squeeze the rootball into the shape of the crevice. If there is any room at all, fill in with good soil or compost, tamped in with a label or other narrow implement; though many alpines need little or no extra nourishment. If the hole is bigger than the plant, wedge the latter with pieces of stone. Keep the plant moist by spraying and, if possible, watering the area in the bed behind, until it is well established. With easy-to-germinate plants such as *Erinus alpinus*, mix some seed in a moist 'dough' of compost and push into the hole.

Once established, rock gardens usually need to be weeded by hand, using a 'touch weeder' filled with weedkiller where necessary. Otherwise, maintenance consists of watering in dry weather (a preference for well drained soil does not necessarily mean a tolerance of drought conditions, merely an

intolerance of waterlogging), and mulching with a fresh layer of grit after the first weeding of the year, in late winter or early spring, adding a light sprinkling of bonemeal at the same time.

In addition, the pockets of rock garden soil will need replacing every few years if vigorous plants are grown in them, or when replanting.

Winter protection of alpine plants means keeping the damp rather than the cold from them; this is particularly important with cushion plants, and those with hairy leaves. Do not, however, exclude all air, or they will rot off even more quickly. Cover with a panel of glass (or perspex if you have children or pets), resting on bricks and weighted down with a stone.

Horticulturally there is little difference between a scree bed and a gravel garden. The scree garden is, however, specifically made to provide an authentic-looking home for alpine plants. It should be on a slope and be covered in

stone chippings, with some larger rocks or stones along the sides and at the ends. It should be very free-draining. A gravel garden, on the other hand, can be constructed to give the impression of a dried-out river bed, with water-washed boulders in the middle, and informal planting augmented by small shrubs and dwarf prostrate conifers; or make no pretence at being true to life, when it will have a wider application. It can be on level ground, and is as suitable for Mediterranean drought-tolerant plants as for alpines.

The disadvantage of gravel gardening is that, once laid, it is difficult to change your mind; removing gravel is much harder than putting it down. It will also need 'topping up' from time to time. So think carefully before committing yourself, and perhaps begin with a small area to see how easy it is to manage.

Screes and gravel gardens have a number of points in common: both aim to achieve an informal look; in both,

CONSTRUCTING A ROCK GARDEN

Choose rock carefully, and if possible use a local stone: it will look better than one that is imported. Enlist help to move the stones, and start by placing one of the larger pieces at a slight angle or 'bedding plane', to simulate natural strata. Match other pieces to this angle, and leave pockets for scree and planting.

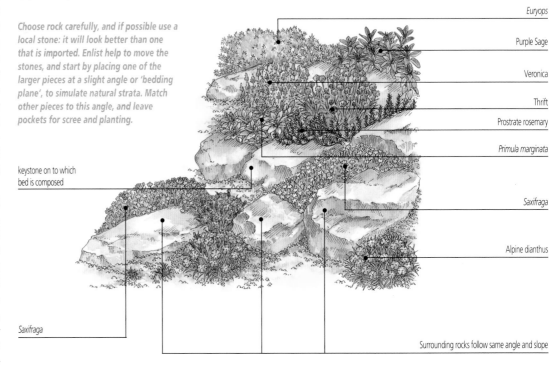

keystone on to which
bed is composed

Saxifraga

Euryops

Purple Sage

Veronica

Thrift

Prostrate rosemary

Primula marginata

Saxifraga

Alpine dianthus

Surrounding rocks follow same angle and slope

plants will self-seed, so there needs to be some element of control; both suit plants such as sempervivums which like a cool root run, and those such as artemisias which do not mind the heat generated by sun on stone; both suit alpines which like very free-draining conditions; and in both, bulbs such as small tulips, which need a summer baking, will thrive. In addition, many doubtfully hardy plants will survive the winter better in gravel than they would in conventional borders.

Both screes and gravel gardens require preparation before the topping goes down. This has to be done thoroughly because it is your only chance. You will first need to kill or remove all existing plant life. For scree, because good drainage is essential, lay 10-15cm/4-6in of broken stone, followed by a good layer of four parts stone chippings, one part leafmould, one part loam and one part sand. If you doubt that you have solved a perennial weed problem effectively, lay permeable polypropylene, fibrous matting, or heavy duty polythene, on top of the prepared soil. Puncture it for drainage, and cover with 30mm/1¼in of chippings.

The gravel garden does not require a special loam mix; only on heavy soils is it necessary to add coarse grit to the underlying soil. Otherwise, simply lay at least 5cm/2in of pea gravel (roughly 4-6mm/¼in diameter), using locally quarried gravel if possible, and roll it firm.

When planting in either gravel or scree, first scrape back the gravel, if necessary cut a hole in the polythene, and use a trowel or even a crowbar to make a planting hole, before replacing the grit. A sprinkling of slow release fertilizer for both scree and gravel gardens will help get plants away to a good start.

Maintenance of a gravel or scree bed is much the same as for rock gardens, although it involves less work. Watering is important in dry weather, as is a yearly grit mulch after weeding in late winter or early spring. Tidy up the area in the autumn if you want to avoid too much self-seeding; otherwise, do it in the early spring. The visual impact of a gravel bed will be enhanced if it is carefully raked over from time to time.

DS There can be few other garden features that are so much abused as a rock garden, though this also applies to cobbles, gravels, and boulders. Yet, if properly used, these natural materials can bring enormous character to the layout in any number of ways.

The 'currant-bun' rockery; a random selection of cobbles set in a sea of concrete; a sprinkling of chippings or gravel to simulate a scree; and boulders set in isolation at the edge of a border, are all too commonly seen. Rocks are natural materials, and the key to their

1 Choosing and using rock needs careful thought, and you should always try to use stone that is local to your area. This rock garden is not intended to emulate a natural outcrop, but has been built to contain a specialist collection of plants. It does this remarkably well, and it is a joy to see how mosses have colonized the surface and softened the outline. Mosses are also a good indicator of a low-pollution environment. A traditional rock garden, with additional bonsai embellishments. Alpine and other small perennial plants do well in the gritty, free-draining conditions that this affords, and its raised nature allows them to be viewed easily, and for trailers to trickle down the rock face. In such a loose arrangement, there is plenty of opportunity for plants to colonize the sides as well as the top. Care must be taken to prevent perennial weeds taking hold.

2 Stones often look at their best in a random arrangement that echoes nature. Summer jasmine, usually grown as a climber, has been encouraged to scramble over these rocks, to mingle with the spikes of terrestrial orchids.

1 A sempervivum in its element on top of these granite rocks. This is one of those alpines which appears to live on air, and can be persuaded to grow in clefts in rock. 'Houseleeks' make a decorative addition to the tops of drystone walls and even house tiles, hence the name.
Natural features are often the most successful in the garden, and the depression in this superb piece of stone forms the perfect miniature birdbath.

successful use lies in using them naturally – whether as independent elements, or together. A series of rock outcrops could, for example, be combined with a water-course, with boulders and cobbles in the stream, and areas of gravel used as a growing medium between the rocks.

Natural materials are individual in form and texture; unlike machine-made products, they will never be identical.

The way in which you move stone is important for safety. Small stones can be lifted by hand, preferably by two people; larger pieces can be slid over a lawn on boards, or dragged over in slings made from sheets of polythene. Don't put stones or rocks in wheelbarrows; they may tip over. Trolleys with pneumatic tyres can be used, or you may have to consider hiring a contractor.

Rock is perhaps the most misunder-stood and poorly used material in the garden. It has great beauty but must be used to simulate a natural setting to look at its best, and if you do not live in stone

country, you should consider carefully whether a rock garden is appropriate to your garden.

Just how you use or set rock in the garden is a sensitive business. If you look at the real landscape, you will see that in most upland areas the rock coming to the surface does so at a set angle to the horizontal; this is known as a 'bedding plane'. Also, like icebergs, only the tops of these outcrops are visible; the main bulk lies below ground. It is this enor-mous visual stability that you want to recreate in your own garden.

Ideally, a rock garden should be in sun for most of the day, facing south, and lying away from the shade of overhang-ing trees. A sloping garden is obviously ideal, and here rocks can be easily set to imitate natural outcrops. Flat gardens are more difficult, but changes of level can be achieved. The soil should be well drained.

When you are ordering rock, choose a type that is as local to you as possible; it will look more comfortable and will

probably cost a good deal less than rock that has been hauled halfway across the country. If possible, select the individual pieces yourself. You could go to a local quarry, where the rock will also be cheaper than in the garden centre. As a general rule, a few large rocks will pro-duce a far better result than a mass of smaller ones. Rock is usually sold by the ton, and depending on its density you will get less or more for your money. Granite is a heavy rock; sandstone is far lighter. Either way, a ton of rock is not very much, and any well-proportioned rock garden or outcrop will almost cer-tainly use at least ten tons.

It is impossible to plan a rock garden accurately at the design stage, as the rock itself will determine the exact outline and final positioning. But the overall outline of the feature should, like the landscape, have a gently ascending 'dip' slope, and a positively formed 'scarp'; it should not give the appearance of an ill-conceived lump in the middle of the garden.

Start by digging out the top 150mm/6in of topsoil and mixing it with grit in a ratio of five parts to one. Replace it on the rock garden site, and use this top layer to infill around the rocks and bed them in. When setting the rock, start with one of the larger good pieces, and bed this well into the ground at a slight angle, to simulate a natural bed-ding plane. This will be the 'key stone' which sets the character of the entire composition. Then start to set other pieces around it, respecting the bedding plane and extending slowly out to the roughly marked-out limits of the finished feature. Sometimes a piece of rock will simply look wrong. Put it to one side; you will always find a place for it later on.

In order to make the rock garden look more natural, use one or two large pieces of rock as 'outliers', away from the main outcrop. Make sure these are set at the same bedding plane. Take your time when setting rock, work care-fully, and enlist help if necessary.

ROCK AND GRAVEL GARDENS

4 A well drained gravel garden, full of Mediterranean-type plants such as euphorbias, verbascums, alliums and the bright carmine *Gladiolus communis* ssp. *byzantinus* in the foreground. It is a pleasure to see such free flowering, although gravel gardens tend to lose their appeal after midsummer, when these plants quickly go to seed in the heat. Self-seeders can quickly take over a path entirely! Gravel paths are not only cheap but provide a good foil for planting that can be allowed to flop over the edge or grow through the surface. Construction is all important and should be thoroughly carried out if the surface is not to be undermined by water.

3

4

2 A feature somewhere between a scree and a gravel garden. It is plain from the vegetation (cordyline, sempervivum, and grey-leaved sub-shrubs) that the conditions are very free draining, while the gravel reflects the heat. These loose water-worn cobbles form a dry stream bed, into which a selection of drought-tolerant plants has been introduced. Such a background acts as a ground-cover and mulch, keeping maintenance to a minimum. It also shows off foliage well.

3 The rocks may belie it, but this is a damp acidic garden, for otherwise these Japanese primulas would not look so rudely healthy. There are many alpine plants which do well in these conditions, most notably *Rhododendron impeditum*, cassiopes and polygalas. These huge pieces of stone are bedded deep in the ground so that only the tops are visible. One or two large rocks will provide great visual stability, and are always more effective than several smaller ones.

If you don't want to go to the lengths of constructing a full-scale rock garden, 'boulders' can be used singly, in limited numbers, or as larger groupings. In outline, boulders may be angular, which normally means that they are freshly quarried, or smooth and water-washed, like those on beaches or in river beds.

Angular pieces of stone bring a rugged feel to a composition. They can be difficult to use, and need careful siting – perhaps as a definite point of emphasis within an area of chippings or gravel. This will, however, provide an excellent opportunity to build up an association of plants with which to temper the outline.

Water-washed boulders are an almost indispensable element in the garden designer's repertoire, and can be used in numerous situations, from larger stones in a Japanese dry-stream bed, to a carefully sited group of smaller ones set at the corner of a path to prevent feet from straying. Once again, the stones need siting carefully by eye. Start with a pile roughly where you need them, and then arrange them, and rearrange them, until they look visually comfortable.

We have already seen that cobbles – smooth, water-washed stones – can be used for paving and paths. When used loose, the effect is altogether less formal, and cobbles can sometimes be used for quite large areas of ground-cover, with planting growing through them.

The fascinating outlines and subtle colours of washed flints can be used in the same way to make a particularly good floor beneath coniferous trees such as Scots pine (*Pinus sylvestris*). If your garden is blessed with these marvellous trees, use flints in great curving drifts and sweeps beneath them.

Cobbles, or flints, can, like boulders, be used for dry-stream beds in the Japanese style; they can also be used as a beach around an informal pool, allowing birds and other small animals to drink easily, and providing a practical mask for a butyl or plastic pool liner. It will be necessary to feather them out around the margins of the pool.

These materials have great potential in the garden, quite apart from their use for drives, paths and general surfacing. Stone chippings can be used in a rock garden to form drifts of scree to run down between larger rocks, making an excellent growing medium for many attractive alpine plants.

There is a trend, and a good one, to use gravel as ground-cover. In an informal garden, areas of gravel can be used for paths as well as for plants to grow and self-seed through. In a more formal situation, the pattern of paths could be more geometric, with plants still acting as a foil. Knot or parterre gardens were traditionally formed by low clipped hedges of box, and were invariably filled with coloured gravels. This resulted in fascinating and far less fussy patterns than those achieved by the infilling of planting that is frequently used today.

Planting Features

TOPIARY

UB Topiary, or the art of training and pruning evergreens to ornamental shapes, can add an element of fun to gardens. It can be as simple as a battle-mented hedge, or as imaginative as a wild, fantastic shape. Topiary is not always appropriate, but in both large formal gardens and in cottage gardens it has an assured place, and is worth considering in any garden, provided that there is space to view it properly, and that you have the time and, most importantly, the will to nurture it.

Most hedging plants which respond to severe pruning can be used for topiary, although yew, box or *Lonicera nitida*, and their golden forms, are most commonly used. These three evergreens all have small close-knit leaves and branches, which makes for dense, well-covered topiary. Yew in particular will regenerate easily from old wood, so if you tire of the shape, or a pheasant begins to look like a saucepan, you can simply start again. For the very small garden, or timid or impatient gardener, ivies planted in pots can be easily trained over small wire structures in the shapes of birds, balls, or hearts.

It is often possible to adapt an existing hedge or bush for topiary; this is quicker than starting from scratch, for a hedge can become a topiary specimen in about four years, whereas it may take a decade to achieve a complex shape from planting. You have an advantage if you are already a practised hedge-clipper, but do not attempt anything too ambitious initially.

If you are starting from scratch, take care to choose your site carefully: you will need a sunny spot, well prepared soil, and easy access to all sides of the plant. Most importantly of all, you will need to find a position where the topiary shape can be seen easily.

Plan the design beforehand, and try to keep the shape simple to begin with; it may be developed into a more complex one in time. Good individual shapes to start with are pyramids and cones;

these look well in any formal situation, and being narrower at the top, allow rain and light to penetrate to the base of the plant. To create birds and animals, you will need either to make or buy ready-shaped wire structures to act as your guide.

Once you have tied in and trained the first leaders of your plant round this wire shape, you can begin to trim the laterals lightly to encourage thickening, but remember to cut off a little at a time to avoid a disaster, which will be slow to grow out. Ivies simply need tying in, although any long shoots should be clipped back.

Once the shape is established, be punctilious about trimming regularly each year. The purists always use hand shears rather than a hedgetrimmer. And, as with all hedge-clipping, take special care when standing on ladders. Finally, feed, water and mulch topiary as you would for any hedge.

TRIMMING A CONE

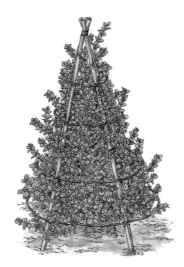

Trimming a topiary cone is made simpler by using a 'wigwam' of canes, with circles of thin wire attached to it at regular intervals. All topiary shapes are best clipped with a pair of hand shears; mechanical hedgetrimmers can too easily run away with you, and damage your carefully constructed shape.

1

2

3

4

5

1 This massive, sinuously shaped topiary specimen is dignified and simple, but unusual. Combined with the surrounding hedges, it echoes the curves and straight lines of the adjoining building.
The rhythm and power of this composition is wonderful, the clipped spiral leading the eye to the pantiled roof.

2 There is humour in these simply cut bird shapes, standing, or rather sitting, sentinel beside an inviting path. The use of the golden form of yew, to contrast with the darker yew behind, is a success. It's the colour break that really does the work here, underlining the point that bright tones draw the eye.

3 Close-clipped evergreens can look particularly good in winter, when snow and frost outline the shapes dramatically and there are no strong flower colours around to distract. These playful but almost sinister shapes are shown off brilliantly by the encircling beech hedge, whose retained leaves make a tawny backdrop.

4 Which came first: the topiary ball or the stone ball set at the end of the wall? This is garden humour at its best.

5 This device is charmingly light-hearted. It could be used for sitting in dry weather. Armchair gardening has always appealed to me. What power there is here.

WATER
PONDS AND POOLS

1

2

DS Water is one of the most important but also one of the most ill-used elements in a garden. To be really effective it must be subtly, not ostentatiously handled: the sound of a bubble jet or a small fall on a hot summer's day can be far more evocative than the torrent of a grandiose fountain surrounded by spouting cherubs.

Water inspires, and for that very reason pools tend to be built on the spur of the moment and with little regard to the rest of the garden. But like all other garden elements they must, if they are to work for the garden as a whole, be designed as an integral part of the overall plan. An ill thought-out design will be uncomfortable to live with.

As we have seen, areas near the house need a more architectural treatment; here you might include a pool in the form of simple rectangle, raised or at ground level, or a series of interlocking shapes that respect the ground plan. Further away from the house, water, like the garden pattern itself, can afford to become softer and less geometric in outline. In the same way, if you want moving water on the terrace or beside steps leading down to the lawn, a series of split-level pools that are part of the surrounding hard landscape will probably work best. In an informal part of the garden you might use in combination a bold outcrop of rock, an informal stream and in a free-form shape.

Think too about water reflecting the sky or a planted area; consider how a central pool would look in a circular drive or as a specific focal point in a formal garden; decide whether an old millstone surrounded by cobbles and with water flowing over the surface would be more appropriate. Whatever the form the feature takes it will be a major visual attraction, so think hard and long before you build it.

As a general rule any pool needs to be sited in a relatively open position, away from shade and a canopy of overhanging trees. You also need to decide on the overall size of your pool: a large sheet of water would be impractical in a tiny courtyard, just as a small pond would be lost in a large country garden. However, the ecology of the pool is important, and it is difficult for a balanced regime of plants and fish to become established in a pool of water less than 2sq m/7sq ft in size. Millstone and boulder features that are not stocked with plants or fish are of course a different matter; such features can be much smaller, and can also be usefully and effectively placed in relatively shady places.

The profile of the pool is crucial, but it does not need to be of vast depth to support life. For all but the largest water lilies, a maximum depth of about 750mm/30in is normally adequate. For aquatics which simply like getting their roots wet, a 'marginal shelf' is invaluable.

225

3

4

If the shelf is in two or more sections this will allow gaps or bays which are ideal spaces for fish to breed in.

The introduction of pool liners has completely revolutionized the construction of ponds today. These liners are usually made from plastic or rubber laminates such as butyl, and are extremely tough and durable. They are easy to lay and you can even get liners 'welded' to fit a rectangular-shaped pool so that creasing in the corners is virtually eliminated. Liners can also be used to form streams and watercourses, and can be pierced to form bog gardens adjoining, or close to the main pool.

Rigid preformed fibreglass pools are also available but these are limited in size

and shape and may not necessarily be compatible with your garden design.

To calculate the size of liner that you will need, add twice the maximum depth of the pool to both the maximum width and length; allow for a 'lip' and you will have ample material. Sheets are normally only available as rectangles so the more complicated your design, the more offcuts and wastage you will incur. Colour is something else to consider: avoid sky blue and also the embarrassingly fake liners that are printed to imitate cobbles and shingle! Black is by far the best as it does not detract from the shape or the planting of the pool, and it sets up surface reflections that help to disguise the actual depth of water.

1 The geometry of this water garden is superb, and the hard landscape features are handled with supreme confidence. Beautifully laid brushed aggregate panels contrast perfectly with the smoothness of the water-worn boulders. Smaller cobbles continue the theme to break the line of the path.

Skilful but restrained use has been made of vertical marginal plants in this strongly horizontal setting.

2 The low, long line of this building sits comfortably against the forest backdrop, and is echoed by the sweeping lawn and large pool. The sound of the generous water slides will be heard from the verandah.

In this expansive landscape, bold foliage plants enliven the banks of the pool, and are reflected in the water.

3 This kind of feature can be used in even the smallest town garden, and is easy to construct. Water is recirculated by a submersible pump set at the bottom of the stone sink, and the cobbles can be supported by a mesh.

This is water at its most understated and domestic, so the planting need take little account of it. The climber growing here is *Humulus lupulus* 'Aureus'.

4 One of the greatest joys of using water lies in the reflections it sets up. Foliage and sky are reflected here, and the globes are probably set on spikes to hold them in place. They look complete: a great visual trick!

Before you embark on the construction of the pool, bear in mind that its edge or coping needs to be perfectly horizontal. If the pool is to be set into a slope, the lower side will have to be retained, either with an informally planted bank or by a wall.

To construct an irregularly shaped pool, first mark out the overall area of both pool and surrounding coping. Next mark out the curves using a line swung from a cane or metal pin like a pair of compasses and making sure that one curve runs smoothly into the next. Turf

1

2

CONSTRUCTING LINER POOLS

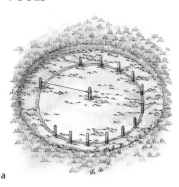
a

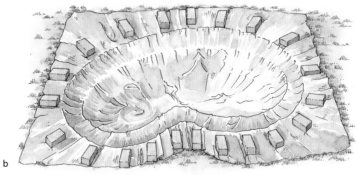
b

a *Mark out the outline of a round pool by swinging a line from a central stake. Strip the turf off to this outer line, and peg out a second circle 225mm/9in inside the perimeter to mark where the coping will go. Excavate the soil within the second circle to a depth of 225mm/9in, which will be the level of the marginal shelf, checking that the sides are at an angle of 20 degrees. Mark off the 300mm/12in width of the shelves, and dig the rest of the pool to a depth of 450mm/18in and at the same angle. Firm up the excavated surfaces as much as possible, removing any sharp stones as you go.*

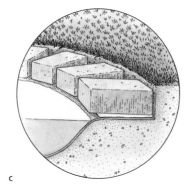
c

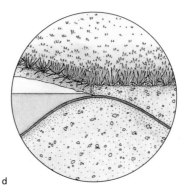
d

b *Once the shape is dug out, trowel damp sand on to the face of the excavation, working up from the bottom. Position the butyl liner loosely over the hole, and hold in place with bricks or coping stones. Run water in with a hose, and the liner will slowly mould itself to the finished shape.*

c *Slit any wrinkles in the liner under the line of the coping, so that it lies flat, and place the coping in position, with an overhang of about 50mm/2in. Mortar it in, turning the liner up behind it, and trimming off any excess. If you intend to have a submersible pump in your pond, lay a piece of plastic pipe under the coping to take the cable, and also an overflow pipe.*

d *Where a natural edge to the pond is required, bring the liner to its highest point and leave an additional 300mm/12in before trimming it off. Roll back the turf, and bury the liner edge. A grass edge will need careful trimming to prevent growth extending into the water.*

3

should be carefully lifted and stacked for future use elsewhere in the garden.

The sides of the pool should be at an angle of 20 degrees. Check this by making a simple plywood template.

Next mark out the perimeter of the pool itself, and excavate all the soil within this to a depth of 225mm/9in, which will be the depth of the marginal shelves. Stack the topsoil for use in a raised bed or as a mix for pots and containers. The shelves should be 300mm/12in wide, so mark the width of these (leaving gaps so that the shelf is not continuous) and

excavate the rest of the pool, checking the 20 degree slope of the sides with your template as you go.

Although liners are tough they are not indestructible; the water itself exerts considerable pressure, and liners can easily be pierced by sharp stones. Any projections should therefore be removed and a layer of damp sand trowelled on to the sides and bottom with a steel float. Place the liner gently and loosely over the excavation and hold it roughly in place with coping stones. Do not try to force it into shape. Then run water into the pool and

the liner will slowly mould itself to the exact shape that you have dug. Once the water level has nearly reached the top, any excess liner can be trimmed off to leave a flap 300mm/12in wide all the way round. Wrinkles in this flap can be slit to allow the liner to lie flat.

Moulded fibreglass pools may not provide the exact shape or size you want but are a good deal easier to install than liners. Mark out the perimeter shape of the pool, then excavate the hole. Bed the pool on sand. Make sure the edges are level by using a straight edge and spirit level.

1 Circular lily pads set up a dramatic pattern, echoed here by the curved edge behind.

2 The charming arum lily, *Zantedeschia aethiopica*, in a formal pool. It flowers in summer and is evergreen in warm climates.

3 The ways in which you can lead the eye to a focal point are numerous. Here, a long pool is crossed by simple stone bridges, with bubble jets just disturbing the water's surface.

4 A succession of formal pools are separated by old brick paths with shallow steps. The water finds its way from pool to pool by a series of rills and falls.

BOG GARDENS

A carefully sited bog garden will substantially improve the look of water-side plantings around pond and pool edges, and will also extend the range of beautiful plants that can be grown. Remember only that these plants may thrive and seed excessively, so the same watchful eye must be kept on them as on the marginal plants.

Concrete and preformed ponds, being impermeable to water and usually sited in a sunny position, generally have very dry soil to the side of them, making them unsuitable for waterside plantings. Ponds made with flexible liners, and natural streams, both lend themselves to the creation of an adjoining area specifically intended to hold moist soil. This is done by creating a large but reasonably shallow depression, 30cm/12in deep, to one side of the pond. Line this depression with thick-gauge polythene, which has had a number of holes punched in it. The reason for puncturing the liner is to prevent water lying permanently in the bog area. Once put in place, these drainage holes should be covered by gravel so that the soil which comes next does not clog them. When adding the soil, bank it up on the side next to the pond, to create a shallow lip which will prevent water from seeping into the bog garden from the pool. The areas will then appear to be connected but will, in fact, be separate.

It is of course possible to create a quite separate bog garden, close to a pre-formed pond or in any other appropriate spot in the same way. Punctures in the liner will ensure that rainwater seeps slowly away. If acid-loving plants are to be grown, the soil of a bog garden should have a low pH and be enriched with fibrous organic material.

Natural streams, with sides which regularly flood, also provide perfect habitats for bog plants. If you are lucky enough to have a stream trickling through your garden, do not miss the opportunity to grow such lovely plants as the marsh marigold (*Caltha palustris*) beside it.

1 What a pretty riverbank planting, flanking a simple stream. These are not, strictly speaking, bog plants, but low-growing perennials and rock plants which look perfectly in keeping.

2 Some of the same colours, but this time provided by true bog plants, such as Japanese 'candelabra' primulas and irises in flower in late spring and early summer. These plants are naturally luxuriant if happy; indeed, they can sometimes get out of hand and may need to be controlled.

MAKING A BOG GARDEN

Making a bog garden at the side of a pool can be achieved by creating a large, shallow depression about 30cm/12in deep, and lining it with punctured polythene sheeting. Pond and bog garden must remain quite separate, so excavated soil should be banked up to form a lip between the depression and the pond itself. There are many handsome and colourful plants that will thrive in these conditions: Japanese irises, Asiatic primulas, many ferns, such as osmunda and onoclea, as well as the huge-leaved Gunnera manicata and Rheum palmatum.

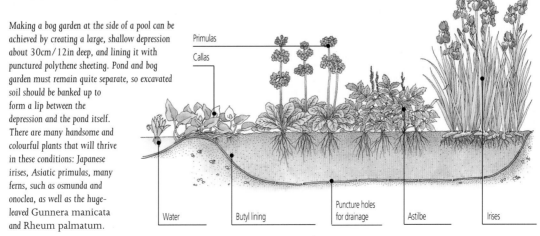

Primulas

Callas

Water

Butyl lining

Puncture holes for drainage

Astilbe

Irises

WATER FEATURES

218 Rock and Gravel Gardens

76 Focal Points

DS Moving water can be achieved in a flat garden by allowing water in a raised pool to fall into another set at ground level, or by using the 'cut and fill' technique to create a raised area from the excavated soil of a depression beside it. A sloping garden provides unlimited possibilities: streams, cascades, water steps, waterfalls are all within your grasp. However, the construction of artificial levels must be immaculately planned and carried out if the whole feature is not to look contrived; any hint of a liner or preformed watercourse will immediately spoil the effect.

Of course those blessed with a spring or a natural stream are the luckiest of all. Here water can be dammed into pools, and waterside planting that needs a moist environment will flourish without resorting to the complicated construction of a bog garden. However, the power and reliability of domestic water pumps has improved enormously in recent years, and relatively small submersibles can now lift and pump large volumes of water with ease.

There are situations where it may not be possible or desirable to have an area of open water, particularly if there are young children. One solution is to build a feature where water is pumped up from a sump through a drilled rock or piece of stone, and then returned to the sump. The classic example is a millstone fountain, which can now be bought in kit form. It is easy to install and can often be fitted into a redundant raised bed or sandpit, though it will work equally well at ground level surrounded by cobbles and planting, or on a suitably reinforced roof garden.

You can of course design something along these lines yourself, and a feature made from a fine piece of rock from a local quarry could be dramatic and will certainly be unique. You could even position spray jets so that they create a fine mist over a sculpture, setting up rainbows and conferring a cooling influence to the entire area.

1

2

3

1 The Japanese influence in this garden is strong, with water playing an important role in a natural stream. Rock and planting have both been used well, the mossy banks providing the perfect foil to the large rough-hewn boulders.

The predominantly green planting and mossy sward which flanks the stream provide a coolly harmonious and tranquil composition.

2 An architectural composition needs architectural planting, and the balance here is just right. The joints between the bricks of the slides have been raked out so that they act as miniature weirs.

The planting is suitably sombre to match this rather hard-edged, if cleverly designed, water feature: bamboos, *Viburnum davidii*, *Acer palmatum* var. *dissectum* and a hebe.

3 Swimming pools often lack sensitive handling, but here the architectural composition and landscape work perfectly together. The geometry of the water slide is in perfect harmony with the simply formed steps, the carefully placed pot, and the surrounding planting.

The shadows cast by the palm and the trailing foliage of other plants enliven the severe verticality of the walls.

4 Millstone fountains are easy to construct, and provide a useful focal point. Since there is no open area of water, they are perfectly safe for children.

The planting here is a happy mixture of foliage and flower, with herbs strongly represented. Grasses often complement cobbles and water well.

5 This cobbled water feature makes an interesting pattern, with the bubble jet just breaking the surface, and providing both movement and sound.

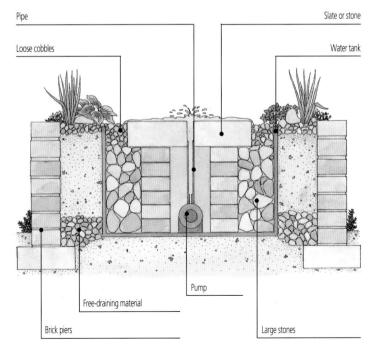

A new type of feature which is stunningly beautiful, and correspondingly expensive, consists of a perfectly machined and polished sphere of granite that fits into an equally perfectly formed granite cup. The diameter of the sphere can be anything from 300mm/12in to 2m/7ft (600mm/2ft is ideal) and it is suspended on low-pressure water jets that are pumped through the cup. This means that the ball rotates at the slightest touch and glistens as it slides over the water. Such a feature is a powerful eyecatcher and needs careful siting, probably as a key focal point on a superbly designed terrace. There are not many features or ideas that I covet; this is certainly one of them. The only drawback is that they are expensive!

If you are going to use a submersible pump in a pool, you will need access for the cable. Cut a piece of plastic pipe of a large enough diameter to accept a cable and long enough to pass comfortably under the coping. Lay it in place then bed the coping on mortar to overhang the water by about 50mm/2in all the way round, when it will cast an attractive shadow. For moulded fibreglass pools, lay a piece of plastic pipe if you want to introduce a pump, and bed the coping on mortar.

Although the construction of a feature like this is relatively straightforward, you would be well advised to hand over large projects and ones that include streams and rock to an experienced landscape contractor or water garden specialist. They will have both the expertise and the equipment to do the job, and you will probably save on time and wasted materials.

Water sculpture provides endless design possibilities, from the sophisticated to the amusing. Here too, a good garden designer or landscape architect should be able either to create a purpose-built piece themselves, or to recommend a sculptor. Your chosen sculpture may be constructed in a wide variety of materials, which might include stone, steel or glass. The design could be unashamedly modern, to reinforce the link with an equally contemporary setting, or something more traditional, such as a figure, or a fish spouting water.

MAKING A WATER FEATURE

A large water tank is either partially or wholly submerged into the ground, or, as here, placed inside a raised bed. The millstone, or slate slab with a hole pierced in the centre, is supported on two brick piers, and a submersible pump placed below. Boulders and cobbles fill the gap, and water is run in.

Pipe — Slate or stone — Loose cobbles — Water tank — Free-draining material — Pump — Brick piers — Large stones

WATER, POND AND BOG PLANTS

UB Water, like fire, is both discreet servant and overbearing master. Water gives us the opportunity to grow plants which will not survive elsewhere, in a unique and highly ornamental setting. Water-gardening also allows us to foster wild creatures.

The rewards are great but water-gardening does require hard work, a vigilant eye, careful forethought when choosing plants, and no fear of getting wet. There are rights and wrongs to successful water-gardening, and fancies cannot always be safely indulged.

Water plants naturally fall into four categories, and the range of genuine, and hardy, water plants is not vast. There are those, like water lilies, which appear to float weightlessly on the surface but which in fact have their roots firmly bedded in the pond bottom or in perforated containers; there are those which genuinely float, the so-called floating

aquatics, such as *Stratiotes;* there are submerged 'oxygenating' plants which are anchored to the pond bed; and there are marginal plants which grow in shallow water at the edge of more informal pools.

For a successful and pleasing water garden, you really need representatives from all four groups, or from the first three if your pond does not allow for marginal plants. The water lilies and other rooted floating plants shade the water from the sun and so inhibit the growth of simple, but highly successful – and undesirable – plant organisms called algae, which give ponds a green look, especially when newly made. Floating aquatics, such as *Stratiotes* and *Trapa,* perform the same vital function.

Oxygenating plants are undistinguished water weeds, invaluable for absorbing the mineral salts derived from fish waste, fertile soil and so on, which

encourage algae growth. It is possible to buy named species, but most people buy a selection in bunches to grow together.

Ideally, half to two-thirds of the water should be covered with surface leaf to keep the algae at bay and to allow fish to be glimpsed. Adding barley straw at a rate of 100g per cubic metre (4oz per cubic yard) of water may be effective at discouraging algae growth.

Marginal plants may also help to shade the water, but their prime function is ornamental. Without them, especially the vertically-growing irises and grasses, the pond might look stark, dull and too horizontal.

Whatever you decide to grow, you will get the best and cheapest plants by ordering from specialist nurseries by mail order, and their catalogues will give you the information you need about planting and caring for water plants. It is important, for instance, to find out the

1 Astilbes are plants that thrive in wet conditions on a bank. Water lilies are invaluable in a pond, but need thinning out periodically, in early summer. **Grass can be run down to the edge of an informal pool in an uninterrupted sweep, or, as here, the junction can be softened with planting. The contrast of leaf shapes is excellent.**

2 Bog plants must be grown in soil that never dries out, even in summer. The leaves of lysichiton and *Primula pulverulenta* would soon wilt in dry weather if this were not the case. The way to achieve this in gardens which do not have soil that waterlogs is by sinking a liner 30cm/12in below ground, puncturing it with a few holes to allow only very slow drainage, and covering it with peaty soil.

3 Marginal plants are grown in shallow water, rather than on the bank. These plants will be in perforated pots, sitting on the pond's bottom or on a shallow shelf round the edge. The pots stabilize the plants, and help restrict their roots. Plant marginal plants in late spring, and aim, as here, to achieve a good mix of leaf shape for the best effect.

Raised beds, and pools, are attractive features, and bring plants closer to eye level. There is a good mix of foliage here, and the mellow colouring of the old brick blends into the background, rather than dominating the scene. If a pool like this one is built about 450mm/18in high, it can also double as an occasional seat, to bring you closer to the sight and sound of water.

4 A lovely and appropriate planting for a woodland stream.

Nature has a haphazard way of doing things, and this is what you need to emulate in your own garden. Then the feature, whatever it is, will look as if it has been there for ever! Here a simple wooden bridge is in perfect keeping with its naturalistic surroundings.

3

4

ultimate planting depth required (the depth from water surface to the top of the plant's roots), and what area of water the plant will cover when full-grown. Water plants can be bought either already planted in perforated plastic containers, or 'bare-rooted'. Containers are the only possible means of growing water plants in concrete pools.

Some plants are so excessively invasive that they should be avoided at all costs. In this category I would include *Typha angustifolia, Glyceria maxima,* and *Azolla caroliniana.*

The hardy water lilies, on the other hand, are indispensable to a successful pond or lake planting. They are beautiful to look at, and varieties can be bought to suit most areas and depths of water, in a wide range of colours which includes red, pink, white, yellow and orange. Some are so vigorous in their growth that they can only be safely

planted in the largest and deepest lakes, while others can be grown successfully in shallow troughs.

In catalogues, water lilies are usually classified by spread: 'miniature', 'small', 'medium' and 'large'. In simplified terms, the 'large' will cover a circular area up to 2.4m/8ft in diameter, and need to have a planting depth of 30-90cm/12-36in; 'medium' will cover an area of up to 1.5m/5ft and require a planting depth of 22-60cm/9-24in; and 'small' will cover 90cm/36in and need a planting depth of 18-35cm/7-15in. 'Miniatures' require even less depth.

Water lilies are best planted in containers, rather than in the soil, if any, at the bottom of the pool. In that way they can be more easily controlled and curbed if necessary. All water lilies are planted when they have come into active growth in the late spring. If they are in containers, attach string to act as handles and

stand them in the water on bricks to a depth of about 25cm/10in. After a few weeks, they will have grown sufficiently for the bricks to be dropped to their proper level. Gravel placed on top of the containers will help stabilize them and prevent the soil washing out.

If you buy bare-rooted water lilies you will see they have rootstocks with short leaves growing from them. Plant them in the soil at the bottom of the pond with the growing tip just above the soil surface; then weigh them down with stones, and cover the entire planting area with gravel.

If you buy your containers and water lilies separately, use a special aquatic compost which contains a slow-release fertilizer, when potting them up. Other surface plants can be treated in exactly the same way.

Oxygenating plants, on the other hand, only need to be rooted in gravel,

as they obtain their nutrients through their leaves. *Stratiotes* and *Trapa* can be simply thrown in.

Marginal plants need to be put in very shallow water, usually where there is less than 8cm/3in between water and soil surface. Preformed pools are designed with shelves at the right height for containers of marginal plants. Many marginal plants are vigorous, not to say invasive, so plant these separately, or they will push out the rest. Try to plant a variety of leaf shapes in close proximity, and leave some gaps on the marginal shelf. The pool will look more 'natural' with a few clumps strategically placed. Marginal plants should be planted when in a period of active growth, from late spring until midsummer.

Water-gardening is not for the idle. Every three years in the case of water lilies, and preferably every year in the case of marginals, the containers should

1 In a semi-wild position such as this, weeds can take hold all too easily; you must keep a careful lookout. Some thinning of plants each spring will be necessary, and if the soil is not naturally acid, a mulch of peat will be beneficial. This is an example of gardening at its most labour intensive! Note the intelligent use of foliage in this composition: rodgersia, on the right, is a must for this kind of situation.

be lifted out. Those plants which have started to 'run', that is, their roots have outgrown the containers, should be cut back. This may mean wading into the water, and, in the case of ponds with butyl or plastic liners, this must be done in bare feet to help avoid punctures.

Vigorous plants that have outgrown their containers should be divided and replanted in fresh soil; this will probably mean using a knife to cut the plant's roots, and much will end up on the compost heap. You may need help if the plants are growing in large and heavy containers.

Another job in the growing season is to rake up blanketweed and remove duckweed with a net, to prevent these taking over; leave them on the side for a while to allow insects to crawl away. At the same time, pick off any plant leaves damaged by pests (nearly all pesticides will harm fish), and in late summer cut back the oxygenators so that they do not die back too much in winter and pollute the water in the process. Before winter

sets in, float an inflated ball on the surface of the water to keep the pond from freezing over entirely.

Most gardeners like the idea of fish in their ponds. Do not introduce them for at least a month after planting up, so that the plants, especially the 'oxygenators', have a chance to establish themselves. On no account introduce carp – Koi or Higoi – because they will damage plants, but go for goldfish and orfe instead, which are not only ornamental but also eat duckweed. You should not buy more than 5cm/2in in length of fish for every 900sq cm/1sq ft surface, to avoid overcrowding.

If you have a small pond containing many fish, you should change about half the water each year; otherwise the fish may suffer from slow carbon dioxide poisoning. Siphon the water out, or remove bucketfuls, and then top the remainder up from the hose. The water will turn green for a time after you have done this because of the minerals present in the fresh water.

Although serviceable, the term 'bog plants' is essentially misleading. Such plants thrive in a very moist soil, which makes them ideal as candidates for planting at the water's edge; they would not, however, last long in the anaerobic and extremely acidic conditions of a true bog. True bog plants, on the other hand, are perfectly suitable candidates for marginal planting in very shallow water, because they can survive without much oxygen at their roots.

The most impressive waterside plants are those with very large leaves. Instantly recognizable are the huge leaves of *Gunnera manicata* and *Rheum palmatum rubrum*, but these are really only for very large natural ponds and lakes. However, there are many other good plants more appropriate for a boggy area close to an average-sized pond: hostas, bergenias, rodgersias, and ferns like osmunda and onoclea. Amongst the flowering plants, the Japanese and Siberian irises (*Iris japonica* and *I. sibirica*) are ideal, especially for providing

vertical contrast, as are the Asiatic primulas (*Primula pulverulenta*) with their beautiful flowers, often held on tall stems, and neat leaves. The wide range of astilbes adds to the choice of summer-flowering plants. Lysichitons are popular in big 'bogs', although the smell of the yellow skunk cabbage (*L. americanus*) may put you off. The white-flowered *L. camtschatcensis* is more acceptable.

If the pond is informal in shape, aim to make the planting look as 'natural' as possible. Plant in drifts, and mix foliage with flower. Keep an eye on the weeds which will enjoy these damp conditions: in late summer, rosebay willowherb can be a lurid-pink pest, and many unwanted grasses and rushes will also thrive by the pond's edge.

If for any reason it is not possible to make a bog garden, yet you wish to soften the edges of a pond or pool, you can 'cheat' by planting drought-tolerant sun-lovers which look like bog plants. Many of the irises, for example *Iris pallida* and the tall bearded irises, will give

2 The double-flowered buttercup *Ranunculus acris* 'Flore Pleno' grows in damp soil beside this informal pond. The water lily in the pond itself serves a dual function: it provides flowers, and also shades the water, which helps to keep green algae at bay.

3 A luxuriant pond setting, with most attractive planting comprising irises, hostas, ligularia, yellow mimulus and *Euphorbia griffithii* 'Fireglow'. The water is clear with no algae or blanketweed.
This is a pool owned by a plant lover, and it burgeons with lush growth. The combination of species is very attractive, and will give foliage colour throughout the summer.

4 What a marvellous colour these primulas are, fringing the water. There are four different types of water plant that can be used in a water feature: water lilies which appear to float weightlessly on the surface; those which genuinely float, such as *Stratiotes*; submerged 'oxygenating' plants; and marginal plants, such as these, which grow in shallow water.

3

4

verticality, yet do not require a wet soil to thrive. *Molinia caerulea* ssp. *caerulea* 'Variegata' looks not unlike a slightly smaller version of *Glyceria maxima* 'Variegata', yet requires a dry acid soil. Hostas are much more resistant to drought than is generally thought, especially if they can be shaded by a taller evergreen that will not drop leaves in the pond. Moreover, there are other primulas, like the auriculas and *P. marginata* 'Linda Pope', which would give a 'bog' feel to the pond's edge without needing moist conditions. *Aruncus dioicus*, the goat's beard, is another substantial plant, tolerant of dry conditions, which has a waterside feel to it.

Another option is simply to treat the pond as an area of water surrounded by garden plants which are suited to the situation. Or, if your pool is a formal one, when any edge-planting would detract from the clean lines you wish to emphasize, restrict your planting to pots, which can be deployed as you wish. This is also effective where the pond is raised.

Water

SWIMMING POOLS

1 A pool is an eyecatching feature, so poolside plantings in pots need to make an equally strong visual impact. The pots here have been carefully chosen, and they stand out in sharp relief against the whitewashed wall.

Nerium oleander makes a good container plant in a hot climate, even though it is poisonous, and should be handled with care. Oleanders flower throughout the summer, and come in several different colours.

2 We have much to thank the Modern Movement for, and this is a good example. The clarity of line, attention to detail, and minimalist approach combine to produce a composition that is totally fit for its purpose. The controlled design contrasts dramatically with the natural landscape, but there is an obvious visual link between sea and pool.

Beautifully set in the *garrigue*, there is no real need for any 'artificial' planting here, although some large pots near the pool might work.

3 The geometry of this design leads to a real build-up of tension, with the drama heightened by the wings of hedging that concentrate the view. But the building prevents the view from continuing, and the tension is released as you reach the water of the pool.

Both hedges and wall climber have been neatly clipped to echo the clean lines of the pool. The yellow ground-cover is the invasive but trimmable *Hypericum calycinum*.

1   2

DS Open-air swimming pools can easily dominate a garden if they are not integrated into the overall design. They may look inviting during a long hot summer but look the very opposite in winter, particularly when empty.

The type and cost of a swimming pool can vary enormously, from an above-ground kit-form temporary structure to the most expensive permanent pool adorned by a purpose-built building containing innumerable additional features. In general, I would advise employing an expert for the construction of any form

of permanent pool; it will certainly save you a huge amount of hard work and possible disaster, and is very likely to save you money in the long run.

There are two main options for the siting of an open-air swimming pool. You can either have it close to the house and designed to fit into the terrace and associated hard landscaping, where it will be visible throughout the year, or you can site it some way away, perhaps screened by a combination of contouring and planting, or hidden behind a wall. Either way, you need to think

carefully about the design of the pool and the hard landscaping, and how to use the site to its best advantage.

Most swimming pool design in northern Europe is remarkably dull, from the ubiquitous kidney shape to the straight rectangle with a 'Roman' semi-circular end. In hot countries, where they have more experience, both the siting and design of pools tends to be more imaginative.

Rectangles are undoubtedly the best shape for serious swimming, even though companies making 'jet stream' type products say you can swim in any

shape or size of pool. As a keen swimmer myself, I feel cheated by battling against powerful streams of water and getting nowhere! There is absolutely no reason why you should not have any shape you like, but you will probably pay a good deal for the privilege.

If you design your own pool, take time thinking about it, peg it out in the garden and see how it relates to everything else. If the sides are to be curved, employ the compass method, swinging a line from a metal pin or cane to ensure that one shape runs into the next.

3

The colour and finish of the pool are also important; you do not have to opt for the predictable blue or turquoise mosaic! Mosaic comes in all colours so you could match a colour scheme used in the garden and even in the house; or, alternatively, you could indulge in exciting polychrome designs or patterns. Rendered pools can be painted either in a solid colour or in any other way you wish. In either case you could successfully work to your own designs or even hire the services of an art-student friend or a professional artist.

Although most pools are naturally 'architectural' in outline, they can be successfully blended into a more natural setting. A spectacular effect can be achieved by running specially filtered water into a pool through bold outcrops. Such rocks can also be positioned so that they also 'outcrop' in an adjoining sitting area. Where a pool is built on sloping ground to overlook a view, the furthest end can be constructed from a thin strip of metal, so that when you are inside the pool, water and sky give the impression of merging together.

Pools are expensive; so too are additional features to go with them. I have worked on outdoor pools that were integrated with the house itself, with a diving board from an upstairs bedroom. Hot tubs, showers, saunas and jacuzzis can all be designed around them, as can separate shallow areas for toddlers. Slides and diving boards have improved greatly over the last few years, and slides in particular can be enormous fun.

The construction of pools varies: they can be made either with concrete sprayed at high pressure on to a mesh of reinforcing rods, or with special interlocking and reinforced concrete blocks that are subsequently rendered, or with liners or semi-rigid shells of various kinds. All have an excellent life expectancy if constructed or fitted properly. Some pools are available in kit form, but these still involve a good deal of hard work. You will need to hire heavy machinery and probably employ some skilled labour as well. Unless you are really keen and competent I would advise getting in an expert to do this job too, and you will have the added bonus of a guarantee into the bargain.

Just as much care needs to go into the design and construction of any building associated with the pool – whether it is simply for changing or for housing the filtration gear, for storing additional features, or for covering the pool itself. If you are lucky you can convert adjoining outhouses for these purposes, or even house the pool in a conservatory; but there are depressingly few good-looking prefabricated buildings available, unless you happen to like wooden chalets and wild west log cabins. Pool buildings generally need to be designed individually, and although they tend to cost more, they can then respect the overall theme of the pool and its surroundings.

A neat and practical solution for a filtration plant, where a pool is built into a slope, is to tuck it into a purpose-built shelter in the bank.

Children adore water and during a hot spell a paddling pool can be invaluable. Pools can be bought in all shapes and sizes, and like portable sandpits can be moved into the sun or shade at will. But as an alternative, why not consider building a permanent paddler on or near the main terrace? It could consist of a butyl lined depression in the paved surface, floored with granite setts, brushed concrete or small rounded cobbles – any of which would provide an excellent grip. If you could also fix an overhead shower to an adjoining wall, enjoyment would be complete!

GARDEN BUILDINGS

1

DS The range of garden buildings is enormous: from the simplest shed to the most elaborate summerhouse or folly. A garden building of whatever kind, whether it looks good or bad, will be a major feature in the garden, and needs emphasizing or concealing accordingly.

In broad terms, buildings are either utilitarian or decorative, and this will largely determine where they are placed. This will have been thought about at the design stage. We now need to consider the building in more detail.

Utility buildings will include sheds, greenhouses, pool and pump houses, workshops, fuel stores, and so on.

A fuel store will need to be close to the house so that wood or coal can be carried easily inside; it can often be economically combined under one roof with a dustbin store and a small separate shed for play equipment, prams and bicycles. A utility area of this kind could form a suitably screened extension of the house itself; or you could use walling to divide it from the main terrace and outside living space. This could then provide a vehicle for overhead beams, built-in seating, and a barbecue on the terrace side, along with space for pots and containers.

A garden shed and greenhouse will probably be at some distance from the house, possibly within a vegetable garden. Good access is essential, and paths of ample width, and a suitably large paved working area, will be useful. Again, screening will be important, and could take the form of hedging, planting, fencing, trellis, or perhaps even espaliered or cordon fruit.

Greenhouses need to be out in the open, and can seldom be tucked out of sight. If you make even a very plain greenhouse the central focus of a growing area, with a surrounding pattern of formal beds, the building becomes an attractive focal point in its own right.

Sheds and greenhouses both come in a wide variety of sizes, materials and styles. Greenhouses are produced in timber, aluminium, or alloy, and in various plastic-coated metals. Manufacturers extol the virtues of the extended life of the plastic-coated metals, but a timber house, regularly treated with non-toxic preservative, can last for a very long time indeed. It will also often blend far more comfortably and attractively with its garden surroundings.

Other specialist buildings, such as pool and pump houses, obviously need to be sited close to the feature they serve. Again, it will make sense if they are integrated with another structure, such as a changing or games room – or even a loggia overlooking the pool.

Decorative buildings reflect a minefield of differing tastes, so be careful! Visit other gardens, look at books, sketch your own ideas, but, above all, consider how the building will look in your own garden. Remember that any such building will almost invariably draw the eye at the expense of everything else, so it must be sited with the utmost sensitivity.

1 This large structure is part gazebo and part arbour. Such structures tend to be painted white, which means they will always be a focal point. This example is a beauty, and the architectural line is softened by old fruit trees. Climbers will need to be taken down for painting and maintenance, and retied once the job is complete.

2 Here is high drama, achieved by setting the gazebo at the tension point between woodland and an open clearing. Gazebos are designed to have a view, and this certainly has one! The strong colour works well, and the ogee roof, which is rarely used to its best advantage, draws the eye dramatically upward towards the light.

Fortunately, there are good-looking buildings available, although they can be pretty expensive, but if all else fails, think about designing and building one, either yourself, or with professional help. You will find marvellous examples in good garden books; some almost good enough to live in.

Play houses come in all shapes and sizes, from plastic 'Wendy Houses' to sophisticated buildings in timber. Tree houses can be good fun, but obviously need to be securely built. Nor need they be just for children: I have visited an aerial dining room, 9m/30ft above the ground, complete with chandelier and seating for twelve people!

There is some confusion concerning gazebos. 'Gazebo' has become a fashionable description of any tatty old garden building, whereas the true meaning of the word is quite simply a small garden building that is sited specifically to embrace a view. And here we are talking about a real vista, perhaps over countryside, across a lake, or down a wooded dell. Once again, the style will be important; a little rustic building with a topknot of thatch will look terrific at the head of a woodland site, but in a suburban garden would undeniably be kitsch. So, unless you have rolling acres, scale your ideas down accordingly!

Follies constitute the most eccentric, beautiful and humorous garden structures you can possess, but they need careful handling if they are to be a success. Traditionally, they were built by rich and sometimes not so rich landowners as straightforward visual jokes or eye-catchers. Whether false church towers, romantic ruins or ornamental grottoes, the idea was to titillate the imagination – and they did! You might argue that today's gardens do not lend themselves to such extravagances, but I would strongly disagree. I personally have created grottoes out of old bomb shelters, arranged broken Corinthian columns across the end of an overgrown town garden, and seen nappies dipped

The most popular buildings, generically known as 'summerhouses', can range from flimsy off-the-peg examples, to beautiful, well-built and unique ones. A summerhouse will act as an ideal focal point within the garden. Remember that the view from a summerhouse or arbour is also important.

After working out exactly what you want to use the building for, shop around. Avoid manufacturers' fantasies, and look for a structure that complements rather than fights with its surroundings. Beware, too, of using your pretty structure for garage overspill; it is fine to store garden furniture in it during the winter, but its point is lost if it is permanently crammed full of general household junk.

in cement hanging like fossilized bats in a grotto in Essex. Ideas like this work!

You could dress up a mundane shed with a gothic façade, build a suitably 'distressed' temple in an open glade, or create your own 'ruin'.

UB Creative planting can go a long way towards reconciling us to the necessity of utilitarian structures in the garden. Dustbin, bicycle and potting sheds can all be softened, even disguised, especially by climbers or evergreen shrubs. The effect can appear to be guileless if the 'softeners' used are those also used in a *bona fide* border scheme nearby. Many of the climbers and wall plants mentioned in the section on climbing plants can be used in this way to blend the offensive object into the gardenscape.

You can also plant scented (and prunable) evergreens, such as *Osmanthus* x *burkwoodii* and *Sarcococca hookeriana* var. *digyna*, in strategic positions to sweeten the daily walk to the dustbins.

In the case of decorative buildings, such as summerhouses or arbours, planting should aim to enhance and accentuate rather than hide the structure. It should also be planting which performs best in the summer months when the building is in use. Appropriate and scented planting in the area surrounding the summerhouse, and along the path leading to it, is also important.

If the summerhouse or arbour is tiled, avoid using very vigorous woody climbers which might undermine the roof tiles; thatch, on the other hand, may be 'fringed' with wisteria or *Clematis montana* attached to its bottom edge, lending an air of mystery to the interior.

If there is room, arrange attractive pots containing summer-flowering scented perennials and even fragile-stemmed climbers on each side of the entrance. An urn or raised pot can make an excellent central feature inside a classical summerhouse but remember to plant it only with shade-tolerant plants.

Living in Your Garden

1 Buildings reflect the mood of the designer, and here the hand of geometry is very plain. This building would make a fine garden room, with ample doors to throw open. The informal planting of grasses is also a major success in this setting.

2 Round houses are wonderful to look at, but complicated to build. This one is a real beauty, and sits comfortably behind a terrace of old York stone, with a superb path of cobbles leading up to it.

Here, the 'soft' elements are designed to enhance the strong 'hard' features. Plants soften the paving, and gravel extensions to the cobbled path have allowed space for more planting.

3 This little gazebo is informal by nature, but has been very positively sited at the end of the well kept gravel path. The borders of clipped hedges concentrate the view, and the soft wings of planting prevent distraction on either side.

The planting – hedges, climbers, pots – all encourages the garden visitor to explore such a charming garden shelter.

4 You have to be bold to like this kind of thing, though in the right setting it can certainly draw the eye! Remember that with anything as visually strong as this, you will need plenty of bold foliage to temper the line.

5 Some of the best garden buildings are low-key and can be built from recycled materials. I love the old weatherboarding and simple window, with the seat below forming a relaxed feature.

The planting is very much in keeping with such an understated building: all the old cottage favourites such as roses, delphiniums, scabious and achilleas.

6 Greenhouses can look delightful in the right setting, and this example sits comfortably within a rambling planting scheme. It is the statue that draws the eye. Where there are tall trees in a garden, a greenhouse needs careful siting to be clear of the shade they cast.

7 This well-detailed little building forms a major focal point, situated as it is on higher ground at the top of solid stone steps. Here is the perfect place for solitude – at the heart of a secret garden.

Two complementary stands of garden-worthy white agapanthus lead up to the garden building. It is best grown where the winters are not too harsh.

6

7

8 A solid no-nonsense building in a strongly vernacular style. Old pantiles on the roof set up an interesting rhythm; the paint colour is good; and it looks fine under the old tree. The trees surrounding this building lend a corresponding air of solidity and permanence to the garden house itself.

9 This composition around a serviceable shed is given colour and life by the snowball tree, *Viburnum plicatum* f. *tomentosum*.

8

9

TERRACES AND PLAY AREAS

DS The terrace, or patio, will be the hub of many garden activities. Its location within the overall composition will have been carefully worked out at the design stage. The important thing is that it links in visual terms with the rest of the garden, and with the house that it normally adjoins.

The terrace will probably be the largest paved area in the garden. Its overall shape and size should be generous; always make it slightly larger than you think necessary. Think in terms of an average room, then allow for furniture, toys and accessories. The terrace is the perfect place for a barbecue and built-in seating, for a raised bed or sandpit, for overhead beams to provide light shade, for pots of plants, and for water used in any number of ways. A minimum space of 3.6 x 3.6m/12 x 12ft should provide room for most family purposes.

If the terrace adjoins the house, the layout can be architectural. Remember to lay it below the level of the damp proof course (dpc), and use materials that match or complement the material used in the construction of the house. Further away from the building, a paved area can be more informal.

Sandpits and paddling pools are essential pieces of equipment for families with small children. Both can be bought off-the-peg, and moved around the garden at will. They can also be built more permanently into a terrace area, where a raised sandpit could later be converted into a raised bed or a pool.

With the former, drainage is all-important: the bottom must be dug out to take 300mm/12in of thoroughly consolidated crushed stone or hardcore, topped first with a layer of clean gravel, and then with 300mm/12in of silver sand. Never use builder's sand; the stains are almost impossible to get out. Some kind of cover will also be needed, which can double as a useful play surface.

When children are a little older, the larger play structures come into their own: swings, slides, see-saws, and climbing frames. All can be built by the determined carpenter, and will be sturdier than the tubular metal varieties. Tailor the features to suit your needs. A swing can be hung in an arch and a slide built into an existing bank.

Large structures are highly visible, but the garden should be seen as a place for the widest range of activities, and your outside room will change as your family grows. Plants and ornaments may be in jeopardy for a few years, and when the ball-game phase arrives, you will have to abandon all hope of a fine lawn. Enjoy it! There will be time enough to repair the wreckage later on.

Children love to escape the eye of adults, but avoid the dreaded plastic Wendy House at all cost. Make a wooden one, hand over a ramshackle shed as a 'den', or put up a tent. For small children, even a blanket slung over a rotary clothes drier makes a fine and secret place. Best of all, of course, is a soundly constructed tree house.

1 The change in level on a sloping site has been well handled, using a combination of old York stone, ample brick steps, and raised beds that soften the architectural outline. Every attempt has been made to soften, without hiding, the well-made 'hard' features. Steps make an excellent showplace for a collection of pots filled with cherished or interesting plants.

2 Children get bored playing in one place. If you can move equipment around, it will also prevent one area of grass from becoming worn out. Buttercups and dandelions are essential ingredients of any garden inhabited by children; as are daisies!

3 The best swings are hung from a stout tree limb. If you are lucky enough to have a suitable tree in the garden, check the branch for any signs of weakness, and use nylon rope that is rot-proof. Safety is paramount. There are many types of swing, many of them improvised by children, but one of the best is a knotted rope. Hang it some distance from the trunk of the tree, if you have a branch that is strong enough, to prevent child and tree becoming too closely involved. Lucky children to be able to swing and climb in this beautiful cherry tree! Even in an enthusiast's garden it is important to find magical corners for children, and this is certainly one such place.

4 It's worth underlining the point that simple things often work best in the garden. In a hot climate overheads may be essential to break the direct rays of the sun, and cast shade. This simple structure does the job perfectly, filtering the light on to the table below. The stone wall defines the space, but is low enough to allow diners to see the view.

5 The terrace here enjoys an elevated position, projecting out over the slope to catch the sea breeze, and there is room for sitting and dining in comfort. The overhead treatment is again important in this kind of climate, and stems have been woven together to form a gently canted roof. Overall construction is mercifully simple, with great plaster columns supporting the round timbers. This is garden architecture in the best vernacular style, using local materials, craftsmen and traditions. Like all good design, it will suit its purpose well.

POTS AND CONTAINERS

DS Pots and containers are your mobile planting stations, but they will vary enormously in character.

Often the position of a group of pots, or of a single large one, will have been obvious when you worked out the design of the garden – either to balance the bulk of a raised bed, or as a focal point at the end of a vista. But you may have been given a pot, or made an impulse buy at a garden centre or antiques market; in this case, a good deal of careful thought will have to go into its siting.

The range of pots and containers today is huge, from brightly coloured contemporary designs in primary colours, through terracotta, stone or concrete, traditional Asian or European glazed earthenware, to lead and copper – or fibreglass copies of the same. Cost may well be a factor in your choice, but so too should be suitability of location and how the pot will relate to others in the garden. Where a group of pots is placed together, a 'mix and match' approach is often the most effective.

Some pots are best left unplanted and treated as sculptures. I have several fine Cretan *pithoi* that make superb focal points, and it would detract greatly from their beauty to sully the line with foliage!

Here, too, is a chance for humour. Think laterally, and do not be put off by horticultural snobbery – the worst kind! If you like something, then have it. I use an old bath for a herb garden, and my garden is adorned with several copper coal scuttles and a chimney pot shaped like a griffin. Things of this kind all have their own place.

UB For those with no garden, pots and containers may provide the only opportunity for growing plants, but for everyone they have their own attractions.

Pots and other containers are immensely versatile: they can be moved around and replanted at will. They can be used to soften or decorate areas of paving,

steps, walls, pools and garden buildings. Depending on their planting and disposition, they can change the entire atmosphere of your garden from year to year.

With the use of pots, a whole tribe of beautiful but tender perennials and sub-shrubs becomes available to you. Tender plants may be moved into the garden during the summer, and returned to a frost-free place in winter. Half-hardy plants from warmer regions will, in summer, withstand lower temperatures in pots than they would if planted out in heavy and damp garden soil. Low half-hardy annuals lend themselves better to container planting than to planting in the border. And alpines can often be seen to their best advantage in troughs.

Pots offer the chance to ring the changes with a variety of mini planting schemes. It is even possible to create two schemes in a year, either in pots or hanging baskets. A successful scheme worked out in a pot one year may form the basis of a border the next.

Containers enable plants to thrive, which would not flourish elsewhere in the garden. Simply planting up a container with an ericaceous or 'multi-purpose' compost, for example, allows a gardener on alkaline soil to grow rhododendrons, azaleas, pieris, and a dozen other lime-hating but highly ornamental plants.

It is also possible to grow good vegetables and fruit in containers. Plastic, clay or wooden pots, tubs and window-boxes are ideal for tomatoes, aubergines, peppers and a host of salad vegetables, together with dwarf fruit trees, bushes and soft fruit. Ornamental vegetables such as ruby chard and 'Lollo Rosso' lettuce can also be grown in this way.

Containers can be used as much for permanent as for temporary plantings: small shrubs, dwarf conifers, and climbers can provide as much beauty as short-lived schemes. And a mixture of permanent and temporary planting can be very effective.

1 These citrus trees can easily be taken under glass in the winter, and brought out again in spring, for they need a minimum temperature of 5°C/41°F. It is just about feasible to move containers of this size, provided there is someone to lend a hand. The hedge, which would otherwise be awkward to reach, could be clipped before the pots were reinstated. Citrus trees require generous watering while in active growth, especially when they are container-grown.

This is an unusual and attractive use of pots, and there is a pleasing contrast in the geometry of the composition, with the low hedges rising from the flat plane of the lawn. The round terracotta containers set up a definite rhythm within the low hedges, and are well set off by the background of sword-shaped foliage behind.

1

Visual impact can be created in several ways. For example, if you wish to emphasize a handsome flight of steps, a pair of identical pots at the bottom, each containing a restrained topiary shape, will be preferable to distracting mounds of lavish helichrysum and argyranthemum. On the other hand, if you have a blank wall and one container to put in front of it, a colourfully harmonious confection of well-fed plants would distract attention from the dull wall.

Large containers can, like raised beds, be used to develop a mini landscape. You just need smaller plants. If you

wish to make a permanent arrangement with, for example, a tall thin conifer, a short ball-like evergreen, and a medium-sized horizontal plant, you could plant *Juniperus communis* 'Compressa', a fiercely clipped ball of *Buxus sempervirens* 'Suffruticosa', and *Hebe pinguifolia* 'Pagei'. Be careful, however, not to make these arrangements look too contrived.

There are some obvious reminders: a tall evergreen plant in the middle of a windowbox may hide the light or the view. Simple planting is best for urns which have elaborate, eye-catching

POTS AND CONTAINERS

2

decoration; but you can smother ugly containers with trailing plants or moderately vigorous climbers such as sweet peas or clematis, and allow them to spill right over. Take account of the background colour when planning a colour scheme. Remember that aspect is as important as it is in the open garden; there are plenty of shade-lovers which will thrive in containers, while for windy sites choose sturdy, bushy, permanent plants, rather than trailing ones which are easily damaged by wind and heavy rain.

Unless the container is very large, with excellent drainage, the growing medium should be not garden soil but an aerated nutritious compost. The type of plant, and the length of time it will remain in the container, will determine what is used for this. John Innes composts Nos 2 and 3 are best for permanent subjects such as climbers, which will stay in the pot for a long time – No 3 has 1½ times the nutrient content of No 2 – while the soil-less 'multipurpose' composts are best for short-term subjects, especially those sited in sunny places, because it is easier to see when they need watering. Soil-less composts also have the advantage of being much lighter – an important consideration when it comes to moving pots about.

All containers need drainage holes. Before planting, put broken tiles or stones over these holes to stop them becoming blocked, then add the compost in layers, pressing down loam composts firmly, but loamless ones quite gently. Never fill with compost right up to the rim; leave a gap so that, when watering, water does not splash out and take the compost with it. To plant, first water the plants in their pots and allow them to drain, then knock each one out and plant it with a trowel, making sure that the compost in the container just covers the compost surface of the plant. Plant the centre plant first, and then fill in round the edges. Leave room for leaf expansion but no large gaps. Sprinkle the soil surface with a coated steady-release fertilizer, and water in well with a watering can fitted with a rose.

Wall plants or climbers in containers will need support: use netting, canes or pea sticks. Tall plants in growing bags also need support. Use a home-made framework of bamboo canes or buy specially-designed frames.

The hanging basket is very popular as a container these days. It should preferably be a deep wire one. If it has a round bottom – and most do – stand it in a suitably sized bucket or large pot to give it stability while you line the bottom, and halfway up the sides, with a 2.5cm/1in thickness of sphagnum moss or moss raked from the lawn, or use a liner made

2 Pelargoniums are ideal subjects for pots, being so tolerant of drought, and requiring little or no feeding; indeed, too much nitrogen tends to promote leaf at the expense of flower. The right-hand plant sits in a terracotta pot placed in the neck of a round-bellied one: this is a sensible solution to the problem of filling very large containers.
A unifying factor to these pots, all of different heights and styles, is the choice of terracotta for them all, in addition to the over-riding drama of the red pelargoniums. The tree provides vertical emphasis, and helps to stabilize the composition at a higher level.

3 There is much to be said for a repeat planting of one type of plant. The ivy-leaved pelargonium in these raised containers is probably perennial in this Mediterranean situation. The shrubs in the attractive swagged pots are lemons, *Citrus limon*.
Containers can be built into almost any situation, and are particularly successful running down either side of this flight of steps. They must be deep enough to retain moisture, particularly in a Mediterranean climate. The steps themselves are an attractive combination of stone or concrete risers with an infill of gravel for the tread.

3

Living in Your Garden

of coir, peat fibre or foam. Gradually add damp compost: you can get special loamless hanging basket compost, or use an ordinary multipurpose one, or John Innes No 2. As you fill the basket, stop at intervals and make holes in the liner with a knife. From the outside, manoeuvre your small plants into the holes, making sure that the roots come into contact with the compost. Gradually add more moss and compost to within 2.5cm/1in of the rim, and continue to plant up in the same way. Water well after planting, and sprinkle the soil surface with a coated steady-release fertilizer to last for the growing season, before covering any bare surface with moss, and, finally, hanging the basket where needed, on a securely fixed hook.

Late spring is the earliest that a hanging basket containing tender summer bedding plants can safely be put outside. Either plant it up then, or plant two to three weeks earlier, and keep it in a greenhouse until ready to be hardened off and put out.

Containers dry out quickly in warm, sunny, or windy weather – partly because of their comparatively large surface area, partly because plant roots soon take up the space available, and partly because plants in containers often grow very fast. Plants wilt fastest in very hot windy weather, and the smaller the container, the more likely they are to be put under stress.

Watering is normally necessary when the compost feels dry to the touch when you stick a finger in a short way. Loam composts in clay pots need watering when the top seems very dry and a sharp tap on the side of the pot with a knuckle produces a hollow sound. With most soil-less composts, excess water will run away quickly and not cause root rot, but it is important not to over-water coir, which absorbs water like a sponge, or loam composts. Never let a peat-based compost dry out completely; not only will plants wilt but the compost will be very difficult to re-wet.

1

Here are some tips that may help reduce compost evaporation, especially useful if you are going on holiday and cannot depend on help from a neighbour. Clay pots dry out faster than plastic ones, so either only use plastic pots, some of which are made to resemble terracotta, or line your clay pots with polythene before planting, making holes at the bottom; only plant in large pots over 25cm/10in in diameter; plant drought-tolerant plants, such as pelargoniums, yuccas, verbenas, or santolina; mulch with woven polypropylene or a bark mulch; or install a drip system on a temporary basis such as a tin can with tiny holes punched in the base, filled with water. Growing bags, especially in greenhouses, dry out very quickly; installing drip trays underneath them will help.

Hanging baskets are always a problem to water. Put them in the shade on hot days or when you are away, and mulch the surface if there is room. To help you water hanging baskets suspended above head-height, you can now buy plastic water bottles which work by pump action, or long curve-ended 'lances' which fit on to hosepipes. It is also possible to buy elaborate pulley systems by which hanging baskets can be lowered and raised for easy access.

I do not recommend mixing 'water-retaining' polymer granules in the compost. In my experience, the plants need watering almost as often as they would without them.

Feeding is far more important for container plants than for those grown in the average garden soil; this is because the

1 This is a perfect illustration of the use of containers in a frost-prone climate. Pots of tender mixed perennials do not come more skilfully designed, or cultivated, than this. The plants are overwintered, usually as rooted cuttings, in a greenhouse, and planted out in late spring into a good quality compost. High potash feeds, frequent watering, and regular deadheading, are essential if such an effect is to be sustained.

2 Containers can also be used for permanent plantings, but although the rose will be hardy in open ground, it is more vulnerable in a pot. If left outside through the winter, both plant and pot should be well protected.

The larger the pot, the happier the plant will be, but the container should also respect the theme of the surrounding garden. Here, the stone jardinière echoes successfully the stone wall in the background.

POTS AND CONTAINERS

roots are restricted in their quest for nutrients. Those nutrients are easily leached when a pot is watered so often, and plants are growing strongly. When the plants have been in the containers for about five weeks (earlier if in coir compost), begin to feed with a liquid fertilizer once a week, unless you put steady-release fertilizer granules on the compost surface after planting.

Those plants grown permanently in containers will need a fillip every spring. Remove at least 2.5cm/1in of compost, replace with new, and apply a long-lasting steady-release fertilizer. Repot completely every few years, especially if the roots seem very constricted, and growth or flowering seems to have become significantly weaker.

Containers become focuses of interest when in flower, and any imperfections are glaringly obvious: flowering plants need regular deadheading, and their dead leaves removed.

In the autumn, you will either have to propagate half-hardy perennial material, or dig it up, repot it and keep it in a frost-free, light place all winter. Alternatively, you can throw it away and buy in new plants each spring, a more expensive proposition, but much easier.

In winter, containers should be moved to shelter for protection from frost; if they are too large to move, or contain permanent hardy plantings and are of clay, marble or stone, they should be wrapped round with protective material to prevent them splitting. Even if clay pots are sold as 'frost-hardy' it is advisable to take precautions in cold situations; a lengthy cold snap can be disastrous for both containers and plants, which are much more likely to suffer damage from frost than they would if grown in the open ground. Plants can be cocooned in the same way as is recommended for plants in the open garden. Alternatively, use bubble polythene secured with waterproof tape to protect both plant and pot, but remember to leave the soil surface and drainage holes uncovered.

1 A collection of houseleeks in pots looks charming and makes a positive impact on these steps.
Stairs can make an excellent platform for pots. In exchange, the pots give the flight variety and help to soften the outline.

2 *Osteospermum ecklonis* is a near-hardy perennial which flowers all summer, opening its striking flowers in the sunshine. It likes a well drained soil.
Planting is often important in tempering the line of an architectural feature. Here, the planter becomes part of the column.

3 *Abutilon vitifolium* var. *album* (left) is a good subject for a large container. It is showy, although a little tender, and the flowers are borne over several weeks in summer.
One of the main aims of a garden designer is to reinforce the link between house and garden. This has been perfectly achieved by the mass of pots and planting that mask the junction of lawn and stonework.

4 Hanging baskets are very popular as a way of growing gay but tender annuals, and small perennials, especially where space is limited at ground level.
There is no historical monopoly on hanging gardens! The planting of these pots, boxes and baskets is so lush that the doorway is almost hidden.

5 This rag-bag of painted second-hand containers looks charming in this unpretentious but highly picturesque setting. Really profuse flower is almost always appealing.
It can be difficult to mix and match materials successfully. The secret here has been to choose pots that are roughly the same size.

6 I like the appealing understatement of this all-green, container-grown shrub group, particularly set against such an interesting floor pattern.

4

5

6

8

7

9

7 The lack of flower bed is no obstacle to interesting gardening here. This courtyard demonstrates the versatility of plants in the hands of an imaginative gardener.
A sense of humour is vital if any garden is to succeed, and the two clipped birds, beaks poised, keep a wary eye on visitors. The apron of granite setts neatly emphasizes the entrance.

8 Ornamental cabbages, more often seen in a potager, are here planted in a sweet terracotta trough, backed by lovely scented lilies.
Terracotta is a versatile material, and is an excellent choice for many pots and containers. Here, it has been used to mimic the effect of basketwork.

9 Alpines, especially saxifrages and sempervivums, are good subjects for small containers; they will stand a certain amount of drought and do not easily get out of hand. Small containers such as these look best in groups.
In some situations the plants themselves become the focus of interest, and the container becomes almost incidental.

FURNISHINGS AND BUILT-IN SEATS

DS While the overall design of the garden is a relatively static affair, at least in terms of the hard landscape, the furnishing of that space will be far more mobile. Here there is room to include both passing fashion and lasting favourites: the choice of a pot; the siting of a statue, a piece of sculpture or an ornament; the colourway of awnings, deckchair fabric and curtains in a summerhouse. Some may stay with you for a lifetime, while others will come and go as the mood takes you.

Having said all that, the garden is often a far more demanding master than the house, and your choices will invariably have to be tempered by practicality.

Why does garden furniture tend to be so uncomfortable, when the garden is supposed to be, above all, a place in which to relax? Of course there are always exceptions, but do make sure you try chairs out before you buy them, and *never* fall for the temptation of buying through mail order.

Materials vary, and there are no real rights or wrongs here; just respect the setting. Run-of-the-mill plastic tables and chairs do not look good beside a classic Georgian façade, nor do wrought-iron replicas alongside a contemporary steel and glass building. Timber is usually a safe bet, but check that the wood has not come from tropical rain forests; there are other environmentally acceptable sources of supply. Timber can be used in many different ways, and in virtually any garden setting. Consider the character of the particular area when you are deciding on a style, and remember to use non-toxic wood preservatives to prolong its life. You will also need cushions, essential if wooden seats and benches are to remain comfortable for any length of time.

I personally love the old canvas deck and directors' chairs. You can have fun with fabrics, perhaps picking up an interior theme, and they also fold up flat for easy storage. Wickerwork is also attractive, and easy to move around, while the woven 'Lloyd Loom' type of furniture is always immensely comfortable.

But my real favourite is the hammock. There is nothing better than gently snoozing above the sweet grasses of an orchard in a hammock suspended from two stout old trees.

Cushions, awnings, tablecloths and bean bags all add instant colour to a composition, in much the same way as annuals in a container. (Bean bags are a favourite of mine, and both children and dogs love them too!) Choose fabrics with care, and if possible link them to your internal colour scheme. There are a number of waterproofed ones that are ideal for outside use and which do not have to be rushed under cover at the first hint of a shower of rain.

One final thought: always have a good quality waterproof sheet available, and if it is brightly patterned, so much the better. It will have many uses, from picnics on the lawn to hanging over the top of overhead beams when you are barbecuing and there is a sudden torrential rainstorm.

There are many ways in which built-in seats can be used in the garden, apart from alongside a barbecue, and they can often double up for other purposes. Walls for raised beds or surrounding pools are discussed elsewhere in the book, and make a perfect perch.

Integral timber seats are an obvious choice for framing the edge of timber decking, or for surrounding a raised planter. Wooden or metal seats around a tree can form a charming focal point, providing somewhere to pause in the shade of overhanging foliage. You can buy off-the-peg designs in wood, but they all tend to look pretty similar, so why not build your own? Choose a tree of ample size and make the seat of generous proportions. A simple design might be rectangular and big enough to double as a table, lounger, or play

1

FURNISHINGS AND BUILT-IN SEATS

1 This informal little outside room has space for sitting, eating, and growing plants. It has the relaxed feeling of a garden in perfect balance. Slopes are always attractive, and here the sitting area overlooks the slope, separated from the path leading to the house. Plants and a well sited tree have been cleverly used to cut off the sitting area from the path.

2 The best place for sitting usually makes itself quickly apparent, and furniture can simply come to hand. This charmingly simple iron seat rests comfortably beneath the curtain draped to break the force of the sun.

3 Simple elegance is not always easy to find. This composition achieves it perfectly and forms an ideal outdoor eating area. The seats look comfortable, and the table is solid enough for a real meal. The floor is beautifully laid with thin stone bricks on edge, and although slightly uneven, provides an interesting low-key background.

4 To lie in a hammock, suspended in dappled shade, is far and away the best way to relax in the garden. The gentle movement on a hot summer's day must be close to heaven. But do check that ropes are non-rot and strong enough, and check that trees or supports are up to the job. A fall could be dangerous.

5 The composition here, with its stunning use of water and paving, is surely art. All the principles of good design are met: the underlying pattern is strong, there is a simple clarity of line, and the colours are powerful. The furniture is sparse, but it and its reflections set off the superbly laid paving.

2

3

4

5

8 This composition is simple and comfortable, just as it should be. A small courtyard is likely to be used primarily for outside living, so chairs and other pieces of furniture are likely to be dominant items. The area can be made doubly alluring with the addition of plants, and pots can be used to ring the seasonal changes.

9 Parasols not only look good in the garden, but are practical, too, where shade is needed. And wicker chairs like these are invariably comfortable, although they will not fare well in wet weather.

10 This controlled sitting space has great appeal. It turns its back decidedly on the more unruly surroundings.
Pots help to domesticate this terrace, a contrast to the wild garden beyond.

1 Whether plants or hard landscape should be allowed to dominate a garden corner is a delicate question; for so often it is a balance between the two that ensures success. In this example, the faint suggestion that the plants could swamp the bench is part of what makes the sitting place enticing. The bench itself is constructed to a classic design.

2 Garden humour at its best – and practical, too. The only thing missing is a family of gnomes picnicking in the forest.

3 & 4 White is a crisp and elegant choice for wrought iron garden furniture. On the left, the profusion of flower colours benefits from a man-made interruption in a neutral colour, while on the right, the bench is set against a dark foliage background for maximum contrast and drama.

5 There can be few more spectacular places in which to swim, or to sit. The water in the pool makes an obvious link with the distant sea, and the lively pattern of shadows from the overhead beams is picked up by the seat's slatted back.

6 Simplicity is invariably the key to good design, and this solid baulk of timber follows the classic rule of form following function, making it extremely appealing.
The ultimate seat for a gardener, made partly of timber and partly of living hedge.

7 Where stone is the dominant material for hard landscaping, echoing it with stone furniture could be a natural choice. Here there is a further echo as well, between the circular table and curving seat, and the curves used in the ground plan.

6

7

8

9

10

Living in Your Garden

surface. Use lots of cushions to brighten it up and make life a little more comfortable, as with movable garden seating. Seats can also be built into the angles of walls. A generously broad flight of steps will offer instant seating as well as providing a pleasantly raised view of the lower level and whatever happens to be taking place on it.

As a final thought, since my definition of a built-in seat is one that cannot be moved, I would include here large boulders set into the edge of a terrace, or huge fallen logs in a woodland setting. The real point is that the setting should inspire the design and that convention does not always provide the right solution. By all means go and see what the garden centre can provide, and look through books; but, even more importantly, look around you to see what others have come up with, or, best of all, create your own designs.

Eating outside must be one of the great garden pleasures, and is the kind of event that needs to happen spontaneously, particularly in a climate that is notoriously changeable.

If you are barbecue addicts, you will have thought out where you want to barbecue, and incorporated this in the overall garden design. It will almost certainly make sense to allocate a space relatively near the kitchen, and you will need an ample area of paving to allow for a picnic bench and the possibility of a large gathering of friends. If you can site your barbecue to achieve the bonus of late afternoon or evening sun, then so much the better.

Swimming pools make a natural barbecue focus, and should be linked to the eating area by a sensible path. The type of barbecue you have really depends on how often you are likely to use it, and you can employ anything from the simplest portable, that can perch on top of a wide wall or raised bed, to a highly sophisticated built-in model that runs on bottled gas or can be even connected to the mains gas supply.

1 & 2 **Tree seats make inviting stopping places around any garden. A classic constructional shape for a wooden seat is a hexagon, and the example below, set amid a sea of golden pansies, shows how its angular design can fit well into a formal layout. Space must be left between seat and trunk to allow for the gradual expansion of the tree's girth. A free-standing, curving stone seat (left) offers no such possibility of constriction to the trunk. Appropriate for its informal setting, this example has rough stone steps leading up to it.**

3 Chamomile (*Chamaemelum nobile*) can form a pleasantly scented 'cushion' for an outdoor seat; this well-constructed example has golden yew to form the seat, back and arms. It is perfect for a quiet garden corner.

When buying off-the-peg barbecues it is safer to get something rather bigger than you think you will need, because, as well as allowing for friends dropping in, it will also allow you to cook in rotation, with food in various stages of readiness. There is a vast range of models and prices to choose from, and there is bound to be something that suits. The cheapest barbecues really only last a season, and are usually best thrown away at the end of the summer; the bigger and better kind can be cleaned up and stored over winter. Never leave them outside; they look dreadfully unseasonal and quickly rust.

If you regularly enjoy eating outside, then a built-in barbecue may be just the thing for you. Assuming that the location of the barbecue is already decided, you now need to think about the exact siting and configuration. Barbecues need a draught, so should not be set up within a confined space where they will not work well. Gas barbecues can overcome this, but I am a firm believer in the taste and smell of charcoal or wood, even if this is a little too pungent at times! Also, a badly sited barbecue, producing the occasional thick cloud of billowing smoke, can upset even the most accommodating of neighbours.

The simplest built-in type can be put together in a matter of minutes from loosely laid concrete blocks or bricks. You can use cooking grids from your oven or, preferably, buy another set that you can use permanently. Such a barbecue is pretty basic, and there is little scope for altering the height of the grids to control the cooking temperature.

A far better proposition would be to build something altogether longer lasting, similar to that shown opposite. You could include a neatly paved worktop with a built-in store beneath to house tools, logs and charcoal, a few toys, and other bits and pieces. The grids slide

4 These friendly and informal structures have been built largely from materials that have come to hand, and have a comfortable air about them. Such a feature could provide a suitable working surface and storage space in a garden where barbecuing and alfresco living are of major importance.

5 Colour co-ordination is just as important outside the house as it is inside, and the strong theme of blue and white picks up the colour of the glazed tiles of the swimming pool. The built-in seat is a practical solution, while the pierced wall and climber combine to soften the severe rear elevation.

along mild steel strips that are built into the brickwork as work progresses, and can be moved up and down to decrease or increase the cooking rate. You can even buy barbecue grid kits that make the job of construction easier.

When planning the barbecue area, it is worth considering how to incorporate built-in seating. The entire arrangement might perhaps fit into a corner formed by two walls, and overhead beams could carry climbers to cast light shade, and offer fragrance. If you plant herbs close by, perhaps contained in a raised bed, they will add their scent and make a useful addition to your cooking.

BUILT-IN BARBECUES

Built-in barbecues provide a practical and permanent cooking area. This one, constructed from brick, includes adjustable cooking grids, worktop, store, and built-in seat. A feature such as this one could fit into the angle formed by two walls, or define the edge of a terrace area.

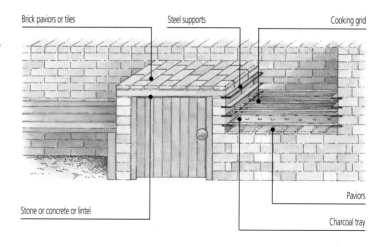

Brick paviors or tiles · Steel supports · Cooking grid · Stone or concrete or lintel · Paviors · Charcoal tray

FURNISHINGS AND BUILT-IN SEATS

LIGHTING

DS Electricity has brought about a revolution in the garden. Apart from its use in the greenhouse, for soil warming, propagation and irrigation, it is also available for lighting and for driving an ever-increasing range of power tools and other equipment.

As far as outside lighting is concerned, the potential is only starting to be appreciated. Not everyone can afford the luxury of a lighting consultant to design and install a specially tailored rig, but it is perfectly possible to create a simpler scheme yourself, that is both practical and highly aesthetic.

There are now a number of 12-volt systems available that are inherently safer than full mains voltage. But whatever system you choose, always follow installation instructions to the letter, and if in any doubt, enlist the services of a qualified electrician.

In designing your own system you must learn to move away from the conventional use of lights. There is little point, for example, in a high level source which lights the top of your head, when what you need is a light to show you where to walk.

The problem, as with many other areas of garden design, is the vast choice of fittings and styles available; these too must be chosen to relate to the house and the rest of the garden, but remember that it is the light rather than the fitting that needs above all to be seen. Georgian coach lamps, for example, belong on Georgian buildings; they look absurd on the front of a 1930s house or on the crisp elevation of a contemporary building, and a better choice would be a plain but well-designed wall light for the first, and something altogether more modern for the second. In the same way, simple bollard lights or entirely concealed fittings will look far better installed along the leafy drive of a mock-Tudor house than a pretentious row of pseudo-Victorian lamp standards.

Garden lighting can be classified into three broad types: functional, security

1

1 This very stage-managed composition, with ruthlessly controlled ground-cover beneath trees, has enormous style, even if there is little here to appeal to the lover of plants. The use of the uplighters positioned at the base of each tree trunk shows the potential of a theatrical approach to lighting outdoors.

Living in Your Garden

1   2

1 Garden lighting can have different aims. Sometimes it sets out to be practical, and sometimes decorative, but it should, if possible, always be attractive. There are also occasions, such as Christmas or other festivities, which require a temporary effect, and in such cases cables and bulbs can be run through trees and around structures to enliven the scene. This is the case here, where the aim has been not to produce long-term subtle effects, but to provide instant colour and a degree of background illumination, perfect for a party or barbecue.

and decorative. Some fittings will be on view, others concealed, but it makes sense to select them all from the same range for the sake of harmony.

Functional lighting is an essential part of any garden. It will provide light for entrances, paths and steps, for a swimming pool or tennis court, for the garage, potting shed or greenhouse; it will extend the use of a terrace for barbecuing, dining and entertaining. Fittings for these purposes should be as simple as possible, and can often be recessed into brick or stonework. For

steps, light can be cast at ground level from a recess in the riser, or in the wall to one side of the flight.

All outside lighting provides some degree of security, and will deter unwelcome visitors. But in certain areas – around the house, for instance – you may want to install movement-sensitive beams that come on when someone walks across them during the hours of darkness – though you must remember that pets and other animals will activate them as well as humans. Lights of this kind are very harsh and it would be

sensible to include an override so that you can deactivate them when you have your other systems switched on.

Decorative lighting can transform the garden at night, highlighting specific features, casting light through trees, and creating dramatic and mysterious effects. During the day, all light comes from above; at night, we can illuminate things from below or to one side, to reveal plants and other features in a new way, or cast shadows in unexpected directions.

Many of the most successful lighting consultants were trained in the theatre,

2 This may be minimal landscaping, but it is breathtaking architecture that is brought alive by the lighting. The secret here is the lack of hard light. Low-wattage bulbs have been used to illuminate the walls gently, rather than plunging them into a harsh glare. Lighting below water can be dramatic, and white is usually the best choice. The uplighters are particularly successful, and reflect the angularity of the composition.

3 Light fittings should be as simple as possible, and pick up the style of the surrounding house and garden. This is a traditional lamp, and it sits comfortably against the soft, floriferous background. Somehow, in this prolific setting, the lamp has escaped being swamped. For both practical and aesthetic reasons, it is important to prune the rose carefully around it each year.

Uplighting is another technique that involves careful positioning. Lights are placed underneath shrubs or trees to highlight the branch and leaf structure. This can be particularly effective in winter, when branches are bare, and as they come into leaf the effect changes; lit from below, the texture and shape of foliage takes on a new and fascinating dimension. Garden lighting is not a static art form; it changes subtly with the seasons and as plants grow, all factors which should be considered when making your final choice.

Backlighting, the reverse of spotlighting, highlights a plant or ornament from behind. The source of light is hidden at ground level, and shines upwards on to the feature. It can be stunningly effective, and because it is positioned close to the object, requires a far less powerful beam than a spotlight.

Moonlighting is where a number of diffused lights are used at high level to filter down through the branches of trees in imitation of moonlight. The effect is beautiful, and if the resulting shadows are cast on to a path or lawn, the results can be breathtaking.

Underwater lighting can be extremely effective; it can also be a disaster, and the key as usual is to keep it as simple as possible. Avoid those floating, rotating displays that children fall for at the garden centre – they are guaranteed to produce a migraine in record time. The water must be clear, and the light preferably positioned to illuminate a feature such as a fountain bowl or statue. Of course pools, and the features within them, may also be lit from an exterior source, using the techniques discussed here.

Mirror lighting is another water technique. Here a spotlight is directed from outside the pool to illuminate a feature which is in turn reflected on the surface of the water. It also has the effect of highlighting a small area around the feature, so that the pool of light merges with the pool of water below.

3

and employ the techniques learned there to stunning effect in the garden. This use of a medium for a quite different purpose is a fine example of lateral thinking, and should remind us that gardens are by no means an isolated art form.

A warning about colour. White light is fine, and so is blue; both enhance rather than detract from the natural colours found in the landscape. But you will find a whole range of coloured lights available, and most create unnatural and distorting effects; green, red and orange are particularly dreadful.

Spotlighting, a traditional lighting technique by which an object is picked out in sharp relief to the pool of darkness around it, is ideal for drawing attention to a focal point such as a statue or container, and if the beam is angled slightly across the feature, it will create surface shadows in a far more interesting way than if it is aimed head-on.

The distance at which the light is positioned from the object it is intended to illuminate will determine the intensity and the spread of the beam; this is particularly important for a spotlight, but

needs consideration for all lighting. Since a spotlight will normally be concealed at some distance from the feature, you will need to use a relatively powerful light.

Grazing describes a beam of light positioned on the face of a building, gazebo or other structure, which 'grazes' the surface; an effect which works by drawing attention to the architectural detail and setting up dramatic shadow patterns that would never be possible with daylight. Lighting of this kind can be directed either from above or below, depending on the effect you want.

ORNAMENTS AND STATUARY

DS A vast selection of statuary and other ornaments is available today; here again the choice is a highly personal one. The real point to remember is that an object should be chosen with its position in mind. Of course, if you already own a feature that you want to use as a focal point, you will have worked out where it should go when designing the garden.

Any ornaments you choose should be in character with your house and the rest of your garden, and should, at the very least, relate to it in a positive way. As a general rule, modern pieces do not look comfortable in a classic setting and vice-versa. Remember, too, that whereas one or two carefully positioned pieces will draw the eye and add to a composition, too many will create a feeling of restlessness, and defeat the object of the exercise.

A feature of this kind need not be 'conventional'; a well-chosen smooth boulder at the turn of the path, or a ball of chicken wire smothered in ivy are both ornaments. Sculpture often gives rise to passionate responses – of both love and hate. Terrific! At least you have elicited a reaction, and reaction is often an indicator of good design.

1 & 2 Contemporary art usually provokes a subjective response, and can be successfully used in a garden to stimulate discussion. The sculpture could be abstract or figurative, as these two examples show. The sinuous acrobats have great movement to them, and look perfectly at home on a flight of old stone steps – illustrating how a contrast between old and new in the ornament and setting can be extremely effective. On the right, an abstract sculpture is set in a small town garden amid a profusion of green leafiness.

5

6

7

8

3, 4 & 6 I am always wary of using classical figures and busts in the garden, but they can form a striking focal point if positioned with care. Since they are often mass-produced, particular attention needs to be paid to their setting.

Plants can usefully surround and smother a classical ornament, setting up appropriate references and suggesting that the object has been there for a very long time. The standing figure is wreathed most attractively in *Viburnum tinus*, and the stone torso is thrown into sharp relief by a positive blaze of magenta bougainvillea in the background.

5 Still water gives the opportunity for some dramatic reflections. Here superb steps rise cleanly from the water, enhancing the effect of the log-crocodile. Both children and adults love this kind of visual trickery.

7 & 8 Two variations on the use of large, unplanted pots as ornaments. On the left, a carefully contrived arrangement using toning colours of brick and terracotta has a raised plinth to add emphasis. On the right, surface patterning on the pot picks up the striking leaf textures in the lush planting around.

THE TOP 100 GARDEN PLANTS

1

This section offers a guide to 100 plants that can be used as a basis for workable and attractive planting schemes. They have been chosen to reflect a wide range of habit, colour and season of interest; they are suitable for a variety of aspects, soil conditions and situations. All are excellent garden plants; most have more than one feature or season of interest to recommend them; nearly all have found a place in one or more of the sample garden designs earlier on in the book.

You will soon find that these 100 plants will whet your appetite for more. There are over 60,000 species and cultivars available – a number large enough to make strong men blench. Practical considerations such as aspect, soil, and hardiness, do much to narrow the field of appropriate plants to a more manageable size; but you are spoiled for choice, and that choice is as satisfying and absorbing as any aspect of gardening.

Professional garden designers tend to use a reliable, if rather limited, selection of readily available plants that can be depended on. You are, in a sense, more fortunate; your constraints are fewer and you can afford to experiment. Remember that availability is no guarantee that a plant will give you pleasure, will be suitable for your garden, or will be rewarding to grow. It is well worth doing some homework before you buy.

Fortunately, information about the habits and requirements of suitable plants is easy to come by. Books, nursery and seed catalogues, magazines, television programmes and instructional videotapes all aim to inform and advise the apprentice and experienced gardener alike. Moreover, there is your own observation. A wander through a friend's garden may well yield up an idea for a good colour scheme or planting association, and a visit to a garden open to the public almost certainly will.

2

1 For many gardeners, the first choice for a brick wall is the climbing rose and it is easy to see why. Even in conditions where there is a limited root run or feeding regime, they will flower wholeheartedly and impressively. The extra warmth they gain from being grown against such a wall helps to ripen the wood and aid flowering, for the sun's rays are absorbed by the brick during the day, and released at night.

2 The joy of evergreen foliage lies in how much it can add to the appeal of the garden in winter. The freshness of the grasses and *Euonymus fortunei* 'Emerald Gaiety' in these obviously very cold conditions is testament to their hardiness and amiability. The space left amongst this ground-cover could allow for bulbs and summer perennials to come up in the spring, and so give added zest to a picture which would perhaps become a little dull if it remained unchanged all the year round.

A botanical garden, arboretum or serious nursery, where plants are labelled, will introduce you to more good plants, and even a visit to the local garden centre to make a note of which plants are in flower at different times of year can be useful.

Take notes of plants which impress you; their season of flower, foliage impact, height, spread, soil and aspect requirements, and colour. Photographs can be helpful, but only in conjunction with notes, because colours do not always reproduce faithfully. Remember also that a plant often changes in appearance at different times of year.

Do not be afraid to make a list of 'hates'; you may be seduced by a photograph in a catalogue, and forget how much you disliked the plant when you actually saw it growing in the ground.

Having looked, read, noted and talked to other gardeners, who are usually happy to share their experience and even their plants, list the plants and plant features that attract you most. Do you like trees, shrubs, herbaceous perennials, annuals, bulbs, ground-cover plants – or a mixture of them all? List colours that appeal to you, and the kind of flowers that you are most drawn to – tiny and exquisite; bold and striking; a cloudy mass. Or are you as much, if not more, interested in foliage; autumn colour; evergreen conifers; 'architectural' plants of all kinds? Do you like ground-hugging dumpy mounds, elegant arching shrubs, fountains of feathery leaves, horizontal tiers, or all of those?

Once you have, in broad terms, decided what you like, you will find it easier to identify the types of plant on which you would wish to concentrate. Of course, your notes are not written on tablets of stone; they are merely aids to making the choice less daunting.

TREES

Trees will be the largest, and most long-lived, plants in your garden so should be chosen with special care. They should be selected for their form and bark almost as much as for their foliage and fruits. A mixture of evergreen and deciduous trees is ideal. Consider the eventual spread (both of branches and roots) as well as the height for, in small gardens especially, this is crucial. Even if you plan to move on in a few years, think ahead when you plant trees and do not select anything that will outgrow its space. Take account of the shade likely to be cast when the tree is mature.

1 *Abies koreana*

Abies koreana, the silver fir, is a small (but not 'dwarf') conifer, which grows to about 5 x 3m/15 x 10ft in ten years and, eventually, 8 x 5m/25 x 15ft. It makes a conical neat shape, and is usually grown for the brightness of its green leaves, intensely silver underneath, and also the abundant upright blue-violet 7.5cm/3in cones which are borne along the branches on even young plants. The silver fir has spirally arranged needle-like soft leaves. It is very hardy, but young shoots can be damaged by spring frosts.
Cultivation and Propagation Likes partial shade or sun and a moist soil, preferably not too alkaline and certainly not chalky. Can be raised from seed shed in the autumn.
Use Makes a good specimen in a confined space, or even as a feature in a large border.
Similar plants A. *koreana* 'Compact Dwarf' (grows eventually to 90cm/36in).

2 *Acer davidii*

This beautiful deciduous small snakebark maple from China grows to about 6 x 4.5m/20 x 15ft in ten years. The leaves are glossy green, ovate, usually about 7.5-12.5cm/ 3-5in long and 7.5cm/3in wide. The flowers are small, yellow, and pendulous, and the fruits the characteristic winged keys of the sycamore family. Its glory, however, lies in the colour of the young stems (sealing-wax red) and the bark which matures to striped green and white. The leaves turn yellow in autumn.
Cultivation and Propagation Will grow in most well drained and fertile soils, provided that they are not too shallow. Best planted in shelter from late frosts and cold winds which burn the young leaves and can split the bark. The stripes develop most clearly in semi-shade.

Propagation is usually done by setting out seeds to 'stratify' over winter outdoors; these should then germinate in spring.
Use Makes a fine small but broad-headed specimen, either grown with a single trunk, or with several stems to show off the 'striations'.
Similar plants A. *capillipes; A. grosseri* var. *hersii.*

3 *Betula pendula*
'Laciniata'
(*B. pendula* 'Dalecarlica')

A fine form of the splendid fast-growing and hardy native silver birch, this tree has the same upright and sparsely branched habit, with long, drooping branchlets, a trunk that whitens with age, and catkins. However, it also has deeply cut leaves which give it a more airy appearance. The tree reaches more than 6m/20ft in time, but its spread rarely exceeds 3-4.5m/10-15ft. The leaves turn golden-yellow before falling in autumn.
Cultivation Grow in full sun and a well drained soil if possible, although this tree is not fussy and will grow in clay. It has wide-ranging shallow roots so do not plant close to buildings or walls. It tolerates wind.
Use An elegant garden tree, casting little shade and requiring no maintenance. It can be grown as a specimen or in small groups. Shrubs with horizontal branches, such as *Viburnum plicatum* 'Mariesii', make suitable contrasting companions.
Similar plants B. *pendula* 'Tristis'.

4 *Carpinus betulus*
'Fastigiata' (*C. betulus* 'Pyramidalis')

The fastigiate, or upright, form of the common hornbeam; a handsome

deciduous tree which grows to about 10 x 5m/33 x 15ft. The leaves are toothed and have prominent veins; they are oval, up to 7.5cm/3in long and 5cm/2in wide, slightly shinier than in the type. The trunk is fluted rather than smooth. This form is remarkable for the dense mass of upward-sweeping branches, giving the tree an oval, or flame-like look, most marked when young.
Separate male and female catkins are borne on the same tree all season; in autumn, the female ones are transformed into clusters of small winged nuts.
Cultivation The hornbeam will grow on heavy wet soils, which makes it more versatile than the beech. It likes sun or partial shade. If you wish to accentuate the shape or grow it as a hedge, prune it in summer. In that way, the dead leaves will not fall.
Use As a good form of a native tree, C. *betulus* 'Fastigiata' is very suitable for country gardens, ideal for gardeners who do not have room for a beech but who appreciate the qualities of these similar, but unrelated, trees. Grow it as a specimen so that its distinctive shape can be properly appreciated. A hedge looks impenetrable.
Similar plants C. *betulus.*

5 *Fagus sylvatica*

The finest of all native trees, the beech (or one of its forms) should be planted wherever there is truly space for it. A fully grown specimen will easily reach 12 x 9m/40 x 30ft, clothed almost to the ground, but it is a beautiful tree even when young. The trunk is smooth and turns grey in time. The leaves, bright green in spring, and turning yellow or gold in the autumn, are ovate and wavy-margined, with conspicuous veins. The flowers are small, but round woody fruits germinate after hot summers.
Cultivation The beech will grow in most soils, provided that they are not too heavy and waterlogged. It likes sun.
Use A specimen tree for a large lawn or conspicuous position. Alternatively, grow it as a hedge, trimming the top and sides back each summer, so that the dead leaves hang on in winter; a lovely effect can be produced using different cultivars of the purple beech with the common green-

leaved form. Beech, like holly and hornbeam, attracts native fauna.
Similar plants F. *sylvatica* 'Aspleniifolia' (deeply cut leaves lend a more delicate look to the tree); F. *sylvatica purpurea* (the famous purple beech); F. *sylvatica* 'Zlatia' (has yellow young leaves).

6 *Gleditsia triacanthos*
'Sunburst'

The fine yellow-leaved form of the hardy deciduous honey locust. It makes a small, broad-spreading, sparsely-branched tree, about 6 x 3m/20 x 10ft. Intensely yellow ferny leaves in spring slowly turn yellow-green before reverting to golden again in autumn. Unlike most other gleditsias, it has spineless stems which turn yellow in winter. The flowers make little impact when they come out in midsummer, and the long, twisted seedpods are rarely seen in northern climates. It is tolerant of shade, particularly when young, and will thrive in any well drained soil, and even in polluted air.
Cultivation Best planted when young, in a sheltered place, and can be hard pruned to achieve as much of the yellow foliage as possible. It can also be pruned as a shrub by leaving the lower branches in place and cutting back all branches by a third before bud-break. A honey locust midge, which has arrived in Europe from the United States, can cause trouble.
Use A tree for use as a specimen in a small garden, or even in the border, for it casts little shade; an excellent alternative to *Robinia pseudoacacia* 'Frisia', particularly in gardens where there are children and a spiny tree is a hazard. In a yellow scheme, it would associate well with *Cornus alba* 'Spaethii'.
Similar plants G. *triacanthos* 'Elegantissima'; G. *triacanthos* 'Rubylace'.

7 *Ilex aquifolium*
'J.C. van Tol'

There are a number of fine hollies suitable for garden cultivation, both green-leaved and variegated. The fastest-growing are the green ones and, of these, the female *Ilex aquifolium* 'J.C. van Tol' is one of the

8

9

10

11

best. Its virtues lie in its practically spineless leaves and its ability to berry even if there are no male hollies nearby.

The leaves are dark green, oval, and up to about 5cm/2in long. The flowers are scarcely noticeable, but the fruits are large, bright red and generously produced. The young stems are purple in colour. The tree will grow to about 3m/10ft high by 1.8-3m/6-10ft wide.

Cultivation and Propagation
Hollies are not fussy as to soil, but do best in a moist loam. They are happy in sun or shade, are tolerant of air pollution, and can be planted in windy positions. If a hedge is required, place young plants 45cm/18in apart and clip in late-spring or early autumn. 'J.C. van Tol' is best propagated by cuttings taken with a heel in late summer and put in a cold frame to root.

Use This holly, like the others, makes a fine stately and inpenetrable hedge; it will stand severe clipping and is clothed to the base. It also makes a handsome specimen tree. Its lack of spines recommends it to gardeners who hand-weed.

Similar plants *I. aquifolium* 'Pyramidalis' (also self-fertile).

8 *Juniperus sabina*
'Tamariscifolia'

Of all the so-called dwarf conifers, this is one of the most versatile, performing either as ground-cover or in an architectural role. A form of the common savin, it makes a prostrate, spreading, evergreen plant, usually about 75cm/30in high by 1.25m/5ft across. The height is achieved in tiers, which adds to the plant's interest.

'Tamariscifolia' has mostly juvenile foliage (junipers have two forms of leaf, juvenile and adult), which emerges at a narrow angle from the crowded young branches. The needles are greyish-green when young, becoming bright green with age. The foliage is dense enough to keep weeds down.

Cultivation and Propagation
Junipers are best grown in full sun but are unfussy as to soil, provided it is not waterlogged. They should be planted in late spring, and protected until well established. All are vulnerable to damage from scale insects. Cuttings, cut with a heel, should be taken in early autumn.

Use Useful for hiding manhole

covers, clothing rocks in a rock garden, or adding horizontal emphasis as a contrast to upright shrubs and perennials.

Similar plants *J. sabina* 'Blue Danube'; *J. sabina* 'Hicksii'.

9 *Malus*
'Red Sentinel'

The ornamental crab apples have gained in popularity in recent years because they are smaller and happier on heavy land than ornamental cherries, less prone to disease than ornamental peaches, and their fruits are edible if cooked. 'Red Sentinel' is remarkable, not so much for its pretty flowers in late spring but for the large, cherry-shaped, deep red fruits which hang in thick clusters until early spring.

It grows to 3-4.5m/10-15ft, and about 2.5m/8ft wide. The mid-green leaves are oval and the flowers 2.5cm/1in wide, cupped, and white. The branches are slightly pendulous; this habit is accentuated by the weight of the massed fruits in autumn and winter. Best planted as a specimen rather than used as an avenue tree.

Cultivation Not fussy as to soil, although all crab apples benefit from a yearly mulch in drier soil. Will grow in sun or semi-shade. The fruit set is best when other malus trees are grown nearby.

Use A great asset to the winter garden. Its relatively modest size makes it suitable for all but very small gardens. It casts only a moderately light shade.

Similar plants *M.* 'Red Jade'.

10 *Metasequoia glyptostroboïdes*

The dawn redwood was discovered in China just after World War II, and has proved itself to be very hardy, pollution-resistant, fast-growing, easy and handsome. There are trees now more than 30m/100ft high from the earliest plantings. Unusually for a conifer, it is deciduous, and has fine autumn colour before the needles drop. It can grow up to 1m/3ft a year, making a conical shape with bright green, feathery foliage which turns bronze as the year wears on. The bark is rusty red, peeling, and the trunk has large indentations.

The cones are dark brown, rather drooping and globose.

Cultivation and Propagation
It is best grown in moist, but well drained and deep soil, and in semi-shade or full sun. In shallow soils it will grow more slowly – which may be a good thing. It is very hardy, but in the early years the top may be frosted, when a replacement leader will have to be encouraged. Plant in mid-spring. Semi-hard cuttings will root easily.

Use A stately, fast-growing tree which makes an excellent specimen where its eventual height will not be a problem. Because it is deciduous, it has great seasonal interest and will not kill off everything growing underneath.

Similar plants Several new forms such as *M. glyptostroboïdes* 'Sheridan Spire'.

11 *Sorbus aria*
'Majestica' (*S. aria* 'Decaisneana')

Simply the most vigorous form of the beautiful common whitebeam, with larger leaves, flowers and fruits. The leaves can be 17.5cm/7in long, and as much as 10cm/4in wide. It makes a broadly conical tree, up to 15m/50ft high in time, and 3m/10ft across. The new foliage is intensely silver on both sides when young; then the hairs on the top disappear, leaving those below, giving the tree an interesting silvery appearance on windy days. The leaves are toothed and oval, and the creamy white flowers are individually small but clustered into large flat-topped flower heads up to 7.5cm/3in across, in late spring. The small round fruits, which are attractive to birds, are bright red and freely borne; the autumn colour is russet and gold.

Cultivation and Propagation
The whitebeam is naturally a tree of chalk soil, but will grow on a wide variety of well drained soils. A robust, usually healthy tree, it is nevertheless, like all sorbuses (and, indeed, other trees in the rose family), vulnerable to canker and fireblight.

Use Grow as a specimen, because it has a fine shape and casts a dense summer shade. It is not a tree for a small garden.

Similar plants *S. aria* 'Lutescens' (yellow leaves in spring).

Shrubs, either with or without trees, provide the permanent planting structure of your garden, and are usually long-lived, so consider every aspect – shape, foliage, scent, flowers, berries, bark, attractiveness and cultivation requirements – when making your choice.

12 Buddleja alternifolia

This deciduous, arching shrub is far more graceful than most other buddlejas, yet just as easy to grow. Its alternate leaves (hence the name) are narrow and dark-green; in early summer clusters of small, scented, lilac-purple flowers are thickly set along pendent flowering stems. It can make a small weeping tree, about 2.4 x 1.8/8 x 6ft, if the lower branches are trimmed off the trunk.
Cultivation and Propagation Likes a place in full sun in well drained loamy soil. Prune by removing flowered shoots in summer. Propagate by taking semi-ripe cuttings at the same time.
Use Can be grown as a specimen, in lawn or longer grass, or in a big shrub border. It needs space to display its full magnificence, but can be underplanted with spring bulbs for interest before it flowers.
Similar plants B. alternifolia 'Argentea' (silvery green leaves).

13 Camellia × williamsii 'Anticipation'

One of the best of the x williamsii hybrids, which have the great advantage over the other camellias in shedding their flowers after they fade. Grows to a height of 3m/10ft by about 1.5m/5ft wide. The leaves are glossy, dark green and ovate, tapering to a point. The 'peony form' flowers come out from early to late spring, a deep bright pink in colour, and up to 12.5cm / 5in across.
Cultivation Slightly frost-tender. Plant in early autumn or spring in sheltered 'woodland' conditions, or against a wall, where the flowers will not be caught by early morning sun and cold winds. Camellias must have a neutral or acid soil, enriched with leaf mould if possible. Mulch every spring. They can also be container-grown in ericaceous compost.
Use Camellias make excellent specimen shrubs, or can be associ-

ated with other early-flowering shrubs and trees like magnolias, shrubby willows, early rhododendrons, and Prunus x subhirtella 'Autumnalis'.
Similar plants C. x williamsii 'Donation' (hardier; a larger, almost tree-sized, shrub).

14 Ceratostigma willmottianum

Blue-flowered shrubs are much too uncommon, so one which flowers in autumn is especially welcome. Ceratostigma willmottianum makes a deciduous, reasonably hardy open shrub, about 90 x 90cm/36 x 36in. The plumbago-shaped flowers are of the most beguiling cerulean blue, borne in bristly terminal clusters over a long period from late summer to late autumn, above a foil of green stalkless ovate leaves which turn red before falling in late autumn. This shrub can be cut to the ground by hard frosts in winter, so it is best to give it the protection of a wall.
Cultivation and Propagation Likes full sun and a well drained soil. Prune by cutting out dead wood. Propagate by softwood cuttings. Protect in winter in cold districts.
Use A plant for shrub or mixed borders. Because of its red leaves in autumn, it associates well with glaucous leaves, for example those of Berberis temolaica and Festuca glauca. Alternatively, use it in conjunction with a red-berried, red-leaved shrub like Berberis 'Rubrostilla'. Autumn bulbs like Sternbergia lutea and Zephyranthes candida can be planted amongst it.
Similar plants C. plumbaginoïdes (sub-shrubby perennial).

15 Cistus × corbariensis

Cistus or rock rose is a beautiful, if not always entirely hardy, genus of Mediterranean sub-shrubs suitable for a warm, sunny spot in a free-draining, even poor soil. Cistus x corbariensis is one of the hardiest

and a good bet for gardens, particularly where rainfall is not high. Cistus do not like cold winds, but will grow happily in mild coastal gardens.
Cistus x corbariensis is a low, dense, spreading shrub (about 60 x 120cm/24 x 48in) with dull green, hairy leaves which are wrinkled, wavy, ovate and toothed. Amongst these come, in midsummer, pure white 3.5cm/1½in in diameter crinkled flowers, with a central boss of yellow stamens. None lasts more than a day but the succession goes on for two to three weeks. The buds are distinctively pinky red.
Cultivation and Propagation Plant in late spring, using container-grown specimens to minimize root disturbance. Prune only the dead and frosted wood and perhaps after flowering remove tips to reshape bush. Older plants do not like being pruned. Take cuttings with a heel in late summer and root in a heated propagator, overwintering rooted cuttings in a cold frame.
Use Its low, bushy nature, reliable hardiness and green-grey leaf colour make it ideal for hot dry schemes; grow amongst sages, teucriums, santolinas, artemisias and tender perennials. A good weed suppressor.
Similar plants C. laurifolius (large bush, white flowers); C. x cyprius (C. ladanifer) (laxer, larger habit; white flowers with red markings).

16 Cornus alba 'Spaethii'

A deciduous hardy shrub with two seasons of interest. In winter there are bright red stems, and in the growing season, beautiful bright green oval pointed leaves with irregular yellow margins and markings. One of the few yellow-variegated shrubs which does not suffer leaf scorch in direct sun and remains bright all season. It makes a thicket of red stems, up to 1.8m/6ft high and broad (less if pruned annually), which almost glow in winter sunshine. Creamy flowers appear in early summer; followed by blue-tinged white berries.
Cultivation and Propagation All Cornus alba forms are easy to grow in a moist soil, thriving even in clay or poor soil (provided it does not dry out in summer), in sun or partial shade. They can stand atmospheric pollution, exposure to wind and cold, and require little maintenance, apart from the biennial cutting back of

12   13

14   15

16

17

18   19

20

stems close to the ground in early spring so that the winter stems are always young and bright. Propagate by hardwood cuttings in autumn, by removing rooted suckers in late autumn, or by layering.

Use Quick to make an impact after planting, and impressive in winter. Plant in a group in boggy ground near a pond or in any moist soil where there is space for it to spread. The stems look well, backed by pampas grass or *Pyrus salicifolia* 'Pendula'. In leaf, it is ideal as a backcloth for a yellow border, giving lasting colour behind more fleeting yellow flowers.

Similar plants *C. alba* 'Elegantissima' (more marginal variegation, white against a grey-green background).

17 Cytisus × kewensis

Like all brooms, *Cytisus x kewensis* is loved by bees. Creamy white or pale yellow leguminous flowers are thickly massed on arching stems, in shoot joints, in late spring, and followed by seed pods. The flowering is later than the well known *Cytisus x praecox* and the flowers larger. It will grow to 45cm/18in high by as much as 1.2m/4ft across, in time. This is a deciduous, hardy, undemanding, ground-hugging shrub, which casts little or no shade because the mid-green trifoliate leaves are so small.

Cultivation and Propagation Plant in spring or early autumn in a sunny place and any well drained, preferably fertile, soil. Take cuttings in late summer. Old stems, if overcrowded, can be trimmed out after flowering.

Use Ideal for hanging over a raised bed, in a dry wall, or on a ledge on a rockery. Will go with other late spring-flowering rock shrubs and plants, such as aubrieta and helianthemums.

Similar plants *C. x praecox* (creamy yellow, flowers in mid-spring); *C. purpureus* (flowers in early summer, purple).

18 Daphne odora
'Aureomarginata'

A neat, bushy, slightly tender, slow-growing evergreen, which can grow to 1.2m x 1.5m/4 x 5ft in time. Oval glossy leaves with a very narrow

creamy yellow edge to them, and very sweetly scented purplish-pink flowers, in terminal clusters, from late winter/mid-spring. These fade as they mature.

Cultivation and Propagation Plant it in early autumn or mid-spring in any well drained soil in a sheltered position; a sunny place will ensure the best flowering. Propagation is easier than for many daphnes; take semi-ripe cuttings with a heel in midsummer.

Use Underplant with dwarf spring bulbs and evergreen ground-cover such as *Stachys byzantina*. Can provide foliage contrast in a hectically colourful border.

Similar plants *D. odora* (green-leaved, less hardy); *D. mezereum* (early spring); *Daphne x burkwoodii* 'Somerset' (late spring flowering).

19 Deutzia × elegantissima

A deciduous, bushy, upright shrub, with a height and spread of about 1.2m/4ft. Its matt green leaves taper to a point. The flowers are scented, white tinted pink, up to 7.5cm/3in wide and shaped like stars, appearing in early summer.

Cultivation and Propagation Will grow in any garden soil that is not too heavy, and in any sheltered position in sun or partial shade. The young shoots are sometimes frosted in spring. Prune by thinning out some old flowered shoots after flowering. Propagate by semi-ripe or hardwood cuttings.

Use Like other dull-leaved shrubs, such as philadelphus or lilacs, deutzias need to be able to blend into the background after flowering. Surround them with late summer perennials and repeat-flowering roses, plant a summer-flowering clematis to scramble through, and underplant with early spring bulbs.

Similar plants *D. x elegantissima* 'Rosealind' (striking, with carmine-pink flowers); *D. monbeigii* (flowers later than other varieties of mid- to late summer deutzias).

20 Erica carnea
'King George'

Erica carnea is one of the few heathers to tolerate an alkaline soil. There are many cultivars widely available, of which one of the best is

'King George'. Its dark green foliage acts as a foil for the deep pink flowers which are borne in short terminal spikes from late autumn until late winter. Like all *E. carnea* cultivars it is evergreen, densely spreading (up to 60cm/24in but only 20cm/8in high in flower), and very hardy. The leaves are needle-like, borne in whorls on the thin woody stems, and the flowers are profuse, pendulous and tubular.

Cultivation and Propagation
A first-rate ground-cover plant if trimmed back after flowering to encourage new growth and prevent legginess. It will take more shade than most heathers, which usually require full sun, but all like a moisture-retentive enriched soil. Plant in early autumn or late spring, and deep enough for all the stem to be buried. Water well until the plants are well established, and in dry periods.
Use Heathers are best planted in substantial groups, making little impact as singletons. They can be associated with deciduous and evergreen shrubs, or with other heathers, and are useful for planting on slopes and rocky ground – their natural habitat. Heathers and dwarf conifer mixtures are rarely successful unless done with great conviction. 'King George' looks well with Lenten hellebores, hepaticas, and *Daphne mezereum* in partial shade, or *Daphne odora* in sun. The dark green neat foliage can act as a foil for colourful summer flowers. *Clematis flammula* can be planted to weave through a patch of it, and can be cut right back in late winter. Alternatively, use the everlasting peas, *Lathyrus grandiflorus* or *L. latifolius*, which die down in winter.
Similar plants *E. carnea* 'Myretoun Ruby'; *E. carnea* 'Vivellii'; *E. carnea* 'Springwood White'; *E. carnea* 'Springwood Pink'.

21 **Euonymus fortunei**
'Emerald 'n' Gold'

Euonymus fortunei cultivars make up a most useful group of plants, because they are hardy, evergreen, long-lived, reliable, and there are many variegated forms, of which 'Emerald 'n' Gold' is one of the best. Bright yellow oval leaves, with central portions of green, are thickly placed on a short shrub, about 60 x 90cm/24 x 36in. Mature plants have

insignificant flowers. This euonymus is attractive to flower arrangers because it is particularly noticeable in winter, when the cold will tinge the leaves with pink.
Cultivation and Propagation
Happy in sun or partial shade and, though unfussy as to soil, grows best in well drained ground and in a sheltered position. Plant in autumn or spring. Propagate by heel cuttings in late summer, putting them in a cuttings mix in a cold frame. Use shears to clip the shrub in summer to retain a neat shape.
Use Associates well with other forms of *E. fortunei*. It also goes with the blue flowers of the hardy geraniums or small ceanothus, and the leaves of silver shrubs. It is most profitably used for winter effect, perhaps as an evergreen understorey to the deciduous *Chimonanthus* or *Cotoneaster horizontalis*.
Similar plants *E. fortunei* 'Emerald Gaiety'; *E. fortunei* 'Silver Queen'.

22 **Fuchsia** 'Riccartonii'

The forms of *Fuchsia magellanica* are among the hardiest deciduous fuchsias; in very mild districts – such as by the sea – can be used as a hedge. In harsher conditions it is cut right back in winter but rarely killed. It makes about 1.2m/4ft of growth in a season, and if not cut back by frost can attain 1.8 x 1.5m/6 x 5ft. Its many erect stems are reddish when young. The pendulous, narrow flowers are scarlet and purple, freely borne over a very long period. The leaves are dark green, lanceolate and toothed in shape.
Cultivation and Propagation
Plant in spring in enriched, well drained soil in a spot sheltered from cold winds. Hedging should be planted 45cm/18in apart. Prune back frosted stems in spring, or alternatively cut all stems back in late autumn close to the ground and cover the roots with protective material. In mild areas, it is only necessary to shape the bush in the spring.
Use Before it flowers, 'Riccartonii' is a good foil for red *Anemone* x *fulgens*. In flower, it contrasts well with green foliage and flowers, or the deep red autumn colour of *Parthenocissus quinquefolia*.
Similar plants *F. magellanica* 'Versicolor' (pink-flushed young leaves which turn grey-green).

23 **Hamamelis** × **intermedia**
'Pallida'

The witch hazels are desirable because they flower in late winter – with 'spiders' of scented ribbon petals on leafless shoots. Although slow-growing and fussy as to soil, they are worth it for the beauty and interest of their flowers and the yellow autumn colour of their leaves.
  Hamamelis x *intermedia* 'Pallida' will grow, eventually, to a height and spread of 3m/10ft as a large shrub or small tree. Its profusely borne scented flowers on ascending branches have broader 'spiders' than other witch hazels, pale sulphur-yellow in colour, with red centres, in mid- to late winter. The leaves are like hazel leaves, ribbed and rounded.
Cultivation and Propagation
Hamamelis will grow in sun or part shade, in well worked fertile soil enriched with humus. In these conditions they will tolerate a somewhat alkaline soil. They need shelter from cold winds. Layering is the safest way of propagating them.
Use Grow with other winter-interest plants which will not detract from the shape of the shrub and its flowers; for example, sarcococca, or an underplanting of *Anemone hepatica*, winter bulbs, or winter heathers. It makes a fine specimen for lawn or border or under deciduous trees, especially where there is a dark background to show off the flowers.
Similar plants *H.* x *intermedia* 'Diane'; *H.* x *intermedia* 'Jelena'.

21
22

23

24 **Hebe pinguifolia**
'Pagei'

A not very endearing but infinitely useful buffer plant, grey-leaved with unexceptional white flowers and a ground-hugging and easy nature. It is also, unlike many hebes, reasonably hardy. Grows to 22cm/9in high but spreads to 90cm/36in. The leaves are small, obovate, slightly fleshy and glaucous-grey. White flowers held in short spikes appear in late spring and early summer and often bloom again in late summer.
Cultivation and Propagation
Plant in spring in any well drained soil in full sun or partial shade. No need to prune unless frosted. It has a tendency to die off in the middle so propagate occasionally by digging

24

25

26

27

and severing natural rooted layers, or by semi-ripe cuttings in late summer. Overwinter these in a frost-free place. **Use** This hummocky hebe grows well in coastal gardens and is excellent for rock gardens, raised beds, pockets in paving, containers, or as ground-cover in any sunny place. It looks very well with low pink flowers such as diascias, with the purple of *Viola labradorica* leaves, or the yellow of *Lysimachia nummularia* 'Aurea'. Medium-sized bulbs like *Allium christophii* can be planted to grow through it.
Similar plants *H. albicans; H. 'Youngii' (H. 'Carl Teschner')*.

25 **Kolkwitzia amabilis** 'Pink Cloud'

The beauty bush from western China makes a hardy, deciduous, arching, twiggy shrub, about 3 x 1.8m/10 x 6ft, and is covered in pink foxglove flowers with yellow throats in late spring and early summer. These are followed by seedheads in midsummer. The leaves are oval, matt and green, and the bark peels. 'Pink Cloud' is the best form.
Cultivation and Propagation A light and airy shrub which can be grown against a wall, even a partially shaded one. It thrives in sun and a well drained soil, even growing happily on chalk. It will sucker or can be propagated by softwood or semi-hard cuttings (taken with a heel). Prune out some of the old shoots after flowering to encourage new ones from the base.
Use Useful for the colour and profusion of its flowers. Mix it with pinks and blues, perhaps shrub roses and blue campanulas. Grow where it can blend into the background after flowering, for the leaves are dull and the habit unexceptional. The sturdy branches can be used as a support for clematis.
Similar plants *K. amabilis.*

26 **Lavandula angustifolia**

Lavenders should be in every garden, for their scent, the attractiveness of their foliage, their usefulness as low hedging, and for their dried flower heads. Their only disadvantage is a tendency to die out in heavy soil.

'Hidcote' is a compact form (no more than 60cm/24in high and across when in flower) with narrow grey-green leaves and deep purple-blue dense flower spikes from midsummer onwards.
Cultivation and Propagation Plant in spring in well drained soil, and preferably full sun. Propagate by short cuttings in late summer, put in a frame, or long cuttings in early autumn, put in a grit-lined trench. Trim and shape in spring, when it will break readily from old wood.
Use A useful plant for associating either with other grey shrubs, especially those with yellow flower heads, or with purple and red flowers and foliage. It can be used to spread over a low wall, to buttress a raised bed, or as an edging to a formal bed or path.
Similar plants *L. angustifolia* 'Alba' (white flowers); *L. angustifolia* 'Munstead' (greener leaves and lavender-blue flowers).

27 **Lavatera** 'Barnsley'

A sport from that well known, long-flowering pink tree mallow, *Lavatera olbia* 'Rosea'. 'Barnsley' is an infinitely preferable colour but otherwise the same, growing to 1.2-1.8m/4-6ft (if pruned back in late winter). The long, thin petals which make up the shapely flower are white, flushed pink, with a darker centre. The leaves are hairy, lobed and grey-green. It flowers from midsummer until the frosts. This shrub has proved tremendously popular for giving height and colour to a border in the late summer.
Cultivation and Propagation A Mediterranean shrub, so happiest with full sun and a well drained soil. Plant in spring from a container into ordinary soil; too rich a soil leads to leaf-growth at the expense of flowers. Not entirely hardy, so best planted in a sheltered position, and staked in an exposed one. It grows well against a warm wall but this is not essential. Shoots of the more vigorous 'Rosea' easily appear and have to be swiftly removed to stop them taking over. 'Barnsley' can be propagated easily by softwood cuttings taken in summer. Seedlings do not come true.
Use Because of its long flowering period, a useful link plant to bridge different seasonal schemes. It associates well with dark blues, such as *Salvia x superba* in summer, and

mauve and blue asters, ceratostigma and aconitums in autumn. It goes well with old roses and foxgloves.
Similar plants *L. 'Burgundy Wine'* (darker in colour).

28 **Mahonia × media** 'Charity'

A marvellous true winter-flowering hardy evergreen shrub, of statuesque appearance and with striking 30cm/12in-long upright racemes of bright yellow scented flowers from late autumn until mid- to late winter. Normally grows to 1.8 x 1.5m/6 x 5ft, but can attain 3m/10ft. The leaves are 45cm/18in long, and consist of two opposite ranks of long spiny leaflets. New ones are made each year, after flowering, at the top of the plant.
Cultivation and Propagation Thrives in a moisture-retentive, fertile (slightly acid for preference) but well drained soil, and flowers best in sun although it will take shade happily. It requires little attention and no pruning, unless it becomes straggly, in which case take out one or two shoots after flowering. Propagation is by leaf cuttings taken in late autumn or early spring; put in a heated propagator or leave on a warm windowsill.
Use Impressive on its own as a specimen but also associates well with other winter flowerers such as *Helleborus foetidus,* clustered around the base. Contrast its foliage with, for example, hardy bamboos.
Similar plants *M. x media* 'Buckland'; *M. x media* 'Lionel Fortescue'.

29 **Philadelphus × lemoinei**

The philadelphus are all worth growing, despite their dull leaves, for the beauty and scent of the flowers. They are bone-hardy, deciduous, twiggy shrubs. *Philadelphus x lemoinei* has masses of small, intensely orange-blossom scented flowers in early summer, on an arching 1.8 x 1.2m/6 x 4ft shrub. It has ovate, green-veined leaves and bright white, open-cupped flowers held in racemes.
Cultivation and Propagation Philadelphus are tolerant of a range of soils, even dry ones, and like sun or partial shade. They flower on the

previous year's wood so prune by taking out the oldest branches in late summer. Occasionally they are assailed by blackfly, but are otherwise free of trouble. Propagate (easily) in late summer or autumn by semi-hard or hardwood cuttings, in a cold frame.

Use Shrubs for large mixed or shrub borders, where they can be ignored or disguised when not in flower.

Similar plants P. 'Manteau d'Hermine' (75 x 150cm/30 x 60in); P. 'Sybille' (1.2 x 1.8m/4 x 6ft).

30 **Potentilla**
'Primrose Beauty'

The potentillas are a first-rate genus of deciduous shrubs with an immensely long flowering season, and a most amiable disposition.

'Primrose Beauty' has grey-green silk-haired leaves, which are round but cut into five leaflets. It grows to about 90 x 120cm/36 x 48in. From late spring until late autumn, it is generously spread with pale yellow, flat-cupped flowers a little over 2.5cm/1in across.

Cultivation and Propagation Thrives in a hot dry spot but is tolerant of aspect and soil, although it will not flower so freely in partial shade. Plant from containers at any time. Pruning is not strictly necessary (except for the periodical removal of entire old branches). Propagate by taking softwood cuttings in early summer. If grown as a reasonably informal hedge, trim in early spring to give plants time to make new shoots, on which flower buds form.

Use 'Primrose Beauty' can be used to make a flowering hedge in sun, as a background specimen in a sunny border, or to give shelter to tender or wind-sensitive plants nearby. The colours go well with the blues and pinks and greys of early summer, and later with Lavatera 'Barnsley' and Ceratostigma willmottianum.

Similar plants P. 'Red Ace' (grow in light shade to preserve colour); P. 'Gold Kugel' (P. 'Farreri') (yellow).

31 **Prunus tenella**
'Fire Hill'

The dwarf Russian almond, a deciduous shrub about 60cm/24in high, flowers as the narrow, oblong, glossy, bright green leaves are

extending in mid-spring. This form has deep rosy-pink single flowers, nearly 2.5cm/1in across, borne in profusion on the erect stems. In time it makes a suckering thicket with a spread of 90 or 120cm/36 or 48in.

Cultivation and Propagation Tolerant of dry soil in full sun, and can be planted at any time, except in hot dry weather. It is easily increased by digging up and severing suckers, or by layering. Alternatively, take softwood cuttings. Pruning consists of cutting back the flowered shoots hard, almost to the base, to encourage new flowering shoots to be made before the following year.

Use The flowers combine well with greys and blues and lemon-yellows, or it can be used as a foreground foil to purple-leaved shrubs such as Corylus maxima 'Purpurea'. Its habit makes it useful for narrow borders in full sun, or even a rock garden, and its flowering time suits bulbs like alliums or narcissi.

Similar plants P. triloba 'Multiplex'; P. glandulosa. 'Rosea Plena' (both double and less hardy).

32 **Rhododendron**
'Vuyk's Scarlet'

This is a small (60 x 60cm/24 x 24in) 'evergreen' azalea, with very striking bright crimson flowers which completely cover the shrub in late spring. They are carried either singly or in pairs, and each is an open funnel-shape, with wavy, overlapping petals about 5cm/2in across. The leaves are small and ovate.

Cultivation and Propagation With only a few exceptions, rhododendrons and azaleas require lime-free soil to thrive. A medium, enriched soil, which does not waterlog, is ideal. They do best in areas of at least average rainfall, sheltered from cold winds, and in partial shade. Plant in early autumn or spring, no deeper than in the container. Deadhead to prevent wasted energy on seed development. Prune out dead wood. Propagate by semi-ripe cuttings or layering in late summer. If leaves show signs of chlorosis, feed with sequestrated iron, and mulch with peat.

Use The low, spreading habit, makes it effective evergreen ground-cover. It can be associated with other evergreen azaleas, and also summer-flowering heathers, which will distract attention from the dreary leaves after the rhododendron's

28

29

30

31

32

33

34

35

36

37

flowering season is over.
Similar plants *R.* 'Orange Beauty' (scarlet); *R.* 'Palestrina' (white with green markings).

33 **Rhododendron**
'Yellowhammer'

A hardy hybrid rhododendron, making an erect shrub about 1.8 x 1.8m/6 x 6ft, clothed to the ground. The leaves are evergreen, dark green, ovate, about 3 x 1.5cm/1½ x ½in long; the flowers are lemon-yellow, held in pairs of 2.5cm/1in- long, funnel-shaped bells in spring. There may be another flush of flowers in the autumn, especially if the first flush is deadheaded.
Cultivation and Propagation
As for *R.* 'Vuyk's Scarlet'.
Use 'Yellowhammer' is small enough to find a place in a shrub border, preferably where other plants will mask it when not in flower, or mix it with naturalized narcissi and other spring bulbs.
Similar plants *R.* 'Curlew'.

34 **Rosa**
'Graham Thomas'

'Graham Thomas' is one of the best known of the 'English roses'. English roses are the result of recent breeding work done with hybrid tea and shrub roses. The mainly lax shrubs fit better than hybrid tea roses into the mixed garden. They are usually scented, the flowers are often cupped and full, and blooms are freely borne all summer and autumn. 'Graham Thomas' is particularly sought after for its generous, rich yellow flowers which do not droop. The habit is bushy, arching and vigorous (about 1.2 x 1.2m/4 x 4ft), and the flowering continuous if the plant is well fed when the fragrant flowers first appear. The foliage is glossy green and healthy.
Cultivation and Propagation
English roses are cultivated with the accent on efficient soil preparation, mulching, watering when conditions are dry, deadheading, and feeding with rose fertilizer, both in late spring and when first in full bloom.
Pruning is basically the same as for shrub roses: weak and dead wood should be cut out in late winter, a proportion of the older shoots removed, and the rest trimmed back to make a neat bush. Prune harder

to produce bigger flowers.
Use English roses are very versatile because of their shrubby habit and recurrent flowering; they appreciate and look best planted with space around them, but with a ground-cover of smaller herbaceous plants. One shrub makes an impact, but a group can be spectacular, particularly of 'Graham Thomas'. These flowers are excellent for cutting, and in turn this stimulates more flower formation.
Similar plants *R.* 'Heritage' (shell-pink); *R.* 'Winchester Cathedral' (white); *R.* 'William Shakespeare' (deep crimson); *R.* 'Gertrude Jekyll' (deep pink).

35 **Rosa** 'Silver Jubilee'

One of the finest of modern hybrid tea roses, 'Silver Jubilee' is useful for exhibition, bedding and general garden use. It has scented apricot-pink, high-centred flowers, shapely in bud, and these are profusely borne on a plant with shiny, disease-resistant leaves. It grows to 90 x 80cm/3 x 2ft if not pruned very hard.
Cultivation and Propagation
A healthy rose, especially if planted in well prepared soil. Roses do best in medium to heavy soil but any well drained, enriched soil is suitable. Plant in late autumn or early spring with the junction of the stock and scion (where the graft is made) 2.5cm/1in below the soil surface. Thereafter prune in early spring and mulch round the base with bark chippings or compost, watering freely in dry summer weather. Take cuttings in late summer.
Use Looks well grouped with others of the same variety, or with other hybrid teas of harmonious colour. It associates well with other pink flowers, so can be underplanted with *Geranium endressii*, garden pinks, the hardier diascias, or the blue and white forms of *Viola cornuta*. Alternatively, place with architectural plants such as yuccas and ornamental grasses.
Similar plants Hybrid tea roses: *R.* 'Royal William' (deep crimson); 'Savoy Hotel' (shell pink); 'Peaudouce' (pale yellow); 'Elizabeth Harkness' (buff); 'Pascali' (white).

36 **Rosa**
'Madame Isaac Pereire'

Said by many to be the most fragrant of all roses, 'Madame Isaac Pereire' is

a vigorous, twice-flowering Bourbon rose which can be grown both as a large shrub or as a wall rose. As a shrub, it grows to about 2 x 1.5m/7 x 5ft, but can get much bigger if trained against a wall. The flowers are large, full of petals, distinctively quartered, and a strong pink, tinged with purple.
Cultivation and Propagation
Plant in the dormant season in good fertile soil, preferably in full sun or only slight shade. Although vigorous, it benefits from generous mulching and, because of the second flower flush, give fertilizer in early summer. Pruning consists of removing deadheads after the first and second flushes, and weak old wood in winter. On a wall, prune as for repeat-flowering climbers.
Use The arching sprays allow an understorey of other plants. Put it with anything on the blue side of red, such as late double peonies.
Similar plants Old fashioned, repeat-flowering shrub roses include 'Madame Knorr' ('Comte de Chambord') (warm-pink, scented); 'Madame Pierre Oger' (globular flowers, palest silver-pink); 'Baron Girod de l'Ain' (dark crimson edged with white).

37 **Viburnum farreri**
(*V. fragrans*)

A hardy deciduous viburnum with strongly fragrant flowers right through the winter, from late autumn until early spring. The drooping clusters of pinky-white tubular flowers are only badly affected by hard frosts. It makes an upright shrub (roughly 2 x 1.5m/7 x 5ft; more if grown against a wall) which can be made into an informal hedge, and pruned in mid-spring. The foliage, which is obviously toothed, ovate, corrugated, and bronze-tinted when young, appears with the last flowers.
Cultivation and Propagation
Plant in a moist, fertile soil, preferably in full sun, although it is not very fussy. Shelter from winds. Propagate by ground layering.
Use Underplant with early bulbs, violas and winter-flowering heathers, or plant at the back of the border to lend solidity to a scheme.
Similar plants *V.* x *bodnantense* 'Dawn' (late autumn to early spring); *V.* x *juddii* and *V.* 'Anne Russell' (spring flowering).

CLIMBERS

Climbers and wall shrubs add an extra dimension to the garden: they can be used either as a backdrop to the borders below, or to add vertical interest. They can even be used as living dividers. Because of the shelter afforded by walls, tender plants may be grown which might not survive in the open garden. Climbers can be encouraged to grow up or through trees, or even scramble up or down slopes. Some are self-clinging (and will not damage walls in good condition); others need to be supported by wires, or encouraged to twine through trellis or mesh.

38 Clematis flammula

A vigorous, hardy, floriferous, late-flowering clematis, which can grow to 3m/10ft or more. It has panicles of 2.5cm/1in flat single white stars, smelling of almonds, between late summer and mid-autumn. These are followed by masses of silvery seedheads. The leaves are bright green, composed of three to five ovate leaflets; they add to the delicacy of this choice but easily grown climber.

Cultivation and Propagation
Not fussy as to soil, although clematis mildly prefer alkaline conditions. Plant in early spring or autumn from a container, a little lower than it was in the pot; this is to give an opportunity for regenerating in case it succumbs to clematis wilt. Like all clematis, it likes its roots in shade and will grow even on a cool, shady wall. If it is to climb it will need early support for its tendrils. Prune by cutting down all stems not required for layering in spring, in late winter.
Use Often successfully trained through a large, sturdy evergreen shrub like *Choisya ternata*. Alternatively, train up a fence, into a tree, or plant on top of a retaining wall to run along and down. Because it can be cut right back in late winter, use it as ground-cover through heathers, or a border which is no longer in flower (for example, one containing peonies). This is the surest way of enjoying the scent.
Similar plants *C. tibetana* ssp. *vernayi (C. orientalis)* (thick-petalled yellow flowers appear in late summer to mid-autumn).

39 Clematis 'Perle d'Azur'

This large-flowered single clematis blooms between early and late summer. It has four to six petals, 7.5-15cm/3-6in wide, which curve backwards at the tips. The colour is a light blue and the anthers a pale green. It grows to a height of 3m/10ft and a width of about 90cm/36in.
Cultivation and Propagation
'Perle d'Azur' does best in a sunny place. For cultivation see previous entry for *C. flammula*.
Use Can, of course, be grown as a specimen up trellis or over a pergola, but its colour and flowering period make it delightful in association with old shrub roses, with pink climbing roses like 'New Dawn', and even for disguising the stiff habit of Floribundas. On a wall, it will climb happily through *Vitis vinifera* 'Purpurea', looking stunning with both the new silvery leaves and the older purple ones. Or grow it through the purple-leaved cotinus. It can be grown with a pink clematis flowering at the same time, like 'Comtesse de Bouchaud' or 'Hagley Hybrid', or with darker ones like 'Madam Edouard André' and *C. viticella*. Alternatively, plant where you can have it scrambling through a golden-leaved shrub, such as *Cornus alba* 'Spaethii' or alternatively *Choisya ternata* 'Sundance'.
Similar plants *C.* 'Ascotiensis'; *C.* 'Lasurstern' (flowers earlier).

40 Hedera helix 'Goldheart'

A restrained form of the native ivy, 'Goldheart' is self-clinging, only reasonably vigorous, and happy in deep shade. It will grow to about 3m/10ft or more in time. The central splash of gold on its small tapering green leaves is most pronounced on young leaves.
Cultivation and Propagation
A wonderfully amenable plant, which will grow in any soil and any aspect, although its leaves can scorch on a sunny wall. It has a mild preference for an alkaline soil. It can be sensitive to wind and frost, so tip back any damaged (and reachable) shoots in spring, or plant in a sheltered place. Only plant against a wall in good repair, because its questing aerial roots *can* do damage to crumbling pointing. Increase by softwood cuttings taken from running growth, or alternatively by layers, if feasible.
Use 'Goldheart' is invaluable for brightening a dark corner or as a background to contrasting, especially deep green, foliage. It will mix successfully with other variegated ivies, such as *H. helix* 'Buttercup'.
Similar plants *H. helix* 'Buttercup'; *H. helix* 'Angularis Aurea'.

38

41 Hydrangea anomala petiolaris

One of the truly great climbers; it climbs unaided, and will also flourish on a sunless wall. Once established it is very vigorous, so is also suitable for clothing tall, rough-barked trees. Will grow up to 15m/50ft in time, has serrated, ovate, dark green leaves, flat heads of creamy white flowers up to 25cm/10in across, in early and midsummer, and yellow leaf colour in autumn. As a bonus, it boasts interesting peeling bark. A mature plant is a very striking sight and makes an effective focal point.
Cultivation and Propagation
Initially rather slow to get going, the self-clinging habit needs to be encouraged at first, by loosely attaching the plant to the wall or tree. Not fussy about soil, provided that it is not very dry. Pruning consists of removing frost-damaged shoots in spring, if necessary. If the plant is outgrowing its space, tip back the spurs after it has flowered, but ideally plant only where there is plenty of room for it.
Use A specimen plant for a wall, which can be fronted by anything that does not need a rich soil, for it will draw out the nutrients for its vigorous growth. It looks effective clothed with delicate tender climbers such as *Eccremocarpus scaber* or *Tropaeolum peregrinum*. In moist soil underplant it with large clumps of different hostas.
Similar plants *Pileostegia viburnoides* (evergreen and rather less hardy).

39

40

41

42

43

44

45

42 Jasminum officinale

The common white jasmine has been popular in this country since the sixteenth century. A reasonably hardy, heavily sweet-smelling, twining climber, it is invaluable for open trellis, pergola or arbour, and also suitable for walls and fences, especially as it requires very little pruning. Deciduous in habit (semi-evergreen in a mild spot), it can grow up to 9m/30ft. The attractive leaves are pinnate, made up of up to nine leaflets, mid- to dark green. The small flowers are borne in axillary clusters from early summer until early autumn (most generously in midsummer). They are pink in tight bud, opening to white, and consist of four- or five-lobed stars. The scent is very sweet and strong, especially in the evening.

Cultivation and Propagation
This jasmine is happiest in full sun. Any ordinary well drained, even poor soil will do. Use simple trellis or netting for support, as it will twine of its own accord. Thin out its shoots after flowering if they have become congested. Sow seeds in the autumn and put in a cold frame, or layer long shoots also in autumn.
Use Jasmine can be associated with other climbing plants such as roses and honeysuckle. If trained round an arbour or similar sheltered place, underplant it with fragrant subshrubs. Its sinuous dense habit makes it a better bet than roses for such a position.
Similar plants J. officinale f. affine (larger flowers, flushed with pale pink); J. officinale 'Argenteovariegatum' (golden variegation).

43 Lonicera japonica 'Halliana'

A stunningly scented evergreen honeysuckle with white, ageing to yellow, flowers from early summer to mid-autumn. The leaves are light green, ovate or oblong. It is a reasonably hardy, vigorous, twining climber, capable of growing to 10m/30ft. The evergreen honey-suckles seem less prone to aphid attack than the more delicate deciduous ones.

Cultivation and Propagation
Honeysuckles are woodland plants, so plant with the roots in shade, in late spring in enriched soil. Mulch annually. Propagation is achieved by putting semi-ripe or hardwood cuttings in a cold frame; or, alternatively, by layering in autumn.
Use Can be used, like Jasminum officinale, for bowers, pergolas and the like. Also recommended by some for ground-covering. Its vigour and enduring leaves make it ideal for hiding ugly buildings. Can be grown as an informal standard, if the old wood is cut out after flowering, but use a substantial support.
Similar plants L. japonica 'Aureoreticulata' (the 'netted honeysuckle') has a network of yellow veining on the leaves but is, in every other respect, the same as 'Halliana' though a little less hardy. L. periclymenum 'Serotina' (reddy-purple flowers, early summer to mid-autumn); L. sempervirens (evergreen, but completely scentless).

44 Rosa 'Aloha'

A very fine climbing hybrid tea rose, really a tall-growing shrub (2.4m/8ft) of erect growth. It flowers continuously and profusely for several months from early summer. The foliage is disease-resistant, glossy, dark green and dense, the large double flowers (7.5cm/3in across) look upwards, are strongly fragrant, and pink with apricot in the middle, carmine-pink in bud. The flowers are full of petals and weather-resistant. The habit is a little stiff, which can be a helpful attribute in a climber.

Cultivation and Propagation
Plant in the same way as other roses and at least 30cm/12in from a support. Prune repeat-flowering climbers by cutting back the flowered laterals close to the main stems in winter, together with all weak, dead and the oldest growth. Propagation, which is not always successful, is by hardwood cuttings.
Use The limited size but generous flowering of 'Aloha' makes it ideal for fences, pillars, trellis, tripods, the walls of a bungalow, or even as a shrub. If grown on a sunny wall or fence, grow pink or blue herbaceous perennials and grey sub-shrubs (cutting off any stridently yellow flowers) in front of it.
Similar plants Other good short climbers include R. 'Bantry Bay' (semi-double, bright pink); R. 'Compassion' (apricot); R. 'New Dawn' (shell-pink).

45 Vitis vinifera 'Purpurea'

The teinturier grape is a most ornamental and useful hardy and deciduous scrambler for a sunny aspect, growing to about 6m/20ft high and 3m/10ft across, if allowed. The ornamental leaves are deep red, ovate or round, deeply lobed, and when young, covered with white hairs which turn them silvery red. It has tiny flowers in early summer in clusters, followed by small, oval, blackish-purple, inedible grapes. The leaves turn a sumptuous purple-red before falling.

Cultivation and Propagation
Like other vines, this likes a well-worked, rich, preferably alkaline soil. After planting, try to develop a framework of upward and horizontal stems. Pruning consists of pinching out some of the growth tips in spring and, if necessary, thinning out older stems in late autumn. Increase by taking hardwood cuttings throughout autumn.
Use An ideal climber for a pergola. It goes well with clematis such as 'Perle d'Azur' and the later-flowering, tulip-flowered, bright red 'Gravetye Beauty'. Its rather heavy purple foliage in late summer is a good foil for the golden perennials of autumn in warm schemes. Alternatively, pair it on a wall to contrast with the silver leaves of Cytisus battandieri.
Similar plants V. coignetiae (more vigorous; larger green leaves turning yellow in autumn).

HERBACEOUS PERENNIALS

This group includes all those plants that die down to a 'crown' in late autumn, and then throw up new shoots in the spring. They are associated with the great borders of grand old gardens, however, there are plenty of excellent varieties which do not need a lot of attention; nor need their use be restricted to borders.

46 *Alchemilla mollis*

The lady's mantle has neat, hairy, grey-green, rounded leaves and sprays of minute greeny-yellow flowers, up to 45cm/18in high, from early to late summer.
Cultivation and Propagation It will grow in all but waterlogged soils, in sun and partial shade, and will even colonize paving. It can be invasive so cut off all flower heads immediately after flowering. Sow seed 3mm/⅛in deep in pots in early spring and keep at 16-21°C/60-70°F until germinated (about four weeks). Move to a cold frame and plant out in autumn or spring.
Use The foliage and flowers of lady's mantle are popular with flower arrangers. It can be used as a repeating feature in a border and as a cool foil for magenta and purple plants. Although deciduous, it makes good weed-suppressing ground-cover.
Similar plants *A. alpina; A. erythropoda.*

47 *Anemone* × *hybrida*
'Honorine Jobert'

Growing to a height of 1.5m/5ft and with a 60cm/24in spread, this Japanese anemone is a handsome late summer and early autumn flowering perennial. Its shallow-cupped pure white flowers, with a boss of yellow stamens in the centre, are held above deeply cut, elegant, dark green leaves.
Cultivation and Propagation Japanese anemones like partial shade and, although not fussy, do best in fertile and well drained soil. They can spread too far at times, coming up even through paving and in walls. Increase either by division or by taking winter root cuttings.
Use Japanese anemones start late into growth, so spring bulbs can successfully be planted amongst them. As they last many years, they make dependable companions for colourful autumn shrubs, such as

hydrangeas. With their attractive flowers, handsome leaves and wiry stems, Japanese anemones are useful plants for flower arranging.
Similar plants *A.* x *hybrida* 'Luise Uhink' (white); *A.* x *hybrida* 'Bressingham Glow' (semi-double, rose-purple); *A. hupehensis* 'September Charm' (rose-pink).

46

48 *Anthemis puncta-*
ta ssp. cupaniana

An invaluable plant for its grey, finely dissected leaves and clear white rayed flowers with large yellow centres. These, some 5cm/2in across, on 15-30cm/6-12in flower stems, appear in early summer and last for several weeks. (Indeed, if you dead-head punctiliously, it will flower all summer.) The foliage is evergreen and makes spreading silvery grey mats which turn greener after rain. The flowers can be picked.
Cultivation and Propagation Plant in spring, about 30cm/12in apart, in a sunny place and in well drained soil. Reasonably hardy but take cuttings in early summer as a precaution in case of winter losses. It can also be divided.
Use Goes well with almost everything, but especially short bearded irises, pink tulips, any yellow-flowered grey-leaved sub-shrub, spurges like *Euphorbia polychroma*, or the taller, yellow-flowered *Anthemis tinctoria* 'E.C. Buxton'. Try it with contrastingly coloured foliage plants such as purple sage.
Similar plants *A. tinctoria* cvs.

47

48

49 *Argyranthemum*
'Jamaica Primrose'
(Chrysanthemum frutescens 'Jamaica Primrose')

A tender but very fine evergreen woody herbaceous perennial, making a bushy plant about 90 x 90cm/36 x 36in. The soft yellow single daisy flowers are carried throughout

49

50

51

52

53

the summer and autumn above the ferny light green leaves.

Cultivation and Propagation Plant out when frost no longer threatens in a sunny place and in well drained soil. Loved by aphids, argyranthemum is nevertheless usually strong enough to withstand an onslaught. Either dig up plants in autumn, pot them up and house them for the winter, or raise new plants each year. Stem cuttings should be taken in late summer or early autumn and overwintered in a frost-free place.

Use Ideal for container-gardening as it will withstand some drought and flowers very freely, and over such a long season. It associates well with other attractive tender plants such as the variegated *Felicia amelloïdes*, *Helichrysum petiolare* and the dark-purple salvias such as *Salvia x superba* 'May Night'.

Similar plants *A.* 'Mary Wootton' (semi-double, pink); *A. frutescens* (single white Marguerite).

50 *Aster* × *frikartii*
'Mönch'

This, the very finest of the Michaelmas daisies, has single, rayed, lavender-blue, yellow-centred flowers (up to 5cm/2in across), borne between midsummer and mid-autumn. The flower stems grow to 90cm/36in, with a spread of 35-45cm/15-18in, but are sufficiently strong not to require staking. The flowers last well in water. It is very hardy and does not suffer from powdery mildew.

Cultivation and Propagation Grow in full sun, in good soil which is well drained but moisture-retentive. Cut back flower stems in autumn. Divide clumps in autumn or spring every four to five years.

Use Its pretty colour, excellent constitution and very long flowering period commend it to summer and autumn schemes of grey, pink and blue; for example, with pink forms of *Anemone x hybrida*, most phloxes and penstemons, and the shrubby tree mallow, *Lavatera olbia* 'Rosea'. It associates well with summer lilies and other bulbs.

Similar plants There are doubts as to whether the plant in commerce is the true *Aster x frikartii* 'Mönch'; no matter, whatever its true name, it is a marvellous plant. *A.* 'Wunder von Stäfa' is very similar.

51 *Dicentra spectabilis*

Although not always very long-lived, the bleeding heart is nevertheless a graceful and intriguing hardy plant which should have a place in every garden. It has fleshy arching stems up to 60cm/24in, from which dangle a string of pendent rosy-red flattened 'hearts', 2.5cm/1in long, with protruding bright white inner petals, in late spring and early summer. The foliage is attractive, deeply cut, ferny and grey-green. It dies down soon after flowering.

Cultivation and Propagation Plant in light enriched soil in sun or partial shade, sheltered from cold winds, about 45cm/18in apart. Can be divided in autumn, but make sure that there are growing buds on each division. Alternatively, take root cuttings of the fleshy brittle roots in early spring and put in a cold frame to propagate.

Use Useful in small gardens because it dies down so quickly and completely after flowering. It associates well with other dicentras and with bergenias in semi-shade, or grey-leaved plants in sun. Underplant it with *Lamium maculatum* 'Beacon Silver'. It also looks well under late spring-flowering cherries and blossoming fruit trees.

Similar plants *D. spectabilis alba* (white); *D. formosa* (this is easier to grow successfully but is a less spectacular plant).

52 *Euphorbia characias ssp. wulfenii*

A tall, imposing perennial, reaching a height of 1.2m/48in with a spread of 90cm/36in. Stems rising from an evergreen base are biennial, producing leaves in the first year and flowers in the next. The leaves are grey-green, lanceolate, up to 12.5cm/5in long, and clustered about the stem below broad, upright panicles of acidulous yellow-green bracts with reddy-brown central flowers in late spring and early summer. The sap is poisonous and can irritate the skin so take care when handling, and wear gloves if you have sensitive skin. This plant differs from *E. characias* which has broader panicles of flowers, greyer leaves and grows to 1.8m/6ft.

Cultivation and Propagation Plant in autumn or spring, preferably when small; large plants do not transplant easily. Grow in full sun or partial shade, preferably sheltered from cold winds, in any ordinary, well drained soil. It will tolerate drought. Cut off the faded flower stems if you want to keep the plant compact. Otherwise leave them after they have finished flowering, to get the benefit of the unique, top-heavy heads. Although basically hardy, if grown in a heavy soil this spurge can be injured or killed by long periods of cold weather. They can be propagated either by basal cuttings in spring or by dividing clumps in the dormant season.

Use Perfect for a sunny courtyard or wide border. Use as a contrast to other bold or coloured foliage plants, such as romneya, artemisia, purple hazel or sage. It is a very versatile plant which will sharpen up soft colour schemes, and which also goes particularly well with blue and purple geraniums, bearded irises or *Ceanothus* 'Cascade'.

Similar plants *E. characias* (purple flower heads); *E. characias* ssp. *wulfenii* 'Lambrook Gold' (golden flower heads).

53 *Geranium macrorrhizum*
'Ingwersen's Variety'

One of the most valuable of the indispensable hardy geraniums. The rose-pink flowers are held 30cm/12in above five-lobed aromatic leaves, which take on reddish tints in the autumn and usually survive through the winter.

Cultivation and Propagation Flowers most profusely in a sunny position and in well drained soil. Geraniums are amongst the most trouble-free of herbaceous perennials, and if deadheaded after the first flush will often produce a second flowering. Propagate either by division in the autumn or in the early spring, spacing plants at least 60cm/24in apart.

Use Makes excellent non-invasive ground-cover in a sunny or partially shaded spot. It harmonizes admirably with a host of early summer flowers such as shrub roses, blue geraniums, polemonium and border pinks. Its usually evergreen habit makes it a useful and attractive addition to foliage schemes.

Similar plants *G. macrorrhizum* (magenta coloured).

54 *Helleborus orientalis*

The Lenten rose is one of the most attractive and useful of late winter-flowering perennials. The many named and unnamed strains vary from cream to deep purple, and there are some interesting spotted forms. The broad five-fingered leaves are evergreen in mild districts, providing useful winter colour.

Cultivation and Propagation The Lenten hellebore thrives in all reasonably moist soils, particularly alkaline ones, provided it is in part or full shade. Best left undisturbed to form a reasonable clump, but divide the roots, if you must, in early or mid-spring. It does, however, self-seed; seedlings can be transplanted when large enough to handle. Seed should be sown as soon as it has newly ripened.

Use Hellebores associate well with shade-tolerant flowering bulbs such as the strong-growing snowdrop *Galanthus elwesii*. They can also be grown successfully with bergenias, hardy geraniums, brunneras and many other partial shade-tolerant foliage plants.

Similar plants Many kinds have been named, and can be found in specialist catalogues.

55 *Hemerocallis*
'Pink Damask'

The day lilies are immensely reliable trouble-free perennials. Although each flower is short-lived, they open over a period from early until late summer. 'Pink Damask' has salmon-pink, broad, trumpet-shaped flowers with a pale central rib, but garden hybrids range in colour from pale yellow to bright orange-red. They grow up to 90cm/36in high and 60cm/24in across. The leaves are fleshy, pale-green, strap-shaped and broadly arching.

Cultivation and Propagation They like a sunny or partially shaded position, with an annual feed of general fertilizer. They are happiest in a moist soil, although they are tolerant of most other soil types, growing well even on clay. They grow well in town gardens, and are best divided soon after flowering.

Use The range of flower colour makes day lilies valuable for border schemes. The soft colouring of 'Pink Damask' can be used to continue the

same colour theme as *Papaver orientale* 'Mrs Perry'. Being rather lax in habit, they are most suitable for informal schemes.

Similar plants *H.* 'Pink Prelude'; *H.* 'Pink Charm'.

56 *Hosta*
'Frances Williams'

One of the real gems of this invaluable genus. A foliage plant which also flowers, 'Frances Williams' has broad glaucous leaves, edged with greeny-yellow margins. The flowers, up to 75cm/30in tall, are pale lilac.

Cultivation and Propagation Hostas will stand more drought than is generally thought but most require at least partial shade and will do best in a reasonably fertile soil. In some situations they are martyrs to slugs. Plant 'Frances Williams' about 60-90cm/24-36in apart. Hostas can be divided after flowering (use a knife to cut the tough rootstock) or sow the seed at a temperature above 20°C/68°F. No variegated variety will come true from seed.

Use Hostas are invaluable for summer foliage ground-cover in partial shade. They are also invaluable as foils to set off hotter colours.

Similar plants *H. sieboldiana* has similar but plain, blue-grey leaves.

57 *Nepeta*
'Six Hills Giant'

Similar to *N. mussinii*, but larger in all its parts and with a great deal more impact. It grows to about 90 x 90cm/36 x 36in, and has ovate, roundly-toothed, grey-green leaves and tubular, hooded, lavender-blue flowers in upright whorled spikes from late spring until early autumn.

Cultivation and Propagation Grows in alkaline soil, in dry or medium-dry places, in sun or partial shade. Although reasonably hardy, plant it in spring. Propagate by cuttings in spring, putting them in a peat and sand mixture, or in sandy soil, in a cold frame. Alternatively, divide the plant.

Use Sets off many plants well, particularly those with yellow flowers and silver leaves like *Santolina chamaecyparissus*, or with pink flowers like *Sidalcea* or *Malva*. It makes an excellent informal edging to a gravel or stone path, even though it

54

55

56

57 58

59

60 61

is very attractive to bees. An indispensable plant, with the attractions of *N. racemosa* but more resilient. **Similar plants** *N. x faassenii* 'Superba'.

58 Paeonia lactiflora
'Duchesse de Nemours'

A particularly free-flowering and fragrant double peony. Growing to a height of 75cm/30in, it carries large incurving outer petals which begin greeny-white but soon become pure white. The inner petals are cream in colour at the base. Flowers from late spring until early to midsummer.
Cultivation and Propagation
Peonies, once planted, like to be left alone. Do not plant the crown more than 5cm/2in under the soil surface (2.5cm/1in in heavy soils). They are quite tolerant as to soil, although a medium soil, fertile and well prepared, suits them best. Plants should be spaced 90-120cm/36-48in apart, and will need some staking. Propagate by division in autumn.
Use Peonies create enormous impact in the border, either as single clumps or as a background to large rock plants and early summer perennials. The foliage is attractive when young, and often takes on autumn tints later.
Similar plants *P. lactiflora* 'Baroness Schroeder' (pinky white); *P. lactiflora* 'Laura Dessert' (yellow).

59 Pulmonaria rubra
'Bowles' Red'

A lungwort with good-sized red flowers and slightly silver-spotted leaves, the earliest of these early-flowering plants, often being out by mid- to late winter, although at its most floriferous in early and mid-spring. It forms a clump about 60cm/24in across, above which rise 30cm/12in hairy flower stems. Flowers are salmon-red and tubular, with five lobes; semi-evergreen leaves are velvety in texture, light green, and broadly ovate.
Cultivation and Propagation
Pulmonarias will grow in any ordinary soil (including heavy clay) but it must be moist. Partial shade is necessary. Tidy up after flowering, when new green leaves will grow. Divide frequently, in early autumn.
Use 'Bowles' Red' makes excellent

ground-cover under deciduous trees. It associates well with ferns and spring flowering plants such as *Omphalodes cappadocica*.
Similar plants *P. rubra* 'Redstart'.

60 Sedum
'Ruby Glow'

A charming, medium-sized stonecrop for the front of the border, with greeny-blue oval leaves (edged with red, as are the stems) and 7.5cm/3in wide heads of reddish-purple small flowers in mid- and late summer and early autumn. It makes a rather floppy clump of stems, growing to 25cm/10in, with a spread of 30cm/12in.
Cultivation and Propagation
Does well in a dry, even poor soil in full sun. It can withstand drought because of the succulent, water-holding leaves, but paradoxically is also quite rain-resistant. Plant in autumn or spring, divide at the same time, or take stem cuttings in spring and early summer.
Use Goes well with tall alliums, like *Allium christophii*, which flower earlier but have silver-purple seed-heads, or with purple or grey foliage such as that of the *Salvia purpurea* or *Stachys olympica*. Contrast it with mossy saxifrages, or the large leaves of *Bergenia*.
Similar plants *S.* 'Vera Jameson' (reddy-purple leaves, pink flowers).

61 Stipa gigantea

A tall, elegant, reasonably hardy perennial grass with flower stems 1.8-2.5m/6-8ft high. The arching stems add grace as well as height to a border planting. The leaves are green, sword-like but floppy, and make a weed-suppressing clump. The airy flower heads, 30cm/12in long, are first silvery purple and then golden – hence the name 'golden oats'. They come in early and mid-summer and last into winter.
Cultivation and Propagation
Likes a very well drained soil in full sun; it may not be quite hardy in cold districts on heavy soil. It should be planted, and divided, in spring. Seed can be sown outside in mid-spring. The heads can be dried.
Use Effective if planted in front of a dark background, or where the sun will catch the golden flower heads.
Similar plants *S. calamagrostis*.

BULBS, CORMS AND TUBERS

'Bulb' is the word we normally use for several types of underground storage organ from which, annually, leaves and flower shoots emerge. By careful choice, you can have flowering bulbs in almost every garden situation and the whole year round. Most are very easy to grow, although tender bulbs do need to be lifted in autumn.

62 *Allium christophii*
(*A. albopilosum*)

The ornamental onions are a big tribe, with many species and cultivars of varying garden worthiness. One of the very best is *Allium christophii*. A startling plant when first encountered, it flowers in early summer and is easy to grow provided that it is given a sunny, well drained spot. It grows to 45-90cm/18-36in, with the usual rather unsatisfactory semi-erect, strap-shaped, grey-green allium leaves, but with very large round umbels, up to 25cm/10in in diameter, made up of masses of silvery lilac-pink star flowers. These are softened slightly by the green incipient seeds in their midst. The dried seedheads are much prized by flower arrangers.

Cultivation and Propagation
Plant the bulbs in autumn in well drained soil, to a depth of 10cm/4in, and 23cm/9in apart. Protect against slug damage in spring. Divide by splitting the bulbs in autumn or spring. Sow seeds ripe.

Use The colour of *Allium christophii* associates well with Old Roses. However, because the stems are bare and the leaves die down very early, it needs an undercarpet. Hostas, bergenias and sedums are good companions, but best is the stunning purple-leaved *Heuchera micrantha* 'Palace Purple', which will stand some sun. Alternatively, match the allium to a strong contrast provided by the yellow flowers of *Cytisus battandieri*, *Genista lydia* or *Berberis thunbergii* 'Aurea'.

Similar plants *A. aflatunense* 'Purple Sensation'.

63 *Anemone blanda*

A delicate, blue-flowering daisy flower with yellow centres and ferny, deeply cut leaves, flowering from late winter until mid-spring. The flowers are up to 3.5cm/1½in across, on 7.5cm/3in stems; the type is blue but there are also pink and white forms, in particular 'Radar' and 'White Splendour'.

Cultivation The flowers show best in sun but it will also grow in light woodland conditions, under deciduous trees. The soil should be well drained and not too acid. The tubers are planted 5cm/2in deep and 10cm/4in apart, with the convex side down.

Use Grow all the colour forms together, or plant the blue one with early narcissi; grow any under an early magnolia such as *Magnolia stellata*, or in pots, with or without other bulbs.

Similar plants *A. nemorosa*.

64 *Asphodeline lutea*

This hardy liliaceous perennial provides clear yellow colour in the early summer border, and evergreen leaves in the winter. It has 90-120cm/36-48in spikes of star-shaped fragrant yellow flowers, which appear above grassy, narrow, glaucous-green leaves.

Cultivation and Propagation
Asphodelines like an ordinary soil and a sunny aspect. Plant and divide in spring.

Use Associates well with yellow-foliaged plants, particularly if leavened with a little purple, such as that provided by *Salvia x sylvestris* 'May Night'.

Similar plants *A. liburnica*.

65 *Camassia leichtlinii*

An early summer-flowering hardy perennial bulb of the lily family, which grows to 90cm/36in in suitable circumstances, and has dense spires of six-petalled white (or sometimes pale violet-blue) flowers. The basal leaves are green, strap-shaped and pointed.

Cultivation and Propagation
Plant bulbs at least 10cm/4in deep and 15cm/6in apart in early autumn. Cut flower heads off after flowering to protect next year's display (unless seed is needed). Split up and replant

only when very overcrowded. Small offsets should be grown on in a nursery bed before replanting.

Use A group makes a considerable impact in a damp border, on a pond's margin, or naturalized in grass on heavy land, perhaps in an orchard. Darker blue forms are available, though not widely.

Similar plants *C. leichtlinii alba*.

66 *Crocus tommasinianus*

A variable species, ideal for naturalizing. It likes full sun and a well drained soil, and can be left to multiply over the years. The 7.5cm/3in narrow-tubed, funnel-shaped, silvery mauve flowers only open in sunshine but are delicate and lovely when they reveal their lilac interiors and yellow-orange stigmas. They are accompanied by narrow leaves.

Cultivation and Propagation
Plant about 3.5cm/1½in deep (crocuses find their own depth if you get it wrong), preferably in sun. This species seeds itself about, but is rarely a nuisance.

Use Use for planting in raised beds, as edgings to borders, for naturalizing in grass, gravel or paving cracks, with or without other bulbs, or planting under deciduous trees, shrubs, and even hedges. It looks well with, for example, winter aconites or *Cyclamen coum*, or under winter-flowering shrubs like viburnums and chimonanthus. A double-act with *C. tommasinianus albus* is successful.

Similar plants *C. tommasinianus* 'Whitewell Purple' (a darker form).

67 *Cyclamen hederifolium*
(*C. neapolitanum*)

The glory of this small (10cm/4in high) autumn-flowering (late summer to late autumn) hardy cyclamen is the marbling and silver marking on the leaves. It is especially successful under deciduous trees, in woodland or the edge of a partly shaded border. The leaves are heart-shaped and pointed, deep green above (with silver markings) and red-purple below. The flowers, 2.5cm/1in long and twisted, are mainly pink, deepest at the mouth. They appear both before, and with,

62

63

64

65

66

67

68

69   70   71

the new leaves and persist until late spring. *Cyclamen hederifolium* scatters its seeds from spherical seedheads on twisted stalks.

Cultivation and Propagation Any well drained soil, enriched with leaf mould, partial shade, and shelter from cold winds. The tubers should be planted with their tops (the side that does not have roots emanating from it) close to the surface of the soil in late summer. Seeds should be sown when first shed and seedlings overwintered in a cold frame. Leave undisturbed.

Use This plant associates well with other autumn bulbs, ferns, pulmonarias, trailing ivies and *Euonymus fortunei* 'Emerald Gaiety'.

Similar plants *C. hederifolium album* (white flowers).

68 *Eranthis hyemalis*

The best clumps of winter aconite are found in old-established gardens where, left undisturbed, they will come up every year, even through snow. It has distinctive yellow upturned cup flowers sitting on a ruff of dissected green leaves, which come out of the ground neck-first. A much-loved late winter flower which grows to no more than 10cm/4in high. It prefers well drained but moisture-retentive soil under deciduous trees. It also dies down by early summer.

Cultivation and Propagation Will grow in sun if the soil is moist. Propagate by lifting the tubers as the plants begin to die down, dividing them up and replanting immediately if possible. Tubers need to be planted 5cm/2in deep and 7.5-10cm/3-4in apart. This is a plant best begged from a friend rather than bought from a nursery. If bought, cover the tubers with moist sand until planted.

Use Combines with other winter flowerers like *Helleborus foetidus*.

Similar plants *E.* Tubergenii Group 'Guinea Gold' (larger and darker-flowered, worth seeking out for its fragrant flowers and bronzy-green leaves; flowers later).

69 *Galanthus* × *atkinsii*

Snowdrops are a must in every garden for their hardiness in the face of the worst of weather and the

promise they give of things to come. They look best grown in thick drifts, so leave the expensive forms alone and concentrate on a good form or relation of the common snowdrop, *Galanthus nivalis*. I suggest *Galanthus* x *atkinsii*, a vigorous, fast-multiplying and easy snowdrop with strap-shaped grey-green leaves, and sturdy stems topped by a slender white flower with distinct green markings on the inner petals. These snowdrops grow anything up to 23cm/9in high.

Cultivation and Propagation Snowdrops like at least partial shade, and a moisture-retentive soil. They can be left to multiply over the years, but if overcrowded, should be lifted while or just after flowering and replanted at a distance of about 7.5cm/3in apart.

Use Snowdrops will enhance most positions, but they look particularly good against a dark background, for example, evergreen ivies. Since they will have died down by early summer they can be grown where there is to be later ground-cover of, for example, herbaceous geraniums.

Similar plants *G. nivalis; G. elwesii.*

70 *Galtonia candicans*

The white flowers of the Cape hyacinth provide useful contrast to the many yellow daisies in the late summer border. Erect, sturdy stems, up to 1.2cm/4ft high, with basal, glaucous, strap-shaped leaves, are topped by a loose pyramidal raceme of pendulous 3.5cm/1½in fragrant, funnel-shaped, waxy white flowers with a hint of green on the petal tips.

Cultivation and Propagation *Galtonia candicans* is moderately hardy, but can be helped through harsh winters by ashes heaped on the soil around it. Best planted in a sunny position, free-draining yet moist. Plant in spring, at least 15cm/6in deep. Protect against slug damage in spring and water in dry summer weather. Propagate by offsets in early autumn, lining these out in nursery rows to grow on for a year. If seed forms, sow it in mid-spring in the open ground and plant the seedlings out, also in spring, two years later.

Use Stately groups of *G. candicans* look well in large pots in the conservatory and will flower earlier than those outside. As small clumps of repeating white 'exclamation

marks' in mixed borders, it associates well with late summer tall daisies or lower-growing variegated hostas. It also goes well with the crimson flowers of *Rosa* 'Frensham', or the orange of *Lilium henryi*. It makes an excellent cut flower.
Similar plants *G. viridiflora* (the same but pale green).

71 Iris histrioïdes
'Major'

One of the bulbous irises, *Iris histrioïdes* 'Major' earns its place here because it flowers very early (often at the same time as the snowdrops), is reliable (its bulbs do not break up into small pieces in its second year, as do those of *I. danfordiae*), and it flowers before the leaves have had a chance to grow up. It has 10cm/4in high bright blue flowers with darker blue spots on the falls, and white markings and a yellow ridge. It is very hardy and the flowers are undamaged by snow or frost. The leaves, which are square, grey-green and pointed, grow to 45cm/18in later on in the season.
Cultivation and Propagation
Likes full sun, and a light, preferably slightly alkaline soil. Feed the bulbs with liquid fertilizer just after flowering. Division is best done after flowering, with the largest bulbs planted *in situ,* and the rest put in a nursery row. Plant new bulbs in early autumn, to a depth of about 7.5cm/3in.
Use Can be grown with other early bulbs, such as yellow crocus and snowdrops, in any kind of container, raised beds, rock pockets, edgings to borders, or shrub borders.
Similar plants *I. histrio aintabensis.*

72 Lilium regale

A summer-flowering bulb, 60-150cm/36-60in high. The narrow leaves grow out from the stem. it produces clusters of very large, fragrant, outward-facing, funnel-shaped flowers in midsummer. The petals are each about 12.5cm/5in long, and are white with a yellow throat inside and pinkish-purple on the outside. The roots grow from the stem just above the bulb, so these bulbs should be planted deeply, at least 15cm/6in and preferably 22cm/9in deep.

Cultivation and Propagation
One of the easiest (and most beautiful) lilies to grow; all beginners should start with it. Plant in the autumn, if possible in a sunny sheltered place and ordinary but enriched well drained soil. The sturdy stems will need staking if planted in windy positions.
Propagate by separating the bulbs in autumn or by sowing seed in deep boxes of seed compost in early autumn, which are then put in the cold frame. The seedlings should be spaced out in nursery rows until large enough to flower.
Use Associates well with summer-flowering hardy perennials such as delphiniums, salvias and foxgloves. The stem roots benefit from some protection and shade, so grow a carpet of ground-cover underneath.
Similar plants *L. regale album; L.* 'Royal Gold'.

73 Narcissus 'Hawera'

There are a myriad narcissi and daffodils worthy of garden cultivation. The taller varieties look best grown in grass, preferably in generous drifts, the grass left uncut until six weeks after flowering; the shorter ones make less garden impact but often have more charm. Of these, one of the sweetest is *Narcissus* 'Hawera', which has pale lemon-yellow, nodding, cup-shaped flowers and swept back outer petals, flowering in mid- to late spring. It only grows to 20cm/8in, but compensates by producing up to six flowers per stem.
Cultivation and Propagation
These narcissi like a fertile but well drained soil, in sun or thin shade. Plant three times as deep as the depth of the bulbs in late summer or early autumn, 7.5-12.5cm/3-5in apart. Then leave them be. Water in dry spells in spring or early summer. Propagate by lifting after the leaves have died down, replanting the large offsets nearby and the smaller ones in nursery beds. They will naturally increase if left to themselves.
Use Goes extremely well with *Muscari armeniacum* 'Blue Spike'; or, for a subtle combination, grow it close to or amongst *Erica carnea* 'Springwood White'. Individual clumps on raised beds look appealing, as do groups in small containers or window boxes.
Similar plants *N.* 'Thalia' (white); *N.* 'April Tears' (yellow).

74 Scilla siberica
'Spring Beauty'

Grown for the intensity of the bright purple-blue flowers which appear in early spring, making it a good companion for early-flowering dwarf narcissi such as 'February Gold', primroses, or the strongly pink *Daphne mezereum*. It has pendent, wide-cupped, 1.5cm/¹/₂in long flowers on 15cm/6in thin, wiry stems, and is reliable provided it is grown in short grass or in fertile, well drained soil in sun or partial shade. The leaves appear before the flowers and are mid-green and strap-shaped. The species, *Scilla siberica*, is bright blue and flowers slightly later than 'Spring Beauty'.
Cultivation and Propagation
The bulbs should be planted about 7.5cm/3in deep and 10cm/4in apart; each bulb produces several stems. The bulbs are best left alone to increase slowly but it is possible to remove offsets in autumn.
Use 'Spring Beauty' is unique in providing such intense blue colour in very early spring. Use it to liven up the ground under deciduous trees and shrubs, not yet in leaf or flower, or as an accompaniment to other dwarf or medium-sized bulbs.
Similar plants *S. siberica* 'Alba'.

75 Tulipa tarda

As reliable and easy as any of the dwarf tulips and one of the most striking. The white flowers with their pointed petals are no more than 15cm/6in tall, but in sunny weather in early spring, the five or so flowers on the top of a short stem expand almost flat to display brilliant yellow centres. Green strap-shaped leaves are borne in a basal rosette.
Cultivation and Propagation
Ideal for crowded raised beds or rock gardens as it does not need to be lifted each year. Likes a sunny position in a very well drained, not rich, soil. Plant about 15cm/6in deep in late autumn. An annual dressing with bonemeal is helpful but not essential; an annual top dressing of grit shows off the flowers and helps drainage. Increases well, but can be lifted after dying down and the offsets removed and grown on.
Use Associates well with many early-flowering rock plants such as *Aubrieta* and *Alyssum saxatile* 'Citrinum'.
Similar plants *T. urumiensis* (bright yellow).

72

73

74

75

ALPINES

76

77

78

79

80

81

82

83

84

85

Most alpines thrive in sun and where they can be given a gritty, free-draining soil, such as in gravel, cracks in paving, troughs, sinks, and rock gardens. Woodland alpines, however, like a peaty, moisture-retentive soil so are best grown in shaded raised beds or under deciduous shrubs and trees. Alpines generally are at their finest in spring and early summer.

76 Campanula
'Birch Hybrid'

A hybrid between two charming but invasive species, C. portenschlagiana and C. poscharskyana, but better behaved than either. It is evergreen, perennial, hardy, and has prostrate stems and green, ivy-type leaves. The many open bell-flowers are deep violet-blue in colour, and come out in midsummer. 'Birch Hybrid' grows to 10cm/4in, with a spread of at least 30cm/12in.
Cultivation and Propagation
Likes a well drained place in sun or light shade, keeping its colour best in shade. Plant in autumn or spring. Deadheading will give another crop of flowers before autumn. Propagate by division in autumn.
Use This is a plant for a raised bed, wall crevice, the foot of a wall, or in gravel. The colour goes well with alpine yellows, pinks and whites.
Similar plants C. poscharskyana 'Stella'.

77 Dianthus deltoïdes
'Flashing Light'

A variety of the maiden pink with particularly dark green foliage and strong cherry-red flowers. It makes a mat of very narrow linear leaves. The flowers are up to 2cm/¾in across, with heavily toothed petals, borne from early until late summer. It has a height and spread of up to 22cm/9in.
Cultivation and Propagation
Plant in autumn or spring in a well drained, even poor soil, preferably in full sun, although it will grow in some shade. Deadheading will encourage more flowers. Seed sown in spring may come reasonably true; otherwise, layer side shoots, or take cuttings in early and midsummer.
Use This plant grows happily in raised beds, in rock gardens, even in gaps amongst paving slabs. It will go with Armeria maritima, saxifrages and other summer-flowering alpines.
Similar plants D. deltoides 'Albus'; D. deltoides 'Brilliant'.

78 Erinus alpinus

Erinus alpinus has a height and spread of only 7.5cm/3in and is not long-lived but it self-seeds, and the cultivars come almost true from seed. It consists of hardy evergreen rosettes of oblong, deeply toothed, soft mid-green leaves and masses of short racemes of charming pink, starry, lipped flowers in summer.
Cultivation and Propagation
An ideal plant for a beginner because it is so easily cultivated. It is not fussy as to soil, provided it is well drained and in sun. Plant in autumn and spring. Sow thinly in spring, where it is to flower.
Use A splendid rock plant for a wall crevice, trough, paving or raised bed. For added effect, plant close to any alpine campanula, phlox or Globularia. The long flowering period and tidy habit recommend it.
Similar plants E. alpinus var. albus (white); E. alpinus 'Mrs Charles Boyle' (brighter pink); E. alpinus 'Dr Hähnle' (crimson).

79 Geranium cinereum
'Ballerina'

A charming little hardy alpine geranium with large (for the size of plant) cup-shaped flowers, lilac-pink, with distinctive and extensive purple veining and a dark purple centre. It flowers from late spring until mid-autumn, from a well-behaved clump. The flowers are held on thin stems above soft, grey-green, deeply divided, semi-evergreen leaves. It grows to about 10cm/4in, with a spread up to 30cm/12in.
Cultivation and Propagation
'Ballerina' likes sun, if possible, and a well drained, even gritty soil. Plant in early spring, divide in autumn or spring. Deadhead for a second flush.
Use Plant it in a rock garden, raised bed, or large trough, or grow between paving stones. It looks effective with Nepeta x faassenii, or even Helianthemum 'Jubilee'.
Similar plants G. cinereum.

80 Helianthemum
'Jubilee'

The helianthemum is a vastly popular alpine sub-shrub, of which there are many named cultivars. They grow to about 15-30cm/6-12in high, with a spread of 30-60cm/12-24in. 'Jubilee' has a mass of double pale yellow flowers, about 2.5cm/1in across, held in terminal clusters, in early and midsummer. The leaves are small, elliptical in shape, dark green above and grey-green below.
Cultivation and Propagation
Plant in early autumn or early spring in any well drained soil and in full sun. You will get a second flush of flowers if the plants are trimmed over in midsummer. At the end of flowering, cut the stems back hard, or the shrub becomes straggly, flowers less freely and is shorter lived. Take short cuttings with a heel after the first flowering, and put in a cold frame to root.
Use A good plant to tumble over a low wall, or in company with other alpines in a raised bed, or even holes in paving or a dry wall.
Similar plants H. 'Wisley Primrose' (single, with grey-green leaves); H. 'Raspberry Ripple' (white flowers with red centres).

81 Saxifraga 'Carmen'
(S. × elisabethiae)

Saxifrages add colour to the rock garden early in the year. 'Carmen' has small upward-looking yellow flowers in early and mid-spring on red sticky stems 5-7.5cm/2-3in above a cushion of evergreen, wedge-shaped, spiny green leaves.
Cultivation and Propagation
More tolerant of hot sun than most saxifrages but best planted out of noonday summer sun. It will tolerate a dry, and certainly likes a well drained, preferably alkaline soil. Propagate by removing a non-flowered side rosette in summer and putting in coarse sand in a pot in a frame or greenhouse.
Use Although 'Carmen' only flowers for a few weeks, the green mats of leaves are neat and pretty and a good foil for later-flowering alpines. Its tolerance of some shade can be a useful attribute.
Similar plants Other saxifrages including S. 'Gregor Mendel' (similar); S. 'Jenkinsiae' (silver-leaved, pale pink-flowered).

82 Sempervivum arachnoïdeum

The cobweb houseleek is a succulent which makes congested domes of conspicuously white and 'cob-webbed' rosettes, due to the many white hairs at the tips of the green and pink leaves. The flowers are reddy-pink, star-like, about 2cm/¾in across, and borne at the ends of 15cm/6in stems from early summer until early autumn. Each rosette is no more than 2.5 x 3cm/1 x 1½in, but a mat of rosettes, 30cm/12in or more across, soon forms.
Cultivation and Propagation
Plant in a sunny place and well drained soil in autumn or spring. Sempervivums can withstand some drought. Propagate by removing any rooted rosettes from the outside of the clump and replanting them.
Use An easy and useful plant for gravel, a trough, raised bed, urn or container, or even the top of a stone wall or house roof. It is just as ornamental when not in flower, and makes a good foil for hot colours.
Similar plants S. arachnoïdeum tomentosum.

83 Thymus × citriodorus
'Silver Queen'

A pretty, upright, reasonably hardy thyme grown for its silver and green variegated leaves, 'Silver Queen' makes an evergreen spreading sub-shrub, up to 15cm/6in high and 25-30cm/10-12in across. The tiny, usually ovate leaves are strongly lemon-scented when crushed. In summer, small lilac flowers are carried on short erect stems.
Cultivation and Propagation
Thymes need a well drained spot in full sun to thrive. Plant in mid-autumn or early spring. If shoots revert to green, they should be cut out, because they are stronger-growing. Trim the plant in spring, or after flowering, to keep it compact and tidy. Take short cuttings with a heel after flowering.
Use An ideal plant for edging, gravel, sinks, raised beds and paving. It associates well with old-fashioned pinks and other low-growing summer-flowering plants like Nepeta x faassenii, Erinus alpinus and Geranium cinereum 'Ballerina'.
Similar plants T. x citriodorus 'Aureus' (golden foliage).

84 Veronica prostrata
'Trehane'

Veronicas are useful for their masses of blue flowers in early summer and for their amiability. 'Trehane' is unusual in having yellow-green, narrowly ovate and toothed leaves to accompany the violet-blue flowers. It is reasonably prostrate and dense-growing, with spikes of small saucer-shaped flowers, which grow up to 20cm/8in high.
Cultivation and Propagation
Happiest in full sun, and any reasonably well drained soil. Plant, and divide, in early or mid-spring. Take short cuttings in late summer and put in cold frame.
Use Combines successfully with the clear yellow flowers of Oenothera tetragona 'Fireworks' and, even better, the yellow and grey of Santolina, or the yellow and green of Alchemilla mollis.
Similar plants V. prostrata 'Mrs Holt'; V. prostrata 'Rosea' (pink).

85 Viola labradorica purpurea

This sweet little violet has almost evergreen purple foliage. Coming from Greenland and Labrador, it is dependably hardy. It comes true from seed and, although prolific, does not grow large enough to be a real nuisance.

It grows to about 12.5cm/5in, with a spread up to 30cm/12in. The leaves are small, heart-shaped, green, but flushed heavily with purple. Its mauve-pink flowers in mid- and late spring consort well with the purple leaves.
Cultivation and Propagation
It self-seeds readily but sow seeds in spring, if you need any more plants. It likes a moist soil and prefers semi-shade, although it will withstand drought and sun well.
Use Ideal for using as a ground-cover under deciduous shrubs; also for adding variety to a bed of alpines, in a border, or between paving stones. Because the leaves are so dark, the effect can be happily lightened by a silver-variegated shrub like Euonymus fortunei 'Emerald Gaiety', or any variegated hosta. Alternatively, associate it with artemisias and coloured grasses in sun, or ferns in shade.

WATER AND BOG PLANTS

86

87

88

89

90

Water planting falls into three categories: true water plants which are rooted in mud and grow in fairly deep water; 'marginals' which prefer shallower water; and bog plants which grow in moist soil. The first group perform best in full sun; the others will thrive in shadier spots. Apart from creating a dense and lush effect, imaginative planting of all three types will attract a welcome range of wildlife.

86 *Caltha palustris*

The marsh marigold is a perennial, deciduous, hardy marginal or very shallow water plant with rounded, dark green leaves and cupped 5cm/2in wide flowers. It grows up to 60cm/24in high with a spread of about 30cm/12in.
Cultivation and Propagation
Plant in late spring in permanently moist, preferably neutral soil; or in a suitable container if in shallow water. Divide the roots after flowering. Seeds can be gathered and sown in summer or autumn, in permanently wet compost.
Use Can be combined with other poolside flowers, such as *Iris sibirica*, *I. ensata*, ligularias, mimulus and hostas. It also looks well with the white bog arum, *Calla palustris*.
Similar plants *C. palustris* 'Plena' (a good double form); *C. palustris* var. *alba* (pure white).

87 *Nymphaea*
'James Brydon'

A reasonably hardy water lily for a medium-sized formal or informal pool. It has double rounded crimson flowers, with a diameter of 15cm/6in, in mid- to late summer until early autumn. These stay open even in dullish weather. The deciduous floating leaves are reddish when young, turning green with age.
Cultivation and Propagation
Plant in a container in good humus, to a depth of up to 90cm/36in, in mid-spring. Alternatively, plant directly into the muddy bottom of a pond. Propagate by taking offsets in late spring. If necessary, thin out the leaves and stems in early summer, to encourage new growth.
Use A plant to take pride of place as a specimen in a pool, although it will also go well with other water lilies, especially pink and white ones (*N.* 'Marliacea Albida' and *N.* 'Pink Sensation').
Similar plants *N.* 'Froebelii'; *N.* 'Attraction'.

88 *Pontederia cordata*

The pickerel weed is not a weed at all, but a very pretty herbaceous, hardy, vigorous without being invasive, perennial marginal plant. It has heart- or spear-shaped, upward-pointing, glossy green leaves and tough 75cm/30in stems with short (up to 10cm/4in) spikes of purple-blue flowers from mid-summer until the autumn.
Cultivation and Propagation
Will grow in water up to 22cm/9in deep. It thrives in full sun and still water. Plant in late spring in the mud, from 7.5-22cm/3-9in deep, and about 45cm/18in apart. It has creeping rhizomes which can be cut with a knife and divided at the same season. Occasionally restrict its spread, if necessary, by removing some of these in late spring.
Use One of the few water plants with blue flowers, it is an ornament in all but very small pools. The yellow-flowered *Nuphar lutea* flowers at the same time, and provides a suitable companion.
Similar plants *Sagittaria japonica* (similarly-shaped leaves, taller, with white flowers).

89 *Primula florindae*

The giant cowslip is a handsome waterside plant. It has large, boat-shaped leaves, up to 20cm/8in long, and 90cm/36in stems topped with heads of fragrant pendulous cowslip flowers in early and midsummer. The stems are loosely covered in white 'meal'.
Cultivation and Propagation
Plant in autumn or spring in a soil which never dries out, in either sun or partial shade. Mulch in spring. Divide, if desired, after flowering. Sow seeds immediately they are ripe (summer) and put in a shaded cold frame; keep moist at all times. Once germinated, plant in nursery rows. Plant out when a reasonable size and able to contend with other vigorous-growing bog plants.

Use Associates happily with many other bogside plants like primulas, *Iris laevigata*, *I. pseudacorus* 'Variegata', and *Calla palustris*.
Similar plants Other tall primulas including *P. bulleyana* and *P. prolifera* (*P. helodoxa*) (both happiest in a peaty soil).

90 *Rheum palmatum*
'Atrosanguineum'

This large ornamental perennial rhubarb is a tremendous asset to a poolside, because of the colour and size of its leaves. It is also hardier than *Gunnera manicata*. Although it will grow in a large wet border, and provides companionship for *Corylus maxima* 'Purpurea', for example, it is best grown in moist soil close to water, where its huge, deeply cut leaves and 1.8m/6ft spires of crimson-pink flowers can be seen to best advantage, and where its girth will not be of any great consequence; it forms a clump up to 1.8 x 1.8m/6 x 6ft. The leaves are intensely purple on both sides when young, although the colour fades on the undersides by flowering time (early summer). The leaves are anything from 60-90cm/24-36in long, rounded, five-lobed and deeply cut.
Cultivation and Propagation
Not a difficult plant to grow, provided there is space for it, and adequate moisture in summer. It will grow in sun or semi-shade. Plant in early winter in soil which has been well enriched with organic humus. Lift and divide at the same time. The seed heads are ornamental enough to be worth retaining.
Use Makes a considerable impact on its own but can be also grown in concert with *Lobelia cardinalis* and a variety of astilbes. The rounded leaves of *Ligularia dentata* make a natural contrast, where space is not at a premium.
Similar plants *R. palmatum* 'Rubrum'; *R. palmatum* (some purple tinging to the leaves, but whitish flower heads).

ANNUALS AND BIENNIALS

Hardy annuals are grown from seed, usually sown in the spring, and they flower, seed and die within one year. Not surprisingly, they are easy to germinate and fast to grow, and are a good provider of inexpensive summer colour. Half-hardy annuals usually need to be sown indoors, and will die with the frosts, but they supply most colourful 'summer bedding'. Biennials make a rosette of leaves in their first year, then flower and die in the second. They are also easy to cultivate and provide much of the 'spring bedding', often planted in association with flowering bulbs.

91

92

91 *Campanula medium*

The well loved biennial Canterbury bell comes in a range of colours in mixed seed packets (pink, dark-purple, blue and white) which blend well together. Its height (90-120cm/36-48in) provides vertical contrast to low-growing annuals. The flowers, which come in early summer, are large, bell-shaped, with backward curving lips. The leaves are retained over the winter in a clump; they are green, lanceolate, toothed. There is a double-flowered version which is not so elegant, and also a 'cup-and-saucer' one – with a ruff of bracts the same colour as the petals.

Cultivation and Propagation
Sow in late spring or early summer in a tray or cold frame. Line the seedlings out in spare ground and plant out in the autumn in the place where they are to flower. They like full sun and well drained soil, but will tolerate some shade.

Use Marvellous for cottage garden schemes, where they lend an air of controlled untidiness. Their flowering time and gardening associations make them natural allies of old shrub roses, columbines, sweet williams and other early summer cottage favourites.

Similar plants *C. medium* 'Bells of Holland' (domed shape).

92 *Cheiranthus cheiri* 'Vulcan'

The biennial wallflower comes in a number of colours. 'Vulcan', a rich velvety red, is one of the best. All are richly scented. Dense spikes of four-petalled flowers (up to 2.5cm/1in wide) in late spring and early summer are held on 35-45cm/15-18in stout erect stems. They are excellent for cutting, not least for their scent. The leaves are dark green and lanceolate.

Cultivation and Propagation
Sow seed in spare ground from late spring to early summer (later if you garden in a windswept place). If possible, transplant seedlings in mid-summer, 23-30cm/9-12in apart, to encourage them to make a more fibrous, and therefore wind-resistant, root system. Pinch out the growing tips to make bushier plants when they are 15cm/6in tall. In early to mid-autumn, plant out tall varieties 30cm/12in apart, rather less for the dwarfs. It is important to establish them in plenty of time before the onset of winter, to avoid damage by frosts. They thrive in an alkaline soil and should only be grown on acid soil which has been limed to lessen the risk of clubroot.

Use Seed mixtures are available, which are suitable for very informal cottage plantings, but for a more sophisticated scheme use, for example, 'Vulcan' with yellow tulips or blue myosotis (forget-me-nots), or with blocks of other wallflowers like the orange-red 'Fire King', or the crimson and yellow 'Blood-Red', with an edging of forget-me-nots. Cheiranthus can also be established with great success in the crevices of old walls.

Similar plants *C. cheiri* 'Blood Red'.

93 *Digitalis purpurea*
Excelsior hybrids

Improved forms of the biennial common foxglove, suitable for large borders or deciduous woodland. Tall spikes (1.5m/5ft) of closely-packed tubular flowers come in a range of colours (pink, purplish, cream, yellow) to flower in early summer. The distinctive feature of the Excelsior hybrids is that the flowers, which open from the bottom first, are held horizontally so that the spotting in the inner flower is visible. If the

93

94

95

96

97

central spike is deadheaded, lateral flower shoots usually form. They make attractive cut flowers.

Cultivation and Propagation
Sow seed in late spring or early summer, preferably in a pot, and put in a cold frame. The plants seed freely but the seedlings are often inferior and it is best to re-sow each year. Plant the seedlings out in a nursery row and plant out in the autumn for flowering the following summer. Do not allow to dry out, but avoid planting in a very heavy soil, for foxgloves are prone to rotting in wet winters.
Use A plant for a semi-wild situation, which looks well amongst shrub roses, flowering at the same time. Useful for its unusual height. Grow it in groups for greater effect.
Similar plants *D*. Foxy hybrids (75cm/30in tall).

94 *Eschscholzia californica*

The Californian poppy is a charming small hardy annual, bringing an echo of West Coast sunshine to sunny places in poor, quick-draining soil. The species has bright orange-yellow, saucer-shaped, single flowers (about 7.5cm/3in across), borne in succession from early summer until mid-autumn, and held 30-37cm/12-15in high above ferny blue-green leaves. The flowers are followed by 7.5cm/3in cylindrical glaucous seed-pods. There are several cultivars available, both semi-double and single, the former usually having wavy tissue-paper petals. They come in a variety of colours from pink through oranges to red: for example, 'Mission Bells' (23cm/9in), and 'Monarch Art Shades' (30-45cm/12-18in). 'Miniature Primrose' is only 15cm/6in tall and lemon-yellow. Californian poppies self-seed, and even if you start with a mixture of different colours, you will soon find that you have mostly orange-yellows.
Cultivation and Propagation
Sow in early spring where you want them to flower, or in early autumn in a sheltered place with cloches over the seedbed. Thin seedlings to 15cm/6in. Deadhead to keep flowering going throughout the season.
Use 'Miniature Primrose' goes well with *Anchusa capensis* 'Blue Angel' or *Phacelia campanularia*, and the others with golden grasses, *Convolvulus tricolor*, red salvias and other bright half-hardy annuals. They look fine alone in crevices in paving.

95 **Impatiens**
Super Elfin Series

Recent breeding work on half-hardy busy lizzies has produced some very good cultivars, usually in mixtures. The Super Elfin Series are some of the best, growing to about 25cm/10in and providing a dense spreading carpet of flowers through the season. Although busy lizzies will flower in sun, in a moisture-retentive soil, unlike most other bedding plants they also flower well in semi-shade, so can be used to brighten up forgotten corners and provide reasonably weed-suppressant ground-cover at the same time. They have flat, open, five-petalled, spurred flowers, 5cm/2in across, held just above the leaves.

Single colours are best, but the mixtures (purple, red, orange, pink, salmon, lilac, white) work surprisingly well, especially in dark surroundings. My preference is for a pastel, rather than brightly-coloured, mixture.
Cultivation and Propagation
The difficulty with impatiens is germinating the seed. They need a high temperature and light but must not dry out, so sow in pots with a thin vermiculite covering at a temperature of 21-24°C/70-75°F. Pot on singly when large enough to handle easily, dropping the temperature to 16°C/61°F. When the seedlings are well established, harden them off gradually before planting out after frosts are over.
Use If grown in single colours, these busy lizzies can be used in a variety of colour schemes. In a mixture, they should be segregated from other plants and grown on their own.
Similar plants *I*. Accent Series.

96 **Lathyrus odoratus**

The sweet pea is a fast-growing annual climber, which uses tendrils to twine round a support and grows to 2.5-3m/8-10ft. A succession of often highly scented keeled flowers in shades of red, pink, blue, lilac or white appear from early summer until early autumn. It is hardy, although seedlings can be killed in an unheated greenhouse in harsh winters. The leaves are oval and grey-green.

There are various types, of which the most commonly grown are the Spencers which have large flowers with wavy petals; the older 'grandi-floras', with smaller flowers, can

claim the strongest fragrance. There are also dwarf types available such as 'Bijou', 'Knee-Hi' and the tendril-less 'Snoopea'.
Cultivation and Propagation
Sweet peas like a sunny place and deep, well drained, humus-rich, slightly alkaline soil, although they will grow adequately in less than perfect conditions. In early autumn or early spring, soak seeds overnight in water, sow a few to a pot, and put in a warm place. Prick the long-rooted seedlings out singly into larger pots, hardening off the plantlings and planting them out in mid- to late spring. Or sow directly into the flowering site in early or mid-spring. Taller varieties will need some support: a wigwam or a line of 2.5m/8ft bamboo canes, trellis, fence, or an upright roll of chicken wire mesh can all be used to give purchase to their numerous tendrils.

Sweet peas should be picked regularly, because flowering eventually ceases if they are allowed to set seed. If deadheading is done on a regular basis, they will have a long flowering season.
Use Grow them on a wigwam of canes in a flower border to create vertical impact. Alternatively, grow the shorter varieties, such as 'Jet Set' (90cm/36in) nearer the front of the border, discreetly staked. 'Snoopea' is self-supporting. All sweet peas look charming when planted with cottage-type summer flowers such as shrub roses, columbines, anchusa and poppies, as well as summer annuals and biennials such as Canterbury bells and cornflowers.
Similar plants *L. latifolius* (purple-pink, perennial).

97 *Lavatera trimestris*
'Mont Blanc'

A hardy annual, often grown as a half-hardy one, started in a green-house in early spring. It makes a bushy erect plant, about 50cm/20in high, and is much more substantial than most hardy annuals. The stems are topped by the most brilliant white, shallow, thin-petalled trumpet flowers (10cm/4in across) in summer, against a background of dark green oval lobed leaves.
Cultivation and Propagation
Sow seed individually in pots in early spring, and place in medium heat. Once germinated, grow on in pots in

98

99

00

a cold frame and harden off before planting out in mid- to late spring. Alternatively, sow in the open ground in spring. The roots dislike disturbance so thin carefully to 35-45cm/15-18in, to give room for each plant to flower well. The soil should not be too rich or you will encourage leaves at the expense of flowers, but it should be in full sun. In a windy place, stake plants.
Use An excellent plant for a white, green and grey scheme; avoid pairing it with off-white plants which will be made to look very dowdy in comparison. White petunias, however, would look well. 'Mont Blanc' also looks effective with *Eryngium* 'Miss Willmott's Ghost', artemisias, and *Nicotiana alata* 'Lime Green'. It will also admirably mask an evergreen shrub no longer in flower, such as choisya or daphne.
Similar plants *L. trimestris* 'Mont Rose' (pink, harder to find); *L. trimestris* 'Silver Cup' (vibrant pink, taller, to 60cm/24in).

98 **Lobularia maritima** 'Snow Crystals' (*Alyssum* 'Snow Crystals')

A sweet alyssum with particularly large white scented flowers, borne over a long period. A hardy annual, it grows to 10cm/4in, with a spread of 20-30cm/8-12in, and makes a compact, dome-shaped plant with short rounded spikes of bright white four-petalled flowers, held above linear grey-green leaves.
Cultivation and Propagation
Sow indoors in early spring, at a temperature of 13°C/55°F or so, or outside where it is to flower. The second course is best for prolonged flowering but, to avoid mildew, thin out seedlings. Successional sowing can also be helpful.
Use This plant is most often to be seen in formal summer bedding schemes, where it can look effective, provided it is planted generously. Useful as a path edging but looks more natural if grown in drifts in gravel, around sun-loving plants such as helianthemums and osteospermum, or individually in holes in paving. It can also be grown in hanging baskets or pots, but must not be allowed to dry out or it will burn up in hot weather.
Similar plants *L. maritima* 'Oriental Night' (purple).

99 **Nicotiana alata** 'Lime Green'

This ornamental tobacco plant is notable for the unusual colour of its evening-scented flowers, which make it popular with flower arrangers. It makes an erect bushy plant, 60-75cm/24-30in tall, covered in sticky hairs and with lax groups of long-tubed flowers which open out into a star at the end, about 7.5cm/3in long. These are freely borne all summer from early to mid-summer, and are unaffected by most weather. 'Lime Green' is a half-hardy perennial which will overwinter, if the weather is mild, and flower early. But it is usually grown as an annual.
Cultivation and Propagation
Sow seed in early spring, in a temperature of at least 18°C/65°F. The seed germinates in two weeks if sown on the surface of the compost and kept damp. Prick out seedlings into small pots to achieve good-sized plants before hardening off and planting out at the end of spring. Plant in a sunny, warm place where the scent can be appreciated, 30cm/12in apart. No staking is necessary.
Use 'Lime Green' is excellent for mid- to late summer blooming yellow/green/blue flower schemes. Mix with the blue-green leaves and white flowers of *Argyranthemum frutescens, A. foeniculaceum,* or *Chrysanthemum maximum,* or the green leaves and deep primrose flowers of *Argyranthemum* 'Jamaica Primrose'; alternatively, with *Alchemilla mollis* as an understorey, mix with sky-blue *Salvia patens,* lavender, or blue *Agapanthus* Headbourne hybrids. Alternatively, try a low-key scheme with *Eucalyptus gunnii* or *Ruta graveolens* 'Jackman's Blue'. Yellow-green is useful in a variety of colour schemes, either to cool down hot colours, or sharpen paler ones.
Similar plants *N. langsdorfii.*

100 **Petunia** Resisto Series

The petunia is a deservedly popular half-hardy perennial (usually grown as an annual), although many petunias, especially those with large flowers, languish in wet seasons. The Resisto Series of Multiflora *Petunia* are the most weather-resistant, and the single flowers and clear colours make them indispensable for tubs, window boxes or a sunny place in the garden, particularly as they have a very long flowering season.
Like all petunias, the Resisto cultivars have oval, green, hairy leaves and wide trumpet flowers, with a height and spread of up to 30cm/12in. The colours range from pure white through rose-pink, blue, to red and even bright red-and-white-striped.
Cultivation and Propagation
Petunias are usually sown in early to mid-spring at a temperature of 18-24°C/65-76°F. Alternatively, buy them as young plants from garden centres. Cuttings, rooted in summer, can be overwintered under glass for early flowering the following year. Petunias do best in a sunny place, and will withstand drought once well established. Like most annuals, petunias benefit from being regularly deadheaded. This prolongs the flowering season.
Use Avoid growing indiscriminate mixtures, or doubles, if you are a stickler for aesthetics. Individual colours, such as pink, chime well with grey-leaved plants like *Helichrysum petiolare,* the variegated *Felicia amelloides,* and *Convolvulus sabatius.* A striking combination can be made using the blue and the white Resisto forms together. Petunias' tolerance of dry conditions makes them ideal container plants.
Similar plants *P.* Super Cascade Series.

GARDENING TECHNIQUES

1

U ntil now, the emphasis in this book has been on the use of plants in the garden, rather than on their cultivation. This is how it should be, for it would not be helpful to burden you with detailed descriptions of cultivation techniques which are simply the means to an end, before the end itself has been established.

However, the time has now come to understand how to encourage plant growth, in order that design schemes can work satisfactorily. If plants languish or die as a result of poor husbandry, the best-laid plans will inevitably fail. Furthermore, many gardeners, myself included, derive enormous satisfaction from successfully cultivating plants, quite apart from fitting them into an overall scheme.

I have assumed very little knowledge, but a considerable degree of commonsense on the part of the reader. I have attempted to explain underlying principles, where these are not immediately obvious, so that your gardening can become as interesting and worthwhile as possible.

I have omitted techniques which I consider to be optional, and have emphasized those remedies, devices and techniques which are up-to-date, in order to try to avoid the repetition of methods now losing relevance in these fast-moving, technocratic times.

Certain areas of gardening activity are covered in more depth than others, but that is intentional. It seems to me that the gardener with other demands on his or her time need not be bombarded by complex and detailed advice on specialisms. There is little, therefore, specifically on the kitchen garden, or the garden under glass, although you should bear in mind that much of what is written generally can be used as a basis for cultivating in particular circumstances.

1 This sub-tropical planting depends for much of its effect on the contrast between the restrained colour of the fan palm in the foreground, and the bright, even garish, massed cinerarias behind. In frost-free conditions, cinerarias are evergreen perennials, and will reliably produce their large and plentiful daisy flowers in winter and spring.

2 Hard and soft elements blend very happily in this town garden. The paving is simple and coherent, the same brick being used also for the shallow steps and the lily pond. Advantage has been taken of the shelter and protection which town gardens can often afford, by planting a variety of hydrangeas, including the slightly tender woolly-leaved *H. aspera*, seen against the end wall. In this shady and damp spot, tolerant perennials such as *Alchemilla mollis* and *Geranium endressii* have been used to good effect in the central bed, with one or two sizeable shrubs to mark off, informally, one side of the garden from the other.

PLANT CARE

UB Plants do not grow in a vacuum: they are intimately influenced by a number of factors, most notably by light, air, the temperature around them and the amount of water and nutrients that are available to them. The reasons are relatively complex but, for our purposes, can be simplified as follows.

HOW PLANTS GROW

Plants require energy to grow, just as we do. They make their own food by photosynthesis. Light is absorbed by chlorophyll, the green pigment in plants, and converted, using carbon dioxide from the atmosphere and water from the soil, into sugars which are then stored as starches. Oxygen is given off in the process. The energy is released for growth when the plant respires: oxygen is used to metabolize the sugars and carbon dioxide is then released into the atmosphere.

In addition, to make the chlorophyll and the enzymes necessary for these chemical reactions to take place, nutrient elements from the soil are also required, the most important of these being nitrogen, phosphorus (as phosphate) and potassium (as potash). Water, which gives plants much of their structural support and is a vital component of photosynthesis, provides the means whereby dissolved minerals can pass into, and up, the plant. Heat is also important, for temperature affects the rate of enzyme activity, which begins at around 6°C/43°F and falls off from about 40°C/104°F. Low light levels tend to slow or even stop this activity.

WHAT CONDITIONS DO PLANTS NEED?

Knowing something of how plants grow surely obliges us to try to give them the conditions that are most likely to suit them. Plants vary greatly in their requirements, usually as a result of the particular conditions to be found in their particular native habitat, be it seashore, desert, temperate woodland, alpine meadow or tropical rainforest.

Plants will often survive in unsuitable conditions but they will not thrive. So sun lovers should not be planted in shady places if they are to flower well, or drought-tolerant plants in permanently wet soil, or tender plants in known frost-pockets. This is only common sense but it is surprising how often we strain the tolerance of plants to suit our design purposes. To my mind, the art of the garden designer lies in achieving the desired effect using only those plants that will flourish in the prevailing conditions.

That said, a number of basic principles of plant growth apply for all plants, so some general observations may safely be made. The first is that since all the plants will be competing for the same available resources, those plants we do not want but which come unbidden – 'weeds' – will need to be eliminated, or at least restricted. It also means that plants have to be sensibly spaced if the soil is not to be exhausted of moisture and nutrients. This is an obvious fact in the vegetable garden but it also needs to be taken into account in the flower border.

WATER IN THE SOIL

The plant's need for both structural rigidity and nutrients from the soil requires that the soil water be conserved, particularly in free-draining soils in summer. Conversely, you must ensure that the soil is not permanently waterlogged, when it will have lost much of the oxygen required by all plants – with the exception of water and bog plants, which are specially adapted to these conditions.

Gardeners often make unusually heavy demands on the soil by growing a large range of plants densely, but, in any event, the conservation of moisture is important in all temperate gardens. This is true almost regardless of the average rainfall, because rain cannot be depended upon to come when required, it easily drains out of the topsoil, and it evaporates from the surface.

MULCHES AND SOIL CONDITIONERS

The most efficient way of conserving moisture, and also warmth, in the soil is to use a mulch; that is, a covering over the soil. Mulches can be made from a variety of materials, both organic and inorganic; inorganic ones such as black polythene or woven polypropylene are probably the most efficient, but organic mulches are to be preferred because in most instances they have a nutritional value and, when pulled down by earthworms, act as a soil conditioner as well. Furthermore, all mulching material, if laid *at least* 5cm/2in thick, should suppress the growth of annual weeds which need light both to germinate and to grow. The soil should be damp before the mulch is laid. Early spring is therefore the best time, before the strongest annual surge of weed growth, when the soil is likely to be damp, and when any warming of the soil is helpful.

In earlier times, rotted cow or pig manure were the favoured choices; but today they are more difficult to find, heavy to barrow, and often contain weed-seeds. Well-rotted horse manure is more readily available, and is helpful for 'opening up' (that is, creating more air spaces in) clay soils when it has been pulled down by worms because of the amount of straw it contains. It is not weed-free, either.

Popular these days, because it is ecologically sound, is home-made compost; important as a source of soil-conditioning humus, and providing nutrients too, it also goes some way towards reconciling us to our wasteful, consumerist natures. However, unless your garden is very small or your family very large, it is highly unlikely you will be able to make enough for all your needs. Unless made very carefully, it is unlikely to be completely weed-free. Also available is spent mushroom compost, a mixture of strawy manure and peat, which is light and easy to handle but contains lime (added to whiten the mushrooms) and therefore should not be used in gardens with lime-hating plants.

All of these materials should be well-rotted: if still in the process of decay, valuable nitrogen may be lost as ammonia into the atmosphere. The heat generated by decaying matter can also, in some circumstances, damage growing plants, especially young ones. So leave your chosen organic matter, covered, in a convenient spot outside until it no longer gives off a strong smell, before using it.

Leafmould is a useful weed-free fibrous mulch which can be made in gardens containing deciduous trees and shrubs. It is slow to form and is best made separately from compost. It is usually acidic.

All of these organic mulches contain a small percentage of the three major nutrient elements, but they are probably more important as soil conditioners and mulches than as feeds. Richer in minerals is cocoa shell. Although a by-product of the chocolate manufacturing process, it is not cheap but it is effective, soon decomposing enough to make a weed-suppressing mat.

A valuable mulch, if you live in the right place, is seaweed. It is best left

---

to rot, which it does comparatively quickly, before being laid on the garden. Spent brewery hops can offer another local alternative.

There are proprietary mulches now on sale, composed of a variety of waste products, such as conifer bark chippings, composted bark, paper and timber waste, straw, coir, and even composted sewage sludge. These will become more important in future years as we try to recycle waste more efficiently.

The impetus to introduce new products on to the market has been strengthened by the current 'peat debate'. Peat has no place as a mulch or soil conditioner because it is both very wasteful of a non-renewable and, in some places, threatened natural resource, and no better at doing the job than a number of other, 'greener', products.

As explained above, the word 'mulch' is also used by gardeners to encompass inorganic materials such as polythene – black for preference because it acts also as a weed suppressant. Polythene is extremely

MULCHING

The value of a thick mulch for plants at the start of the growing season, to conserve moisture and discourage weeds, cannot be overstated. Leave a gap unmulched around the base of the plant, to avoid stem rot.

effective but ugly and so, in the flower garden, should be hidden by bark chippings or gravel. Lately, UV-stable woven polypropylene materials have appeared on the market. These can be cut to shape and are handy for laying around permanent plantings, being unobtrusive, durable and not impervious to rain. Even old carpets, and newspapers anchored with a thin layer of soil or wood chips, can be used as temporary measures. In beds where alpines are grown, or in 'gravel gardens', grit of varying sizes can be used as a weed inhibiting mulch.

MULCHES
- Black polythene
- Carpet
- Coarse bark
- Coarse grit
- Cocoa shell
- Coir
- Composted bark
- Composted sewage sludge
- Composted straw
- Farmyard manure (cow; horse)
- Fibre fleece
- Garden compost
- Gravel
- Leafmould
- Newspaper
- Paper and timber waste
- Perforated plastic film ('floating cloche')
- Seaweed
- Spent hop manure
- Spent mushroom compost
- Woven polypropylene ('geotextile')

SOIL CONDITIONERS
- Clay (to very light soils)
- Coarse coir
- Coarse grit
- Coarse sand
- Composted bark
- Composted straw
- Farmyard manure
- Garden compost

- Green manures
- Gypsum
- Leafmould
- Lime
- Paper and timber waste
- Seaweed
- Spent hop manure
- Spent mushroom compost
- Sulphur

NUTRIENTS

Plants require a variety of nutrients to help them grow. Therefore, if the essential ones are exhausted, or have been leached out of the topsoil in rainwater, they must be replaced, and in the right quantities to be efficient and economic. The availability of some nutrients to plants is affected by the acidity or alkalinity of the soil – the pH value; so it is important to establish what the pH of your soil is and, if necessary, adjust it accordingly, to prevent plants suffering from deficiencies. The optimum pH for growing a wide range of plants is 6·5. Small kits or, even easier, meters can be bought so that you can do your own analysis.

Altering the pH of your soil is possible, temporarily, by adding dressings of 'lime' (calcium carbonate) or calcified seaweed, to make it more alkaline, or sulphur to make it more acidic. Neither option works permanently because these elements are washed out easily by rain. However, liming is essential in the vegetable garden if, for example, you wish to grow plants in the cabbage family in a soil with a low pH. It should be applied in autumn, and never at the same time as manure or sulphate of ammonia, with which it reacts chemically to give off gaseous ammonia, and hence the nitrogen is dispersed into the air and lost.

Quantities of pine bark and leafmould can be used to help lower a soil's pH sufficiently to grow lime-hating plants but their efficacy is,

again, short-lived. Peat is wasteful so should not be contemplated except for growing acid-loving plants in containers. Flowers of sulphur and aluminium sulphate are alternatives which also have only a temporary effect.

The three major nutrients needed by all plants for healthy growth are nitrogen (N), phosphorus (P) and potassium (K). Three other intermediate elements, magnesium (Mg), calcium (Ca) and sulphur (S), are needed by plants in lesser quantities, while trace elements such as iron (Fe), boron (Bo), molybdenum (Mb) and manganese (Ma), although very important, are required in even smaller amounts. You can buy a kit to test your soil for deficiency of the three major nutrients but the surest way of detecting nutrient deficiencies is to examine plants exhibiting symptoms.

FERTILIZERS

A certain amount of nutrient comes from organic mulches and soil conditioners but some (although by no means all) plants will benefit from additional feeding, both in the spring, and halfway through the growing season. For this, we use fertilizers, which work in one of three ways: 'quick-acting', 'steady-release' and 'slow-release'. The quick-acting ones have an almost immediate but usually short-term effect, while steady-release feeds not only begin to work quickly but continue to release nutrients over a long period of time. Slow-release fertilizers take time to become available to plants.

Fertilizers can be used for a number of purposes, depending on how they are formulated, and what they contain: as a base dressing, forked or raked into the top layer of the soil before sowing or planting; as a top dressing scattered round established plants; as a liquid feed watered around the roots, or as a liquid foliar feed sprayed on to the leaves. The last two are only available as liquids but the others come in granular, powder, and resin-coated forms.

Common examples of quick-acting fertilizers are sulphate of ammonia, general proprietary mixes like 'Growmore', dried blood, and all liquid and foliar feeds. Steady-release fertilizers come as small resin-coated pellets which can be placed on the soil round a plant at the beginning of the growing season and will last until the autumn. Steady-release fertilizers are invaluable, particularly for feeding shrubs and other permanent plants. However, the nutrient is released more quickly in warm weather, so there can be 'accelerated depletion', in which case a later, additional liquid feed may be necessary. The coated fertilizers are widely used in the nursery trade and are often to be seen on the surface of containers in garden centres.

Not to be confused with these are the slow-release fertilizers, such as bonemeal, and hoof and horn. Some of these are organic, so it takes some while for soil organisms to break them down into a form available to plants. This makes them useful for putting around bulbs, for example, in autumn, to give these a boost as they start flowering in spring. Blood, fish and bone is a popular general fertilizer because its nutrients are released both immediately and over a period of time. Other slow-release fertilizers are derived from rocks so take time to dissolve and become available.

There is a further division (although it is an artificial one) between organic and inorganic fertilizers. The assumption that organic fertilizers are naturally made, while inorganic ones are artificially produced, is not always correct; for

example, slow-release fertilizers derived from natural rock, such as rock phosphate, are, strictly speaking, inorganic, because they contain no carbon. Nevertheless, because they are naturally occurring they are acceptable to most organic gardeners. It must be said that it matters not a jot to plants whether they are absorbing 'organic' or 'inorganic' fertilizers from the soil water.

COMPOST

There are a great many theories about good compost-making but you can leave most of them to the compost-hobbyists. All you need to know is that, although you *can* make compost by piling vegetable waste in an untidy heap, it is messy and takes longer to rot down into something useful than is necessary. The microscopic fungi and bacteria which cause decay need warmth, humidity, air and nitrogen. These elements can be provided by erecting a retaining structure (timber, brick, plastic or wire mesh), insulated sufficiently to keep in warmth and moisture yet with small gaps or holes to let in some air, with a lid or covering to prevent the heap becoming waterlogged and to keep in the heat which the bacteria will generate, and a front panel which can be removed easily. The only other requirement is a proprietary 'activator', sulphate of ammonia or dried blood, to provide the nitrogen which the bacteria need in order to work efficiently.

The heat generated speeds decomposition which is why the top covering should be removed as little as possible. However, this heat will not inevitably kill all weed seeds and plant diseases so it is unwise to put any roots of perennial weeds, or flowering annual weeds, or diseased leaves or prunings in a compost heap. Either bag these up for the

refuse collectors or chop them up small and burn when dry.

If you construct a wooden bin, it should be about 1-1.2m/3-4ft wide and deep, and up to 1.5m/5ft tall. It is most easily made up of a number of slats fitted together with thin gaps between them. These gaps will allow in the oxygen which the bacteria need, without letting out all the heat that is generated by bacterial activity. If you make the bin with no holes in the sides, place a deep layer of brushwood in the bottom instead. Site the bin in a sheltered place, to prevent the wind from drying out the edges of the compost; or line the inside of the bin with windbreak material.

Manufactured plastic or wooden bins, with a capacity of between 0.2 and 0.6 cubic metres/7 and 20 cubic feet, are the answer for those with small gardens or for those who do not want to make their own structure. Pick a sturdy construction, with some side holes, which is easy to dismantle when you want to get the rotted compost out. Place a plastic bin on earth rather than concrete to provide better insulation.

The compost 'tumbler' is a plastic bin, with holes in the sides, fixed on a stand so that it can be turned over easily. This is a simple way of turning a small compost heap but, for best results, it must be done daily, so is only practical if the tumbler is conveniently placed.

Efficient composting requires a good mixture of materials: kitchen vegetable waste; some leaves; shredded, healthy, dry, woody material (use a compost shredder or cut into very small pieces with secateurs); shredded newspaper; green annual weeds (not in flower) with the soil still attached to the roots; and lawn mowings. There should, ideally, not be too much of any one thing, particularly grass clippings which

degrade very quickly and become slimy and smelly if added in large quantities. As you fill the bin, add compost activator (which contains nitrogen) or a nitrogenous fertilizer after each 15cm/6in layer, to encourage the bacteria to work faster. I suggest that you turn the top layer of the decaying compost with a garden fork every two weeks as you fill the bin, so that the outer parts reach the centre of the heap where it is hottest. You may need to water the heap occasionally to keep it moist, though not soaking; put on a lid or covering to hold the heat and prevent the rain getting in.

In a perfect world, a bin would be filled in one go and would then rot in two to three months. In practice, most gardeners have to add waste in small layers; this means making compost can easily take twice as long, particularly in cold weather when bacterial activity is slow or even halted. Start a bin in spring, if you can, so that you have the compost ready by the following winter and spring when it is most needed for digging in or mulching. Your compost is properly decayed when it has cooled down, is dark brown in colour and its constituents are no longer recognizable. Empty the bin of its decomposed contents, which can be piled up in a convenient place, covered to prevent nutrients leaching out in rainwater, while you begin once more to fill the bin with fresh material.

If you have room, place two bins side by side, so that once one has been filled and the compost made, it can be raided when needed, while you are still filling the other. It is silly to put new waste on fully decomposed material. Any material left undecayed on the first pile should be added to the new bin.

It is also possible to make compost anaerobically, that is, without any oxygen being present. Use a bottomless plastic dustbin with a lid, or black bin liner without holes, and add a 2.5cm/1in layer of soil for every 25cm/10in or so of waste material. Do not add activator, or turn the heap. This method takes much longer to achieve good compost, and can be rather smelly, but is much less work.

Leafmould, although invaluable, takes longer to decay than other plant remains, being food more for fungi than bacteria. So, either put your deciduous leaves into a double thickness black plastic bag, water if dry, and leave for at least one year, or, for fine leafmould, two to three years; or make a simple structure of wooden posts and chicken wire, into which the leaves can be put to stop them flying about. As with compost in a bin, you will have to water the heap if it dries out. If you have only a few leaves, add them to your compost bin. Leafmould is ready for use in potting composts when it is very friable and dark brown in colour but it can be used before that – as a soil conditioner and mulch. It contains about the same amount and kind of nutrients as farmyard manure. The best leaves are oak and beech but use whatever you have. However, thick evergreen leaves, like holly, are best added to the compost heap.

Organic gardeners swear by the worm bin, usually a plastic dustbin full of brandling worms which live on kitchen and garden green waste, but this is not entirely straightforward to handle, so has to come into the category of a compost-hobby.

ORGANIC GARDENING
The debate about organic gardening is a lively one, with strongly held views on each side. Organic gardeners believe that manufactured pesticides alter the natural balance of friend and foe in the garden, by killing too indiscriminately; and that artificial plant foods should be avoided because they require fossil fuels for their manufacture and, in the case of fast-acting nitrogenous fertilizers, leach too easily into the groundwater where they may contaminate water supplies.

The true organic gardener feeds the soil, not the plant: the theory is that, if a soil is fertile, plants will grow well enough without artificial fertilizers, and be healthy enough to withstand some damage from pest and disease. It is certainly possible with the help of liberal quantities of home-made compost, well-rotted animal and seaweed manures and the contents of a worm bin, to keep even an intensively cultivated garden fertile. However, if pests and diseases are to be kept at bay, soil fertility is not the whole answer. Observant and consistent attention to garden hygiene is an article of faith to organic gardeners, as is the use of so-called biological controls, and, even more important, tolerance of damage. Furthermore, although this may conflict with design considerations, they must also rely on the most pest- and disease-resistant varieties of plants.

Organic gardeners will only buy products which are labelled as being 'organic' but there is still much confusion (some of it fostered by the manufacturers) about which products can genuinely be called that. Furthermore, even an obviously organic material like poultry manure is unacceptable to many organic gardeners if it comes from a battery farm. Non-purists will accept the use of 'natural' (that is, naturally-occurring) pesticides, such as derris, which, though very poisonous to beneficial insects and fish, is of short persistence. Unfortunately for organic gardeners, the use of several 'natural' remedies is not specifically recommended for amateur gardeners, and is therefore not authorized under Pesticide Regulations.

It seems to me that, in most instances, the development of a truly organic garden is admirable, time-consuming, and not entirely realistic. The difficulty lies in the fact that what happens in your garden is strongly influenced by what goes on in your neighbours' or the surrounding farmland, making it hard to achieve a natural balance between predator and pest, for example. For some time to come, true organic gardening is likely to remain the preserve of hard-working and idealistic people, while the rest of us continue to use chemicals, but for ever more specific and circumscribed purposes.

COMPOST BIN

A typical pair of compost bins, made of wood, with removable front panels. Compost from one bin can be used while the other bin is being filled. An old piece of carpet laid on top will help to retain warmth and moisture, while the spaced slats provide ventilation.

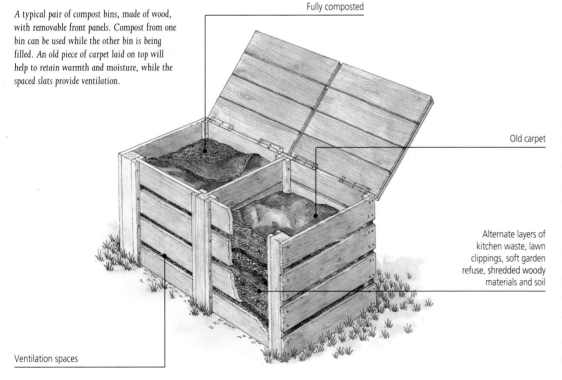

Fully composted

Old carpet

Alternate layers of kitchen waste, lawn clippings, soft garden refuse, shredded woody materials and soil

Ventilation spaces

BUYING AND PLANTING

UB There are many ways of acquiring plants. The most congenial and haphazard is accepting cuttings or grown plants from friends. Many gardeners are naturally generous and can see the point of spreading good plants around, if only because they may lose them themselves in the future. Almost as agreeable, and haphazard, is buying plants at local markets or at sales held at garden openings. You may well find interesting and unusual plants this way but these are gap-fillers; as a method of acquiring plants to fulfil a garden plan, it is next to useless.

SOURCES OF PLANTS

Having planned a border on paper, or indeed the planting for your whole garden, your best course is to visit, or obtain the catalogues of, a variety of specialist nurseries; many of these also send plants by mail order. Large flower shows are also good sources of information and catalogues. This process may sound laborious but it is most unlikely that your local garden centre will be able to provide the entire range of plants you are after, especially if it includes any rare or unusual varieties.

Mail-order buying usually costs less per plant than at the average garden centre, although there are the additional expenses of postage and packing to consider, and plants do not always arrive in immaculate condition – or when you want them. It is important to state that substitutions are not acceptable.

Garden centres provide a more instantly gratifying kind of plant buying, for many plants can be bought in containers when they are flowering. However, although it is useful to be able to *view* plants when you are planning a garden, try to avoid impulse buying if you want to retain the integrity of your plan. If you are not planning whole borders,

merely augmenting or replacing piecemeal, then garden centres can be a good source of plants; shrubs, particularly, are usually well represented and organized.

Steer clear of large DIY stores that do not look as though they have adequate facilities for looking after living plants well. Some plants may be bought in high street stores, but usually only house plants (and not all of these) will thrive in the conditions which occur there.

It is possible to order cheap plants from newspaper advertisements, but the quality of those you receive is variable and often unacceptably low. The range of plants offered is limited, and often only mixed collections are available.

Seeds may be bought by mail order from a variety of seedsmen who issue free glossy catalogues each autumn. Seeds are also available in garden centres and DIY outlets in sufficient range to please most people. The larger mail-order

seedsmen also send out both pre-germinated seedlings and small plants, called plantlets or plugs, in the spring. The choice is small but this is a good way of acquiring young plants of, for example, geraniums and begonias, which are difficult or expensive to germinate. Garden centres also carry a range.

BUYING PLANTS

Plants may be bought in plastic or terracotta pots (containers), or 'polythene wrapped', that is, in a flexible variant of the rigid pot. Deciduous and hardy plants can also be bought, especially by mail order, 'bare-rooted'. Evergreens are usually sold in containers although conifers especially may occasionally be obtained 'root-balled', that is wrapped in hessian or similar, to prevent the soil falling away from the fibrous roots.

Choosing a good plant for your money is important, but not always straightforward. Large plants in

large pots may look expensive but often offer better value. This is particularly so in the case of herbaceous perennials, which may be divided up into several plants after purchase. Shrubs and trees are best bought reasonably small, as they establish more quickly in the ground than very large plants.

If you are buying in the growing season, don't choose plants which have a lot of dead wood, yellowing or brown leaves, or obvious signs of pests or diseases. Evergreen shrubs should be bushy; with deciduous shrubs, look for a balanced shape. Reject variegated plants with green 'reverted' shoots.

Do not be afraid to lift a containerized tree or shrub off the ground by the stem(s). It should remain firm; if the roots and the compost look in danger of parting company, it has not been in the pot long enough. Then examine the bottom of the pot; if there are a lot of roots pushing through the air holes,

A CONTAINER-GROWN SHRUB

Buy container-grown plants when they have been long enough in the pot not to part company with the compost when lifted off the ground, but not so long that the roots are well out of the drainage holes at the bottom, the label faded, or the compost surface weedy and mossy.

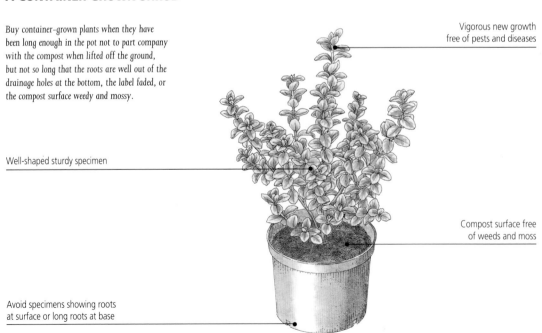

Vigorous new growth free of pests and diseases

Well-shaped sturdy specimen

Compost surface free of weeds and moss

Avoid specimens showing roots at surface or long roots at base the plant is probably pot-bound. Other tell-tale signs of this include faded colour photograph labels and weeds growing on the compost surface. In the case of trees over 2m/7ft tall, be wary of those which have fallen over, because they are probably in too small pots. If you are at all uncertain, ask an assistant to remove the plant from the pot for you. If the roots are encircling the inside perimeter of the pot, known as 'girdling', the plant may well be slow to establish itself in the ground and might remain vulnerable to the wind blowing it over for a long time.

At certain times of the year, a plant which looks half-dead may actually be fine. Herbaceous perennials, for example, are a good buy in early autumn but, as some naturally die down early, may look most unimpressive at the time of sale.

Bedding plants are usually sold in strips, packs, or trays; the packs have compartments for single plants so are easier to handle, but are, *pro rata*, more expensive. Do not be tempted to buy half-hardy bedding plants until the risk of a late frost in your area is minimal, unless you are happy to protect them yourself until the time for planting out. Bedding plants begin to appear in garden centres long before it is suitable to plant them outside.

You will get a better choice if you grow from seed, particularly if you want to grow plants in single colours rather than mixtures, but, generally speaking, garden centres are good for bedding plants, and offer a better choice than other outlets such as greengrocers and market stalls. Do not buy plants that are leggy, have prematurely yellowing outer leaves, or precocious flowers: early flowering in an annual may be a sign of stress.

Generally speaking, although there have been improvements in recent years in quality control and customer information, buying plants can still be a haphazard business. Gardeners can encourage improvements by avoiding second-rate plants, asking for information when it is not available, and complaining when they consider standards are not satisfactory.

WHEN TO PLANT

Container trees, shrubs and perennials can be planted, in theory at least, at any time of year; in practice, frosty or summer drought conditions must be avoided. That is because, until the roots are well-established, a ready supply of moisture is critical. Conversely, autumn is not advised if the site is vulnerable to extreme winter conditions, or if the soil is very heavy, as roots may rot. The best plan for deciduous plants is, therefore, to plant hardy plants in autumn and more tender ones in spring. A stricter time-scale should be followed for evergreens, which are even more prone to desiccation and weather damage: namely, to plant in either early autumn or late spring. Evergreens especially also benefit from a windbreak placed round them for at least the first winter and spring; woven polypropylene netting, attached to canes, is best because it allows a certain amount of wind through and also gives some protection from frost.

Bare-rooted deciduous plants are sent out from nurseries in the dormant season, after leaf-fall, between mid-autumn and early spring; that is the time to plant them, in so-called 'open weather', when the ground is not frozen or covered with snow. Avoid planting into waterlogged soil, or into frozen ground because, if the topsoil is buried, it will not easily thaw and can damage roots. Planting when

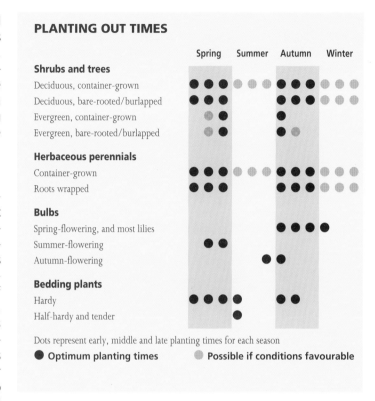

PLANTING OUT TIMES

	Spring	Summer	Autumn	Winter
Shrubs and trees				
Deciduous, container-grown	●●●	○○○	●●●	○○○
Deciduous, bare-rooted/burlapped	●●●		●●●	○○○
Evergreen, container-grown	○●		●	
Evergreen, bare-rooted/burlapped	○●			
Herbaceous perennials				
Container-grown	●●●	○○○	●●●	○○○
Roots wrapped	●●●		●●○	
Bulbs				
Spring-flowering, and most lilies			●●●	
Summer-flowering	●●			
Autumn-flowering		●●		
Bedding plants				
Hardy	●●●●		●●	
Half-hardy and tender	●			

Dots represent early, middle and late planting times for each season

● **Optimum planting times**   ○ **Possible if conditions favourable**

the soil is still relatively warm, that is, until the end of autumn, also helps root development, which is generally at its most active between early and very late autumn.

If conditions are not suitable for planting when bare-rooted plants arrive, 'heel' them in in spare ground in a sheltered place. This consists of digging a hole, leaning the plant at an angle, with the roots in the hole, and covering the roots with soil. If the roots are near to the surface, cover them with insulating material. Of course, if the ground is frozen you will have to keep the plants protected from frost, in a cool shed or store, with the roots wrapped in wet newspaper, until conditions improve. If stems and leaves arrive wrapped, even loosely, in polythene, this should be removed; as the plant transpires inside, water will condense on the polythene, and this may well invite

fungal infection. Plants in containers should be placed in a light place where the compost cannot freeze or become waterlogged. A cold greenhouse or cold frame is ideal for hardy plants, although you will have to remember to water them from time to time.

Bedding plants should not be planted out until you are reasonably sure that the danger of frost is passed, which depends, of course, on where you live. Alpines, half-hardy perennials and shrubs should be left until late spring.

Spring-planted subjects are likely to suffer from drought in their first year. The importance of watering them well in dry weather cannot be overstated. Generally, large and shallow-rooted plants, such as azaleas, need most water, although climbers such as clematis, which may look delicate, also have substantial water requirements.

HOW TO PLANT

Successful planting generally follows the same basic procedures, whatever the subject. For all plants, except alpines and half-hardy annuals which do not benefit from rich soil, the topsoil (which must not be waterlogged) of the planting area should be forked or dug over well and enriched with organic matter, preferably well before planting to allow the soil time to settle again. This area should be as large as you expect the roots to expand in the first five years. The hole into which the plant is to go should be dug out with a spade and made large enough to take the roots amply. A good rule of thumb is twice the diameter of the container. The bottom of the hole should be forked over to help drainage, especially in heavy soils, and watered if dry. In spring, a slow-release root-promoting fertilizer, such as bonemeal, can be mixed with the dug-out soil but this is not essential.

It is not necessary to add a proprietary planting mixture to the hole. Indeed, those with peat as a major constituent can induce rather than prevent water shortage around the roots in dry weather. What is essential is a good watering after planting, especially if fertilizer has been added to the soil which might burn the roots if left undissolved; and a thick surface mulch, laid in a wide diameter round the plant to help prevent water evaporation, insulate the roots from winter cold, and keep away competing weeds. Drought and competition are the major factors which inhibit the quick, healthy, and strong growth of new plants. Indeed these two evils can easily kill perfectly good plants.

Some hours before planting, water **container-grown plants** so that the roots will slip easily out of the plastic pot or bag when needed. If the border soil shows signs of being dry, water the hole as well. When the moment comes to plant, carefully remove the plant from its pot; a bag is best slit with a knife. If a container plant has girdled roots, gently pull those that you can away from the rest, and as you put the plant in, lay them round the inside perimeter of the planting hole. Cut off the most intractably girdled roots with secateurs. Lay a cane across the hole, so that you can check that the plant is sitting in the hole with the top of its compost just below the cane. If it is too low or too high, adjust the depth of the hole and check again.

The soil should be filled in round the compost up to the cane and firmed down with the ball of the foot several times. The idea is that, once the soil is firm, the plant should be at roughly the same depth as it was in the pot. If the soil is clay, be careful not to firm it too much. Then stake if necessary, water and apply a mulch.

Bare-rooted trees and shrubs should have their roots soaked in a large container of water first, and trimmed if broken or disproportionately long. After that they can be

PLANTING A CONTAINER-GROWN SHRUB

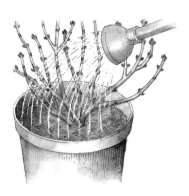

a Water the shrub well some hours before, to ensure the compost is wet before planting. If the growing medium is peat-based it may need several successive waterings to become thoroughly wet.

b Put the entire container in the hole, and lay a bamboo cane across the surface to check whether you have dug it to the correct depth. The surface of the compost should be level with that of the surrounding soil.

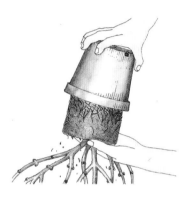

c Grasp the main stems of the plant firmly, turn the pot upside down and gently ease out the shrub. If the compost has been thoroughly watered previously, the plant should slip out quite easily.

d Tease any long roots that have encircled the root ball free of the rest, and place the plant gently in the hole, laying any free roots around the perimeter. Slowly fill in with soil all round, keeping the plant upright and at the right depth.

e Carefully tread the soil down round the plant until it is even and reasonably firm. Add extra soil if necessary. Be careful not to firm it too much by applying excessive pressure, or you may risk compacting the soil.

f Stake the plant if necessary, water in, and mulch to retain moisture and repel weeds. Be careful to avoid mulching too close to the stem of the plant. Water regularly, especially in dry weather, until the plant is well established.

planted in much the same way as container plants, except that care must be taken to shake the soil down between the roots, so that no large air spaces are left. When planting bare-rooted trees, put in the stake, if used, first, on the windward side. Always aim to achieve the same level at which the plant grew in the nursery; this is usually obvious as a darker line just above where the roots begin. Never leave roots showing on the surface. Too shallow planting can lead to water-shortage for the plant, and suckering from rootstocks.

Treat **root-balled plants,** (known as 'balled and burlapped' in the USA), like those grown in containers, but remove the wrapping material carefully after the plant has been put in the hole. This is done by first tilting the plant one way, and then the other. Two stakes may then be put in, one each side of the root ball.

Small trees and shrubs, say those grown from seed or cuttings, planted in rural situations, can be protected by tree or shrub 'shelters'. These are translucent, plastic, open-ended tubes, usually 1.2m/4ft tall, which guard against rabbits and deter weed competition.

Smaller plants, such as hardy perennials, transplanted vegetables, annuals and alpines, need only shallow holes, slightly bigger than the pot from which they have been knocked out, or the ball of soil with which you have lifted them. The roots should be damp; a dip in a proprietary root dip can help quick establishment. A trowel is the most useful tool for planting, while hands are best for firming the soil afterwards. Again, these plants should be left at the same level as they were in the pot. Alpines benefit from a grit, rather than organic, mulch. Give short-lived plants like annuals and leaf vegetables a base-dressing of general balanced fertilizer, rather than bonemeal.

There are particular plants which like individual treatment. For example, **conifers** have thin, fibrous roots which drop soil easily; therefore the plants should be carefully removed from the containers so that the soil does not fall away.

Unlike container plants and bare-rooted deciduous plants, which are put in the ground at the level they were in the nursery, some informed guesswork is needed for **bulbs**. As a rule of thumb, they should be planted with their bases at a depth which is two to three times their length. If you garden in a light soil, err on the deep side: this is because in subsequent years bulbs such as daffodils will not flower if the soil around them is dry in autumn. If the bulbs are to grow in grass, plant them with a 'bulb planter'. Otherwise dig out a square of turf and plant several bulbs in the soil beneath, before replacing the turf.

Alpines are straightforward if planted in raised beds, where they need to be planted into a gritty soil and mulched with a 5cm/2in layer of grit. If going into a crevice, or vertical stonework, the plant roots can be patted and squeezed into an oval shape to facilitate their planting into the gap; the hole should be large enough to receive such a rootball and should, preferably, contain some soil to help hold the plant until its roots can reach the earth behind. When the plant is put in, any gaps there are should be filled with soil and small stones, and tamped in. Make sure that the plant does not dry out until well established.

When **planting into containers,** use a pot that is large enough for the subject, put drainage material at the bottom and surround the root ball with a potting compost. Plants need feeding and watering when growing, and may need staking and protection in winter.

PLANTING A BARE-ROOTED TREE

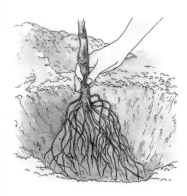

a *Soak roots well before planting. Dig a hole and check, by placing the plant gently in the hole, that it is deep enough and wide enough to contain the roots comfortably and without any restriction.*

b *If using a stake, hammer it in on what will be the windward side before you plant, or you may damage the roots. Stakes are usually only necessary in exposed positions. They should be no higher than a third of the plant's height.*

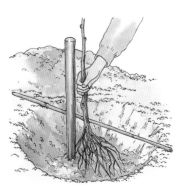

c *The tree should be planted to the same depth as it was in the nursery. Lay a cane across the hole, and lower the plant until the darker soil line on the stem is level with the cane. Shake the soil down between the roots.*

d *Tread the soil down firmly and evenly after planting, water in, and mulch the soil well to conserve moisture. Remember that a stake, if used, should be removed after two or three seasons at most.*

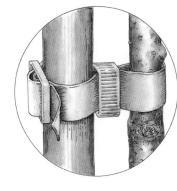

e *The last task is to secure the tree to the stake with 'tree ties'. Check the ties regularly, and loosen them as the trunk expands. A young fruit tree need only be secured at the top of the stake; larger trees need two ties.*

PRUNING

222 Topiary

160 Hedges

UB When you begin to garden, it is not long before the necessity of 'pruning' is borne in on you. You will know the word, of course: for, apart from its horticultural use, politicians are fond of talking about pruning budgets or expenditure, and anyone with a passing knowledge of the Bible will know that pruning hooks can, where there is a will, be fashioned out of spears. But why so much emphasis is laid on pruning may well still be a mystery.

THE REASONS FOR PRUNING

The reasons for pruning are various, but not complicated. Most plants, especially established ones in the open ground, will thrive and flourish perfectly satisfactorily for extended periods without being pruned, and some never need anything done to

them in the whole of their existence. This suits today's rather more naturalistic approach to garden planning. After all, no pruning takes place in the wild; only a gradual process of death, decay and drop of branches. However, many plants cannot, in the highly artificial environment of the garden, be allowed to grow as they like indefinitely. Despite the most careful planning, plants may outgrow the space allotted to them, and will need to be controlled (this is especially true of plants grown against walls); plants die back for one reason or another; weak growing plants can be encouraged by pruning, and neglected ones restored to health and vigour. However, some shrubs, such as hedging and topiary specimens, may well be pruned and shaped simply for aesthetic reasons.

Pruning stimulates young growth, which may, as in the case of roses, be necessary for good future flowering; excessive growth may need cutting back for the same reason. Pruning is necessary for young woody plants, so that a balanced framework can be established to show off the plants' attributes to best advantage. From time to time, plants need the removal of growths which are dead, diseased or damaged, or so weak that they will not support good flower or fruit. Disease enters through wounds and spreads if left unchecked, and weak wood, often the result of overcrowded growth, can spoil the look of an otherwise healthy plant.

The idea behind pruning, therefore, is to ensure that woody plants give of their best by living long, having a good general appearance,

flowering well and in the case of fruit bushes and trees, yielding good crops. It simplifies gardening to know the theory behind pruning and the requirements of plants.

THE THEORY BEHIND PRUNING

The theory behind pruning relies heavily on the fact that every plant exhibits 'apical dominance'. In layman's terms this means that, if the apex of a branch or shoot is cut off above a dormant bud, that bud will be stimulated to break into growth, while hormones called 'auxins' suppress the 'breaking' of buds further down the shoot. This feature of plant growth is clearly visible in newly pruned modern roses: in late spring, the new leaves can be seen developing from the buds situated just below the pruning cuts. It is also the reason why so much emphasis is put on cutting to an outward-facing bud, which will then break to produce shoots that grow away from the centre of that plant. Thus a balanced framework can develop, and the plant will not become congested in the middle.

There are other ways in which pruners make use of the immutable laws of plant physiology. For example, if you cut away a substantial proportion of a shoot, the plant's root system will compensate for the loss by initiating vigorous new growth. If, however, you merely trim back a small part, the resultant growth will be correspondingly modest. To take the case of roses again: if you cut back most of the shoots to a few buds from the ground, and remove the weaker shoots completely, you will get a limited number of shoots, carrying big flowers. If you prune lightly, or give the bush a trim with a pair of shears, you will get smaller flowers but many more of them.

When in the year you prune shrubs depends on when their flowering wood is produced. Spring and early summer-flowering shrubs, such as philadelphus and hydrangea, make this wood in the year before. It is, therefore, important to prune them soon after flowering, to provide maximum time for developing new shoots and flower buds. Prune only very lightly in the first and second seasons, but once a shrub is well established, it is advisable to cut back about a third of the older, just-flowered wood, to strong, newer lateral shoots. The act of pruning will stimulate these into growth. As with pruning all shrubs, cut out any diseased, dead or weak wood at the same time.

Different plants will, however, respond to pruning in different ways. If you prune a forsythia, for example, the flowers it produces next year will not be larger but they will almost certainly be carried in much greater profusion.

Many plants, such as roses, can suffer dieback after pruning if the cut is not carried out sharply and correctly. Cutting the shoot on a slant sloping away from and just above the bud that you wish to stimulate into growth should minimize the likelihood of this occurring.

Perfect pruning technique is not difficult to achieve and is, generally, beneficial. That said, if you have to fall short of the ideal for any reason it will comfort you to know that your plants will almost certainly survive your shortcomings.

Incidentally, if 'deadheading' is used to stimulate growth for another flowering, this too is pruning. Repeat-flowering roses, for example, benefit from being generously deadheaded for this reason but so

DEADHEADING

Repeat-flowering roses, and many herbaceous plants, benefit from being deadheaded after their first blooming. In the case of roses, cut off a generous amount of stem, down to an outward-facing bud, to stimulate it into making new flower-bearing growth.

also do garden pinks, hardy geraniums and even delphiniums. If what you are doing is simply removing the dead stems of perennials at the end of the season, that is not pruning, but tidying up.

WHEN TO PRUNE

There is one basic principle that rules the timing of deciduous shrub pruning; once you have mastered this, much else becomes clear. It is this: those shrubs which flower in the first half of the year, like forsythia, *Jasminum nudiflorum*, philadelphus, syringa and early clematis, nearly all grow ('make' is the expression used) their flowering growths during the previous growing season. If pruning is necessary, therefore, it should take place soon after the flowering is finished, to allow the plant plenty of time before the winter to make new flowering growth. Those plants which flower on growths made during the current season (shrubs which flower on 'new' wood, as opposed to 'old'), and which usually flower in the second half of the summer and in the autumn, should be cut back in late winter, to give them plenty of time to grow their 'wood' before flowering time. Good examples are most buddleja and late-flowering clematis.

The principles of pruning outlined above should always guide you. However, as the ways of plants are various, you may find it helpful to refer to a specialist book on pruning for the odd occasion when a plant's habit or its situation seems particularly individual. If these books have a fault, it is that they usually provide counsels of perfection; it is important not to feel intimidated by them.

PRUNING TOOLS

Pruning is done with a pair of secateurs for thin stems and branches, a

pair of 'loppers' for cutting tougher branches, and a saw for thick ones up to 30cm/12in in diameter. I find the curved Grecian saw invaluable for general shrub or light tree work, and a pair of 'parrot-bill' loppers for close encounters with the larger branches of shrubs and roses. In the case of trees, anything too large for these to deal with should be left to trained tree surgeons. Chainsaws are not suitable tools for amateurs, in my opinion; there have been cases of horrifying injuries inflicted by them. Power-operated hedge-trimmers are recommended for pruning hedges with small leaves, and can be used on your modern roses if you are pressed for time. An electric shredder is invaluable for cutting up small prunings so that they can be added to the compost heap, although diseased wood should always be burned.

TREES

In the general way of things, trees do not need annual pruning: only if

branches are dead, dying, diseased, inconveniently placed or sprouting too low down the trunk, need you take action. If you have any doubts about the health or safety of a garden tree, consult an expert. Professional associations often supply lists of accredited tree surgeons.

Work on deciduous trees should be done either after midsummer, or in the dormant season, because a tree's sap may 'bleed' from cuts made from the late winter onwards, when sap pressure is high. This loss of sap can weaken a young tree. Evergreens, on the other hand, are best tackled once the risk of frost is past, in late spring or early summer.

Tree surgery, in the way of bracing trees, cleaning cavities, felling, removing large branches, and stump chipping, is best left to tree surgeons. However, with care, you should be able to saw off easily reached dead or dying branches under 30cm/12in in diameter yourself. In this case it is advisable to cut a long branch off in 45cm/18in

CUTTING A TREE BRANCH

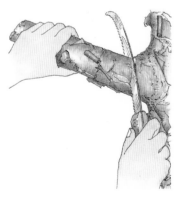

Although most tree surgery should be done by professionals, it is possible to cut off small branches yourself using a curved-blade Grecian saw. Long branches should be cut off in 45cm/18in sections working from the end of the branch, to prevent too much falling at any one time. The tree shown here is Acer griseum.

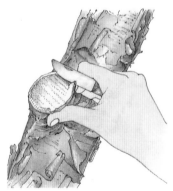

Do not cut flush with the main stem, but leave a slight stub or 'collar'. Cut at a slight angle so that rain can run off easily. In order to encourage callus formation (healing) trim around the edge of the short stub that is left with a sharp garden knife. It is usually unnecessary to paint the cut with wound sealant.

1 The garden is a highly artificial environment. That being the case, trees and shrubs cannot be allowed to grow unchecked indefinitely, if they are to look their best. Sensible pruning can curb exuberant plants, which are grown in a restricted space; it can encourage flowering and fruiting; it can check the spread of disease; restore neglected plants to health and vigour; and generally improve the look of a plant. It can also help shape the garden: hedge-trimming is, after all, a kind of pruning.

POLLARDING AND COPPICING

Right: Pollarding is a pruning regime in which a head is established at a given height on the main stem of a tree or shrub, all shoots that grow from the pollarded part above, being cut back annually in spring.

Below: In coppicing the pruning regime is similar to that followed in pollarding but growths are cut back at or near ground level, new shoots sprouting from the permanent woody base or 'stool'.

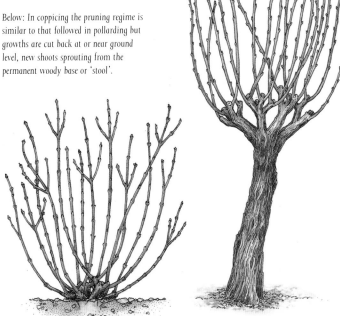

sections so that the weight does not cause the branch to tear the bark from the trunk. Cut halfway through the branch from underneath, and then cut from the top. In that way, the branch's weight will cause it to break at the point where you have first cut. Once most of the branch is removed, cut the stub close to the trunk, at a slight angle so that rain runs off easily, leaving a short 'collar'. On no account cut flush with the trunk. Trim the edge of the sawcut with a sharp knife to aid callusing (healing). Most experts now consider that the use of wound-sealant paints is generally unnecessary.

Young trees may need attention after planting. They are often bought 'feathered', that is, with shoots all the way up the trunk, and all should be removed to the height where you wish the branches to start. You may have to do this task several times in the early years. The exceptions are columnar trees, such

as poplars, which you will want to see clothed with erect branches almost down to the ground.

Young trees sometimes suffer dieback on the main leading shoot, soon after planting. If this occurs, cut back the shoot to healthy wood in the dormant season. If the tree, for example a maple (*Acer*), has opposite leaves (and, therefore, shoots), this will have the effect of stimulating two shoots to grow out opposite each other. In the next dormant season, cut out one of these shoots and encourage the other one to grow vertically by tying it to a long bamboo cane placed in the soil next to the trunk.

There are ancient pruning techniques called 'coppicing' and 'pollarding', which can be practised to good effect on some shrubs or small trees to emphasize such positive attributes as beautiful bark or leaves. Both techniques were used to maintain a cycle of wood production from trees and shrubs such as willow and hazel, which shoot again after the removal of a crop of branches. In 'coppicing' (also known as 'stooling'), the shoots are cut back almost to ground level after the first year, and very close to the base of the resulting shoots each year thereafter; in 'pollarding', a stem, or 'leg', is allowed to develop first, with all the shoots being cut back almost to the stump each spring, or at longer but regular intervals.

Coppicing enables the gardener to grow a large shrub in a small space, and encourages it to produce particularly large and decorative leaves (*Paulownia tomentosa*, *Catalpa bignonioides*, purple hazel, the coloured leaf forms of elder), or to emphasize beautiful stems (*Cornus alba*, *Rubus cockburnianus*), or else to retain juvenile leaves (*Eucalpytus gunnii*,) although this last example is often pollarded on to a single stem. Pollarding is especially suitable for willows, and this is a traditional way of dealing with them along riverbanks.

SHRUBS

Formative pruning of shrubs is often done in the nursery. Once planted, many shrubs can be left quite alone, apart from the removal of dead and diseased wood, unless they outgrow their allotted space. The viburnums, camellias and skimmias, for example, need little or no attention. However, it is sometimes necessary to continue the building up of a balanced, open, permanent framework. This is especially important for evergreen and deciduous shrubs which do not readily make basal shoots once they are mature – examples include rhododendrons, magnolias, potentillas and cotinus. In the early years, therefore, remove weak shoots, those growing inwards, and those too close to others. Once a reasonably balanced plant has emerged, little need be done to these plants in future years.

Once spring and early summer-flowering deciduous shrubs (deutzias, forsythias, weigelas, philadelphus, lilacs) which flower on the previous season's growths are established, cut back about a third, but let your eye guide you, of older, flowered wood after flowering, to strong, newer lateral shoots. Cytisus are treated slightly differently, because, although early flowering, they do not appreciate having their older wood pruned. Either leave them alone or just trim back the flowered shoots to young shoots.

Late summer-flowering deciduous shrubs (for example, *Buddleja davidii*, caryopteris, ceratostigma, the deciduous ceanothus and perovskia) are best cut back very hard between late winter and early spring, to within two buds or so of

PRUNING A SPRING-FLOWERING SHRUB

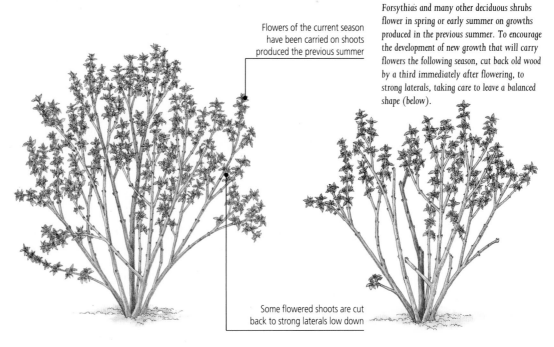

Flowers of the current season have been carried on shoots produced the previous summer

Some flowered shoots are cut back to strong laterals low down

Forsythias and many other deciduous shrubs flower in spring or early summer on growths produced in the previous summer. To encourage the development of new growth that will carry flowers the following season, cut back old wood by a third immediately after flowering, to strong laterals, taking care to leave a balanced shape (below).

PRUNING A SUMMER-FLOWERING SHRUB

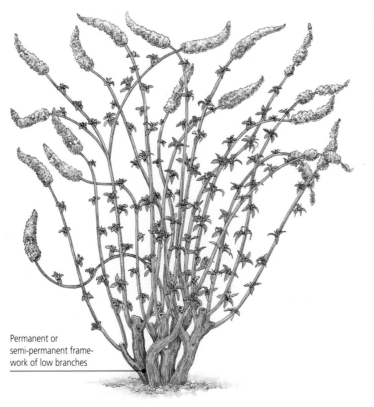

Permanent or semi-permanent framework of low branches

A suitable pruning regime for established specimens of Buddleja davidii *and other deciduous shrubs that flower in late summer encourages the development of new growth from a permanent framework. For buddleja, which is vigorous and so can be pruned very much harder than other shrubs, cut back old growths in late winter or early spring, leaving two or three buds above the framework branches (below).*

From late winter new shoots develop on wood which will carry the flowers

the old wood. However, this hard pruning is only appropriate after the shrub has had a year or two to build up a short framework of main stems unhindered.

Mophead hydrangeas (hortensias) are an exception. By rights, they should be pruned hard in the same way because they flower in late summer; however, this treatment does not ensure the best flowering. Instead, leave them for two to three years to make a framework, and then cut out only a proportion of the older shoots in late winter or early spring. Do not deadhead the faded flowers in autumn, because these help to protect the frost-tender buds over the winter. The flower-heads are removed during the normal pruning procedure.

Most evergreen shrubs can be left alone completely, or just lightly trimmed in spring if they are lopsided or have frosted young shoots. Tender hebes and evergreen ceanothus, for example, which are prone to winter damage, can be cut back to live, sprouting wood if shoots have been killed or damaged by cold weather.

Some of the evergreen Mediterranean sub-shrubs, for example lavender, santolina and artemisia (as well as summer-flowering heathers), become woody and straggly if not pruned at least every other year. This is done in early or mid-spring, when the worst weather is past, and you can see the new growths beginning to sprout on the main stems. Clipping with shears or cutting back with secateurs to those new growths will keep these shrubs neat. Do not attempt it with a very old, neglected plant without recognizing that there is a risk that the shock of drastic treatment may kill it.

Vigorous evergreen shrubs such as rhododendrons and cherry laurel (*Prunus laurocerasus*) that have a tendency to outgrow their space may need to be cut back. Remove one or two of the most extensive

SHEARING

Santolina, lavender, artemisia, and other evergreen Mediterranean sub-shrubs which have become straggly benefit from being clipped over with garden shears in early or mid-spring.

1 Roses are easily the most widely grown garden plants, and justifiably so. Although many species and cultivars flower once only, their clusters of blossom are always a beautiful sight. With climbing roses, pruning and training should go hand in hand: training horizontally or with the stems arched over encourages free flowering. Often, however, the support dictates how the rose is to be trained. Repeat-flowering climbers and pillar roses are well suited to clothe free-standing vertical structures.

PRUNING

shoots to suitable side branches each summer. Avoid, however, drastic pruning of this kind, for it can put an evergreen under enormous strain.

A few evergreens tolerate close trimming and are suitable for topiary.

ROSES

There has been a conspicuous absentee from the descriptions of deciduous shrub pruning: the rose. This most popular of garden shrubs is best dealt with in isolation, partly because any pruning should have the additional aim of discouraging diseases, and partly because the techniques vary slightly, depending on whether the roses to be pruned

are bushes (hybrid tea or large-flowered, and floribunda or cluster-flowered); shrubs, including old roses; or climbers and ramblers. It is difficult to generalize, because roses have very different parentages, which means that some flower on old wood and some on new. In general, HTs and floribundas, and climbers derived from HTs, together with perpetual modern shrub roses, flower on new wood; while single-flush roses such as ramblers, species and old roses flower on older wood.

If left to themselves, unpruned, most single-flush shrub roses (that is, old varieties like the gallicas and damasks, and species roses) will

flower adequately, even well, especially if fed and watered enough. However, it is always well worth encouraging a good framework initially, by tipping back shoots after planting and, later, removing dead and very weak wood, especially from the centre of the bush, to create freer air circulation (which helps discourage diseases), and to allow the sun to ripen all the wood equally. It is also worth cutting back really long arching stems, both for the look of the bush and to stop it rocking in the wind in winter. But remember that these roses flower on old wood, so trim them back in summer, after flowering, rather than in spring.

Modern shrub roses, and old roses which are repeat-flowering (such as bourbons), are best tackled in early spring. Do the job when the buds have just started to swell, and preferably before they have burst into leaf. (The 'bud' will, incidentally, only appear as a semi-circular line on the shoot in late winter.) Otherwise, a late frost may inflict severe damage on the young and, therefore, highly vulnerable leaves.

Remove any flowered side-shoots close to where they emanate from the main shoots. Cut out a good proportion (say 25 per cent) of any sparsely-flowered old wood, and cut back, by about a third, any very

PRUNING A REPEAT-FLOWERING MODERN SHRUB ROSE

The following regime also suits repeat-flowering old roses. In early spring take out all dead, diseased and damaged wood and prune to remove crossing shoots. Cut back any remaining

flowered sideshoots at the main stem. Cut out about a quarter of old wood and shorten any very long new growths by a third.

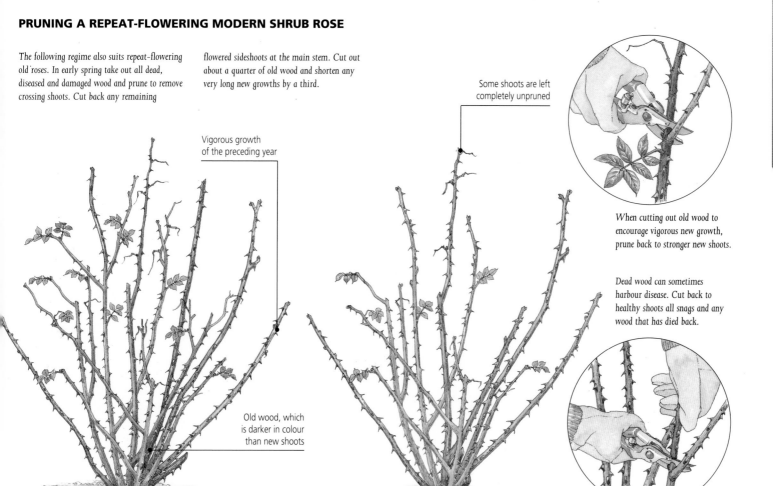

Vigorous growth of the preceding year

Old wood, which is darker in colour than new shoots

Some shoots are left completely unpruned

When cutting out old wood to encourage vigorous new growth, prune back to stronger new shoots.

Dead wood can sometimes harbour disease. Cut back to healthy shoots all snags and any wood that has died back.

PRUNING A HYBRID TEA ROSE

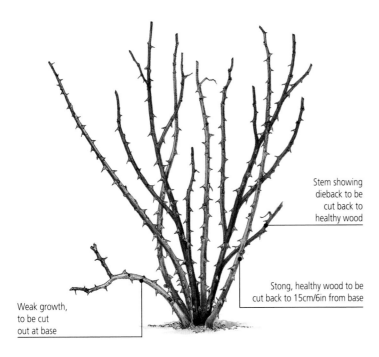

Hybrid tea (large-flowered bush) roses should be pruned harder than floribundas (cluster-flowered roses), because they tend to be less vigorous. Remove dead, diseased, weak or crossing stems first, then cut the remaining sturdy stems to outward facing buds, between 15cm/6in and 25cm/10in from ground level. This promotes the growth of an open-shaped bush, and therefore good air circulation, which is important to minimize mildew infection.

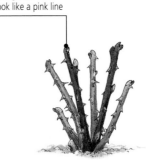

Cut to an outward-facing bud: it will look like a pink line

Stem showing dieback to be cut back to healthy wood

Stong, healthy wood to be cut back to 15cm/6in from base

Weak growth, to be cut out at base

PRUNING A FLORIBUNDA ROSE

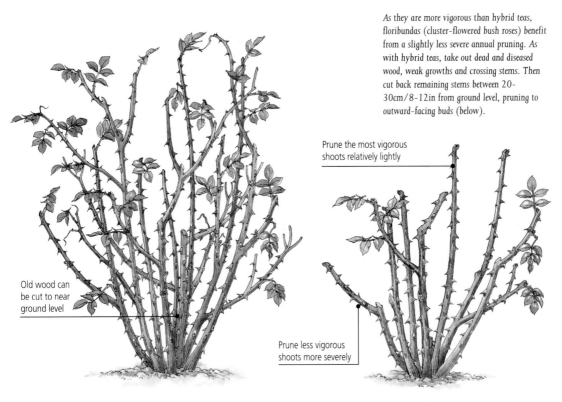

As they are more vigorous than hybrid teas, floribundas (cluster-flowered bush roses) benefit from a slightly less severe annual pruning. As with hybrid teas, take out dead and diseased wood, weak growths and crossing stems. Then cut back remaining stems between 20-30cm/8-12in from ground level, pruning to outward-facing buds (below).

Prune the most vigorous shoots relatively lightly

Old wood can be cut to near ground level

Prune less vigorous shoots more severely

long new shoots, which were produced from the main stem after the flowers went over. Deadhead after the first flush of flower to stimulate abundant later flower production.

Bush roses are also pruned in early spring. Prune hybrid tea roses harder than floribundas, because they are naturally less vigorous. Cut to an outward-facing bud about 15cm/6in from the base to make a balanced open bush; remove some of the weak shoots, and all the dead ones right back to live wood, which is greenish-white rather than brown inside. Floribundas should be cut to about 20cm/8in from the base of the bush. Take your cue from the vigour of the cultivar itself; 'Iceberg', for example, which is a very strong growing rose, will usually need only a light trim.

Prune the shoots of ramblers at planting to about 30cm/12in from the ground to encourage vigorous growth. They flower once, so cut flowered shoots back almost to the main stems after flowering, in late summer. Take the whole rose off its supporting structure, if possible, by cutting all the string ties and gently easing the shoots down. This is the best scheme for all climbing roses, where practicable. Cut out, or cut very low down, one or two vigorous main shoots; this should encourage buds, which may be quite invisible, near the bottom to produce strong new shoots. Another group that can be treated in the same way are the climbing roses that flower only once a year.

Climbers derived from HTs, including climbing 'sports', are usually repeat-flowering and flower on the current season's wood. They require no early pruning; indeed cutting back hard at planting time may cause a climbing 'sport' to revert to a bush. Instead, build up the framework gradually by tying the stems, and pulling them down as horizontal as is possible. Pruning consists principally of cutting back the flowered sideshoots to within three buds of the older wood. Do this after the first flush, if you have time and energy, and certainly after the last flowers. Once the plant is established, cut one or two of the main shoots out in the late autumn (early spring in cold areas) close to the base, if they have lost vigour. This pruning should encourage one or two new growths to come up in spring. At the same time, tip back any very long shoots which might whip about in the wind.

The trick for making climbers flower well lies in the training and tying in. The more horizontal a potential flowering shoot is, the more floriferous it will be. When training and tying in shoots, therefore, avoid near-vertical fans but arrange stems near the horizontal, even if it means crossing shoots over each other. Provided that they are firmly tied, there will be no damage from chafing.

Pillar roses pose something of a problem in this respect. Pillar roses are those not very vigorous roses (up to 2.4m/8ft or 3m/10ft) which are trained vertically up posts or pergolas. Encouraging flowers midway up the pillar is not easy, nor is preventing overcrowding by shoots round the pillar. These roses are best left alone initially and their shoots simply tied in. After two seasons, prune them in late autumn by cutting back one or two of the older shoots by two-thirds, to encourage new shoots from near the base. If there are many shoots, cut out the oldest ones completely near ground level. Tie in any loose shoots. Trim back any which have grown above the pillar.

All repeat-flowering roses should be deadheaded after the first flush,

PRUNING A RAMBLING ROSE

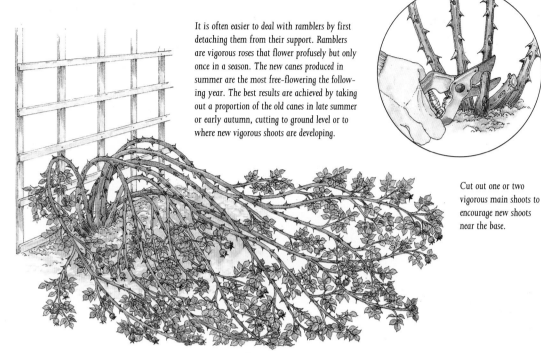

It is often easier to deal with ramblers by first detaching them from their support. Ramblers are vigorous roses that flower profusely but only once in a season. The new canes produced in summer are the most free-flowering the following year. The best results are achieved by taking out a proportion of the old canes in late summer or early autumn, cutting to ground level or to where new vigorous shoots are developing.

Cut out one or two vigorous main shoots to encourage new shoots near the base.

PRUNING A CLIMBING ROSE

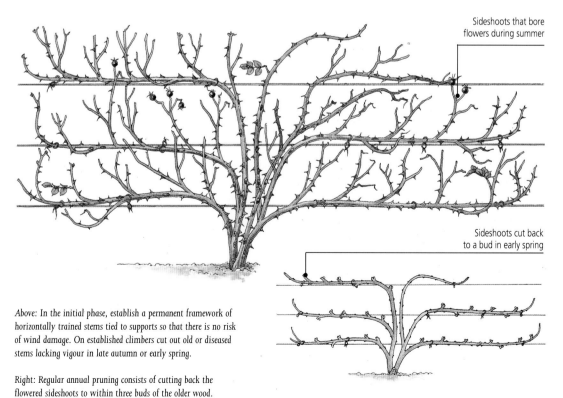

Sideshoots that bore flowers during summer

Sideshoots cut back to a bud in early spring

Above: In the initial phase, establish a permanent framework of horizontally trained stems tied to supports so that there is no risk of wind damage. On established climbers cut out old or diseased stems lacking vigour in late autumn or early spring.

Right: Regular annual pruning consists of cutting back the flowered sideshoots to within three buds of the older wood.

by removing several inches of stem, where possible, cutting to an outward-facing bud. Do not take trouble to deadhead one-flush roses unless, like 'Albertine', they hang on too obstinately to their faded flowers and look untidy.

CLEMATIS

Another popular group of climbing plants which need pruning, especially if they are to be trained, neatly illustrates the point about the importance of taking into account the season when the flowering shoots have been made.

Clematis fall into three categories: those which flower on last year's wood, before midsummer; those which flower in early summer and again in late summer, first on 'old' wood then on 'new'; those which flower after midsummer and flower exclusively on 'new' wood.

Examples of the first group include the spring-flowering species *C. montana*, *C. macropetala* and *C. alpina* and their relatives. The second includes large-flowered hybrids such as 'Barbara Dibley', 'Belle of Woking', 'Lasurstern', 'Marie Boisselot', 'Nelly Moser' and 'Vyvyan Pennell'. Among the third group are 'Ernest Markham', 'Hagley Hybrid' 'Royal Velours', *C. orientalis*, *C. tangutica*, *C. flammula*, and all the *C. x jackmanii* and *C. viticella* types.

The easiest to deal with are the last-mentioned: those which flower in late summer and autumn. Because they flower on the current season's growth, simply cut the shoots back to a pair of buds about 90cm/36in from the ground in late winter; this will encourage strong new shoots from close to the base.

The spring flowerers (the first category), on the other hand, can be left alone entirely. If they become very tangled in time, as they tend to do, simply take the shears and trim

them over after flowering, removing any obvious dead growths completely. If you want to do a really professional job with your *C. montana*, especially if you are prepared to restrain it by annual pruning of its vigorous growth, cut back all the flowered shoots close to their bases in early summer.

The trickiest clematis appear to be those which flower on both old and new wood. The fact that flowering is repeated is a valuable attribute of these plants but heavy injudicious pruning will result in only one season of flower. The easiest solution, if you want both flushes of flower, is to prune in late winter: cut some of the old growths back to the highest pair of obviously strong buds, which will just be breaking then. These will flower last. Leave some unpruned to flower early. Then, after the first flush, cut out about a quarter of the flowered shoots to ensure a good early flowering next year.

If you inherit an established garden, you can prune existing clematis even if you do not know their names. Provided you note exactly when they flower, you will have the information you need with which to prune them properly.

With clematis, whatever the kind, it is important to keep tying or training in the new shoots, whether on wires or through trellis. Growth is extremely rapid in the spring, and the fragility of the stems makes them vulnerable to wind damage. Also the last two mentioned groups will be easier to prune if the 'vines' (growths) have been separated from one another. Twining these shoots carefully by hand round the support is preferable to using string to attach them; better still is the careful use of green plastic-coated ties. This sounds laborious but can be an agreeable evening task, undertaken every week or so.

OTHER CLIMBING, TWINING, OR WALL PLANTS

I have discussed climbing roses and clematis at length, but there are, of course, many other climbing, twining or wall plants which need to be pruned, often only because they are trained against a structure. As with other shrubs, forming a framework in the early years is often important. Once again, you can be guided as to the best way to prune them by whether they flower on old or new wood, by their hardiness, or lack of it, and by how much they need to be kept under control.

Jasminum nudiflorum is hardy and early flowering and should have its flowered shoots removed completely in spring, once it has reached the height and spread required. The really vigorous spring-flowering climber wisteria needs pruning twice a year, both to keep it under control and to encourage the formation of flower buds. In high summer cut the flowered side-shoots back to four to six leaves (15cm/6in). These should be cut back still further, to two to three buds (about 7cm/3in) in late winter.

Honeysuckles *(Lonicera)* benefit from losing some of their older wood after flowering. It is a matter of taste whether you tie in the newer shoots or allow them to hang in an informal way. *Passiflora caerulea* and *Solanum crispum* flower from midsummer onwards so should have many of their sideshoots, especially the weak ones, cut back almost to the main stems in spring, while *Actinidia kolomikta* and ornamental vines, which are vigorous and grown for their leaves rather than flowers, should have their sideshoots cut back to about 10cm/4in during the dormant season.

WALL SHRUBS

Chaenomeles and pyracantha, which can be grown as wall plants, are, like apples, members of the rose family and will develop flower and, therefore, fruit spurs if the unwanted sideshoots (especially those pointing away from the wall) are cut back to four to six leaves (7-10cm/3-4in) in midsummer. See that a well spaced framework of branches is produced by tying in extension growths at the same time. As the years pass, cut out old wood if there are replacement sideshoots to tie in their stead. It is worth remembering that these, like other hardy wall shrubs, will grow quite well without regular pruning.

Tender wall shrubs, such as *Abutilon* x *suntense*, should have their frosted shoots removed in spring, as disease can enter the plant if these are left. Otherwise, if the plant is not getting too crowded or growing too many shoots away from the wall, it is best left alone. If shoots must be removed, do so according to whether the shrub flowers on new or old wood.

FRUIT TREES

Probably, the type of pruning most likely to worry you is that of fruit trees. However, even here, your knowledge of the basic principles of pruning will still apply.

After flowering, most fruit trees grow long, leafy shoots. These have flatter buds than the short and fat fruit (flower) buds. If these leaf shoots are shortened as growth slows down in late summer, or later, in winter, they will probably initiate fruiting spurs (clusters of buds). A

1 Clematis often cause anxiety to gardeners, because it is not immediately obvious when and how to prune them. However, they do fall into three basic groups according to when, and on what wood, they flower. Provided that you note their time of flowering, you should encounter no difficulties with their pruning.

WALL-TRAINING A SHRUB

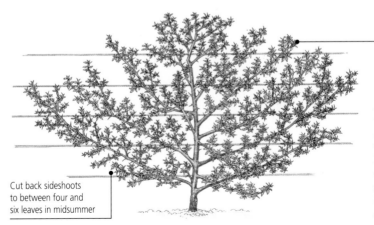

Cut back the leader and main laterals annually in early to mid-spring when they have reached the desired height

Cut back sideshoots to between four and six leaves in midsummer

Pyracantha and some other shrubs can be wall-trained with branches tied down horizontally either side of a central stem. Once the framework has reached the desired size, cut back the leader and main laterals in spring to summer. Cut back sideshoots to four to six leaves in midsummer. At the same time cut back to the main branches any sideshoots growing into or right away from the wall.

1 Apples are most commonly grown in bush or standard forms. The aim of initial pruning, carried out between late autumn and early spring, is to create a balanced, open-centred head with a framework of three or four main branches. Generally, established trees need only light pruning to maintain the overall shape, but specialized pruning will encourage the development of fruiting wood. Many apples are spur-bearers, carrying fruit on short shoots, the spurs, that develop on older wood; these need their branch leaders and young laterals shortened in winter. Some apple trees bear their fruit buds at the tips of shoots, and it is helpful to remove a few of these to the base after fruiting.

1

any laterals to four buds. Mature trees do not normally need to be encouraged in vigour by hard pruning unless they look weak, so cutting back leading shoots becomes less important. On the other hand, fruit spur systems become rather crowded on older trees, and may well need thinning out.

Several varieties of apple trees, such as 'Bramley's Seedling', bear their fruit not on spurs but at the tips of shoots. 'Discovery' is both tip and spur bearing. If you prune back too many shoots of 'Bramleys Seedling', you will get little fruit. With 'Discovery', the fruit usually comes at the end of the short shoots, so only prune the long ones.

Plum and damson trees do not need to be pruned once established; indeed, it is better to leave them because of the risk of silver leaf diseases entering through wounds. When they are young, cut all shoots back by at least half, and thin out if there are more than four of them. Trim back shoots coming from the trunk. In the second year, let some sideshoots grow, and then cut them back by half in winter. In later life, if you *must* prune, do it in early summer, in dry weather, to keep the tree tidy and well shaped.

good balance between leaf growth and fruiting spurs is obviously ideal, with the leaf growth providing sufficient energy for the trees to crop satisfactorily.

Standard or bush apple and pear trees, such as you are likely to encounter in established gardens and which you may well want to plant yourself, should be pruned in winter. If the planted tree is a 'maiden', that is, without sideshoots, let these grow in the first season, and reduce the primary branches which then develop to four. If you buy a tree with primary branches already present, in the winter after planting cut out all dead and crossing wood, wood containing canker, and any shoots on the trunk. Then cut all the primary branches back by half, and

FRUIT BUSHES

Blackcurrants fruit on wood made the previous year. After planting, cut back all shoots almost to ground level. Thereafter, in autumn (or when picking the fruit if that is easier), cut out a quarter or so of the older wood down to ground level and the rest to a vigorous new shoot. Be careful to cut out those growths with signs of big bud mite.

When planting gooseberries, prune out the lower sideshoots, if any, so that there is a clear 15cm/6in 'leg'. Tip back leading shoots. Prune gooseberries in winter, unless

PRUNING A BLACKCURRANT BUSH

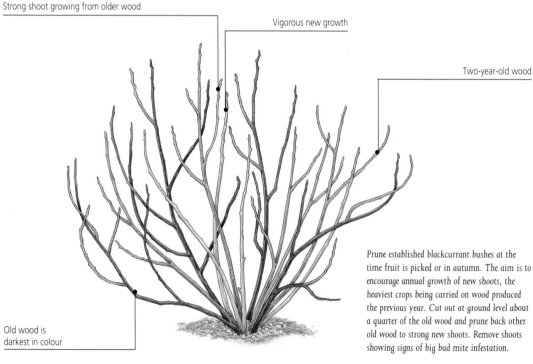

Strong shoot growing from older wood

Vigorous new growth

Two-year-old wood

Old wood is darkest in colour

Prune established blackcurrant bushes at the time fruit is picked or in autumn. The aim is to encourage annual growth of new shoots, the heaviest crops being carried on wood produced the previous year. Cut out at ground level about a quarter of the old wood and prune back other old wood to strong new shoots. Remove shoots showing signs of big bud mite infestation.

PRUNING

birds are prone to stripping their buds, when spring is better because the stripped stems can be seen and cut out. Try to build up a framework of eight to ten main branches. Thereafter, each year, cut back the sideshoots to 7cm/3in and tip back the leading shoots. Cut out all crossing and central branches, to make life easier for the picker and discourage mildew. Long-handled 'loppers' are useful because gooseberries are intensely prickly.

Raspberries either fruit on last season's wood (summer-fruiting types) or on the current season's wood (autumn-fruiting varieties). Prune summer-fruiters after fruiting: cut out all the old fruited shoots almost to ground level, and tie in the new growths, keeping them about 10cm/4in apart on the horizontal wires so that they can develop fully.

Cut all shoots of autumn-fruiting raspberries almost to ground level in late winter. The shoots will grow quickly but flower and fruit later than the summer-fruiting varieties.

Prune blackberries and loganberries by removing the fruited canes. The best system for training is to separate canes that will flower this year from those that will flower next, tying the first in one direction, and the second in another.

SUCKERS

Many plants are grafted or budded on to a rootstock of a vigorous, closely related plant. The rootstock may well push up 'suckers' from the roots. These will eventually overwhelm the 'scion', which is grafted on to the stock. If suckers appear around roses, lilacs, poplars, *Rhus typhina*, bush fruit trees and other grafted plants, follow their course back to the roots and pull them cleanly away. Cutting at ground level encourages the production of yet more suckers.

PRUNING A GOOSEBERRY BUSH

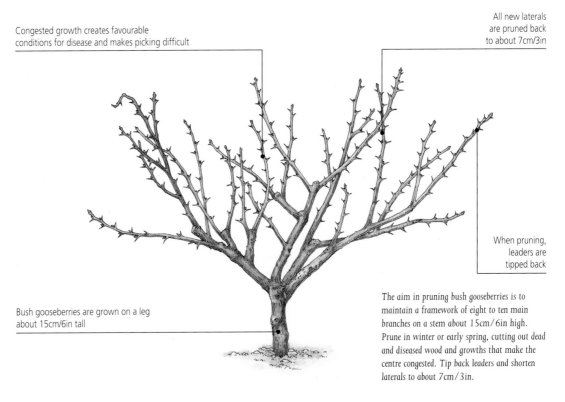

Congested growth creates favourable conditions for disease and makes picking difficult

All new laterals are pruned back to about 7cm/3in

When pruning, leaders are tipped back

Bush gooseberries are grown on a leg about 15cm/6in tall

The aim in pruning bush gooseberries is to maintain a framework of eight to ten main branches on a stem about 15cm/6in high. Prune in winter or early spring, cutting out dead and diseased wood and growths that make the centre congested. Tip back leaders and shorten laterals to about 7cm/3in.

PRUNING RASPBERRY CANES

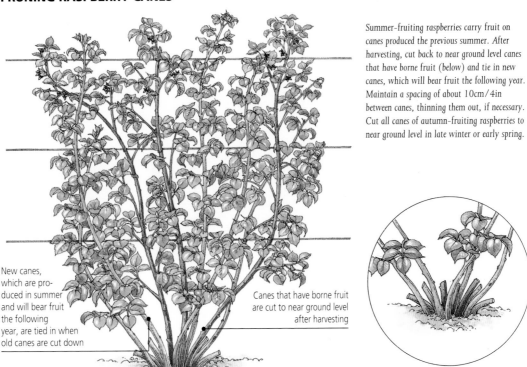

Summer-fruiting raspberries carry fruit on canes produced the previous summer. After harvesting, cut back to near ground level canes that have borne fruit (below) and tie in new canes, which will bear fruit the following year. Maintain a spacing of about 10cm/4in between canes, thinning them out, if necessary. Cut all canes of autumn-fruiting raspberries to near ground level in late winter or early spring.

New canes, which are produced in summer and will bear fruit the following year, are tied in when old canes are cut down

Canes that have borne fruit are cut to near ground level after harvesting

RENOVATION

UB It is often the case that when you move into a 'new' house the garden will have suffered some time of neglect, at least a few months and sometimes many years. So the first thing to do is to assess what will need to be done. This should focus first on the condition of garden structures and 'hard' features, such as paving, ponds and pergolas, the priority being to see that they are safe, and then serviceable. Trees also should be assessed for condition, preferably by a trained arboriculturist. The lawn, which will almost inevitably be overgrown and weedy, will need inspection, as will shrubs, climbers, the rock garden if there is one, water plantings, and perennial borders. Only then can you decide what must go and what can stay. Most structural plants, however neglected, can be brought back into shape and condition in the end. There are exceptions, of course: whereas a yew hedge can be cut back 'to the bone' and will resprout satisfactorily, many overgrown conifer hedges take time to recover from hard pruning and are best scrapped. Tree stumps should be removed by a professional, as they can feed fungal infections like *Armillaria*, a common problem in neglected gardens.

Lawns rarely need to be dug up and resown, unless there are severe bumps and hollows, or there is poor drainage.

After the initial assessment, a plan for the new layout can be worked out, and a timetable for action drawn up. For this, you need to be clear about the best time to carry out the different tasks.

Use systemic weedkillers while perennial weeds are growing strongly, in late spring and early summer, but take care to avoid spraying ornamental plants. If you decide to remove perennial weeds physically, do it either when they are dying down, and you can dig up the roots more easily, or during the growing season when there is a chance of desiccation.

Digging new borders, and sowing or turfing lawns, is best done in early autumn, but early spring is also an option. Use the winter months for spreading, or incorporating, manures, to allow time for them to break down and settle before spring planting, but apply moisture-retaining and weed-suppressing mulches in early spring.

Moving existing, or putting in new, plants should be done in autumn and early winter if they are reliably hardy, and in late spring if they are not. Container-grown stock, however, can be planted at any time, except during hard frost and periods of drought.

Tree repair work can be done at any time, except early spring, when cuts may cause 'bleeding' of sap.

Pervasive perennial weed is the most universal problem in neglected gardens, and the most important consideration when first renovating one. In badly affected permanent borders and rock gardens, herbaceous perennials should be removed, their roots minutely examined and cleaned of perennial weed root, and then 'heeled-in' in spare ground while weeds are removed from the rest of the border. This can be done either by hand, or by spraying with glyphosate, preferably twice, at a six-week interval. The latter is expensive, but is far and away the most effective method; glyphosate has low mammalian toxicity and degrades quickly in the soil.

The neglected garden may well contain woody weeds, such as sycamore seedlings and brambles. The former should be dug out, but the latter can be hacked right back in winter, and the regrowth treated with a systemic weedkiller in the spring. Once you have the weeds under control, you must take action to prevent them from getting out of hand once more.

If you are making a new border from lawn, or you suspect years of neglect, or there is a compaction problem causing waterlogging, it is best to double-dig the soil. Only when borders are clear of weed, and they have been dug over and manured, should they be replanted.

Major tree surgery is a task for experts, because of the safety implications, but the removal of small, dead or diseased branches is possible, particularly if they grow close to ground level. Do this either in the summer, when dead branches are most visible, or during autumn or early winter.

Both trees and shrubs, if grafted, may be subject to sucker growth from the stock below ground. This is a particular problem with neglected gardens, not only because suckers are allowed to develop unchecked but also because rain, over time, may wash the soil away from the roots, exposing them to the air and encouraging them to sucker. 'Water shoots' – thin, upright shoots growing from

RENOVATING A SHRUB

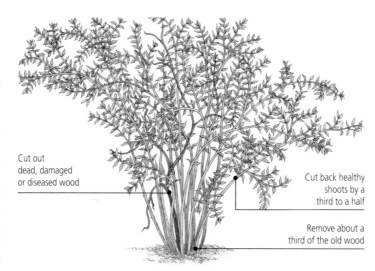

Cut out dead, damaged or diseased wood

Cut back healthy shoots by a third to a half

Remove about a third of the old wood

Many old, neglected shrubs can be successfully renovated by pruning over a two- or three-year period, at a season dictated by the flowering of the particular plant (this example is a philadelphus). In this way, old wood can be removed gradually without shocking the plant, and with adequate feeding and watering, plenty

of new shoots should be produced until the plant ultimately renews itself. In the first year, remove any dead or diseased wood. Identify about one-third of the oldest stems, and cut these back to the base. Cut back a further third of the stems to a bud about halfway along their length. Feed, water and mulch the plant well.

In the following season, the plant will send out new shoots both from the base and from below the cuts on the stems. Remove a further third to a half of the oldest stems, cutting back to a bud. As before, feed, water and mulch the plant well. Further removal of old wood may be necessary in the following year.

RENOVATION

stems and branches – on lime trees and walnuts, for example, should also be cut off close to the trunk, as they waste the plant's energy. Congested shrubs may take two, or even three, seasons to be restored to a well-balanced framework. All dead wood can be removed at once, but take care not to cut all the superfluous live wood away in one go, if you do not want to give an old shrub a potentially life-threatening shock. The oldest wood should go first. Take care to prune at the right season, depending on whether the shrub flowers on the 'old' or 'new' wood. Feed with a slow-release fertilizer and mulch afterwards.

Climbers should be treated as shrubs in this respect, although in addition – even if it is detrimental to their flowering – you may have to cut them right back, in order to repair wall ties and wires. Variegated shrubs may well have 'reverted' – that is, started to

throw out branches bearing plain green leaves. These must be removed if you wish to retain the variegation.

Neglected roses can usually be saved and rejuvenated, but if they are very old and weak, dig them up because they do not live forever and are easily, and relatively cheaply, replaced. If you are saving modern bush roses, cut out all dead, diseased, damaged and weak wood in late winter, prune back some of the youngest and strongest growths, and cover the rootstock with fresh soil, if this has disappeared. Feed with a balanced fertilizer and mulch with organic material. With climbers and ramblers, cut out the oldest stems as well as the dead ones, to encourage new growth, but do not be too drastic in the first year. You will generally find that once the dead wood (which often dies because of lack of light) is removed, together with crossing stems, so that

the plant is 'opened up', things will immediately improve. Cut back dead wood as low down as is practicable.

Remember, if you do wish to plant new roses where old have been, you will have to replace the topsoil with fresh from elsewhere.

Lawns can usually be renovated, although badly neglected ones will take a couple of seasons to recover. If you do not want to spike, scarify, weedkill and feed, as well as regularly mow, then kill the grass with glyphosate in spring and turf or re-seed in autumn. I favour renovation as being less expensive and wasteful. If the grass is very high, cut it initially with a nylon-corded strimmer, wearing protective goggles and gloves when you do it. Then cut it with a rotary mower with the blade set at its highest, and regularly and frequently thereafter, with the box on, gradually dropping the height of the blade.

Frequent mowing will discourage coarse grasses and weeds, and together with other aspects of lawn care, should ensure a reasonable sward in two seasons or so.

Rock gardens are often overgrown with bad perennial weeds, because it is hard to weed effectively in such restricted, and well planted, spaces. If grass weeds are a problem, use a specific grass herbicide. Broad-leaved weeds must either be dug out by hand (not an easy matter amongst rocks) or painted with glyphosate gel. Alpines themselves can become weeds, so if they are smothering others, you may have to take stern action with hand fork and secateurs.

Ponds and their margins are so often planted with potentially invasive plants that a neglected one is almost sure to be overgrown. Be ruthless in pulling out unwanted plants. This is best done in spring, which is also the time to rake out blanket weed.

Deciduous hedges can often be renovated, although beech and hornbeam will take longer than privet, say, so are best done one side at a time. As with other shrubs, renovate in easy stages. Evergreens such as holly, *Lonicera nitida*, and Portugal laurel can also be cut back hard if necessary, but conifers are, with the exception of yew, more problematic, because you should not cut into old wood. After hard pruning, feed, water and mulch.

There is no ready answer to the question 'How long will all this take?' Many people find it best to leave well alone for a year to see what 'comes up' first. Certainly, too hasty action may mean you lose plants that could be salvaged. In the case of mature trees, the loss may be keenly felt later on. Moreover, although it is neither possible nor desirable to sort out all the problems of badly overgrown or neglected plants in one season, at least most plants are amenable to renovation, if it is done with care.

RENOVATING A HEDGE

Deal with deciduous hedges in late winter, evergreen hedges in mid- to late spring. In the first year, cut back the top to the required height, followed by the branches on one side only, close to the main stems. Treat the other side the following year, or even two years later. Feed, water and mulch regularly.

REMOVING SUCKERS

On roses and many other plants the rootstock on which a selected cultivar is grafted will often send up suckers to the detriment of the cultivar. These are usually paler in colour and may have rather different leaves. Expose the junction of the sucker and the plant and, if possible, pull it away rather than cut it off.

REVERSION

Many variegated plants have a tendency to produce shoots that have reverted to the non-variegated form. These are generally more vigorous and will soon dominate if allowed to grow unchecked. To prevent this happening, cut out shoots that have reverted, pruning back to a stem that is variegated.

PROPAGATION

UB Propagation is the name given to the various means employed by gardeners to initiate the growth of plants, or to multiply those which they already have. It is a fascinating aspect of gardening and no one who considers themself a gardener, rather than simply a garden owner, will go through life without propagating plants – even if they do not always recognize what they are doing.

The instinct to make new plants, and look after them once made, is even more deeply ingrained in gardeners than the desire to acquire something for almost nothing. Moreover, propagation provides the opportunity to rear those plants which are not widely available and to keep a supply of those plants which are generally short-lived or liable to die in cold winters.

Although you may find mentioned in books a variety of arcane techniques such as 'twin-scaling' daffodil bulbs or 'saddle-grafting', the most useful forms of propagation for the amateur can be reduced to the following: seed sowing, taking cuttings, ground-layering, and dividing plants.

Seed-sowing is the best way of rearing hardy and half-hardy annuals, biennial flowers, and vegetables, and a good way of growing many hardy perennials. It is certainly suitable for propagating tree and shrub species too, although it is slower than other means.

It is not, however, necessarily suitable for hybrids or cultivated varieties ('cultivars'), which cannot be depended upon to come 'true' from seed. For these, asexual or vegetative propagation is necessary. If you propagate a plant asexually, you replicate its genetic make-up, so you know precisely what the resulting plants will be like. Taking cuttings, layering and division are all forms of vegetative propagation.

We take cuttings of many types of plant, most particularly shrubs, which would take too long to grow from seed, but also of hardy and half-hardy perennials, which we may need to propagate in case of winter losses in the garden or just to increase stock.

Layering is, in essence, a form of taking cuttings; the difference is that shoots of a plant are encouraged to make roots *before* being severed from the mother plant. This technique is helpful for clematis, and for shrubs which grow branches close to the ground.

Division is an easy way of replicating hardy perennials and many alpines, and has the bonus of revivifying existing clumps.

Most propagation is reasonably straightforward and you will usually find yourself blessed with countless surplus divisions of, say, hemerocallis or rooted fuchsia cuttings. As it goes against the grain to put on the compost heap something you have brought into existence in the first place, you will find yourself giving these plants to visitors, plant stalls and fêtes. This is an excellent state of affairs, for gardening is not, nor should it be, simply a nicely judged deployment of human and financial resources.

That said, all gardeners know, or should know, that failure can attend these operations. Not every type of plant germinates like cress, strikes roots like the fuchsia, or divides as successfully as a rudbeckia. Indeed, some plants are so difficult, even for experts, that they are rare in gardens, and expensive to buy. Providing the right circumstances for propagation and obeying a few basic rules is therefore important. These are not complicated and can be summarized as follows.

Equipment, tools and composts must be clean, as fungi which feed on seedlings and young plants thrive in unhygienic conditions.

Care must be taken to choose the right time for propagation. This has less to do with calendar dates than with the coincidence of a range of environmental factors. In very general terms, plants propagate most easily in temperate conditions, when there are good light values, and the plants can be shielded from certain stresses – that is, drought, starvation, wild temperature fluctuations, and excessive heat, sunshine or cold, not to mention pests and diseases to which they are particularly vulnerable.

Aftercare must be watchful and consistent to limit, or relieve, the possibility of 'checks' to growth caused by adverse circumstances. These checks can cause far greater problems to young plants than they do to mature ones, and should be avoided if at all possible. So keep the greenhouse or windowsill well ventilated in sunny weather (automatic vent openers, which are adjusted to open at a predetermined temperature, are invaluable for this), shade the greenhouse or frame from strong, direct sun, keep plants well watered without waterlogging them, and feed them when necessary.

Having so-called 'green fingers' merely consists of taking advantage of a pool of knowledge about the ways of plants, coupled with personal experience, a natural sympathy and an adventurous spirit. If you do not know, or cannot discover, exactly the propagation requirements for a particular plant, it is nonetheless always worth taking a chance. If someone gives you some seed of a coveted plant, for example, sow half of it at once, and half at another season. There is a strong possibility that, one way or another, you will be in luck.

EQUIPMENT

Every would-be propagator needs to have pots into which to put seed sown, or cuttings taken. In my opinion square pots are best because they take up less space on the greenhouse staging or windowsill than round pots. (Round plastic pots are a strange leftover from the era when clay pots were the norm; the difference is that clay pots *had* to be made round whereas plastic ones do not.) A wide range of containers – for example, polystyrene coffee cups – will do, however, and almost anything goes as long as it is possible to pierce holes in the bottom and at the lower sides to allow excess water to drain away.

Large or half-size seed trays are necessary to sow seed into or to receive 'pricked out' seedlings. A seed pot of small seedlings will fill at least one large seed tray, often more, if all the seedlings are to be grown on. Expanded polystyrene trays, divided into cells, are an alternative but, in my experience, no less fiddly and inclined to break easily. However, the individual bottomless compartments do enable you to push up and remove the contents of any one cell when it is ready for planting, without disturbing the rest. This is useful when you are sowing large seed such as that of runner beans, and is particularly appropriate for 'multiple seeding'. These trays, quite intriguingly, seem to defy the law of gravity: when you fill them with loamless compost, hardly any of it falls out of the bottom.

It is as well to know from the start that ordinary garden soil on its own is not a suitable medium for growing plants in pots, because it is not sterile, and is unlikely to be free-draining enough. For seed-sowing, taking cuttings, and growing on young plants, you need a compost in which to grow your plants. This is

PROPAGATION

not the compost that results from decaying vegetable matter, but a free-draining fibrous 'soil' in which seeds can germinate and plants can grow before they are ready to go out into the garden. Some composts have soil, described as loam, as an important ingredient; others do not and are called 'loamless'.

Modern loamless 'multipurpose' composts have been formulated for seed sowing, taking cuttings, and growing on young plants. They all contain nutrients to sustain the young plants for a greater or lesser period. However, in the long term, most composts need supplementing with liquid or granular feed.

For simplicity's sake, it is probably best to use a multipurpose peat or reduced-peat compost as the medium. One alternative is a loam-based compost in a John Innes formula. These are composts made up of sterilized loam, peat and grit, and contain fertilizer. The formula number (1, 2 or 3) refers to the strength: No. 3 has three times as much fertilizer as No. 1.

If you object to using composts with peat in them on environmental grounds, try an alternative such as coir seed and potting compost, but be prepared to start feeding the plantlings earlier. Take care not to over-water because these fibrous composts have great water-holding capacities. Even if the top is dry, the compost beneath may still be wet.

You will also need a small watering-can with a very fine 'rose' attachment or a hand-held mist sprayer; a pencil or plastic dibber (a small implement with a pointed end) for making holes in the compost; small labels and a waterproof marker pen; either sheets of polystyrene which you can cut, or newspaper; and a supply of copper fungicide. A small 3mm/⅛in sieve sometimes comes in handy.

Cuttings takers will also need either a 'multipurpose' compost or special cuttings compost, a selection of clear polythene bags, such as are sold for the freezer, and large rubber bands; some thin, flexible wire; either a straight-bladed gardener's knife and attendant oilstone or, alternatively, a Stanley knife and spare blades; a pair of secateurs; and some hormone rooting powder, which can be used to stimulate rooting in many plants.

If your seeds or cuttings need to germinate or strike root in heated conditions, (and many either require or benefit from that) a thermostatically-controlled general propagator or windowsill version is very helpful because it creates a small, heated (usually to 18-21°C/65-70°F), moisture-retentive, sanitary environment. It obviates the need to heat the whole greenhouse and can be easily shaded. If electricity is not available in the greenhouse, put your propagator on a windowsill in the house or on a shelf in the conservatory.

Home-made propagating cases containing soil-warming cables, heated 'blankets' for the greenhouse staging, and mist propagation units, are all refinements which are not necessary, unless you wish to make a hobby out of propagation. Most often, they hasten the process of rooting cuttings rather than providing the difference between success and failure. What they will do is quickly, but stealthily, cause costs to rise out of all proportion to the benefit gained.

Whether you have a greenhouse or not, you will ideally need a cold frame into which to put plants when they need to be hardened off, that is, acclimatized to outside conditions before being planted out. A cold frame can also be a suitable place for sowing the seed of hardy perennials or early vegetables, which are hardy and simply benefit from a little more warmth at germinating time. Some cuttings, notably hardwood, can also be put straight in. Cold frames are best sited near the greenhouse for convenience, if you have one, and on the sunny side for preference. If you intend to sow directly into one, simply erect the frame over reasonable, free-draining soil. If, however, you want only to put pots in it, cover the base with polythene to keep out weeds and cover the polythene with a layer of gravel, raked level. If you intend raising just a few plants each year, a cloche will do as a cold frame.

If you have neither greenhouse nor cold frame, you can still be a successful propagator. Use either a windowsill propagator or the airing cupboard to provide the warmth to germinate seeds and strike cuttings, and a cool windowsill, out of direct sunshine, on which to place them for growing on. When hardening-off, plants can be put directly outside in a sheltered, not too sunny place in the day, and brought in at night for two to three weeks.

SEEDS

For seed sowing directly outside you will require a garden line for making straight lines in the vegetable garden; a straight piece of wood on which you have marked off inches or centimetres; wire netting to keep birds and cats off seedbeds; and plastic cloches to protect tender seedlings from frost early on in the year or mature plants at the other end of the season. Spun polypropylene fleece, or clear polythene sheeting punctured with neat regular holes, can be used as an effective alternative to cloches.

Seed packets are covered in useful and accessible information about sowing times, spacings, temperatures, potential difficulties, even the number of seed in the packet and the likely number of plants that will be raised from them, or the length of row they will furnish.

Information which may not be available, but which you also need to know, is what constitutes an 'F1 hybrid' and what advantages it represents. This is not academic because F1 seed is very expensive, and there are often few seeds in a packet. An F1 hybrid cross has been made between two pure-breeding parents to produce offspring which have particular positive characteristics: uniform size and shape and vigour, floriferousness, even uniformity of maturity. They often, although not inevitably, mark a significant advance in plant breeding. Some F1 seeds – for example, pelargoniums and Brussels sprouts – make a sound investment. However, for many other plants – for example, tomatoes – 'open-pollinated' seed is readily available and far cheaper. There is no point in saving any seed made by F1 hybrid flowers or vegetables, because the offspring will turn out to be a mixed batch and, possibly, a mixed blessing.

Seed is sold well packaged, in many cases in vacuum-sealed packs, but it can soon lose its viability if left in warm, humid conditions. It is best kept in a tightly-closed tin, in a cool and dry shed, or even in a fridge compartment if it is not to be used for a while.

It is helpful to have a supply of vermiculite or perlite to put on top of the compost. The seeds can be sown directly on to these expanded micas (volcanic rocks) which drain water very freely and allow a free passage of air. Fungal attack is less likely in what is essentially a sterile medium, and vermiculite also lets in some light, which is necessary for many seeds to germinate (there are few seeds which can only germinate in complete darkness), yet protects the seeds from being washed about when watered, and stabilizes them as they make their young shoots and roots.

Fill a clean pot, 7cm/3in in diameter, two-thirds full with seed compost and very lightly tamp it down with the bottom of a same-sized pot. Add vermiculite to within 6mm/¼in of the rim, to allow for watering without splashing over. Sow tiny seed directly on top of this and water it carefully in. Very fine seed can be mixed with a little silver sand so that it is easier to distribute evenly. Watering with a copper fungicide helps to prevent the common 'damping-off' disease of seedlings.

Sow seed by rolling it between thumb and forefinger so that it falls singly, or make a channel of the seed packet so that it can drop out slowly and evenly. If the seed is large enough to handle easily, do not fill the pot right up to the top with vermiculite initially, but sow on to the top of the compost and add the vermiculite after sowing.

Water well with a fine rose on the watering can. You can cover the pot with either a square of clear perspex, or a piece of the expanded polystyrene in which electrical goods are packed for delivery, cut to the right size. These materials stop evaporation from the surface of the compost, necessary because all seed needs moisture to germinate, guard against overheating on hot days, and are safer to handle than glass. However, if you are prepared to be attentive with watering and the pots are going straight into a propagator with a clear lid, this covering is not strictly necessary. Put a label with the name and date of sowing on it at the back of the pot or on top of the polystyrene. Put the pot in the propagator or airing cupboard, at the advised temperature if possible. Check frequently to see how the seeds are progressing.

As a general rule, half-hardy annuals germinate most quickly and uniformly at 18-21°C/65-70°F. This includes plants such as petunias, as well as frost-tender vegetables like tomatoes and cucumbers, which can be sown inside in warm conditions from early spring. However, in my experience there is no advantage in sowing the seed until mid spring. They may flower a week later than they would if sown a month earlier but they will be very much cheaper to produce, will germinate faster and will suffer fewer losses than they would in bad light and cold conditions. Nor will they hang around growing 'leggy' in trays until the weather is sufficiently fine for them to be hardened off in cold frames. The urge to start propagating early in order not to feel too pressed in late spring is strong, but the answer to that is to sow little and often, so that the 'pricking-out' is also staggered.

The only half-hardy annuals that really do need to be started off in late winter are *Begonia semperflorens*, pelargoniums, gazanias, lobelia and African marigolds.

Hardy perennials need less heat to germinate so can be sown in late spring in pots inside, or sown directly into the soil in a shaded cold frame which is opened on sunny days. Hardy perennials can also be sown in nursery rows outside, like biennials. They will take slightly longer to germinate and develop than they would under glass, but urgency with these things is often quite illusory. Only those plants which must grow and flourish in a season need to be treated to artificial warmth.

Alpines often need a winter spent outside, for frost to break down inhibitors in the seed coats before they will germinate. Sow them in midwinter in pots of compost topped with horticultural grit, and put them in the cold frame. The topping of grit facilitates the removal of weeds, prevents rain dislodging the seed, and deters mice. The seed of some trees and shrubs also needs to be treated this way. Make periodic checks to see if they have germinated. Germination can take up to two years so contain your soul in patience.

Seedlings, once germinated, should be given more space quickly, not only to prevent them from damping-off but also because

SOWING SEEDS

a *Fill a clean 7cm/3in pot two-thirds full with seed compost, and lightly tamp down the surface with another pot. Be very careful not to firm modern loamless composts too hard, or precious air holes which allow the roots to penetrate may be lost.*

b *Water with a weak solution of copper fungicide, and for tiny seed add vermiculite to within 6mm/¼in of the rim. Sow the seed, mixed with a little silver sand, on top. Sow larger seed on the compost, and cover with vermiculite. Water well with a fine rose.*

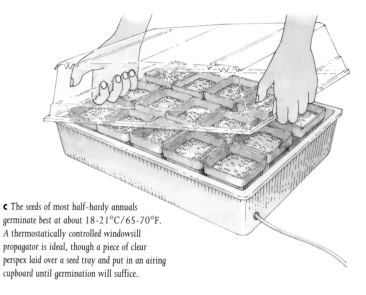

c *The seeds of most half-hardy annuals germinate best at about 18-21°C/65-70°F. A thermostatically controlled windowsill propagator is ideal, though a piece of clear perspex laid over a seed tray and put in an airing cupboard until germination will suffice.*

growth is soon checked in crowded conditions. This usually means removing the perspex immediately after germination, and then 'pricking out' the seedlings into trays when they are large enough to handle safely. Use a potting or multipurpose compost as the medium, tamped down lightly but evenly in the tray, and space the seedlings out so that there are at least 48 per large standard seed tray (eight along, six down) or even more for small-growing seedlings. Plant small seedlings, like lobelia, in little clumps as they are too tiny to be handled separately. Handle seedlings only by the first seed leaves if possible. Use your dibber to dig the seedling's roots gently out of the compost, to make the hole in the potting compost, and to firm the seedling in afterwards. Settle in with a light watering. Memory is fallible; transfer the label from the seed pot to the back of the tray.

These seedlings need cosseting for a few days, under a plastic cover, or in the propagator if there is room, until they are acclimatized to their new state; then the trays can be put on to the greenhouse staging or windowsill – remembering in the latter's case to turn them through an angle of 90 degrees every few days, to help prevent the seedlings being drawn too strongly towards the light. This should happen much less in the greenhouse because light comes from all sides. After a month to six weeks, feed the seedlings with a weak liquid feed, or even sooner if they have been planted in a peat-free compost.

When the seedlings begin to crowd each other in the trays, it is time to pot them on individually, in the case of large annuals such as nicotiana, or harden them off prior to planting them out. This is the process of acclimatizing them gradually to the temperatures outside. As nights are colder than days, the trays can be put outside, either into a ventilated cold frame which can be closed at night, or lined up in a sheltered place, and cloched or covered with newspaper at night. The process generally takes two to three weeks in late spring.

It is possible to sow seed so thinly in a seed tray that it is not necessary to prick the seedlings out, although seed that doesn't germinate will leave gaps in the seed tray. Alternatively, sow a few seeds at regular spacings in the seed tray and, at germination, thin each clump to the strongest seedling.

There are modern ways of making the business of seed sowing slightly more predictable. It is possible, for example, to buy what is called 'primed seed' from large mail order seed firms. This seed has undergone a process to bring it to the point of germination, but no further, before it is put in a state of suspended animation, packaged and posted. This type of seed is, of course, more expensive than the ordinary kind, but is worth considering for those plants that can be difficult to germinate, like begonias and verbenas, or those which need high temperatures initially, like pelargoniums. If you lack confidence or experience, this seed may help you.

You can also obtain plants from mail-order seedsmen at a variety of stages: germinated seedlings; plugs grown in modular trays (often known as 'plantlets' or 'speedplugs'); and 'pot ready' plants. The last mentioned really take the uncertainty out of propagation but also much of the fun. What kind you choose depends on how confident you feel in your abilities or equipment.

Seedlings come in 100s and need to be pricked off into trays and perhaps later into pots before being planted out. Plugs, in 35s, need to be potted on and kept under glass until hardening-off time. 'Pot-ready' plants come in biodegradable peat pots and can be planted straight out into ornamental containers or hanging baskets. These seedlings and plantlets are not expensive considering the costs of propagation, and particularly that of heating glasshouse space early in the year. The only problem is that, by buying them, you are inevitably limiting your choice of variety for the sake of convenience and flexibility.

Much easier than all this is sowing seed outdoors: a method suitable for hardy annuals, many hardy

PRICKING OUT AND POTTING ON

a *When seedlings are big enough to handle by their first leaves, prick them out at wider spacings in trays. Hold on to a leaf rather than the stem, and gently prise each seedling up, using a purpose-made dibber, a pencil, or even a plant label.*

b *In a prepared tray of compost, make a hole with the dibber and lower the seedling in. Allow about 48 seedlings to a large seed tray – diagonal rows are the most economical – and use the dibber to firm the soil gently round them. Water in, and cover again for a few days.*

c *Young plants should not be planted out until the danger of frost is well past, and in late spring it is possible that they might have outgrown the tray before they can be planted out outside. If so, pot them on into new compost to avoid any checks to growth.*

SOWING SEEDS OUTDOORS

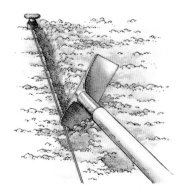

a *Sow when the soil is no longer cold. It is important to firm the earth before you sow. Rake the soil flat, then shuffle over it with your feet close together and your weight on your heels. You may need to repeat this. Rake again carefully to finish with a level tilth.*

b *Straight lines enable seedlings to be easily differentiated from weeds. Stretch a garden line, making sure it is at right angles or parallel to the edge of the bed, and draw out a 'drill', using a draw hoe or the edge of a garden rake to make a shallow furrow.*

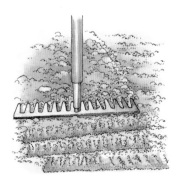

c *Water, if the soil is dry. Sow large seed individually, dropping each one into the drill close to the line, and spaced out according to instructions on the packet. Sprinkle smaller seed evenly along the row, using the packet as a funnel.*

d *Use a garden rake to draw the soil back from the sides carefully over the drill, and tamp the soil down gently afterwards. Unless the soil is very damp, water in using a very fine rose on a watering-can.*

e *If you are sowing seed in early spring, when the soil is still cold and air temperatures low, lay a sheet of polypropylene fleece to give protection. Anchored with soil at the edges, it will be pushed up gradually as the crop grows.*

perennials and hardy vegetables. Biennials and perennials are usually sown outside in early summer, while hardy annuals and vegetables are sown in late spring and early summer. Many can be sown where they are to grow, while some, such as large leaf vegetables, and biennials, are best sown in a seedbed first, and later transplanted to a main bed at wider spacings.

Whatever is sown, prepare the soil properly in advance, at least a week before sowing, fork over the soil and sprinkle 115 grams per square metre (4oz per square yard) of a general fertilizer. The point of the fertilizer is to provide something immediately for the emergent seedlings to take up.

Do not think of sowing until the soil is no longer cold to the touch, nor when it is so wet it clings to rake or spade. When you are ready to sow, tread down the soil until it is level and reasonably firm, using a shuffling walk with the weight on the heels. Rake it to form what is known as a tilth, that is, a surface of fine and moist soil particles. Making a level tilth takes practice, but less than perfect raking will not prevent seed germinating so do not worry too much if the surface is uneven.

For vegetables and perennials, stretch a line straight and taut between two pegs, just above soil level, and score along the line with the edge of the head of a rake or hoe to form a straight shallow furrow, called a drill. The point of sowing in rows is to make the position of young seedlings easy to see, so that weeds can be identified and hoed off. Seed packets will tell you how deep to make the drill, and usually how far apart to space the rows and thin the seedlings. Sow the seed as sparsely as you are able, rolling it into the drill through thumb and index finger or pouring

it slowly out of the seed packet, made into a narrow funnel. Even with tight quality controls, not all seed germinates, which is why we go through the seemingly wasteful procedure of sowing close together and thinning the seedlings later.

After the seed is sown, rake the soil gently back from the sides of the drill, and tamp it level with the back of the rake. Use a home-made measuring rod or a stiff metal tape-measure to space the rows accurately. Label each row.

Make shallow drills for hardy annual seed using the end of a short cane; a series of close and criss-crossing drills will ensure good flower coverage and make it easy to tell annual from weed seedlings when they germinate. If you wish to sow a variety of annuals informally (and if you can recognize weed seedlings!), divide their allotted spaces with lines of sand trickled out of your hand, and simply sow broadcast, distributing the seed evenly. Rake lightly over afterwards just to cover and stabilize the seed.

Once the seedlings are through the ground, you will probably have to thin them at least once, and possibly twice, to give them room to grow. In the case of lettuce and carrots, the second thinnings are large enough to be eaten.

Biennials and perennials can be thinned once but after that should be transplanted. This helps develop their root systems, which is important for plants that will be in the ground over the winter. Mark out a new row with the garden line, lift the little plants up carefully with a hand trowel or fork under the roots, replant them at the required spacing and water them in. Young roots are vulnerable to drought so cover with newspaper. A proprietary 'root dip' helps to establish transplants, but is not essential.

CUTTINGS

Vegetative propagation takes advantage of the amazing capacity of plants to reproduce from portions of themselves.

The commonest, and easiest, form of cutting is the stem cutting, classified as 'softwood', 'semi-hardwood' (semi-ripe) and 'hardwood', depending on the age of the stem from which the cutting is taken. Softwood cuttings are taken in late spring or in summer, and are suitable for plants such as pelargoniums, fuchsias, herbaceous perennials, and also tender perennial plants which you might lose in the winter outside. Semi-hardwood cuttings tend to be taken in late summer and autumn, and are suitable for a range of deciduous and evergreen shrubs. Hardwood cuttings are taken in late autumn and early winter when the plants have become dormant; this method is useful for climbing roses, blackcurrants, poplars, willows and a host of other easy-to-strike deciduous

plants, as well as evergreens like rhododendrons and holly. Heel cuttings are those semi-hard or hardwood cuttings taken with a small piece of older wood still attached. Suitable subjects are evergreen shrubs.

Although nodal (leaf-joint) cuttings are most widely used, it is also possible, especially with herbaceous perennials like delphiniums and lupins, to take 'basal' cuttings, that is, to remove an entire sideshoot when small (10-15cm/4-6in) in early spring and root that. With carnations and pinks, the best course is to root a 'piping' (stem tip) which can be removed from an established plant by taking hold of the top leaves and pulling sharply upwards. 'Internodal' cuttings, that is, stems that are cut halfway between leaf joints, work particularly well for propagating clematis.

Soft and semi-hard cuttings strike best in a sterile and humid atmosphere, as they still have their leaves and would otherwise lose moisture

easily by transpiration, and with heat beneath their cut stems to encourage rooting (18-25°C/65-80°F is a good range for striking many plants). They are best put in pots of free-draining cuttings compost. A mix of 50 per cent perlite or horticultural grit and 50 per cent moss peat is usually recommended but pure perlite also works, provided that the cuttings are kept continuously damp and are potted up straight away on rooting. Alternatively, any multipurpose compost will do, especially if extra grit or perlite is added to aid free drainage.

Place the pot either in a heated propagator or cover it with a clear plastic bag, held clear of the cuttings by hoops of flexible thin wire tied with a rubber band, and put in a warm place but not in direct sun. Even better than polythene bags are purpose-designed perspex domes, which are available to fit different sizes of round pot. Because the sides are rigid, they are less likely to touch the cuttings and cause them to rot.

The best length of stem cutting, generally, is about 10cm/4in long, taken from a non-flowering sideshoot, or one from which the flower bud has been removed. A slightly longer shoot should be cut with secateurs from the plant, the bottom leaves removed, and the cutting put in a polythene bag so that it does not dry out at the cut end. Then, when the pot of compost is ready and has been watered with a copper-based fungicide, the end should be cut very cleanly with a sharp knife just below a leaf joint. This should be clearly visible even after a leaf has been removed from it. Most cuttings benefit from having their cut ends dipped in hormone rooting powder, which contains a fungicide and stimulates rooting at the cut end. However, it is important to use only a little hormone powder: too much can be counterproductive by causing harm to immature tissue.

Cuttings of any kind with large leaves should have some leaves removed and others cut down by

TYPES OF CUTTINGS

Softwood cuttings from plants such as pelargoniums are prepared by taking off a healthy shoot just above a joint and then making a clean cut just below a joint. Remove the lower leaves before inserting the cuttings in a free-draining cuttings compost.

Heel cuttings, usually hardwood or semi-hardwood cuttings of evergreen shrubs, have a piece of older wood attached. Trim the heel with a clean knife or razor blade and remove lower leaves before inserting the cutting in compost.

Internodal cuttings, that is cuttings where the cut is made halfway between leaf joints, are commonly used to propagate clematis. Remove one leaf before inserting the cutting in the compost, taking care not to damage the buds in the leaf axils.

Stem tips (pipings) provide an easy way of propagating pinks and carnations. Take the cuttings from vigorous sideshoots in summer and insert in a sandy compost. Keep cuttings lightly shaded until they root.

1 Propagation – the process whereby new plants are made – adds another dimension to gardening, and is a popular reason for acquiring a greenhouse. Most plants reproduce easily and in a variety of ways, but many will only do so dependably if provided with sheltered and consistent growing conditions. The most common forms of propagation carried out are sowing seeds, taking cuttings, layering and dividing plants.

TAKING CUTTINGS

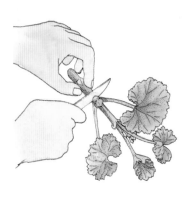

a Here a softwood cutting of pelargonium is removed from the parent plant in spring. Make a sharp cut just below a leaf joint to give a cutting of 10-15cm/4-6in. Remove the bottom leaves carefully with the knife, to keep water loss to a minimum, which is essential while the cutting is rooting.

b Dip the cut end immediately into a fungicide and then in fresh hormone rooting powder, and tap off any excess. If there is a delay between taking the cutting and potting it up, put it in a sealed polythene bag so that the end does not dry out. This would substantially reduce its chances of rooting successfully.

c Make a hole in moist cuttings compost with a dibber, a pencil or a plant label, and insert the cutting sufficiently deep that the leaves are just clear of the compost. Take care not to leave an airspace between the cutting and the bottom of the hole which would hamper successful rooting. Water in well.

d To prevent evaporation, cover the pot with a purpose-made clear perspex cover, or, alternatively, use a clear polythene bag and secure it around the pot with an elastic band. A simple, semi-circular wire hoop can be used to ensure that the bag does not touch the cutting as it grows and so encourage rot.

half to help slow down the rate of water loss before rooting.

With a dibber or pencil-end make a hole, about one-third the length of the cutting, in the compost and push the cutting down as far as the bottom of the hole; it will not root so easily if there is an air pocket beneath the cut stem. Firm the compost gently round the cutting with your fingers. Put up to six cuttings in a small pot, making sure that they do not touch each other, then press the soil gently round them, and water in well, preferably with a weak solution of fungicide.

You can usually tell when a cutting has rooted because it starts to grow leaves at the top, but you can check by pulling the plant gently. If it resists the pull it has rooted. If not, it will have to be put back and firmed in. There is enormous variation in how long cuttings take to root. Provided they have not obviously rotted off, you should be patient and leave them alone for as long as it takes.

Potting on should be done once good roots have been made because, without liquid feeding (there being no nutrients in a grit-and-peat cuttings compost) growth will be slow. Turn the pot upside down, using your fingers and palm to retain the cuttings, and knock the rim against the bench or staging to separate pot from cuttings. Disentangle these carefully, making sure to retain as many roots as possible. Pot on, either into a potting or multipurpose compost, and keep the pots in the propagator for a few days until the plants are well recovered, if that is where they were growing before.

Rooted cuttings should then be potted on as they require and kept well fed with weak liquid fertilizer in the growing season to prevent stunting in such restricted circumstances. They should be hardened off well before planting out. Cuttings of hardy plants can, in theory, be planted out once they have been carefully and gradually

hardened-off but, if struck in autumn, they are best protected in a cold frame until spring. In either case, once planted out, they are vulnerable to being trodden on in the border so it is better to plant them out in a line in a spare piece of the garden until they have grown to a sufficient size to be able to hold their own.

Hardwood cuttings are treated rather differently. In autumn, take them about 22cm/9in long from growths made in the current season, trim below a bud at the bottom, then place each about 7cm/3in apart in a 15cm/6in deep slit trench, made with a spade and lined at the bottom with a few centimetres or so of sharp grit. This trench is best made in a sheltered place, but not underneath trees or shrubs that drip. Once the cuttings are all lined up in the trench, close it by pushing the soil together with your boots. These cuttings may only take a few months to root but ideally are left at least a year before being dug up and then

HARDWOOD CUTTINGS

a *Some shrubs and some soft fruit; such as black- and redcurrants, can be propagated by hardwood cuttings in late autumn. Cut off a 22cm/9in stem below a node, leaving the buds, and place in a narrow 'slit' trench.*

b *Your slit trench should be about 15cm/6in deep. Make it by pulling a spade to and fro in the soil. Put a thin layer of grit in the bottom to aid drainage and stimulate rooting.*

c *Use your boots to close up the trench, so that the cuttings are held upright by the soil. They shouldn't need any further support. The cuttings should root within a year, and can then be transplanted in the following dormant season.*

POTTING ON

First water well and allow to drain. Then knock the plant out by tapping the pot rim against a firm surface, holding the plant stem between two fingers. Place the plant into a larger pot on a bed of new compost so that the surface of the old compost is 8mm/¼in below the rim, and fill in with more compost round the edge. Shake the compost down gently, and water.

ROOT CUTTINGS

a It is not always necessary to dig up a plant, such as Papaver orientale, before taking root cuttings in the dormant season; simply scrape away the soil from one side. Make the cut nearest the crown straight, and cut the root end at a slant, to avoid confusion.

b Place root cuttings in cuttings compost, with the flat end level with the compost surface, and cover in a shallow layer of grit or sharp sand. Water, and keep in a cold frame until shoots appear. Use this method for Japanese anemones, phlox, romneya and gypsophila.

transplanted, by which time they will have a sufficiently extensive root system to survive being planted out.

If you have room, it is quicker to root hardwood cuttings, about 15cm/6in long, in pots in the cold frame, shaded in sunny weather.

There are some herbaceous perennials which can be propagated most easily by root cuttings: examples include phlox, brunnera, Oriental poppies (*Papaver orientale* forms), verbascum and *Anemone japonica* cultivars. Cuttings can be taken at any time in the dormant season and it is not always necessary even to dig up the established plant to take them.

Scrabble round the edge of the clump and remove 5-10cm/2-4in pencil-thick lengths from the roots of the plant, cutting the end nearest the crown straight and the other end slanting so that you will know which is the top when putting the cuttings in a pot. Place the cuttings upright in a pot, fill round them with seed compost, keeping the level ends just below the surface. Several cuttings will go into a 12.5cm/5in pot. Label it. Phloxes have very thin and pliable roots, so simply lay them flat on compost in a seed tray and cover lightly with more compost. These cuttings need to go in a cold frame or cold greenhouse for the winter, to give them protection until they have rooted. Keep them moist. In the spring, shoots should appear at the top. Transplant to a nursery bed and put out in their final places the following autumn.

LAYERING

Layering is a method of rooting cuttings before they are severed from the mother plant, often used on rhododendrons and viburnums. Make a nick on the underside of a suitably low-growing shoot (right), to aid rooting. A small pebble may be forced into the nick to keep it open. Bend the shoot down, secure it with a piece of U-shaped wire, and cover the bent section with good soil. Tie the rest of the shoot to a short cane to keep it free of the soil. The method is slow but sure: you may have to wait up to 18 months before the layer has made sufficient roots to be cut from the plant and transplanted.

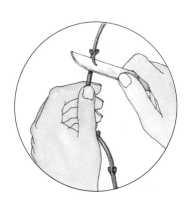

TIP LAYERING

Blackberries, like other members of the Rubus genus, will readily make a new plant by 'tip-layering' in summer. Simply place the tip in a shallow hole, using a piece of bent garden wire to hold it in place, and cover with soil. It should have rooted by late autumn, and can then be severed, and transplanted in spring.

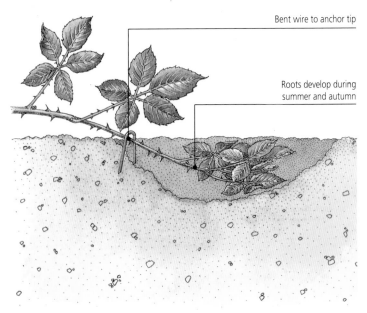

Bent wire to anchor tip

Roots develop during summer and autumn

LAYERING

The technique called layering is slow but simple, usually successful, and demands no aftercare. It is a way of rooting cuttings before they are severed from the mother plant. It is particularly useful for plants, like magnolia, which do not strike easily by other means, or for shrubs which naturally grow branches near ground level, like viburnums and rhododendrons. It is carried out in the dormant season.

The most usual way of doing it is to bend a young shoot, stripped of its leaves except at the tip, down to the ground, make a sharp cut on the underside and halfway through the shoot, and then peg it to the ground with wire bent into a U-shape. The shoot should be covered at ground level with good soil and preferably a heavy stone to keep it secure. The rest of the shoot should be tied to a short cane, pushed vertically into the ground. It may take anything up to 18 months before the layer is sufficiently well-rooted to be severed from the mother shrub and transplanted.

A variation of this is 'tip layering' which takes advantage of some plants' capacity to strike roots wherever a stem tip touches the ground. This is true of the *Rubus* genus – ornamental species as well as blackberries and loganberries. All you do is to push the tips into loose soil in summer and peg them in position until the autumn. By this time roots will have formed and the stem can be cut and the new plant transplanted.

There are some shrubs, such as *Clematis flammula* and *Jasminum nudiflorum*, which are not always easily grown from cuttings; these also can be propagated by layering. Their long flexible shoots can be pegged to the soil in several places between the nodes and new roots should form at each spot.

DIVISION

Probably the easiest technique of all is division of plants. Herbaceous perennials and some alpines can be divided up to form several plants, all with roots, which are then replanted. Not only is this a good way of making new plants but it is actually a necessary procedure every few years in order to keep many herbaceous perennials vigorous and flowering freely. It is usually done in very early autumn or early to late spring, so that the roots can develop in reasonably warm soil. The exception is the bearded iris which is divided straight after flowering because it rots easily in winter.

Detaching the plants can be done in several ways. The most commonly advised method, especially for fibrous-rooted plants such as Michaelmas daisies, is to dig the clump up intact, place it on the ground, take two border forks (or one border fork and one larger fork, if that is all you have), put them back to back through the centre of the clump and push and prise the plant into two halves. This process is then repeated until there are several little plants, all with buds and roots. It is the centres which lose their vigour, so concentrate on replanting the outer parts. If you have difficulty with this technique, try using hand forks or your bare hands to pull apart the crown.

Irises are divided by pulling apart the newer portions of rhizome, each with some leaves attached. They need to be planted very shallowly, with the top of the rhizome showing just above the soil, and preferably facing towards the sun, which will then have every opportunity to bake them in summer. As irises need dividing in midsummer, cut back all the leaves by half to minimize water loss until the roots have had a chance to establish.

DIVISION

Here a plant is being pulled apart to form several different plants. This can be done with two forks, but hands are often more effective with fibrous-rooted herbaceous plants such as geraniums. Make sure that each division you make has buds as well as roots, and discard the worn-out centre.

1 Division is not just an easy way to propagate many herbaceous plants, such as hemerocallis; the technique is also necessary every three or four years, to revitalize herbaceous plants.

PROTECTION AND STAKING

UB Growing plants which are on the borderline of hardiness both expands the range of suitable plants and adds a not unpleasant *frisson* of uncertainty to the business of making a garden. Hardiness here refers not just to tolerance of frost but also of other climatic stresses which affect some plants' chances of survival, such as excessive wet in winter, and cold winds in the early spring. Gambling with a plant's hardiness is, however, foolhardy from a design point of view, for the premature death of a key plant can rip the heart out of a scheme and it may take months or years to grow a substitute or rework the design. Fortunately, it is possible to protect, to some degree, those plants that if left to themselves might perish in the winter or early spring.

Ingenious gardeners will, perhaps, devise their own ways of protecting shrubs through spells of bad weather, improvising from a range of materials to hand. There are, however, some materials widely acknowledged to be helpful.

The best is the polypropylene mesh, known as 'shading and windbreak material', which is available on metre-wide rolls from garden centres. This is a flexible, permeable mesh, 50 per cent of which is air. It therefore allows some light, air and rain to penetrate but breaks the force of cold winds, whose desiccating effect is often the chief reason that plants die in winter; and it provides some protection from frost. The material is certainly preferable to the cheaper clear polythene, for it does not promote humidity and the growth of fungal diseases. To provide protection for a group of plants, insert several free-standing canes and attach the mesh to them. Tender shrubs are often given a degree of protection by being grown against a wall. Provide additional shelter for these wall shrubs by nailing mesh to upright stakes, or by attaching it to the wall on both sides of the shrub.

An alternative is to use some form of home-made wire structure. Chicken wire is highly suitable, being relatively cheap, flexible, and capable of being cut to suit the size and shape of individual free-standing plants. If two concentric cylinders are made, one with a slightly wider diameter than the other, and placed round a plant that is not hardy, insulation material of one kind or another can be stuffed between them to provide protection.

Dried bracken is suitable for this, if available. Straw will provide a good substitute, otherwise newspaper, wood waste packaging, dried leaves, or even the trimmings from a Leyland cypress hedge should serve the same purpose.

Hardy plants which have frost-tender flowers early in the year, for example, wall-trained peach trees, can have their blossom protected by windbreak material that is carefully let down on a roll from the top of the wall at night.

Permanent plantings in free-standing containers are often damaged in the winter because the water in the compost freezes and expands. Some containers are themselves liable to be cracked or chipped during spells of frosty weather. However, it is possible to enclose tightly the whole container, including the lip, in polythene, with just a small opening at the top to allow water in. If this polythene surround is lined with insulating material, such as shredded newspaper, so much the better.

Many shrubs are sufficiently tender to lose their top growth in cold weather but, because soil is an insulator, their roots will survive the average winter. Their survival will be ensured if the soil around the plant is covered with 15cm/6in of coarse bark chippings in autumn. This also works for half-hardy perennials. Ashes, sometimes proposed as an alternative, are no longer easy to find. Peat is unacceptable: it does not insulate when wet, blows away when dry, and its use unnecessarily depletes peat-bogs. If you have nothing else available, heap earth around the plant.

Alpine plants resent winter wet far more than cold winds, so a cloche or piece of glass or clear polycarbonate placed over the plant and secured by bricks will help save a particular treasure. Simple plastic cloches will protect over-wintering vegetables, such as lettuce, or autumn-sown annuals.

STAKING PLANTS WITH BAMBOO CANES AND STRING

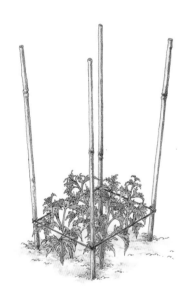 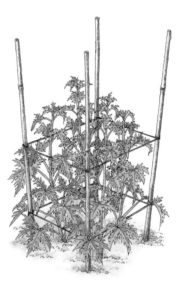 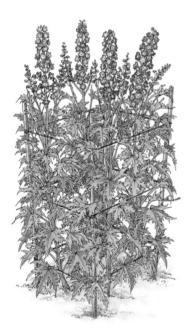

a In spring, push a number of canes into the ground around the plant or group of plants, close to the leaves. Tie string to one cane using a reef knot, then loop it round the others and tie it off.

b The careful gardener adds more string to support tall-growing plants progressively, always tying it around the canes at a level just below the top of the new growth.

c The last length of string should come just below the base of the flower spikes. By summer, the bamboo and string should be largely hidden by luxuriant foliage.

STAKING

However casual your approach to gardening techniques, you will need to provide support for a variety of plants: most particularly, climbing plants, especially twiners, and wall shrubs; thin-stemmed herbaceous perennials; and newly-planted trees.

In the past, gardeners have erred on the side of overstaking where young trees were concerned. The custom has been to use wooden stakes, as tall as the trees and painted with preservative, and to leave them in the ground until they eventually rotted. Tree experts, however, recommend that, if possible, a young tree should not be staked at all. If the tree is in an exposed position it will need a stake, but only a short one. The stake should come up no higher than one-third of the trunk's height, should be attached to the trunk with two proprietary tree ties, and should preferably be left in place for just two or three seasons. A tree that has had the opportunity to sway with the wind 'tapers' better, that is, the stem grows thicker at the bottom, and so is better able to withstand gales.

Herbaceous perennials are another matter. The appearance of the border is easily spoiled by too many tall plants flopping over the path, especially after rain. These days, traditional bamboo canes and string have in many gardens been superseded by linking metal stakes. These come in several heights, can be easily inserted as the plant is growing, and can be extended to accommodate broad clumps. An alternative is a circular metal frame, divided into segments, and standing on legs. Substantial twigs cut from deciduous trees and shrubs, called 'pea-sticks', the bases of which are pushed into the ground to create a kind of thicket, are an alternative. Whatever is used should be in place before flowering, and should never exceed in height the bottom of the flower spikes. The art is to stake effectively, without supports being visible once the border is in bloom.

It is possible to buy semi-circular metal hoops on legs to support arching shrub roses. However, for really vigorous plants, it may be better to make a simple structure out of four stout stakes, connected to each other by horizontal battens. The roses can grow up through such a structure, in a loose and naturalistic way but remain manageable.

Climbing plants, with the exception of the 'self-clingers', such as ivies and *Hydrangea anomala petiolaris*, will almost certainly need a support. Large gauge plastic mesh, sold for sweet peas and runner beans, is garish and fiddly: I prefer four 2.4m/8ft bamboo canes, put in the ground to form a wigwam, and tied at the top. More substantial trellis is necessary to support heavy and semi-rigid climbers such as rambling roses.

Plastic ties are available for tying many kinds of plants, but I favour strong garden twine. It is cheaper, can be cut easily at pruning time, is degradable and all but invisible.

A WIGWAM OF CANES

A simple wigwam of canes can be used as an effective support for climbers. As the plants grow upwards, some sort of tie will become necessary. Soft garden twine allows a certain amount of 'give' and should not slip.

Always push any support for the plants into the ground before planting them out; this is particularly important for sweet peas, which have long roots that can be damaged.

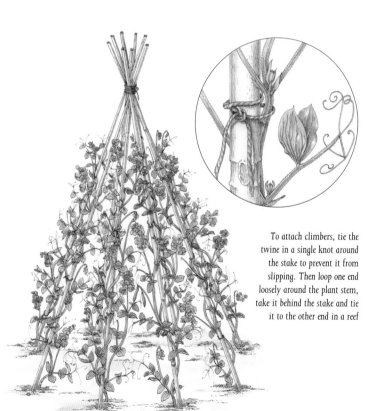

To attach climbers, tie the twine in a single knot around the stake to prevent it from slipping. Then loop one end loosely around the plant stem, take it behind the stake and tie it to the other end in a reef

STAKING A YOUNG TREE

If planted in an exposed position, a young tree needs a short stake to support it. To avoid damage to the roots, bang in the stake first. Stakes are only used to keep the roots firm until re-established, so remove the stake in the second spring after planting. The tie should be nailed close to the top of the stake to prevent slipping.

Gardening Techniques

UB Weeds are plants which grow where we do not want them. It is a sad fact of gardening life that weeds occupy as much, and sometimes even more, of our thoughts than the plants which they threaten. There are plenty of perfectly sensible reasons for minding about weeds, of course: many are ugly, and all are aggressive and get in our way. Their greatest disadvantage, however, is that they represent competition – for space, light, water and food – and that is inherently wasteful.

The reason that weeds do so well is because those which are native are suited to their environment, and those which are exotic have adapted all too well to the prevailing conditions, at the expense of other, more delicate plants. Indeed, many weeds do much better in the garden than outside because of the favourable conditions for growth which exist there.

The situation is complicated by the range of weeds and their adaptation to different circumstances. Some are annual, some perennial and, while some grow mainly in lawns, others prefer open borders, while yet more are to be found principally on paths, in vegetable patches, by water or in shady woodland.

On the face of it, perennial weeds seem the worst menace because their deeply penetrating and persistent root systems ensure that they come back to haunt us each year. Examples include bindweed, ground elder, couch grass, dandelion, and perennial nettle. Many, such as couch and bindweed, have the ability to regenerate from very small pieces of root.

However, annual weeds can also be very troublesome in some circumstances particularly if, like hairy bittercress and chickweed, they seed heavily or often. Groundsel will not only set seed after uprooting if it is already in flower but it can also produce several generations of plant from seed in one season

Nor should we forget the imported weed, the invasive garden plant which has been deliberately introduced and then later regretted because of its capacity to invade other plants' space. Examples include Japanese knotweed, Himalayan balsam, and the Peruvian lily (*Alstroemeria*).

Fortunately, not all weeds do well in all circumstances so the chances are that there are some very troublesome plants which you will never see in your garden. Dog's mercury, for example, can be very persistent but will only thrive in shade, and is most common in gardens on the edge of woodland.

It is as well to learn to know your adversary early on in your gardening career, even if you are determined not to become obsessed with weeds. Most likely to appear in most gardens are: (*annual*) shepherd's purse; hairy bittercress; goosegrass or cleavers; annual meadowgrass; groundsel; rosebay willowherb; nipplewort; black nightshade; chickweed; common speedwell; annual nettle; petty spurge; sowthistle; (*perennial*) ground elder; couch grass; creeping thistle; field bindweed; bryony; horsetail; white dead nettle; creeping buttercup; lesser celandine; oxalis; stinging nettle; plantain; broad-leaved dock, common ragwort; dandelion; slender speedwell; colt's foot; elder and brambles.

We now come to the question of what to do about them. Above all, it is important not to let them grow as rankly in your psyche as they do at the back of the bonfire heap. Weeds in your garden are not only inevitable but sometimes almost desirable, particularly if you are interested in providing food plants for butterfly larvae. There are even weeds, like dandelion leaves, which can be eaten.

WEEDKILLERS

That said, you will, from time to time, have to consider the use of chemical or mechanical means to eradicate or control weeds. Herbicides, as chemical weedkillers are called, are most usually watered on, although one or two are applied in granular form.

Herbicides can be divided into the following categories: contact, residual and translocated. They can be either total or selective. The contact herbicides, such as paraquat or glufosinate ammonium, kill all green leaves and stems, but are neutralized when they touch the soil; whereas a residual weedkiller, such as simazine, enters from the soil through the roots and can continue to affect plants over a long period.

Systemic, or translocated, weedkillers enter through leaves and are carried down to the roots. Their use as killers of perennial weeds is obvious but they must be given the chance to work by spraying when the leaf growth is strong. More than one application is necessary to extirpate stubborn perennials like nettles and docks. Glyphosate is a good example of an effective translocated weedkiller, without residual effect; however, more than one application may be necessary for stubborn or well-established weeds. It is, however, generally slower in taking effect than a contact herbicide.

Touchweeders or ready-to-use sprays containing glyphosate are helpful in controlling perennial weeds, such as bindweed, in permanent plantings.

Selective weedkillers kill only broad-leaved weeds and so are invaluable for lawns. They are sometimes called hormone weedkillers because they work by stimulating plant growth – lawn weeds often grow spectacularly before keeling over. Examples include MCPA and mecoprop. Lawn weedkillers can be delivered from a 'touchweeder' or ready-to-use spray.

These days, most gardeners are reasonably tolerant of lawn weeds, digging out plantains and daisies by hand, keeping others suppressed with close mowing. However, if clover becomes a problem, try 2-4-D and mecoprop, or a specific mosskiller based on chloroxuron, ferrous sulphate, or dichlorophen if moss is troublesome. Speedwell and mind-your-own-business can be invasive in lawns, and both are resistant to lawn weedkillers.

There is yet another kind of weedkiller, described by what it does rather than how it does it. This is the pre-emergent granular weedkiller which leaves established woody plants alone but creates a chemical cap on the soil to prevent weeds breaking through. The active ingredient is dichlobenil.

Paths may be tackled with a contact herbicide such as paraquat, and then dichlobenil to prevent further germination. An alternative is the translocated herbicide amitrole, combined with the residuals simazine or atrazine. No path weedkiller will remain effective for more than a season.

If you have a tree stump which you wish to kill, use granular ammonium sulphamate which is totally non-selective, so avoid the roots of other plants. However, in time it breaks down in the soil to harmless sulphate of ammonia. Woody weeds, such as brambles and elder, can also be tackled with ammonium sulphamate.

Of course, herbicides, like pesticides, are not sold by the name of the active ingredients. Therefore, it is important when buying any chemical to check carefully on the label that it can be used for the purpose that you require.

MECHANICAL SUPPRESSION

If, despite what I have written, you do not believe that chemical weedkillers are justified (particularly the persistent ones, such as simazine), you will have to consider other options. The first is to tell yourself that some weeds are inevitable so you must learn not to mind too much. The second is finding 'mechanical' and prophylactic means of suppressing and eradicating them.

Thick old carpet laid right-side down, woven polypropylene 'ground-cover' material, newspaper overlaid with bark or straw, or light-excluding black polythene laid undisturbed for at least two seasons, have a reasonable chance of starving out perennial weeds, however extensive their root systems. If these are covered with bark chippings, the effect can be quite ornamental. The problem is finding enough old carpet.

Despite what you may read, other mulches such as home-made compost or leafmould do not always suppress even annual weeds entirely, unless several centimetres thick, although the weeds are much easier to extract through a mulch than from naked, baked soil. Growing dense 'ground-cover' plants can be an effective alternative, provided that they themselves do not become weeds. Nor, contrary to popular mythology, is methodical, regular hoeing of the shoots of perennial weeds likely to weaken well established clumps enough to kill them. It is also very laborious and, in the case of a crowded border, difficult to carry out without damaging other plants. Carefully hand-digging and picking out will be more successful as it is in many other parts of the garden. If possible, hoe off or hand-pick annual weeds before they flower.

Taking care not to disturb soil unnecessarily is one way of stemming the annual weed populations for, in that way, long-lived weed seeds are not regularly being brought to the surface where they can germinate.

If perennial weeds have infested herbaceous plants, your best chance is to dig the plants up in spring or autumn, and remove every piece of weed root before replanting. This may mean dividing up your plants. This is laborious but can be successful. However, you will have to retain a watching brief.

For paths, an alternative non-chemical method is the flame gun, used several times in the season. But watch out for precious plants nearby, especially hedges and shrubs, because fire is as undiscerning as paraquat but less easy to control.

Although lawn weeds are most easily dealt with by specific lawn herbicides, isolated weeds can be removed by hand, if care is taken to remove the roots of perennial weeds. Moss can be temporarily controlled with chemical mosskillers but if the lawn is shaded, or the soil badly drained, it will always return.

1 The well maintained border will quickly become a glorious mass of intermingling plants, with little soil left bare for annual weeds to colonize. Perennial weeds can become a problem if left unchecked, so it is vital that these are assiduously cleared before planting, and a watchful eye kept on them. Gravel makes an excellent surfacing for paths in the informal garden, allowing border plants to seed and spread into it. Weeds can likewise, however, and may need to be cleared at least once a year by mechanical or chemical means.

PESTS, DISEASES AND DISORDERS

UB If you are a gardening beginner, you will be in a state of ignorant bliss (and I mean no disrespect), intent on growing beautiful flowers and creating a haven of peace and harmony, scarcely aware of the forces massed against you. This state does not last. Soon, pests and diseases will loom large – too large in fact – in your consciousness. Books will inform you, in even tones, of chafer grubs and rhynchites, oedema and magpie moth. It is only with experience that you begin to realize that, although you need to be aware of major pests and diseases, and there will be a few which will be a constant source of irritation, the importance of most of them is overstated.

What follows, therefore, is worth reading, and certainly worth referring to, from time to time, but should not cause loss of sleep. Even when you know about a problem, you do not necessarily have to do anything about it. Much of the damage done by pests and diseases in gardens is either tolerable or fundamentally irremediable. By the time you have seen the damage, it is often too late to do anything constructive about it.

What is more, even serious diseases are not found in all gardens. Club root, for example, thrives in acid soils, so there are millions of gardeners who have never, and never will, see the disastrous effect it has on brassicas.

Furthermore, some problems are only bad in certain years. Climatic conditions materially affect the incidence of well known problems such as potato blight, powdery mildew, thrips and red spider mite, so that there are seasons when they will not bother you at all. Nor should it be forgotten that some kinds of plants are more likely to incur problems than others. If you want a trouble-free garden, you should avoid those groups of plants that cause most trouble: brassicas, modern roses, chrysanthemums or greenhouse plants.

PREVENTION

As no doubt you are used to being told, prevention is better than cure. Prevention means being observant and looking out for trouble. Prevention also means good garden hygiene and practices. For example, many pests find shelter and sustenance amongst weeds and debris. Garden hygiene means clearing up leaves, prunings and dead wood, and weeding conscientiously. It is harder in the more natural garden, in vogue these days, and can sometimes have unsought consequences. For example, some weeds are the food plants for butterfly larvae. And some slugs, annoyingly, feed upon green shoots after, rather than instead of, decaying matter. Garden hygiene is, of course, an article of faith for organic gardeners, and is one of the mightiest weapons in their armoury, but no gardener can afford to ignore it.

Pests and diseases cause most problems with plants which are already under stress. Strong-growing plants can shrug off problems which prove fatal to weaklings. This is one of the main reasons why we feed and water our plants so assiduously, and why we must take particular care of seedlings.

Prevention also means the encouragement of natural predators to do the job of pest control for us, and here we have some useful allies. For example, it has been estimated that if a single blackfly and its offspring were allowed to reproduce unhindered for three months in the summer, they would produce 2,000,000,000,000,000 progeny and we would be knee-deep in them. However, their populations are kept down to more or less tolerable proportions by a variety of pest predators, the beneficial insects: hoverflies, ladybirds, lacewings, even wasps. Any assault against pests must, therefore, take this into account and be aimed specifically at discouraging the pests that cause serious damage while leaving the beneficial insects (and that includes wasps!) unscathed.

We can encourage these pest predators by providing food plants and shelter. Frogs and toads, for example, eat a wide range of flies, beetles, grubs and even slugs, so a small pond dug to foster frogs might be a good addition to the garden. Lacewing and hoverfly larvae, together with ladybirds (adults and larvae), live off aphids, so do not kill them with unspecific insecticides. Hoverflies can be encouraged by planting French marigolds, which they visit for nectar. Tiny parasitic wasps enjoy the flowers of fennel and the daisy family, and slug-eating ground beetles are grateful for the shelter which you can provide with mulches and thick planting. Centipedes eat pest grubs so think hard before applying a soil insecticide. Hedgehogs will eat slugs, so do not poison them accidentally. Always check bonfires before lighting them in case hedgehogs have hibernated within them.

Some birds, such as blue tits, blackbirds and thrushes, are predators of pests and should be encouraged with water, food in the winter, and nesting boxes.

Prevention can also mean providing mechanical barriers, traps and scaring devices. If these sorts of prevention fail to work, we can either spray with a chemical developed for the purpose, or limit or perhaps even eradicate potential damage using biological or mechanical means.

BIOLOGICAL CONTROL

Biological control describes keeping down pests by the introduction of natural enemies: predators, parasites and diseases.

Such controls are not enormously expensive but do require at least a rudimentary knowledge of insect life cycles, and of the conditions which suit particular predators. The specificity of biological control is immensely attractive to the gardener, and it is becoming more and more popular: there are now several different pest predators available (by mail order from specialist firms), to kill whitefly, red spider mite, leaf miner, mealybug, scale insect, thrips, and vine weevil in the greenhouse. There is also a bacterium which can be bought, with which to spray caterpillars. Some gardeners may find the requirement to keep the greenhouse above a certain temperature (especially in the case of the red spider mite predator) a difficulty; nevertheless, this kind of pest control, which is narrowly targeted, is obviously the way forward.

Scientists have also developed a number of synthetic sexual attractants (pheromones) specific to various pests, particularly moths. One, for example, is used to trap the males of the codling moth, a common pest of apples.

CHEMICAL WARFARE

In the end, despite good cultivation methods and the use of biological control and other measures, there comes a time when spraying with chemicals may be necessary.

As a general rule, you should spray for diseases just before experience suggests that you can expect trouble, and, in the case of pests, at the first sign of damage; early action may, if you are lucky, pre-empt the need for yet further spraying.

Pesticides either have a contact/ fumigant action (that is, they kill those pests immediately sprayed, with little or no residual effect), or they work through the plant's system, drawn up through the roots or taken in through the leaf pores. 'Systemic' insecticides of this kind are obviously suitable for killing sap-suckers but may be inappropriate for food crops. Read the information on the label, follow the instructions with great care, and never exceed the recommended dose.

Introducing alien chemicals into the garden's environment imposes a duty on us to take as much care as possible. In particular, any pesticide which is potentially harmful to bees and other beneficial insects should only be sprayed in the very late evening when they are no longer working the flowers.

Those who do not wish to have a shed full of rarely used chemicals may find the following shortlist helpful. All the names given are those of the active chemical ingredients of proprietary products, often sold in mixtures.

An all-in-one insecticide and fungicide (pirimicarb, bupirimate and triforine) which will not kill beneficial insects, is suitable for aphids, mildew and black spot on roses. Metaldehyde is a suitable slug-killer. Permethrin or pyrethrum can be used for a wide range of insect pests generally. For most fungal diseases use thiophanate-methyl. Perennial weeds can be eradicated with glyphosate, woody weeds with ammonium sulphamate, and path weeds, for a whole season, by a mixture of amitrole and atrazine (or simazine). Additionally, it may be wise to have a lawn mosskiller (chloroxuron, ferrous sulphate, or diclorophen), and a spot-application selective lawn weedkiller (2-4-D with mecoprop) at the ready.

Organic gardeners will want a supply of insecticidal soap, quassia, derris or pyrethrum and the fungicide sulphur, which are considered 'natural' products and are of short persistence. Aluminium sulphate is a remedy for slugs.

Pest and disease attack of any kind is debilitating to a plant. It is therefore no more than common sense to feed with a general fertilizer after an attack. Use a foliar feed if you suspect root damage, which will have made the uptake of nutrients from the soil difficult.

PESTS

Chief amongst ubiquitous pests in the garden are the **sap-suckers**. Their effects are always unwelcome and can be devastating. Sap-suckers are insects and mites which weaken plants by removing sap from them, thereby causing cells to collapse; this distorts the growth of leaves and stems, often yellows or blisters the leaves, and generally spoils their appearance. The best known sap-suckers (probably because the most visible) are aphids, of which there are several types, the most common being greenfly and blackfly. Capsid bugs, whitefly, mealybugs, scale insects, thrips, root aphids, and a variety of mites, including red spider mite and big bud mite, are also sap-suckers. Some, particularly aphids, can be blamed for spreading debilitating viruses in their saliva.

Aphids can be active at almost any time, both inside and outside. Control consists of encouraging beneficial insects and spraying with a contact insecticide such as pirimicarb, which does not harm lace-wings or ladybirds, or the systemics dimethoate or heptenophos. Most organic gardeners use insecticidal soap. In the greenhouse, a predatory midge called *Aphidoletes* will give useful control in summer.

Capsid bugs are elongated shield-shaped winged insects, active in spring and summer, which distort buds and make holes in new leaves. If this is a consistent problem, spray likely candidates with dimethoate or permethrin, although you may be unsuccessful, for capsid bugs are unpredictable in what and when they attack. Organic gardeners tolerate the damage or use derris.

Red spider mite is a tiny animal, difficult to see with the naked eye, which lurks on the underside of leaves and turns them yellow. In bad attacks, the mites spin webbing from leaf to leaf. Active all through the season, the mites thrive in hot dry conditions, particularly in the greenhouse. *Phytoseiulus persimilis* can be bought as a biological control for the greenhouse. Alternatively, keep the humidity high by regularly spraying plants with water and damping down the floors.

Outside, on fruit trees, red spider mite can be sprayed with pirimiphos-methyl or dimethoate but will probably need more than one application. Do not use a winter tar oil wash if you can avoid it because this kills natural predators. Organic gardeners use insecticidal soap.

Big bud mite affects blackcurrant bushes; small mites breed inside the buds, making these swell. This mite spreads 'reversion virus', which stunts the growth of leaves and cuts fruit yields. Pick off enlarged buds in autumn or winter, and burn them. If the infestation is bad, cut all stems back to ground level in autumn, or even replace.

Thrips, or thunderflies, are about 2mm/1/16in long and come in a variety of colours, although they are often black. They are especially numerous in the country in hot, dry summers. They suck sap from flowers and leaves, causing speckling. Outdoors the damage is usually

sustainable but in the greenhouse can be more serious. There, use insecticidal soap, derris, permethrin or pirimiphos-methyl smokes.

Root aphids attack the roots of lettuce and also some greenhouse plants, causing plants to wilt or even die. They are distinctive, because they are covered in a white 'flour'. If you do not wish to drench the soil with malathion, grow resistant varieties of lettuce such as 'Avoncrisp' or 'Avondefiance'.

In the greenhouse, the worst sap-sucking villain is the **whitefly**. It has an easily recognizable triangular shape and floury appearance, and multiplies quickly at high temperatures. It attacks myriad soft-tissued plants, particularly fuchsias and tomatoes. A parasitic wasp called *Encarsia formosa* is a well established means of biological control. Alternatively, yellow sticky traps are quite effective, although you will catch other insects as well. A small hand-held vacuum cleaner will suck them up, if they are disturbed and flying. Otherwise, spray greenhouse plants with dimethoate/permethrin regularly in summer, or use permethrin insecticidal smokes. As with red spider mite, pesticide resistance is a frequent problem with this pest.

Outside, whitefly attack brassicas, settling underneath where they are difficult to spray. Dimethoate/permethrin is worth trying, provided the undersides of the leaves are well drenched, but success may be limited. Organic gardeners spray with insecticidal soap, or pick off the lower leaves where the larvae are usually to be found.

Less horrid than sap-suckers, but nevertheless disagreeable, are the **maggots** and **caterpillars** – the larvae of a variety of flies, moths, butterflies and sawflies. These chew or tunnel through soft plant tissue. One of the most serious of these is the **carrot** fly larva, which spoils carrots by burrowing into the roots, turning the foliage bronze and rendering the roots useless. Although these pests can be stopped with chlorpyrifos and diazinon put in the seed drill, the more ecologically sound remedy is to erect a polythene barrier, at least 50cm/20in high, so that the adults, who can smell carrot foliage from several metres away, do not lay their eggs by the young carrots. An alternative is to place polypropylene fleece over the young foliage, which allows sunlight and rain through, but not flies.

Onion flies are also attracted to their hosts by scent. The grubs tunnel into onion bulbs, which often collapse and have to be pulled up and burned. Onion fly is less of a problem if onion sets rather than seed are grown, because there is no need to thin onion sets and so release the scent which attracts the adults. The chemical solution is chlorpyrifos and diazinon applied at planting time.

Cabbage root fly lays its eggs by seedling cabbages. Protective barriers (called 'brassica collars') placed on the soil round the stems prevent the maggots attacking the roots and causing plants to collapse.

Leaf miner grubs make tunnels in the leaves of many types of plant, most seriously chrysanthemums. Some damage is tolerable; unacceptable injury can be prevented by spraying with malathion or picking off the affected leaves. There are parasitic wasps available for control in the greenhouse.

The damage caused by **apple sawfly** and **codling moth** is often confused. They both tunnel into apples, and scar them on the outside. However, the sawfly grub gets to work straight after petal fall, whereas the codling moth is active in high and late summer. Both will

succumb to permethrin or fenitrothion sprayed at petal fall for sawfly, and in early and midsummer for codling moth.

Codling moth can also be trapped by special pheromone traps. These are corrugated plastic tents, with sticky floors, hung from fruit trees, which give off a synthetic pheromone (sexual attractant) similar to that which the female codling moth emits. Males are caught, and so eggs laid by the females may remain unfertilized. For organic gardeners, these traps are a way of controlling infestations.

Other **caterpillars**, in several shapes and sizes, do damage by chewing holes in leaves. They are particularly troublesome on fruit bushes and brassicas – or, rather, that is where their damage matters most. Cabbage white caterpillars are well known, even to non-gardeners, but there are others such as winter moth caterpillars which do damage to fruit trees. Damage on ornamentals can often be tolerated. If not, pick the caterpillars off by hand or spray with permethrin or *Bacillus thuringiensis*, a bacterium which only harms caterpillars. Adult female winter moths can be trapped with greasebands or sticky grease when they climb up the trunks of fruit trees in late autumn to winter.

Earwigs, whose distinctive looks even non-gardeners know, do damage to flower petals in summer and autumn. They are a particular nuisance to dahlia and chrysanthemum growers. They find shelter amongst garden rubbish so good hygiene helps keep numbers down. They can also be trapped by the traditional upturned pot full of straw, set on top of a 1m/3ft bamboo cane. Remember that this method only traps them; you will have the burden of killing them or, more humanely, removing them elsewhere.

Wasps can be a tremendous bore in high summer around fruit trees, damaging the skins, eating the flesh, and stinging fruit gatherers. Jam-jars full of a sugar solution and hung on trees will trap many but it should not be forgotten that earlier in the season wasps are a scourge of another pest, aphids.

There are a number of pests which are related only by their habitat, the soil, and the fact that they are all slow-moving. Some, such as slugs and snails, are as bad pests as any gardeners are likely to encounter, whereas others, such as wireworm, are only a real problem in new gardens.

Wireworm is a generic term for the larvae of click beetles. They are about 2.5cm/1in long, and yellow-brown in colour. They feed on roots, tubers and bulbs, and they are especially partial to potatoes in late summer. Digging the soil helps, as this brings the larvae to the surface for hungry birds to eat. Other measures include sensible crop rotation and harvesting potatoes by early autumn (this also limits slug damage). Chlorpyrifos and diazinon will kill the larvae in seed beds.

Leatherjackets, the larvae of the crane fly ('daddy-long-legs'), are also troublesome in new gardens and in lawns. They have unattractive, fat, grey-brown, leathery bodies, up to 3.5cm/1½in long. Indeed, nothing could resemble less the fragile, long-legged crane fly. They cause yellow patches in the grass and will come to the surface in warm wet weather, and eat plant stems and seedlings. Keeping the lawn well spiked (therefore drained) helps, as does weeding the vegetable plot. Treat lawns with carbaryl in the autumn.

The counterpart to the leatherjacket on dry, sandy soils is the **chafer grub**. The chafer grub has a

distinctive, fat, creamy-white body, in the shape of a 'C', with a brown head, and it eats the roots of many plants. Cultivation, and hand-picking, are helpful, with chlorpyrifos and diazinon as a last resort.

More serious are **vine weevils**, particularly in greenhouses. These are smaller than chafer grubs, and uncurved. The larvae burrow through the contents of pots and into bulbs, and the adults (small and black) chew the edges of leaves. Vine weevils are very partial to cyclamen and tuberous begonias inside, and strawberries and alpines outdoors. There is now a parasitic eelworm available, called *Heterorhabditis*, which can be put in the potting compost in summer; the alternative is pirimiphos-methyl or HCH in dust form, which is mixed into the compost. Any grubs found in pots, when you are repotting, should be destroyed.

Cutworms are other soil pests which may cause problems by cutting through plant stems at ground level. They are the larvae of several moths. They are fat and fleshy and up to 5cm/2in long. Like chafer grubs, they like dry weather and light soils. Birds enjoy them, so bring them up to the surface by digging. Otherwise use chlorpyrifos and diazinon when transplanting seedlings.

Far, far worse than these, however, in the eyes of gardeners at least, are **slugs and snails**. Not all species are villains, indeed some feed largely on dead or dying vegetation, but it is true to say that the most common garden species are the most harmful. The problem is that no soft green plant tissue is really safe from them in springtime, especially if the conditions are wet, and bulbs, alpines, delphiniums, hostas and lettuce are especially delectable to them. Many species live underground or in wall crevices and come out to feed at night. Their voracious appetites, the fact that they are so good at hiding under debris, in containers and on garden plants, and their ability to climb, makes them serious pests in many, though not all, gardens.

It is possible to expose slug and snail eggs to the birds in midwinter by digging, but they are so ubiquitous that it seems wiser simply to protect vulnerable plants. This can be done in a number of ways. Organic gardeners favour taking out a torch at night and hunting for the creatures but this is rather time-consuming and necessitates stamping on them or drowning them in salty water once they are caught. Older gardeners seem to favour beer in margarine cartons, which is not only unglamorous but kills other creatures too, some of which, like ground beetles, eat slugs. Laying crushed eggshells, grit, wood or coal ash around vulnerable plants are other remedies which take advantage of the molluscs' need to slide smoothly over the ground on a trail of slime. Bark chippings and cocoa shell mulches are also off-putting to the slug and snail. Much advocated are plastic barriers, for example, cut-down lemonade bottles, pressed into the soil round plants such as lettuces or alpines. This is a desperate remedy, for, though effective, the bottles look awful so their use must be restricted to the vegetable garden. No two gardeners will agree on the relative merits of these remedies but all are worth a try, at least once.

Slug pellets, containing methiocarb or metaldehyde, kill by dehydrating the slug but they are potentially harmful if eaten by other animals or children so should be used with care and scattered *very* sparingly. Renew them after rain. Better still, cover securely with an upturned pot or curved tile. Mulches foster slugs because they give protection from, for example, birds, but on the other hand they do provide cover for slug pellets and slug predators. Aluminium sulphate will kill slugs by contact and is harmless to humans, pets and wild creatures.

There are ranges of plants which are mainly left untouched by slugs, and any of these are worth growing. For example, spiny or prickly plants like acanthus and eryngium are unpopular with them, as are most herbs, and plants with rough or glossy leaves. Lastly, encourage natural slug predators, such as birds, hedgehogs and frogs.

Garden plants are sometimes at the mercy of a variety of **large animals**, ranging from domestic pets to deer and rabbits. Most dogs can be trained not to wander on the flower beds, or dig holes, but cats need to be deterred with netting from digging up or lying on seedbeds. Nonylmethyl-keytone, which comes in strong-smelling, jelly-like crystals, will help deter both cats and dogs, if applied regularly, until the animals learn to avoid it.

The only really efficient way to keep out **rabbits**, which eat a variety of plants and 'bark' young trees, is to fence your garden with wire mesh with holes less than 5cm/2in in diameter, buried in the ground to a depth of at least 30cm/12in. PVC flexible tubing, such as is used by farmers for new hedgerows and foresters for planting young trees, will protect young trees from rabbits. **Deer** are only a local problem but seriously troublesome where they do occur, being very partial to roses and the bark of young trees. Deer fences, at least 2m/6ft high, are the only sure deterrent.

Squirrels can also be troublesome, often in town gardens on the edge of green spaces, where they steal nuts and fruits, and dig up bulbs. Netting of bulbs, fruit bushes and trees will help; otherwise you may have to resort to humane traps which can catch these agile and clever creatures alive. There is the obligation, however, of finding somewhere suitable to set them free.

Moles can damage lawns by pushing up molehills; they also like freshly worked soil, such as that in the vegetable garden. The most effective and humane way of ridding yourself of them, temporarily at least, is to use a device which sends high-frequency soundwaves along the underground tunnels. This device is expensive so is only justified when there is major and permanent infestation of lawns. The alternatives are smokes and traps, both of which are drastic and unpalatable solutions.

Birds of various kinds do damage. Pigeons eat brassicas, bullfinches eat fruit and ornamental shrub buds, and smaller birds like sparrows peck the petals off crocuses, polyanthus and wisteria. Netting, especially if laid over a metal or wooden structure to form a fruit cage, is the most effective deterrent. 'Scaraweb', a biodegradable cord made up of fibres of ultrafine rayon, can be put over small fruit trees and bushes, wall fruit and spring-flowering shrubs, such as forsythia. Humming wire strung between two posts is helpful in the kitchen garden. Black cotton strung between small pegs over low-growing plants will discourage birds from landing to peck crocuses. Bird repellants can be used but must be reapplied after rain.

Finally, **mice** often steal bulbs, as well as pea and bean seeds. It is possible to put down animal repellants, baits or set traps; the latter must be set in a place where birds and pets cannot find them.

DISEASES

Diseases are normally classified into three main groups: fungi, bacteria, and viruses. All groups give trouble from time to time but it is very unlikely that the average gardener will see even a majority of the afflictions listed below in the course of a lifetime. The odds are lengthened if the garden is kept clean of dead leaves, wood and weeds, although there are some diseases whose success is strongly influenced by weather, making other control measures sometimes unavoidable. There is only a limited range of fungicides available to the amateur and it is worth remembering that resistant strains of diseases can evolve, so it is best to use one for a single season, and then change to another which is unrelated chemically.

FUNGAL DISEASES

Of all fungal diseases, the most important, because they have so many hosts, are honey fungus, powdery mildews and grey mould. Control these and you have controlled much of the disease in the garden. Also widespread and sometimes serious is potato blight. There are also a variety of leaf spots, rusts and scabs.

Honey fungus attacks many types of plants, particularly trees and shrubs. It is properly called *Armillaria*, and colloquially the 'bootlace fungus', because it spreads by black, stringy fungal strands. Other signs include white mycelium at the base of the trunk or stem, under the bark and, sometimes, honey-coloured toadstools in autumn. There are plants with some resistance to it, such as beech, holly, yew and clematis, but the best defence against honey fungus is to grow plants well. Old and sickly trees and shrubs are more vulnerable than vigorous young plants.

If you diagnose a plainly dying tree as suffering from honey fungus, have it cut down, and the stump dug up and burned if possible. Dead wood in the soil acts as a food source to prevent this fungus dying out; that is why it is such a problem in old-established gardens. When replanting in an area you suspect of harbouring the fungus, remove as much old root and woody debris as you can, and make sure that you replace the soil to a depth of 60cm/2ft where any plant is to go.

Powdery mildews of different kinds attack a variety of plants, such as roses, Michaelmas daisies, gooseberries, apples, brassicas and strawberries. Showing as a white powder over buds and leaves, they sap a plant's vigour. They are worst in hot, dry summers and where the circulation of air is bad, which is why climbers on warm walls are particularly prone to attack.

Resistance to mildew has been bred into some roses and gooseberries; catalogues refer to the best varieties. Do not grow rambler roses on warm walls (they are not easy to manage against walls, anyway) and spray with propiconazole or carbendazim or, if you garden organically, sulphur, although this can defoliate some cultivars of gooseberry.

Downy mildews are not closely related to powdery mildews, as you might think, and are less serious. They do, however, attack lettuces and onions, for example, in wet seasons. The leaves become yellow on the top, white and furry underneath. Control is best achieved using mancozeb and taking care not to overwater. There are some resistant lettuce cultivars like 'Avondefiance'.

Grey mould (*Botrytis*) appears in autumn and winter in greenhouses as a fluffy grey fungus, sometimes with black spots in it. It attacks a wide range of plants, particularly in damp conditions, both inside and out. Cleaning off dead or dying leaves, flowers, stems and fruits limits its spread, because these act as initial hosts. Spraying with carbendazim or other systemic fungicide, airing the greenhouse well in winter (on sunny days), and being careful not to splash water about in damp weather, all help to keep *Botrytis* within bounds. Some strawberries, such as 'Pandora', have resistance.

Sooty mould is the name given to the fungus which forms on leaves which are covered with sticky excretions from aphids and scale insects. It is washed off by heavy rain so is only a problem in greenhouses and houses, where it looks unsightly and can also undermine healthy growth. The obvious answer, where practicable, is to control the pests that are the indirect cause.

Damping-off is most often seen in seed pots where seedlings are growing too close together, and in damp weather. It is worst in unhygienic conditions so clean up the greenhouse, water sparingly and carefully, use seed composts which drain quickly, and sow thinly.

Potato blight attacks both the potato and the closely related tomato and is most likely to attack in wet summers. Potato leaves become blotched and sometimes a white mould forms on their undersides, before the leaves collapse altogether. Tomato fruits rot. The organic gardener sprays with Bordeaux mixture (copper sulphate and slaked lime), and everyone else with mancozeb, at intervals between early summer to early autumn.

Leaf spots are usually more unsightly than serious. An example is chocolate spot of broad beans. The exception is **rose black spot** which can defoliate bushes and needs to be tackled with propiconazole or triforine with bupirimate or other systemic fungicides. Some varieties are more-or-less resistant. Other leaf spots need no action, except perhaps the removal of affected leaves.

Rusts soon make themselves known, and are common diseases of hollyhocks, hypericum, pelargoniums, antirrhinums, mints and roses. The rusts are composed of small brown, yellow or orange pustules which cover leaves, which then die off. Spray with propiconazole (myclobutanil for roses) or, possibly, sulphur, and burn affected leaves. Edible mints are best cut back and allowed to regrow.

Scabs show themselves by the presence of corky scars or lesions. Apples, pears, pyracantha and potatoes can be affected. Potato scab (which also shows up on beetroot) is most common on light, alkaline soils which are short of organic matter. If that fault is corrected nothing more need be done. The apples 'Lord Derby' and 'Discovery', the pears 'Conference' and 'Dr Jules Guyot' have some resistance. The leaves of affected apples and pears should be picked off, where possible, and the fallen leaves swept up.

Coral spot is widespread on trees and shrubs, its distinctive raised orange pustules appearing on wood at any time of year. This is a disease which has lately become more aggressive. No longer confined mainly to dead wood, it now also colonizes and kills live wood. Affected wood has to be cut out; if it is left, the whole shrub will eventually be killed.

A serious disease of plum trees (and sometimes of other *Prunus*, such as ornamental and fruiting cherries, and several other types of ornamentals) is **silver leaf**, showing itself, not surprisingly, as a silvering on the upper surface of the leaves. If you cut off an affected branch, the inside will be stained brown. The remedy is to prune the tree in dry weather in early summer, for the spores can enter even tiny wounds in damp conditions at other seasons. Remove dead twigs and branches punctiliously as it is on these that the fungus fructifies. If treatment does not do the trick, have the tree cut down and the wood burned.

Peach leaf curl produces depressing red blistering on peach, nectarine and almond leaves, which fall prematurely, causing stunted growth. Pick off affected leaves, spray with mancozeb or copper fungicide at leaf fall and again in late winter. Wall-trained fruit can be protected in winter by a simple wooden frame attached to the wall, on which is tacked polythene sheeting. This will keep the trees dry and substantially lessen the risk of the fungal spores reaching the plant.

Wilt is an alarming condition because it appears to attack a plant suddenly and dramatically. A clematis, for example, will swiftly collapse. Other affected plants include michaelmas daisies and peonies. All wilted shoots should be cut out. Do not plant vulnerable plants in infected ground. In the case of clematis to be planted in a garden known to harbour the fungus, plant specimens 15cm/6in deeper than you otherwise would; that way, if they do become affected, there is a good chance that new shoots will emerge. Spray them with benomyl. Feeding and watering after an attack helps regeneration.

Apple and pear **canker** manifests itself as round, sunken patches on the branches, which gradually encircle them. If that happens, the branch will be killed. The remedy is to cut back the branch beyond the canker to healthy wood and spray with Bordeaux mixture after the fruit is picked in autumn. Parsnip canker looks like a browny-orange rot on the shoulders of the root. Grow resistant varieties, such as 'Avonresister', and lime the soil if the pH is below 6.5.

Club root is a devastating disease of brassicas and wallflowers – but only on acid soils. The roots swell to form nodules and then rot. The disease can stay in the ground for as long as 20 years. Effective crop rotation is difficult in anything but large gardens, so lime the soil in winter, dip all transplants in a thiophanate-methyl solution and burn any affected plants immediately.

Rots are usually caused by fungi or bacteria. The symptoms are decay of plant tissues. The most commonly seen is brown rot of apples, which can be controlled although never eliminated, by punctiliously removing affected fruit in store, picking rotted fruits that hang on the trees and burning them, and keeping the ground clear of weeds and debris round the tree.

Onion white rot can be serious. It manifests itself as fluffy white mould around the roots. Although, traditionally, onions are often grown for years on end in the same bed, this facilitates the build-up of this pernicious disease. Sensible crop rotation is necessary, therefore, as is burning affected bulbs, and not overfeeding the soil with nitrogenous fertilizers which promote soft, lush growth.

BACTERIAL DISEASES
Bacteria cause a number of diseases, some of little consequence but others very serious. One of the most dangerous is probably **fireblight**. This can affect members of the rose family such as apples, pears, cotoneasters, hawthorns and pyracanthas. The first sign of it is the browning and withering of leaves,

which do not fall. It looks just as if a bonfire had been lit too close to the plant, hence the name. All affected branches should be removed to 60cm/24in beyond the point where the reddish internal staining ends, and burned. This is a widespread disease on the continent and is now well established in southern England.

Bacterial canker is a serious disease usually seen on plum and cherry trees. The leaves develop spots, then shot-holes, and lesions form on the bark and exude a sticky gum. The affected branches have to be cut off. Spraying is difficult but copper fungicide administered three times in late summer and early autumn may help.

VIRUSES
More and more common these days are the plant viruses, for which, like human viruses, there is usually no cure. They range, also like human viruses, from the symptomless to the devastating. They are spread on tools, hands, and on the saliva of various sap-sucking pests, aphids being among the most troublesome.

The presence of viruses can cause a variety of unwanted conditions in plants. They include: stony pit of pears; striping in narcissus leaves; 'reversion' in blackcurrant leaves; distortion of many types of flower; and yellow mottling of cucumber and tomato leaves.

As good luck would have it, viruses usually lag a cell or two behind the growing tips of plants, so virus-free stock, particularly of fruit bushes, can be bought, which has been propagated from these growing tips. These plants may be more expensive to buy but they are more vigorous and fruitful, and well worth any extra money. Plants badly infected by virus should be burned and replacements planted elsewhere in the garden.

PHYSIOLOGICAL DISORDERS
We are inclined to forget that plants can also suffer from physiological disorders, and often mistake frost or heat damage for disease, wasting valuable time in the process. The worst disorders are caused by poor light, waterlogging, irregular watering and nutrient deficiencies. Moreover, any one of these stresses will promote the establishment and spread of pest and disease damage, which is a very good reason, if any more were needed, for trying to give plants the growing conditions which suit them.

Poor light is particularly a problem in greenhouses in winter and early spring, causing leaves to yellow and plants to become weak and drawn. This is why the glass should be cleaned off well, particularly if it has been painted with shading in the summer. Seed should not be sown too early. Pots of seedlings on windowsills need turning through 90 degrees every few days so that the plants do not become 'drawn'.

Too low humidity is a common problem in greenhouses in summer, promoting poor growth, browning of leaves, and bud-drop on semi-tropical plants. It also encourages the red spider mite. However, **too high humidity** can also cause trouble, encouraging the development of raised scaly patches on leaves known as oedema, as well as diseases such as blight on tomatoes and grey mould in autumn. These symptoms may also be seen outside.

Drought shows up as wilting which can cause permanent damage or even death, and it can also lead to starvation because nutrients are absorbed in soil water. Drought causes scorching and browning of leaves, with premature leaf and fruit fall. Plants respond favourably to a continuous, reasonable

supply of fresh water. **Irregular watering** – be it natural or man-made – leads to cracking and splitting in root vegetables and fruits, flowers which do not 'set', shooting up to premature flower ('bolting'), and fruit drop. Within the confines of the greenhouse, and even the vegetable garden, it is possible to control this by watering. But water is a precious commodity which should not be squandered, and it is far better to mulch borders adequately in spring than sprinkle wastefully with water in summer.

Of course, the converse – **waterlogging** – is also undesirable because plant roots become asphyxiated in waterlogged soil, and may die. Waterlogging also slows down the process of soil warming in spring and as a consequence plants may be slow to make strong growth.

Low temperatures in spring can cause tomato plants to curl their leaves, and seedlings to be checked, often acquiring a silvery sheen on the leaves. Even worse is a **frost** at the wrong moment: it can do more damage than a plague of aphids. Harmful late frosts not only kill fruit blossom, often wiping out fruit harvests as a result, but also crack bark and twist leaves in the bud. The answer is to grow only late-flowering fruit varieties and hardy plants if you garden in a cold district, on high ground, or in a frost pocket. Measures that are worth taking in many gardens include: putting polypropylene fleece or cloches over low-growing, tender plants, such as potatoes; throwing windbreak netting temporarily over small trees and wall shrubs; and keeping winter protection materials on plants until the danger of frost is past.

The reverse – **too high temperatures** – can slow or stop growth altogether, particularly in greenhouses, and cause scorching of leaves and flowers. Adequate ventilation helps considerably; automatic vents are a boon to all gardeners, not just to those who are away from home all day. Damping down the floor of a greenhouse or conservatory with water on hot days temporarily lowers the temperature as well as increases humidity, which is helpful in itself and slows the evaporation of water from pot composts.

Strong winds can be harmful, particularly in winter and early spring; not only can they blow trees over but they desiccate plants, browning the evergreen leaves of conifers and killing more tender plants which have come through frosts intact. Physical protection is the answer.

Although **snow** can protect plants by insulating like a blanket when it comes before hard frosts, it will also damage evergreens if it lies heavy and frozen on the branches. The answer to this is to beat or shake the snow off the branches before it has the chance to freeze.

NUTRIENT DEFICIENCIES

Nutrient deficiencies are hard to avoid completely, because they arise on a variety of different soil types, but if the problem has been properly analysed it is possible to help considerably.

Nitrogen deficiency shows up as a yellowing or reddening of the leaves, particularly in springtime. Growth is stunted. It is most likely to be seen on plants which are mainly leaf, such as cabbages and grass, and is very common.

Lack of necessary **phosphates** leads to poor growth, and leaves which turn a dull green with purple tints. Sometimes the leaf margins become slightly scorched. Phosphates are most likely to be missing on clay soils, and in areas where there is a particularly high rainfall.

Potash deficiency leads to small fruits and leaves, with the latter showing scorched margins, which fall early. Lack of potash also undermines the frost-hardiness of plants. It is most likely to occur on light soils.

Calcium is only deficient on very acid soils: it shows up as curled leaf tips of, for example, Brussels sprouts. Bitter pit of apples is due to a deficiency of calcium within the fruit but it can occur where there is enough calcium in the soil but it is unavailable to the plant.

Sulphur deficiency has not been very common in the past because it is a constituent of the traditional compound fertilizers and is also an element of industrial air pollution. However, with cleaner air and a wider range of fertilizers available, it can occur – as yellow leaves and woody, thin growth.

Lack of **magnesium** is much more of a problem, manifesting itself as yellow patches between green veins on leaves, bringing the veins into relief like a green fishbone. It happens particularly to the older leaves and is most likely on soils that are acidic, after rain, and if there is a lot of potash in the soil.

Iron is made unavailable to plants ('locked up') by calcium, and so iron deficiency is most likely to occur on alkaline soils, manifesting itself as yellowing of young leaves. It often occurs in conjunction with **manganese** deficiency, which shows itself in the same way as a lack of magnesium.

Trace elements are needed in such small amounts that they are rarely deficient if organic matter is dug in regularly.

CHEMICAL AND MECHANICAL INJURY

Of all physiological disorders the most avoidable are those caused by human agency: chemical and mechanical injury. The first refers to the abuse of chemicals. **Chemical damage** can occur if a bottle of hormone lawn weedkiller is put in the greenhouse, where the vapours will affect the growth of sensitive plants like tomatoes, or if grass clippings from weedkilled lawns are spread on the compost heap. It can also arise from using the wrong chemicals for the wrong problem or the wrong plant. So-called 'phytotoxic' chemicals affect sensitive plants such as members of the cucumber family, for example, which are very sensitive about what is sprayed over them; plenty of plants are killed by the use of unselective weedkillers, carelessly applied. So-called spray-drift is a common problem, the result of spraying on windy days. Spilling petrol or oil on the lawn when filling the lawnmower will kill the grass underneath.

Mechanical damage covers a multitude of sins. One of the most common forms is the 'barking' of trees by lawnmowers. If this is a recurrent problem, the best course may be to alter the shape of the lawn or to have longer grass close to the base of trees. The strangulation by ties of the trunks of staked trees and the branches of trained shrubs and climbers can be avoided by periodic checks, when tight ties can be loosened. Many plants suffer their worst damage during pruning. Ragged saw cuts and badly placed cuts can provide entry points for disease that may threaten the plant's life. Pruning of certain trees in spring may lead to bleeding, with subsequent weakening. Most injuries are easily avoided or rectified, but many happen to the most assiduous of gardeners. Keeping a watchful eye as you walk around your garden will ensure that no plant injury is sustained for too long, and that your garden remains beautiful and productive.

SAFETY AND EQUIPMENT

UB The garden can be a dangerous place, particularly for the unwary, but there are many ways of making it safer.

Before you move to a new garden, check it over for potential hazards, especially if you have children: ponds, rickety paths, broken fencing or gates on to a road, dangerous rubbish, disused buildings, poisonous plants and possibly unsafe trees. You may well have to take immediate action: fencing off or filling in a pond; calling in a builder or landscape contractor to clear rubbish or sort out problems in the 'hard landscaping'; repairing fences; removing plants which might be a hazard to yourself or to children; calling in a trained arboriculturist to check the trees.

When you buy equipment, fertilizers or pesticides (even 'organic' ones) to be used in the garden, take care always to read, follow and retain the manufacturers' safety instructions concerning dosage, storage, protective clothing and accidents.

Only use pesticides or herbicides for the purpose specified on the label. They will have been approved under the Pesticide Regulations for this use alone and it is illegal to use them for any other purpose.

Store concentrates safely, tightly closed, in a locked cupboard in a frost-free place. Lids are now usually, though not invariably, childproof. Do not keep chemicals for more than two years, and throw away anything that has an indecipherable label or which is no longer an 'approved' product; never decant chemicals into unmarked containers; do not ask for, or accept, agricultural chemicals. Keep children and pets away from concentrates; should they eat or drink any, take them immediately to the doctor or vet, showing them the container from which the concentrate came.

Dispose of all unwanted chemicals safely. Current recommendations are: clean out sprayers and other receptacles in plenty of running water from an outside tap before and after use; get rid of any excess mixture down the drain or into a hole dug in the garden, and never pour it away into or near fishponds or streams. If you wish to dispose of a concentrate, hand it in to the office of your local waste disposal site.

Always wear gloves when handling concentrates; do not make up more than you anticipate needing; never exceed the recommended dose; stick to the correct dilution; keep a separate sprayer or watering can for weedkillers. Use a face mask to prevent inhaling spray, and wash any exposed skin well after spraying. If you should get any concentrate in the eye or on the skin, use plenty of clean water to wash it out or off, and consult your doctor immediately, remembering to tell him or her what the chemical was.

When spraying, take care to avoid spray drift, especially on to edible crops, and keep pets and children away until the chemicals have dried. Protect wildlife: spray insecticides only in the late evening when the bees are no longer active, and remember that fish are very sensitive to pesticides. Try not to spray in strong sunshine, as damage to foliage can occur. If using an aerosol, pay particular attention to the instructions about spraying distance; it is not desirable to give the plants a complete wetting.

When gardening, wear protective clothing as appropriate: ear-defenders when using rotary lawn mowers, hedgetrimmers and compost shredders, indeed any noisy machinery; goggles when using strimmers, shredders, hedgetrimmers and when pruning generally; gloves when handling manures and fertilizers and when pruning roses; gloves and mouth mask when spraying; strong boots or shoes when digging or when using powered machinery, especially on rough ground.

Much trouble can also be avoided by common sense and a ready understanding of the potential dangers, even of innocent-seeming gardening activities:

always reading, and retaining, manufacturers' instructions before using any power tool; checking machinery, hired or owned, carefully for defects before use; not using electrical equipment in wet conditions; putting a residual current device in the electric socket when using a power cable to reduce the risk of electrocution if the cable is cut; always disconnecting the power supply and turning off the engine before cleaning, inspecting, dismantling or servicing an electrical or mechanized tool; locking away equipment and chemicals; taking particular care when using a sharp knife, secateurs, or saw; not leaving tools around to be tripped over; avoiding eye injuries by putting guards on the tops of bamboo canes; and always being aware of just where your young children are, especially when you are lighting bonfires or using machinery of any kind.

Any and every tool can be dangerous if proper care is not taken, but problems can be most anticipated with chainsaws, flame-guns, lawn mowers, hedge-trimmers and shredders. It is possible today to find machines with lock-off switches and 'dead man's' handles; these models should be sought out. Rotary mowers with plastic cutting blades do less damage to flesh and bone than those with metal blades; alternatively, you can buy 'safety-blades' to fit to conventional small hover and rotary mowers.

Frequent servicing of power tools also minimizes the dangers posed by unsafe machinery. Take care when hiring these tools to check their condition. As a consumer, you should put safety at the top of the list of desirable features, above cost, when buying machinery.

Think hard before installing water for ornamental purposes, or before planting poisonous plants (it is not only children who can suffer after handling toxic plants). Protect small children from water with fencing or netting, and discourage them from eating anything in the garden except under supervision.

EQUIPMENT

Equipment divides into two sections: tools and machinery. Of these, by far the most important are tools, because every gardener must have forks and spades, trowels and secateurs, whereas all of us could, by dint of hard work, get by without any mechanized equipment. Whatever you buy, see that it is both comfortable to use and suitable for the job. Maintaining all tools (and machinery) punctiliously makes obvious sense.

There is an almost unlimited variety of tools but you will probably only need at the most about twenty basic items, and not all at once. One option is to buy a range of tool heads that all fit on to the same handle.

Stainless steel tools are a pleasure to use, do the job efficiently, and require barely any cleaning. Carbon steel tools are usually much cheaper and do a serviceable job, but need cleaning, oiling and, in the case of spades, periodic gentle sharpening. Coated or 'non-stick' tools also need little cleaning but the coating can peel off in time.

You will need a large garden fork and spade (a specially adapted one with a lever to move the blade if you have back trouble). Look for tools that you can use without excessive bending. Tall people usually find the standard shaft of tools too short. You will also need a smaller border fork and hand trowel and fork; a long-handled hand fork will enable you to weed without bending.

A Dutch hoe (or onion hoe if you grow your vegetables in 'deep beds') is fine for the kitchen garden, but not for crowded flower borders. A draw hoe is the best for making seed drills and earthing up potatoes, so is not necessary if you do not grow vegetables. A garden rake is necessary for levelling soil and creating a fine tilth, while a besom, or a rubber or bamboo rake, is best for raking up leaves. For raking out a 'thatch' of dead grass and clippings you will need a spring-tine rake; motorized lawn rakers with collection boxes are available. A

Gardening Techniques

metal or plastic 'grabber' allows you to pick up weeds and leaves, without any unnecessary bending.

For pruning, a curve-bladed Grecian pruning saw is invaluable, and a pair of long-handled loppers helpful. Hand shears are useful, even if you also have an electric or engine-driven hedgetrimmer. A pair of secateurs for pruning soft material and woody stems up to 1cm/⅜in thick is a must; buy the most expensive that you can afford. They work either with a scissor- or anvil-action, but the scissor-action types are best. If lack of strength in the hands is a problem, use a pair with a ratchet system. Long-handled shears are necessary for clipping lawn edges. All pruning tools should be cleaned and oiled after use; from time to time, the blades will need sharpening.

A hosepipe, preferably with a reel on to which it can easily be rolled, will be needed in all but the tiniest gardens.

A wheelbarrow is essential: if you have only lawn to cross, buy one with a large ball for a front wheel, to minimize pressure on the grass. A 'donkey' (a large polypropylene sheet with a handle at each corner) will enable you to carry weeds and lawn mowings to the compost heap easily if your garden has steps.

For a large garden, a wheeled sweeper with rotating brushes and a collection bag can make the task of leaf-sweeping much easier. If you care deeply about your lawn you will require a plastic-hoppered wheeled fertilizer spreader. If you intend to use pesticides you will need two hand-pumped sprayers (one with a spray hood), or one sprayer and a watering-can with dribble bar; the first for spraying pesticides and the second for applying weedkillers.

Smaller pieces of essential equipment include: a pair of kneeling pads, a pair of tough gardening gloves, a garden line, plenty of twine, plant ties, wire, a dibber, labels, a waterproof pencil, a gardener's knife and whetstone, a light watering-can with a fine 'rose', a small hand

sprayer for misting plants in the greenhouse or windowsill, bamboo canes, plastic netting, polypropylene fleece and a variety of pots and trays.

When considering the purchase of potentially expensive mechanized equipment, be careful not to buy a larger machine than you need. The costs are inclined to rise exponentially, especially as far as lawn mowers are concerned. You should consider safety features as a priority and bear in mind the cost of servicing. It may be better to hire rather than buy large items, such as rotovators, that are used infrequently.

Choosing the right lawn mower depends on the type and size of lawn, and how easy to manage you want it to be. Unless your lawn is very small, when a push mower would be adequate, you will need either a petrol-driven or an electric cylinder or rotary mower. A cylinder mower has its cutting blades on a revolving cylinder; on a rotary mower a blade rotates underneath the machine. Some rotary mowers also 'hover', that is, work on a cushion of air. Mini-tractors also have rotating blades underneath; they and other types of ride-on mowers can only be justified, in terms of cost, where large areas must be regularly mown. A motorized lawn rake or 'scarifier' is invaluable for removing thatch and moss in a lawn.

Rotovators, either petrol- or electric-powered, are useful for cultivating large areas, but are heavy to use unless they have powered wheels. Buy a hedge-trimmer if you have a long hedge to cut or if using shears tires you; and a strimmer with a nylon line for trimming grass round trees, under walls and shrubs, and in other awkward places – one with a swivel head will also cut lawn edges. Despite its drawbacks – it is noisy and needs to be operated with care – a compost shredder is definitely worthwhile for larger gardens, as it means much more valuable compost material will become available, and you will make far fewer bonfires or trips to the tip.

A BASIC TOOL KIT

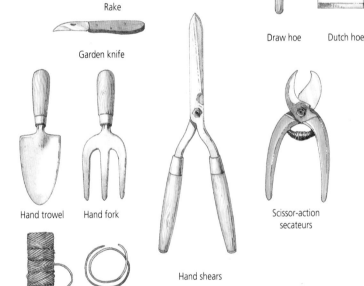

Fork

Rake

Spade

Draw hoe

Dutch hoe

Garden knife

Hand trowel

Hand fork

Hand shears

Scissor-action secateurs

Garden twine

Grecian saw

Garden line

Tough gardening gloves

INDEX

ACKNOWLEDGMENTS

The publisher thanks the photographers and organizations for their kind permission to reproduce the following photographs in this book:

1   Christian Sarraman;
2   Brigitte Perdereau;
4-5   Andrew Lawson;
6   *above right* Jean-Pierre Godeaut;
    above left Jerry Harpur (designers: Oehme, van Sweden Associates, Washington D.C.);
    centre left Peter Baistow;
    centre right W A Lord;
    below Jerry Harpur (Old Rectory, Sudborough, Northants);
7   *above* Jerry Harpur (designers: Oehme, van Sweden Associates, Washington D.C.);
    below Jean-Pierre Godeaut;
8   Peter Baistow;
9   *above* W A Lord;
    below Jerry Harpur (Old Rectory, Sudborough, Northants);
10-11   1 S&O Mathews;
    2 Gary Rogers;
12-13   1 Jerry Harpur (designers: Oehme, van Sweden Associates, Washington D.C.);
14-15   1 S&O Mathews;
16-17   1 Jerry Harpur (designers: Oehme, van Sweden Associates, Washington D.C.);
18-19   1 Jerry Harpur (Annie Lambton, Tangier);
    2 W A Lord;
20-21   1 DIA Press;
    2 Noel Kavanagh;
22-23   1 George Lévêque (designer: Jacques Wirtz, Saint Niklaas);
    2 Clive Nichols (designer: Sir Roy Strong);
    3 Brigitte Perdereau;
24-25   1 Steven Wooster;
    2 Jerry Harpur (designers: Oehme, van Sweden Associates, Washington D.C.);
26-27   1 *Belle* Magazine/Warwick Kent;
    2 Balthazar Korab;
    3 Elizabeth Whiting & Associates/Tim Street-Porter (designer: Allee Willis);
28-29   1 S&O Mathews;
    2 Jerry Harpur (Heide Garden, Melbourne, Victoria);
30-31   1 Gary Rogers;
    2 Brigitte Perdereau (Cotelle);
    3 Marijke Heuff (Mr & Mrs Groenewegen-Groot);
    4 Jerry Harpur (Eastgrove Cottage Garden, Sankyns Green, Worcester);
32-33   1 Brigitte Perdereau (designer: Jean Mus);
    2 George Lévêque (designer: Jean Mus, Saint-Jean-Cap-Ferrat);
    3 Marianne Majerus;
    4 Gary Rogers;
34-35   1 Gary Rogers;
    2 Elizabeth Whiting & Associates/Michael Dunne;
    3 Stylograph (Côté Sud de Lerins);
36-37   1-2 Michèle Lamontagne;
    3 S&O Mathews;
    4 Balthazar Korab;
38-39   1 Linda Burgess/Conran Octopus (Terence Conran's vegetable garden);
    2 George Lévêque (hamlet of Chantemerle, Samoens);
    3 Brigitte Perdereau (Heak House);

40-41   1 Andrew Lawson;
    2 Jerry Harpur (Essebourne Manor, designer: Simon Hopkinson);
    3 Noelle Hoeppe;
42-43   1 Elizabeth Whiting & Associates/Jerry Harpur (Sir Peter Finley, Sydney);
    2 Marianne Majerus;
    3 George Lévêque (designer: Mireille Ferrari, Bormes-les-Mimosas);
    4 *Vogue Living*/John Hay;
44-45   1 George Lévêque (designer: Etienne Van Campenhout, Rhode-St-Genese);
    2 Jerry Harpur (designer: Simon Fraser, London);
46-47   1 Jerry Harpur (designers: Joe Eck & Wayne Winterrowd, Readsboro, Vermont);
    2 Jerry Harpur (designer: Gunilla Pickard);
    3 David Massey;
    4 George Lévêque;
    5 S&O Mathews;
48-49   1 Clive Nichols (East Lambrook Manor, Somerset);
    2 George Lévêque (designer: Elisabeth Chesini/Kurt Salathe, Hofstetten);
    3 W A Lord;
50-51   1 Jean-Pierre Godeaut;
52-53   1 Jerry Harpur (Felicity Mullen, Johannesburg);
    2 Peter Baistow;
54-55   1 Elizabeth Whiting & Associates/Jerry Harpur;
64-65   1 Gary Rogers;
    2 Jerry Harpur (Kevin Newman, Launceston, Tasmania);
    3 Jerry Harpur (Park Farm, Chelmsford);
    4 Andrew Lawson, (Broughton Castle);
66-67   1 Brigitte Perdereau (designer: van Vassenhove);
    2 Marijke Heuff (Mr & Mrs Steeg van Zweers, designer: Harry Esselink, planting: Piet Oudolf;
    3 Gary Rogers;
    4 Brigitte Perdereau;
68-69   1 John Miller;
    2 Jerry Harpur (designer: Christopher Masson);
    3 Tim Street-Porter (Smith-Miller Hawkinson House project. LA);
70-71   1 Christian Sarraman;
    2 Steven Wooster (designer: Anthony Paul);
    3 Brigitte Perdereau (designer: Chevalier Frinault);
72-73   1 Jerry Harpur (designer: Arabella Lennox Boyd);
    2 Andrew Lawson;
74-75   1 Jerry Harpur (designer: John Brookes);
    2 Jerry Harpur (designer: Christopher Masson);
    3 Jerry Harpur (Park Farm, Chelmsford);
76-77   1 Elizabeth Whiting & Associates/Jerry Harpur;
    2 Jerry Harpur (Hazelby House, Nr Newbury, Berkshire);
    3 Jerry Harpur (designer: Edwina von Gal, New York);
    4 Steven Wooster (Hugh & Judy Johnson, Saling Hall);
    5 Brigitte Perdereau;
    6 Jerry Harpur (designer: Bobbie Hicks);
78-79   1 Andrew Lawson;
    2 Gary Rogers;
    3 Marijke Heuff (Sijtje Stuurman);
80-81   1 Jean-Pierre Godeaut;
    2 Brigitte Perdereau (Brook Cottage);
    3 Fritz von der Schulenland;
    4 Marijke Heuff (Tove Geluk Hjet, designer: Jan van der Horst);

82-83 1 Andrew Lawson;
2 Steven Wooster (Martin Lane-Fox, Hazelby House);

84-85 1 Andrew Lawson;
2-3 S&O Mathews;

86-87 1 Marijke Heuff (Little Chart, Kent);
2 Fritz von der Schulenburg (V Stourton);
3 S&O Mathews;
4 W A Lord;

88-89 1 Steven Wooster (Mien Ruys garden);
2 Marijke Heuff (Smerpertuin-Hippolytushoef);
3 S&O Mathews;
4 Marijke Heuff (Sijtje Stuurman);
5 Jerry Harpur (RHS Wisley);

90-91 1 Clive Nichols (Hazelbury Manor, Wiltshire);
2 Steven Wooster/Upper Mill Cottage;
3 George Lévêque (designer: Jean-Pierre Hennebelle, Boubers-sur-Canche);

92-93 1 Brigitte Perdereau (designer: Jean Mus);

98-99 1 S&O Mathews;
2 Marijke Heuff (Mr and Mrs Adraanse Quint);
3 Michèle Lamontagne;

104-105 1 Jerry Harpur (designer: Claus Scheinert);
2 S&O Mathews;
3 Jerry Harpur (designer: Martin Haward);
4 Christian Sarramon;

108-109 1 Jerry Harpur (Prue Herda, Sydney);
2 Jerry Harpur (designer: Christopher Masson);
3 Jerry Harpur (designer: Peter Place);
4 Clive Nichols (Turn End, Buckinghamshire, designer: Peter Aldington);

112-113 1 Steven Wooster;
2 Christine Ternynck;
3 Jerry Harpur (designer: Michael Balston);

116-117 1 Jerry Harpur (designer: Pascal Cribier, Paris);
2 Brigitte Perdereau (Chenies Manor);
3 W A Lord;

120-121 1 Clive Nichols;
2 S&O Mathews;
3 Fritz von der Schulenburg;
4 S&O Mathews;

126-127 1 Marijke Heuff (Renata Hendriks Muller);
2 Jerry Harpur (Hobart, Tasmania);
3 Gary Rogers;

128-129 1 Jerry Harpur (designer: Keith Corlett, NY City);
2 Elizabeth Whiting & Associates/Tim Street-Porter;

132-133 1 Marijke Heuff (Teffon Magna Village);
2 Garden Picture Library/Marijke Heuff (Mr & Mrs van Dyk-Hoefsmit);

134-135 1 John Miller;
2 Jerry Harpur (designer: Edwina von Gael, NY);

138-139 1 Jerry Harpur (Marguerite McBey, Tangier);

140-141 1 Vogue Living/Mark Chew;
2 Andrew Lawson;
3 Vogue Living/Mark Chew;
4 Brigitte Perdereau (design: A. J. van der Horst);

142-143 1 Peter Baistow;

144-145 1 Juliette Wade;
2 George Lévêque (designer: Hélène d'Andlau, Remalard, France);

146-147 1-2 Christian Sarramon;

148-149 1 Marijke Heuff;
2 S&O Mathews;
3 Dia Press;
4 Christian Sarramon;
5 Peter Baistow;
6 Garden Picture Library/Joanne Pavia;

150-151 1 Annette Schreiner;
2 Marijke Heuff (Garden Centre Koelemeyer, Holland);
3 Gary Rogers;
4 Michèle Lamontagne;
5 Gary Rogers;
6 Edifice/Philippa Lewis;

152-153 1 Balthazar Korab;
2 Jerry Harpur (Ballarat, Victoria);
3 Garden Picture Library/Gary Rogers;
4 Jerry Harpur (designer: Edwina von Gal, New York);
5 Garden Picture Library/Kate Zari;
6 Balthazar Korab;
7 Jerry Harpur (designer: Ann Griot, LA);
8 Marijke Heuff (Mr & Mrs Broekhuis);

154-155 1 John Neubauer (Simmons Design Shimizu Landscape Corp);

156-157 1 DIA Press;
2 W A Lord;
3 Christian Sarramon;
4 Balthazar Korab (Vens Vensen E.E. Ford, Grosseapoint);

158-159 1 Eric Crichton;
2 Christian Sarramon;
3 Tim Street-Porter (Van der Kamp);
4 Jerry Harpur (designer: John Keges);

160-161 1 Eric Crichton;
2 George Lévêque (designer: Alain de Conde, St-Pey-de-Castets, France);

162-163 1 George Lévêque (designer: Patricia van Roosmalen, Rekem);
2 Garden Picture Library/Nick Meers;

164-165 1 Eric Crichton;
2 Brigitte Perdereau (designer: J. Wirtz);
3 Andrew Lawson;
4 Peter Baistow;
5 Marijke Heuff (Garden Mien Ruys);
6 Jean-Pierre Godeaut;
7 Biofotos/Heather Angel;
8 Clive Nichols (designer: David Hicks);

166-167 1 Christian Sarramon;
2 John Neubauer;
3 George Lévêque (Alain de Conde, St-Pey-de-Castet);
4 Elizabeth Whiting & Associates/Andreas von Einsiedel;
5 Jerry Harpur (Terry Moller, Johannesburg);
6 Michèle Lamontagne;

168-169 1 Jerry Harpur (designer: Chris Rosmini, LA);
2 John Miller;
3 Hugh Palmer;

170-171 1 Jerry Harpur (Heide Garden, Melbourne, Victoria);
2 Linda Burgess/Conran Octopus (Terence Conran's vegetable garden);
3 Fritz von der Schulenburg;
4 Christian Sarramon;
5 Peter Baistow;
6 Gary Rogers;
7 Marijke Heuff (Mrs B Brand-Sema-Koekkoek);
8 Brigitte Perdereau;

172-173 1 Brigitte Perdereau (Les Moutiers);
2 Jerry Harpur (designer: Keith Collett, NY City);
3 Vogue Living/John Hay;
4 Elizabeth Whiting & Associates/Rodney Hyett;
5 Fritz von der Schulenburg (Miguel Servera, Majorca);

174-175 1 Brigitte Perdereau (Old Rectory);
2 Brigitte Perdereau (Chenies Manor);
3 Brigitte Perdereau (designer: J. Wirtz);
4 Jerry Harpur (designer: Gus Lieber, L.I.);

176-177 1 Brigitte Perdereau (The Priory);
2 Andrew Lawson;

3 George Lévêque (designers: Rosemary Brown/Susan Dewees, Delgany);
4 Edifice/Philippa Lewis;
5 Brigitte Perdereau (designer: Dino Pellizzaro);

178-179 1 Garden Picture Library/David Russell;
2 Brigitte Perdereau;
3 Garden Picture Library/Steven Wooster (Coldham, Kent);
4 W A Lord;

180-181 1 George Lévêque (private garden Grasse);
2 Clive Nichols;
3 Garden Picture Library/Vaughan Flemming;
4 Brigitte Perdereau;
5 Andrew Lawson;
6 Marijke Heuff (Hoven van Groot-Buggenum, Holland);
7 Steven Wooster (The Manor House, Chaldon Herring);

182-183 1 Jerry Harpur (designer: Ruth Shellhorn, LA);
2 Brigitte Perdereau (Poley);
3 Christian Sarramon;
4 George Lévêque (designer: Jean Mus, Grimaud);

184-185 1 Jerry Harpur (Francesca Watson, Capetown);
2 Garden Picture Library/John Glover;
3 Jerry Harpur (designers: Arabella Lennox-Boyd and Michael Balston);

186-187 1 Marijke Heuff (Mrs N Hummelen-van-Nood);
2 Elizabeth Whiting & Associates/Jerry Harpur;

188-189 1 George Lévêque (designer: François Chevalier/Michel Frinault, Orleans);
2 Laura Jeannes;
3 George Lévêque (designer: Marieva Gastaud, Marseille);
4 Jerry Hapur;

190-191 1 Brigitte Perdereau (designer: A. J. van der Horst);
2 Jerry Harpur;
3 Christian Sarramon;
4 Marijke Heuff (Anja Keepers);

192-193 1 John Miller;
2 Jerry Harpur (designer: Victor Nelson, NY);
3 Elizabeth Whiting & Associates/Rodney Hyett;
4 Jerry Harpur (Bradenham Hall, Norfolk);

194-195 1 George Lévêque (designer: Jean Mus, Grimaud);
2 Jerry Harpur (Shute House, Donhead St Mary, Dorset, designer: Sir Geoffrey Jellicoe);
3 Andrew Lawson;
4 Jerry Harpur (Hall Place, Leigh Kent);
5 S&O Mathews;

196-197 1 Jerry Harpur (Chenies Manor, Bucks);
2 Christian Sarramon;

198-199 1 Andrew Lawson;
2 Jerry Harpur (designer: Ann Griot, LA);
3 Jerry Harpur (Tudor Place, Washington);

200-201 1 George Lévêque (designer: Jean Mus, Cabris);
2 Steven Wooster;
3 S&O Mathews;
4 Edifice/Gillian Darley;
5 Nadia Mackenzie;
6 Christian Sarramon;
7 Elizabeth Whiting & Associates/Jerry Harpur;

202-203 1 Brigitte Perdereau (designer: J. Wirtz);
2 Jerry Harpur (Ablington Manor, Glos);
3 Clive Nichols (University Botanic Garden, Cambridge);
4 Andrew Lawson;
5 Clive Nichols (Coates Manor, Sussex);
6 Brigitte Perdereau (designer: Joop Braam);

204-205 1 Gary Rogers;
2 Steven Wooster (Hugh & Judy Johnson, Saling Hall);
3 George Lévêque (on the road to Chalet Joux-Planem, Samoens);
4 Elizabeth Whiting & Associates/Karl Dietrich-Bühler;

206-207 1 Jerry Harpur (Lady Barborolli, Hampstead);
2 Jerry Harpur (designer: Preben Jakobsen, Cheltenham);
3 Jerry Harpur (designers: Oehme, van Sweden, Washington D.C.);
4 Jerry Harpur (Park Farm, Chelmsford);

208-209 1 George Lévêque (designer: Christiane Engel/Camille Muller);
2 Christian Sarramon;

210-211 1 Gary Rogers;
2 Andrew Lawson;
3 Gary Rogers;
4 Jerry Harpur (Stone House Cottage, Stone, nr Wolverhampton);
5 Andrew Lawson;
6 Peter Baistow;

212-213 1 Gary Rogers;

214-215 1 Jerry Harpur (designer: Ragna Goddard, Connecticut);
2 Clive Nichols (Barnsley House, Gloucestershire);
3 Fritz von der Schulenburg;
4 Andrew Lawson;

216-217 1 George Lévêque (designer: Etienne Van Campenhout, Rhode-St-Genese);
2 Jerry Harpur (designer: Mirabel Osler);
3 S&O Mathews;

218-219 1 Andrew Lawson;
2 Jerry Harpur (Manwallok, Victoria);

220-221 1 Dia Press;
2 Jerry Harpur (designer: Trevor Frankland);
3 George Lévêque (designer: John and Shirley Beatty, Carrickmines);
4 S&O Mathews;

222-223 1 Jerry Harpur (Château Gourdon, Alpes-Maritimes);
2 Brigitte Perdereau;
3 Marijke Heuff (Jaap Niewenhuis and Paula Thies);
4 Christian Sarramon;
5 Jean-Pierre Godeaut (Canovias);

224-225 1 Elizabeth Whiting & Associates/Karl Dietrich Bühler;
2 Jean-Pierre Godeaut;
3 Steven Wooster (designer: Anthony Noel);
4 Marianne Majerus;

226-227 1 Jerry Harpur (Wave Hill, NY);
2 Steven Wooster (designer Anthony Paul);
3 Jerry Harpur (Shute House, Donhead St Mary, Dorset, designer: Sir Geoffrey Jellicoe);
4 Christan Sarramon;

228-229 1-2 Andrew Lawson;

230-231 1 Michèle Lamontagne;
2 Elizabeth Whiting & Associates/Jerry Harpur (Michael Branch);
3 Tim Street-Porter (designer: Luis Ortega);
4 Jerry Harpur (Terry Moller, Johannesburg);
5 Garden Picture Library/Ron Sutherland;

232-233 1 Brigitte Perdereau (Lower Hall);
2 Marianne Majerus;
3-4 W A Lord;

234-235 1 W A Lord;
2 Brigitte Perdereau (West Kinton);
3 Andrew Lawson;
4 W A Lord;

236-237 1 Jerry Harpur (Sam Hellinger, LA);
2 Christian Sarramon;
3 Steven Wooster (Château Erignac);

ACKNOWLEDGMENTS

238-239 **1** Marijke Heuff (Little Haseley);
2 Edifice/Weideger;
240-241 **1** Christian Sarramon;
2 Jerry Harpur (designer: Sir Hardy Amies);
3 Fritz von der Schulenburg/IPC/Robert Harding Syndication;
4 Jerry Harpur (designer: Bob Dash, Sagaponck);
5 Christian Sarramon;
6 Marianne Majerus;
7 Jerry Harpur ('Nooroo', NSW);
8 George Lévêque (designer: Françoise Bessy, La-Croix-Valmer);
9 Marijke Heuff (Sijtje Stuurman);
242-243 **1** Jerry Harpur (designer: Christopher Masson);
2 Brigitte Perdereau (Brook Cottage);
3 Brigitte Perdereau;
4 Karl Dietrich-Bühler (designer: Francesca Marzotto Caotorta);
5 Bent Rej;
244-245 **1** Brigitte Perdereau (designer: J. Wirtz);
2 Christian Sarramon;
3 Garden Picture Library/Gary Rogers;
246-247 **1** Clive Nichols (Mrs Merton, The Old Rectory, Burghfield, Berkshire);
2 Noel Kavanagh;
248-249 **1** Juliette Wade;
2 Clive Nichols (Tintinhull House, Somerset);
3 Brigitte Perdereau (designer: Dino Pellizzaro);
4 S&O Mathews;
5-6 Christian Sarramon;
7 George Lévêque (designer: Yves Taralon, Richebourg);
8 Clive Nichols (designer: Anthony Noel);
9 Andrew Lawson;
250-251 **1** George Lévêque (designer: Jean Mus, Grimaud);
2 Marie Claire Maison/D Christope/ Postic/Joseé;
3-4 Christian Sarramon;
5 Vogue Living/Scott Hawkins;
252-253 **1** Christian Sarramon;
2 Balthazar Korab;
3 Noel Kavanagh;
4 Jerry Harpur (Tania Young, Perth, W.A.);
5 Agence Top/Robert Tixador;
6 Brigitte Perdereau (Dekker Fokker);
7 Andrew Lawson;
8 Jerry Harpur (Vernon Edenfield,

Fredericksburg, Virginia);
9 Marijke Heuff (Mr F de Greeuw & Mr F Tiebout);
10 Brigitte Perdereau (designer: Delgado);
254-255 **1** Jerry Harpur (Felicity Mullen, Johannesburg);
2 Mike England;
3 Brigitte Perdereau;
4 Gary Rogers;
5 Tim Street-Porter (designer: Nancy Goslee Power);
256-257 **1** Balthazar Korab;
258-259 **1** Garden Picture Library/Nigel Temple;
2 Vogue Living/Richard Ludbrook;
3 Brigitte Perdereau;
260-261 **1** Clive Nichols (Hazelbury Manor, Wiltshire, sculpture: Patrick Barker);
2 Christian Sarramon;
3 Andrew Lawson;
4 Noel Kavanagh;
5 Clive Nichols (Parnham House, Dorset, designer: Jerry Burgess);
6 Christian Sarramon;
7 Gary Rogers;
8 Andrew Lawson;
262-263 **1** W A Lord;
264-265 **1** Marion Nickig;
2 S&O Mathews;
266-267 **1-2** Andrew Lawson;
3 Photos Horticultural;
4 Ursula Buchan;
5-6 Andrew Lawson;
7 Photos Horticultural;
268-269 **8-9** Tania Midgley;
10 Andrew Lawson;
11 Harry Smith Collection;
12-14 Andrew Lawson;
15-16 Photos Horticultural;
270-271 **17** S&O Mathews;
18 Tania Midgley;
19 Andrew Lawson;
20 Photos Horticultural;
21 A-Z Botanical Collection;
22 Garden Picture Library/David Russell;
23 S&O Mathews;
24 Photos Horticultural;
272-273 **25** S&O Mathews;
26 Andrew Lawson;
27 S&O Mathews;
28 Harry Smith Collection;
29 Tania Midgley;
30 Garden Picture Library/Brian Carter;

31-32 Tania Midgley;
33-34 S&O Mathews;
35 Tania Midgley;
36 Andrew Lawson;
37 Tania Midgley;
38 S&O Mathews;
39-41 Andrew Lawson;
274-275
276-277 **42** A-Z Botanical Collection;
43 Andrew Lawson;
44-45 Photos Horticultural;
46 Clive Nichols;
47-48 Andrew Lawson;
49 Photos Horticultural;
278-279 **50** Andrew Lawson;
51-52 S&O Mathews;
53 Photos Horticultural;
54 Andrew Lawson;
55 S&O Mathews;
56 Andrew Lawson;
57 Andrew Lawson;
280-281 **58** Garden Picture Library/Sidney Moulds;
59 Photos Horticultural;
60 S&O Mathews;
61 Andrew Lawson;
62-63 S&O Mathews;
64 Photos Horticultural;
65 A-Z Botanical Collection;
66 Andrew Lawson;
282-283 **67** John Glover;
68 S&O Mathews;
69 Garden Picture Library/Stephen Jury;
70-71 Andrew Lawson;
72 S&O Mathews;
73-74 Photos Horticultural;
75 Tania Midgley;
284-285 **76** Photos Horticultural;
77 Harry Smith Collection;
78 Biofotos/Heather Angel;
79-80 Photos Horticultural;
81 Harry Smith Collection;
82 Andrew Lawson;
83 Tania Midgley;
84 Photos Horticultural;
85 Andrew Lawson;
286-287 **86-87** Photos Horticultural;
88 Garden Picture Library/Ron Sutherland;
89-91 Andrew Lawson;
92 Harry Smith Collection;
93 Andrew Lawson;
288-289 **94** Andrew Lawson;
95 Harry Smith Collection;

96 S&O Mathews;
97-98 Andrew Lawson;
99 Photos Horticultural;
100 Tania Midgley;
290-291 **1** Jerry Harpur (Old Rectory, Sudborough, Northants);
292-293 **1** Jerry Harpur/Villa Taylor Marrakesch;
2 Marijke Heuff (Mr & Mrs Arends-Buyning, designer: Els Proost);
302-303 **1** Garden Picture Library/Brian Carter;
304-305 **1** Steven Wooster;
306-307 **1** Gary Rogers;
310-311 **1** Michèle Lamontagne;
312-313 **1** Tania Midgley;
322-323 **1** S&O Mathews;
328-329 **1** Jerry Harpur (designer: Chris Grey-Wilson);
325-326 **1** S&O Mathews;
339 **1** Peter Baistow;
352 Marijke Heuff (Walda Pairon).

Illustrations

Vanessa Luff: pages 92, 94-5, 97, 148-9, 155, 158, 159, 160, 161, 162, 172, 176, 185, 187, 190, 191, 192, 193, 196, 200, 210, 213, 218, 222, 226, 229, 231, 255, 295, 297, 298, 300, 301, 303, 304, 305, 307, 308, 309, 311-315, 318-327, 338

Liz Pepperell: pages 27, 29, 48, 57 (colour), 63 (below), 100-1, 102-3, 106-7, 110-11, 114-15, 118-19, 122-3, 124-5, 128-9, 130-1, 135, 136-7, 138

Paul Bryant: pages 57 (black-and-white), 58-9, 60, 62, 63 (top), 72, 73